History and Computing

Edited by
Peter Denley *and* Deian Hopkin

Manchester University Press

Published by Manchester University Press
Oxford Road, Manchester M13 9PL

British Library cataloguing in publication data
History and computing.
   1. Historiography——Data processing
   I. Denley, Peter   II. Hopkin, Deian
   907'.2   D16.12

Library of Congress cataloging in publication data applied for

ISBN 0 7190 2484 6

Printed in Great Britain
by Biddles Ltd, Guildford and King's Lynn

Table of Contents

PART I. Applications

viii

Introduction

This volume has its origins in a conference held in March 1986 to attempt to inaugurate an association for historians who used or wished to use computers in their work, whether that work was research or teaching. The conference was summoned by open invitation and the programme was compiled from the response. The outcome was a programme as varied as it was disconnected. Several themes had been suggested at the outset, including databases, quantification, text processing and the teaching of computing skills to historians, but the conference was consciously organised to reflect the enormous variety of the papers offered. Without doubt, the most enduring result of the conference is the Association for History and Computing; this book is offered primarily as a record of that event but also as a reflection of the range and quality of work currently being conducted in historical computing. It is, in this sense, an 'arena' book.

The three main themes of the book are those around which the conference was organised, but the editors have added a number of subdivisions in order to impose some order on the contributions. The essays are as brief as were the original conference papers; in this respect, the opportunity to expand individual contributions was sacrificed in order to maintain the number and variety of the whole.

Four cross-currents emerge from among the themes around which this volume has been organised. In the first place, it is evident that historical computing has evolved considerably from the early days of quantification and basic data processing. This is not to decry the achievements of the pioneers, but inevitably the evolution of the technology has led to an evolution of the means for problem-solving.

This is not the place to debate the relative advantages and disadvantages of computer-based over more conventional modes of historical explanation. As the essays in this volume clearly show, computers can be used at all levels of historical enquiry, from hypothesis and model-building to narrative. It may well be that computers require unusually precise formulations of hypotheses and more rigorous definitions of the routes of explanation. This in turn may alert the historian to the shortcomings of evidence and the inadequacy of other modes of explanation although there is always the parallel danger that computers can offer a deceptively reassuring sense of order where, in reality, no order exists. Yet, as many of the essays show, this is not a danger into which many historians have yet fallen; there is a paradoxically strong sense of uncertainty amongst all the technological certainty.

In the second place, computers provide common ground between historians who otherwise inhabit segmented and secluded worlds. Through the search for standard implementations and procedures, historians with very different chronological and thematic interests have come together — historians of Ancient Greece and of modern British politics exchange ideas and opinions in a way which may not have been seen since the breakdown of the 'generalist' school of history and the rise of specialism. This may yet prove to be a false dawn, a coincidence not a synchronicity. Yet at Westfield, and in this volume, an unusually eclectic gathering of historians came together. And not just historians. In the exploration of new media, historians, geographers, linguists and lexicographers come together to share experiences, to exchange disaster stories, and to enthuse over new discoveries. If the process of the integration of disciplines is widely observed, nowhere is it more evident than in this field.

In the third place, there is common understanding of the logistical problems — of the need for training, and of awareness of the technology. Perhaps, above all, there is a sense of common cause in the face of economic and financial uncertainty. For the first time, historians are making claims on resources which match those of some of the sciences. And why not? History is as labour-intensive as any laboratory-based subject — indeed, it might be argued that the massive task of resource building poses greater problems for the historian than for most scientists.

Finally, in a world of sharply divided national loyalties and increasing protectionism, it is reassuring to witness historians from so many different countries finding common cause. At Westfield participants from 19 countries, representing over 150 institutions and agencies, came together. Through the search for common solutions to common problems, the important priorities become, for a time, intellectual, not institutional or territorial.

The gaps in this volume are many and inevitable — the product of the fortuitous nature by which people responded to the call for papers. That so many different people responded is a measure of the success of the conference. In consequence, this volume is catholic; it is not, nor is it intended to be, compendious. Like the conference itself it is, we believe, an inauguration.

There is an optimism in this corner of history which is conspicuously lacking elsewhere, perhaps because through the mastery of computing, historians are demonstrating a utilitarian value and a modern relevance which is so much stressed. This cannot be a justification for the use of historical computing. That would be a path to disaster. Yet there is no gainsaying the fact that in the present age of diminishing resources and the search for justifications, this blend of qualitative and quantitative, of insight and deduction, of old-fashioned instinct and modern processing power, offers a rare combination; something of which historians can, for once, be proud.

Deian Hopkin
Peter Denley

February 1987

The Association for History and Computing

The AHC is a federal organisation with national and regional branches which exists to promote the use of computers in the research and teaching of history.

The proposed constitution of the Association allows for the election of a group of officers, including a President, Secretary General, Director of Finance, Director of Publications and Newsletter Editor, and for an international representative Council.

A Steering Committee was elected during the inaugural conference with a broad representation, including colleagues from Germany, Denmark, Sweden, France and Portugal; later a distinguished colleague from Italy joined the Committee . Through the generous support of the Nuffield Foundation and the European Science Foundation, two extended meetings were held in London and Strasbourg at which a number of developments were discussed and initiated. Constitutions were drafted for the federal organisation as well as model national constitutions. Dr Bob Morris and Professor Bill Speck were appointed as Editors of the new newsletter of the Association. Preliminary arrangements were made for the second annual conference, and provisional plans laid down for future international conferences in a number of European venues as well as provision for national conferences in each country in which a branch was formed. At this stage, it was felt that the Association should concentrate on developing its links in continental Europe, although it is intended to forge links with North America and the rest of the world as soon as possible; indeed, there are already a number of members from the USA, Canada and Australasia. Finally, a series of initatives have been launched, including several major collaborative projects and educational training programmes.

Further details of the Association's activities are available from Peter Denley, Department of History, Westfield College (University of London), London NW3 7ST.

Acknowledgments

This book was photoset on Oxford University Computing Service's Monotype Lasercomp phototypesetter. It was prepared using facilities generously provided by the Computer Unit, Westfield College. Valuable assistance was received from the Data Preparation Services of the University College of Wales, Aberystwyth and the KDEM service of the University of London Computing Centre. The editors gratefully acknowledge the help given by the staff of all these bodies.

List of Contributors

Peter Adman *Computer Centre, University of Hull*
Charles Anderson *Department of Education, University of Edinburgh*
P. Anstey *Computing Centre, University of East Anglia*
Andrew Ayton *Domesday Unit, Department of History, University of Hull*
John Beckett *Department of History, University of Nottingham*
Frances Blow *Centre for History Education, Trinity and All Saints College, Leeds*
Francesca Bocchi *Department of History, University of Bologna*
Harold W. Booton *Dunfermline*
Caroline Bourlet *Institut de Recherche et d'Histoire des Textes (C.N.R.S.), Paris*
Jonathan Briggs *University of Exeter*
Peter Britton *Durham*
Lou Burnard *Oxford University Computing Service*
R. Burt *Department of Economic History, University of Exeter*
David Cairns *Department of Humanities, North Staffordshire Polytechnic*
Brenda Collins *Institute of Irish Studies, Queen's University, Belfast*
P. J. Corfield *Department of History, Royal Holloway and Bedford New College, University of London*
Valerie Cromwell *School of English and American Studies, University of Sussex*
Virginia Davis *Domesday Unit, Department of History, University of Hull*
Jackie Dean *University of Exeter*
Peter Denley *Department of History, Westfield College (University of London)*
Ian Diamond *Department of Social Statistics, University of Southampton*
Rob Dixon *STIPPLE Database Services Ltd, Culham, Oxon.*
David Doulton *Computing Service, University of Southampton*
Joseph Ehmer *Institut für Wirtschafts- und Sozialgeschichte, University of Vienna*
Nesta Evans *University of Cambridge*
Renée-Arlette Faugères *Institut d'Histoire Moderne et Contemporaine (C.N.R.S.), Paris*
Trevor Foulds *Department of History, University of Nottingham*
Jean-Philippe Genet *University of Paris I*
Michael Gervers *University of Toronto (Scarborough Campus)*
Anne Gilmour-Bryson *Glendon College of York University, Toronto*
Michael Greenhalgh *Department of the History of Art, University of Leicester*
Eric C. Griffiths *Department of Computing Mathematics, University College, Cardiff*
Charles Harvey *Department of History, Royal Holloway and Bedford New College, University of London*
Noel Heather *Faculty of Humanities, Polytechnic of North London*
Adam Hodgkin *Oxford University Press*
Deian Hopkin *Department of History, University College of Wales, Aberystwyth*
Arno Kitts *Department of Social Statistics, University of Southampton*
R. A. Lewis *Department of Economic History, University of Exeter*
Fernando Lugli *Centro Ricerche, Carpi (Modena)*
Michelle Magdelaine *Institut d'Histoire Moderne et Contemporaine (C.N.R.S.), Paris*
Hans Jørgen Marker *Danish Data Archives, Odense*
David Marshall *Department of Law, North Staffordshire Polytechnic*
David Mealand *University of Edinburgh*
Rainer Metz *Zentrum für Datenverarbeitung, University of Tübingen*

Hélène Millet   *C.N.R.S., Paris*

Jean-Luc Minel   *Institut de Recherche et d'Histoire des Textes (C.N.R.S.), Paris*

Nicholas J. Morgan   *Department of Scottish History, University of Glasgow*

R. J. Morris   *Department of Economic History, University of Edinburgh*

Harold Mytum   *Department of Archaeology, University of York*

Jon Nichol   *School of Education, University of Exeter*

Mark Overton   *Department of Geography, University of Newcastle upon Tyne*

J. H. Porter   *Department of Economic History, University of Exeter*

John Power   *Department of Geography, Queen's University, Belfast*

Elizabeth Reis   *University of Southampton*

Timothy Reuter   *Monumenta Germaniae Historica, Munich*

David Rheubottom   *Department of Social Anthropology, University of Manchester*

Shaun Richards   *Department of Humanities, North Staffordshire Polytechnic*

T. E. Rihll   *School of History, University of Leeds*

Kevin Schürer   *Cambridge Group for the History of Population and Social Structure, University of Cambridge*

Josef Smets   *Institut de Recherche Historique par l'Informatique et la Statistique, Montpellier*

Gun Stenflo   *Demographic Data Base, Umeå University*

Jan Sundin   *University of Linköping*

David Taylor   *Department of Humanities, Teesside Polytechnic*

Peter Taylor   *Bristol Polytechnic*

Manfred Thaller   *Max-Planck-Institut für Geschichte, Göttingen*

Richard H. Trainor   *Department of Economic History, University of Glasgow*

John Turner   *Department of History, Royal Holloway and Bedford New College, University of London*

Will Vaughan   *Department of History of Art, Birkbeck College, University of London*

Peter Wakelin   *School of Humanities and Cultural Studies, The Polytechnic, Wolverhampton*

Peter Wardley   *History Department, University of Durham*

Lorna Weatherill   *St. Andrews*

Ron Weir   *Department of Economics and Related Studies, University of York*

Martyn Wild   *Prolog Education Group, University of Exeter, and Advisory Unit Microtechnology in Education, Hatfield*

Richard G. Williams   *Haldane Library, Imperial College London*

A. G. Wilson   *School of Geography, University of Leeds*

Ulrike Winkler   *History Department (ÖHB), University of Klagenfurt*

Robert L. Woods, Jr.   *Department of History, Pomona College, Claremont, California*

PART I

Applications

Computers and Medieval Historical Texts: an Overview

First let me state how pleased I am that a society on History and Computing has been founded at last. For too long historians at conferences have had to be content with a few history papers swamped by ten times as many devoted to literary or linguistic computing. In this overview of medieval history and the computer I will describe a number of representative projects; I have not chosen the best projects, but instead a representative selection.

One cannot discuss computer textual treatment without mentioning the herculean task successfully brought to completion by Father Roberto Busa with his production of the *Index Thomisticus*, in 56 volumes as at 1980. Father Busa and his team worked for 30 years using less than 10,000 computer hours and more than one million man hours. I am not surprised that one hundred man hours were required for every computer hour. Computerisation does not always result in less work. As the *Index* prospectus states:

It [the project] was the pioneer of [the use of] the computer in the humanities and is still a model of it. [And most important] The computer has not been used principally to speed up operations, but most of all to enhance the qualities of the method: completeness, accuracy, in-depth systematization of linguistic categories.

In April of 1974, Lusignan, Bullough, and Ohlgren published a report on computers and medieval studies in *Speculum*. As the authors stated: 'Computers imply quantification and quantification is nothing new to medievalists . . .'[1] At that time, two hundred medieval scholars were known to the authors to be using the computer, although the variety of research carried out by computer was very much smaller than it became even by 1979. Few historical projects were underway, although the earlier outstanding work by David Herlihy on the Florentine Catasto of 1427–1430, and Theodore Evergates on Champagne nobility, surely encouraged many of us to use the computer on our own projects. Literature and linguistics still make up the majority of computer-aided projects undertaken by medievalists. At that time, the *Speculum* report stated: '. . . medieval historians have not shown a willingness to experiment with computers, and . . . have been slightly more conservative . . . than their colleagues in other parts of the medieval vineyard'.[2] To contrast 1983 with 1974, the *Index* to the newsletter CAMDAP[3] lists historical projects in the following descending order of frequency, biography-prosopography (13), diplomatic sources tied with fiscal sources (7), judicial sources tied with cadastral records (4), real estate documents *ex aequo* with epigraphy (3), followed by a cluster each with two listings: accounting documents, legal sources, onomastics, administrative sources, and wills; one project reported to the newsletter on demography, genealogy, heraldry, canonical sources, and notarial sources, for a total of 56 historical projects reported.

An interesting source for the state of computing in 1975 is found in the proceedings of the 1975 conference jointly sponsored by the École Française de Rome and the Institute of Medieval History of the University of Pisa. As Professor Giulio Battelli said then, regarding the slow progress of printed volumes of papal registers in the past century: 'The fruits obtained in 100 years with traditional methods are not encouraging if one wishes to extend the research to later periods when the amount of documentation is even richer'.[4] Regarding integral text entry, the situation as it existed in 1975 forced Professor Battelli to conclude:

The new technology using computer systems is perfectly capable of registering whole texts in a way which would satisfy every future query from researchers. This perspective, it seems to me is not feasible with regard to the pontifical registers because of the sheer mass of the documents.[5]

In 1975, as now, it was the economic and social historians who where particularly interested in future computer assistance with their documents.

The first project I will describe is the largest scholarly project I know of, containing 70 million words already, the Responsa Project initiated in 1966 and headed by Professor Yaacov Choueka since 1975 at the Bar-Ilan Center for Computers and Jewish Heritage in Israel. These questions and answers addressed by the faithful to their rabbis for judicial resolution were written in Hebrew over the last 1500 years at least. All texts were entered in their entirety, and can be retrieved using simple search techniques. Of great interest to all medievalists is the next project of the Choueka group that of building up a database of thousands of medieval manuscript facsimiles using optical disc technology.

For the historian, as well as the specialist in literature, manuscript edition is a long, painstaking task which can be helped considerably by the use of computer techniques. My critical edition of *The Trial of the Templars in the Papal States and the Abruzzi*[6] was the first computer-published edition which the Vatican ever published. Critical editions are often prepared with the help of methods developed and used by Dr Wilhelm Ott in Tübingen. His interlinked programs can undertake manuscript collation, concordances, word indices and every facet of publication itself. Index generation and critical apparatus are created automatically. Best of all from the point of view of the author is that this system requires far less proof reading and makes it impossible for the publisher to make any changes to the text.

Another problem common to almost all manuscript editors is that of the creation of a *stemma codicum* tracing the probable transmission of the manuscript across space and time. Several new methods to accomplish this feat automatically have appeared in the last three years. Great caution is advisable as the community of scholars is certainly not yet convinced that any of these is completely reliable.[7]

If one looks back to James Powell's *Medieval Studies*,[8] to the essay on computing by David Herlihy,[9] we find much useful information on the state of computing in the early 70's. Nevertheless, computing has become so much easier in the intervening ten years that one can only admire the dedication of those such as Herlihy who paved the way for the rest of us. We would see far fewer humanists using computers if the following citation from the same source were still true: 'Quite obviously, the use of computers requires from him (the medieval historian) a considerable effort, if he is to gain even a rudimentary familiarity with the art; computer-assisted research also demands considerable sums of money'.[10] In the same essay, Professor Herlihy stated: 'Several medieval scholars, for example, have been seeking to prepare "machine-readable" editions of the large collection of private charters and notarial acts . . . but a truly workable system has yet to be achieved'.[11]

Historians have special needs in the computer field, hence Dr Manfred Thaller's workshop on the creation, linkage and usage of large-scale interdisciplinary source banks in the historical disciplines held in July of 1985 by the Max-Planck-Institut für Geschichte. Among the matters discussed were the description and collection of sources including coding conventions, legal and organisational access to historical data banks, and an attempt to standardize and provide access for data in the Humanities and the Social Sciences throughout Europe. As Dr Thaller mentioned, the comparative ease of data entry and the continually lowering cost of processing may make it possible for us to see in our lifetime some of the projects discussed and abandoned over the last twenty years because of the time and money it would once have cost to carry them out. For medieval historians the immediate need is for computer access to such collections as the *Monumenta Germaniae Historica*, Migne's *Patrologiae*, all the Papal *Registers*, and some of the collections of chronicles. But if these resources are to be really useful to historians who have no computer training or background, the query procedure will have to be simple and crystal clear.

Many projects today computerise notarial archives as do Professors Hébert, Lavoie, and Shatzmiller at the town of Manosque in Provence. Criminal cases are coded numerically by category, a solution which certainly reduces tremendously the size of the database but which also makes it impossible to differentiate between various acts which receive the same code.

Another project in French history was directed by Elizabeth Brown of New York in which she studied the last wills and testamentary documents of the French Royal lineage. Professor Brown lists all information relevant to the provenance of the will and then uses a complex coding system providing every detail of the document itself and finally reproduces the full text. Her system is so thorough that I imagine all demanding scholars would approve of it. Unfortunately, such truly thorough hand-made systems of transcription and data entry are highly time-consuming.

Diane Frappier-Bigras of the Université de Montréal is the author of a study of the *Livre de la taille de Paris* of 1292. The complete computerisation of this document has permitted Frappier-Bigras to carry out a study of professions by street, or by sex, or by the amount of tax paid. It is also possible to prepare a map of Paris including the frequency of various professions. An earlier computerised map project also came out of the Université de Montréal in 1977 when Denise St-Michel and Guy Tiphane prepared a map to all the places mentioned by Gregory of Tours in his

Historia Francorum.

In the area of population figures and statistics, Hans Bächler and P. Rück of Switzerland have undertaken a thorough study of medieval Freiburg using naturalization registers from the period 1341 to 1416. The authors used a simple relational database model Query by Enquiry method to produce results or to ask questions.[12] When the authors undertook their project, only mainframe systems could use QBE; some database software such as Paradox now allows micro computer users to experiment with QBE, one of the simplest query methods. Michele Luzzati, and his group, made a population study in Pisa, using baptismal records from 1457 to 1509, in order to construct tables of persons and family relationships.[13] This type of historical work is the most usual computer-assisted research today.

A much later project on late medieval Franconian nobility is underway directed by Hans-Peter Baum. He is conducting an analysis of five *libri feudorum* of the prince-bishops of Würzburg between 1303 and 1510 in conjunction with supporting source material from the bishops' chancellery or registers kept by the princes. Baum is using a custom-made adaptation of TUSTEP the programming and editing program developed at Tübingen.

An interesting project on English History was that of Joel and Bernice Lipkin who studied the educational status of the beneficed clergy of the diocese of Hereford from 1289 to 1539. The Lipkins used a program written in SAIL (Stanford Artificial Intelligence Language), a high-level Algol type language which seems particularly well suited to quantitative history.[14] Still in Great Britain, Janet Williamson carried out a project with Professor Hilton, and others, on manorial court records.[15] The amount of data to be input was impressive, some 125,000 entries covering an eighty-year period of the mid-fourteenth century. The team adapted an input and record-handling system entitled GENDATA developed at Cambridge for such purposes. One of the best features of the GENDATA record input system is that relatively few changes have to be made to the document prior to input. Relatively little coding is necessary. Neither is it necessary to know exactly how the material will be used before it is entered.

Turning to France, a project undertaken by Jean-Philippe Genet in Paris is of particular interest.[16] In the course of a study on polemic works, Genet decided that factorial analysis would be useful in order to demonstrate closeness or distance between concepts as expressed in terms of key words. In order to process his data, Genet and others developed the ALINE program for linguistic analysis.

One more very complicated and important project continues still at the CNRS under its director Gian-Piero Zarri: the RESEDA project which began in 1975.[17] The project concerns French history from the end of the fourteenth to the mid-fifteenth centuries. The nucleus of this unusual attempt to create a historical database able to answer questions posed by the scholar is the breaking down of historical events into separate 'episodes'. Each episode must then be written out, accompanied by the appropriate codes, in a completely unambiguous fashion. 'Correlators', or 'cases' in artificial intelligence terminology, accompany the data so that the computer recognised who or what is the subject or object of any action.

As a specialist in the military Order of the Temple, and most particularly in the Templar trials which took place between 1307 and 1311 throughout Latin Christendom, it became obvious to me that the 140,000 different answers in the depositions of some 910 witnesses remaining to us could only be thoroughly analysed with the help of the computer. For that purpose, I developed a coding scheme which listed the standard 127 accusations used throughout the trials and translated the answers into a maximum of 15 letters and numbers signifying not just guilt or innocence but who committed the act, whether or not it was performed under threat, which acts the witness observed occur, who was responsible for the order to commit the sin, and whether the answer contained specific or vague hearsay. The data was then treated with SAS. The research was sponsored by the Social Science and Humanities Council of Canada, Glendon College, York University, and the Université de Montréal.[18]

In 1982 I was retained by the Attorney General of the Province of Ontario to assist the Homicide Squad of the Metropolitan Toronto Police by designing and implementing a database to the medical charts of some 46 children whose deaths were deemed suspicious in a murder investigation concerning a local hospital. I eventually input relevant data from another 150 charts for purposes of comparison.[19]

Between 1983 and 1985 I directed computerised research for a Royal Commission of Inquiry into those deaths and other matters. The post involved computerising a considerable range of material from the 45,000 pages of hearing transcript to some 100 police officers' notebooks and various technical reports submitted to the inquiry by expert witnesses. For that project I designed another simple relational database using mainframe FOCUS the software I had used for the patients' charts.[20]

In conclusion, historical research began with large, complex, difficult projects carried out by a few extremely courageous historians with the stamina to tackle all the horrors of punching cards, learning programming languages, and limiting themselves to database formats fixed in stone, with computer use available only to those with fairly large university grants or those belonging to the few institutions which offered free computer use to all qualified staff projects. When computers became easier to use, and university computing centres became more receptive to the needs of the computer-illiterate members of non-scientific departments, computer use proliferated. Some of these projects were flawed by a naïve belief that whatever statistics or results the computer churned out were valid. Not enough emphasis was placed on the quality or completeness of the data which eager computer users were inputting.

Only six years ago, we were forced to learn dBASE programming and to deal with its truly dreadful manual if we wanted to manipulate historical databases on our tiny 16, 32 or 64K CP/M based early micros. As I typed this article on my IBM PC AT with its 1·2 megabyte floppy disk, its 20 megabyte hard disk, making automatic backups on its 20 megabyte tape backup system, and printed it on an 8 page per minute laser printer, it was hard to believe that such progress had taken place in six years. Readily available software with a type of artificial intelligence interface enables the novice to build a database, query it, and report from it within a few hours at most.

But does the use of computers improve historical accuracy or completeness? Is our work better because we are using computers? Obviously a bad project remains a bad project after the computer is finished with it. In the vast majority of cases though, the amazing possibility we now have to try out literally hundreds of hypotheses by asking a few questions of our database allows us to find solutions to problems in the data which would not have been solved before the present day. Not because these problems could not have been solved by other means but because the time and/or manpower needed would have been prohibitive. I am most definitely optimistic about the benefits computers will bring to the study of history provided that obvious precautions are taken to ensure that the data entered be as accurate as possible, that the proper software be chosen to process the data, and that no unusual conclusions go unchallenged simply because the computer provided what appears to be accurate results. It seems evident at this point that larger, more ambitious historical data banks will be created throughout the world now that the hardware and software will permit the development of such systems at much lower cost, much faster, and more easily. It is also apparent that our colleagues are in general far more convinced of the desirability of computerising the medieval vineyard than they were only twelve years ago.

Notes

1.   Vern Bullough, Serge Lusignan, Thomas Ohlgren, 'Computers and the Medievalist, a report', *Speculum*, April, 1974, pp. 392–402. This quotation can be found on page 400.

2.   *Ibidem*, p. 401.

3.   *Computers and Medieval Data Processing*, available from the Institut d'études médiévales, Université de Montréal, Montréal, Québec.

4.   Giulio Battelli, 'Una proposta per un indice dei registri pontificti,' *Informatique et Histoire Médiévale*, Ecole Française de Rome, Rome, 1977, p. 21.

5.   *Ibidem*, p. 25.

6.   *Studi e Testi* 303, Biblioteca Apostolica Vaticana, 1982.

7.   Check the *Index* and the bibliographies published in CAMDAP for articles on this subejct.

8.   James Powell (ed.), *Medieval Studies — An Introduction*, Syracuse University, 1976.

9.   David Herlihy, 'Computer-assisted Analysis of the Statistical Documents of Medieval Society', in Powell, *op. cit.*, pp. 185–211.

10.   *Ibid.*, p. 195.

11.   *Ibid.*, p. 196.

12.   See Hans Bächler, 'The Use of a Relational Data Base Model for the Implementation of an Information System . . .', in Anne Gilmour-Bryson (ed.), *Computer Application to Medieval Studies*, Medieval Institute Publications, Western Michigan University, 1984, pp. 89–106.

13.   See Luzzati *et al.*, 'The Use of Computers in Editing Medieval Baptismal Records in Pisa . . .', in Anne Gilmour-Bryson (ed.), *Medieval Studies and the Computer*, Pergamon Press, 1978, pp. 155–64.

14.   Bernice Lipkin and Joel Lipkin, 'Data Base Development and Analysis for the Social Historian: The Educational Status of the Beneficed Clergy of the Diocese of Hereford 1250–1529' in *Medieval Studies and the Computer*, *cit.*, pp. 113–25.

15.   Janet Williamson, 'One Use of the Computer in Historical Studies:

Demographic, Social and Economic History from Medieval English Manor Court Rolls', *Computer Applications to Medieval Studies, cit.*, pp. 51–61.

16. See Jean-Philippe Genet, 'Automatic Text Processing and Factorial Analysis . . .' in *Computer Applications to Medieval Studies, cit.*, pp. 147–76.

17. See, for example, Gian Piero Zarri, 'An Overview of RESEDA, an Artificial Intelligence Question Answering System . . .', *ibid.*, pp. 177–94.

18. See Anne Gilmour-Bryson, 'Coding of the Testimony of Prisoners in the Trial of the Templars in the Papal States 1309–1310' in S. Lusignan and J. North (eds.), *Computing in the Humanities*, Waterloo, Canada, 1977, pp. 135–60; 'Coding of the Depositions of the Templars', in A.A.Martino (ed.), *Deontic Logic Computational Linguistics and Legal Information Systems*, North Holland Press, Amsterdam, 1982, pp. 451–67.

19. See my articles: 'FOCUS, a data base for use by the Homicide Squad', *International Conference to the ALLC San Francisco, 1982* (in press); 'Manuscripts to Homicide: the Investigation at the Hospital for Sick Children', Sarah K. Burton and Douglas D. Short (eds.), *Sixth International Conference on Computers and the Humanities*, Computer Science Press, 1983, pp. 206–14.

20. 'Computers and Legal Indexing', *Advances in Computing in the Humanities* (in press).

Communities

2 *T. E. Rihll and A. G. Wilson*

Model Based Approaches to the Analysis of Regional Settlement Structures: the Case of Ancient Greece

Introduction

History, said Montaigne, is of all subjects that one to which our minds apply themselves in the most various ways.[1] This paper concerns a collaborative project, between a member of the School of History and a computer modeller in the School of Geography at Leeds, to build a conceptually simple but mathematically rigorous model of settlement hierarchy development, specifically in Ancient Greece. A mathematical model is a set of equations which represent a formally defined hypothesis or theory about some real-world system of interest.

The paper is organised as follows:

First, a brief introduction to the problem, namely, the emergence of the *polis* or city-state, and the approach taken to explore it, that is, spatial analysis. Second, a brief review of theoretical desiderata in model- and theory-building, and an account of how and why the survey area was selected and what evidence was used as the database. The main section is a discussion of the model components with special emphasis on the major subroutines, followed by examples to illustrate its potential contribution to history and archaeology. In the concluding comments we will indicate what we take to be the most valuable and important aspects of model-building in history at this time, and try to locate such work in the wider academic spectrum of social studies, i.e. disciplines having as their subject people and society.

I. The emergence of the *polis* symbolises the transformation from European prehistory to 'the Western Tradition'. The dividing line, for analytical purposes, is conventionally drawn at 700 BC, the start of the Archaic period of Ancient Greece. Such a radical transformation, needless to say, involved social change at the level of structural principles — society was more or less completely reorganised along new lines.[2]

Cities are at the core of 'civilisations'; citizen, civic, civil and civilised are all historically and etymologically intertwined with the phenomenon of the city, and nowhere more so than in the city-states. Attempts to define 'the city' in terms of urban structure have now been abandoned by geographers and sociologists as futile and misdirected,[3] and the city is instead conceptualised in terms of a storage container and crucible for the generation of power.[4] Cities are, above all, loci of social interaction, places where social action is concentrated and focussed. To analyse why some settlements became cities whereas others did not, and why some cities became greater than others, we can enlarge the historical armoury with tailor-made spatial interaction and location models based on recent developments in geography.

II Theoretical desiderata in model-building are (i) a clearly defined problem and sharply defined hypotheses which are compatible with the available evidence. Elaborate hypotheses require elaborate evidence. In these early days, the simpler the model the better. (ii) The evidence available may be alternatively sparse, superabundant, incommensurate or highly subjective, and is always partial, especially in more remote periods. Consequently a model should be independent of the database, and this renders the model *pro tanto* independent of the data used to test it. (iii) The model should be sensitive to slight changes in parameter values and be able to simulate a variety of possible situations and conditions. (iv) It should be robust, that is, it should perform reasonably well even if the data are imperfect, for example, if there are errors or omissions in the database. (v) For this kind of analysis, sites included should be contemporaneous to the nearest degree possible;[5] in our case the most reasonable minimum span was 200 years (900–700 BC), the duration of the Geometric pottery style. This was selected as the criterion of admission on the grounds that (a) pottery is ubiquitous and practically indestructible. (b) This is a distinctive, easily recognised style associated with the period under consideration. (c) Its presence at a site is likely to be recorded no matter how brief the report.

The data the model requires has been pared down to the minimum of a site's existence and location, nothing more, given in the form of Cartesian co-ordinates. This minimisation of input data not only makes the model independent of an inadequate database and of the evidence used to test it, but also has the additional benefit of giving the model a predictive potential to identify important sites even if evidence is lacking, or exists but hasn't yet been organised or utilised to bear upon the problem posed.

There are two methods by which additional information can be incorporated without changing the equations (e.g. adding sub- and/or superscripts to the variables or additional elements): sites can be weighted individually or by sets during a program run, allowing the user, for example,

Figure 1

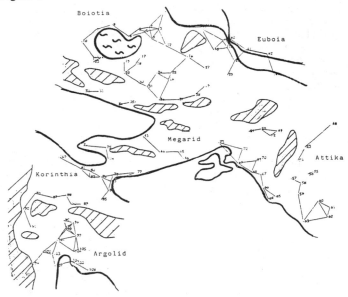

to modify the isotropic landscape and model topographic or social (e.g. language) barriers occurring within the survey area. Our survey area[6] was selected in order to include several major *poleis* about which a great deal is known, such as Athens and Korinth; two regions which are seriously neglected in the surviving documentary sources but which have recently received extensive archaeological attention (Boiotia and the Argolid); and the general area in which the earliest *poleis* are thought to have arisen (Argolid-Korinthia). Within this area there is a total of 109 known sites thought to have been occupied *c*.900–700 BC.

III   We begin with the assumption that, initially, all sites are approximately equal in population and 'importance'/'size'. At the risk of oversimplification, the hypothesis expressed in the spatial interaction and location model (see equations 1 — 4 in the appendix) is that:

interaction between two places (S_{ij}) is proportional to the population at the origin zone (G_i), multiplied by the 'size', or resources available, at the destination zone (W_j). The model also involves a negative exponential function of the distance between i and j (c_{ij}). The parameter (β) allows the relationship between interaction and distance to be 'fine-tuned'. It may — but need not — be interpreted as the media 'strength' by which resources are communicated across spatial and temporal gaps. A constant of proportionality is calculated for each zone i (see equations 2 and 4), and this can be interpreted as representing the effect of competition between centres.

The prediction of settlement 'size' or 'importance', expressed through the variable W_j, is rather more complex, involving the solution of nonlinear simultaneous equations. The mathematics and brief explanation are given in the appendix (see equations 5 — 8).[7] Suffice to say that the hypothesis here is that resource availability at a site is proportional to the total inflow attracted to that site as calculated by the interaction model. On the feedback version, indicated by the addition of a capital F, we add the hypothesis that the population of a place is directly proportional to the resources available there, and rerun the model using the results of the first iteration to provide the population estimate for the second.

The mathematics are derived from entropy-maximising methods, which can be understood as finding the most probable overall state of the system at a given time subject to the known constraints.[8] That is, of many possible 'ends' this method finds that one which can be arrived at via the greatest number of different 'means'. It recognises that individuals have many options open to them, between which it does not presume to choose on their behalf. At any point in history there are many possible futures, and what actually happens is generally the unintended outcome of a multiplicity of contingent human actions. Using this method allows us to find the most probable overall state whilst making the least assumptions about the particular actions or intentions of the actors involved.

The concepts of resources and media through which the model can (but need not be) interpreted are derived from the theory of structuration as formulated by Anthony Giddens.[9] We do not distinguish in the model between allocative resources, which are material resources deriving from man's dominion over nature, the natural environment, physical artifacts and technologies; and authoritative resources, which are non-material resources deriving from the dominion of some people over others, the capability to organise and co-ordinate the activities of other people. Both types, which are distinguished by Giddens for the purposes of analysis, can be expressed through the variable W. The media by which social interaction is carried across time and space, such as writing and vehicles, can be expressed through the parameter β. High values of β represent media of short 'range', 'duration' or 'penetration', low values those of long or deep 'reach'.[10]

IV Let us look briefly at some results (see Figure 2). An extended version of the Nystuen and Dacey procedure,[11] written in GHOST 80, has been incorporated into the program to provide another analysis of hierarchy which also offers a visual indication of the output. The result accords very well with the overall picture of Greek settlement hierarchy which is suggested by literary and archaeological evidence. I would like to use this result also to illustrate the predictive potential of the model: Akraiphnion, ranked 7, is sorely neglected in the surviving documentary sources. Although long known to archaeologists, it was also neglected by them until 1974, when a third cemetery was discovered here. Within one season some 400 richly furnished graves had been excavated, producing over 2000 vases from Attika, Korinthia and Euboia as well as Boiotia.[12] Although the results have not yet been properly published, this is recognised as a major find in Greek

Figure 2

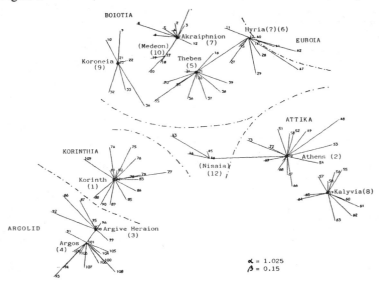

Figure 3

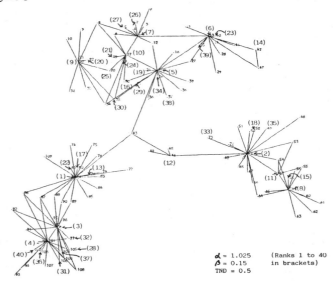

Figure 4

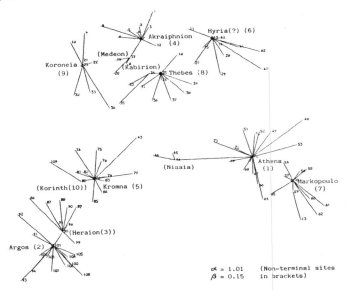

$\alpha = 1.01$ (Non-terminal sites
$\beta = 0.15$ in brackets)

archaeology. If it had not been discovered, the model results would suggest that an examination of the site might be profitable. As it is, the city itself is still neglected.

The extension of the Nystuen and Dacey technique allows us to see rather more of the interaction flows: Figure 3, for example, depicts the same analysis as Figure 2, but all flows over 50% of the maximum are plotted. Regional structures are now more apparent.

The program has been run over 200 times, exploring parameter values and testing for sensitivity and robustness. To illustrate the model's sensitivity, compare Figures 2 and 4. Whilst the overall appearance is very similar, note that: Athens now ranks 1; the Korinthia has 'lost ground' to the Argolid; and the 'centre' for the Korinthia has shifted from Korinth to Kromna, another little known and unexcavated site, but one at which extensive habitational remains and a large cemetery were discovered in 1960[13] and the sherd-scatter suggested to another visitor a large and substantial settlement occupied for over 1000 years, from at least the seventh century BC to the fourth century AD.[14] I might add that Kromna is regularly predicted to be an important site by the model. We also note that Argos and the Heraion have switched rank order. Other changes and similarities the reader can identify for him or herself. These differences result from a 0·015 change in the alpha parameter, where alpha has a possible range from 1 to around 3.

Rather than present a selection of individual results, I will refer to an analysis which illustrates the results of a large number of runs and which demonstrates how location can affect a site's fortunes over changing conditions. The predicted rank and terminal status of a representative twelve

Figure 5 *Exploration of parameter space*

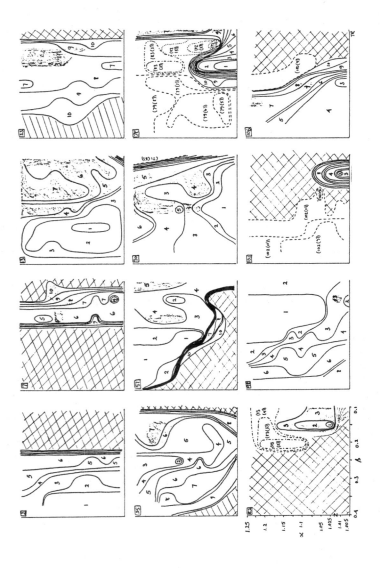

sites[15] were plotted across a range of parameter values (see Figure 5). A site is defined as a terminal if the total inflow attracted to it is greater than the total flow attracted to that site which receives the highest flow from it. The number indicates predicted rank (within only the top ten for simplicity and clarity), hatching indicates terminal status but rank less than ten (out of 109), shading indicates non-terminal status but rank within the top ten, and cross-hatching indicates rank less than ten and non-terminal status (i.e. relative unimportance). Those sites about which we know a great deal can be used as 'controls' to establish which region of parameter space is appropriate for Greece of the period — which is the lower middle to right quarter. We can then use this kind of analysis in two distinct ways.

In the first place, we can use it to deduce the relative importance of sites about which we know a great deal less, by finding how they perform in the appropriate parameter space. This then acts as a sort of practical bibliography, guiding archival and archaeological research towards those sites we expect to be more important.

In the second place, we can begin to work back from the model towards the social structure, using the empirical evidence to disaggregate specific structural systems, such as religious structures, from the higher-level abstraction of the model components. I take religion as an example because whilst every city had its temples, the major regional and panhellenic sanctuaries were not in, sometimes not even near, cities large or small. This suggests that one area of parameter space may be particularly appropriate for this kind of Greek religious structure.

This analysis also allows us to see whether a site is so located *vis-a-vis* other sites as to be practically unaffected by changing conditions — shown by consistent performance at whatever level across a broad area of parameter space, e.g. site no. 70, Athens; or profoundly affected by such changes — shown by dramatic 'cliffs', rapid and severe rank changes over small changes in parameter values, e.g. site no. 101, Argos.

V   We would like to conclude with a few remarks of the value of model-building in history, emphasising the benefit of building upon a decade's research in geography which underlies this model's structure.

There are basically three kinds of benefit to be gained from building a simulation model. 1. Conceptual. Model-building demands explicit structure and a clarity which forces one to rethink current concepts and assumptions, and to do so at the beginning. It was at this stage, for example, that the weaknesses in the concepts *'polis'* and 'city' became painfully apparent, which suggested that the problem would have to be redefined. 2. Developmental. This is the benefit arising from trying to translate a verbal hypothesis into a mathematical model, or, as in this case, trying to develop a verbal hypothesis for an adopted (and adapted) mathematical model which appears to work in a society, space and time very different from that in which it was developed.[16] Either way, the process forces the model-builder to give clear and sharp expression to his/her ideas and the relationships between ideas, to work through the hypothesis in a consistent and coherent manner. 3. Output. This is the benefit which may arise if the model is sharply defined and successfully tested, and the results may be expected to be realistic, that is, useable.[17] Although this particular model, chiefly because it rests on so much previous work by a team of geographers, seems to have output utility — which cannot of course be proved until someone excavates currently neglected sites predicted to be important by the model — the major benefits of model-building at this time are, we believe, in the conceptual and developmental areas. Stale concepts, shoddy thinking, unjustifiable assumptions, poorly formulated or poorly grasped hypotheses, gaps in knowledge or data; all are brought into sharp focus in the attempt to build a model, irrespective of whether or not it ultimately 'works'.

History and the social sciences, if we may call them that, are coming together in a new and deeper recognition of their respective merits. Geographers and sociologists in particular are attempting to bring the temporal dimension into the heart of their perspectives, by building new theories of power and elegance which break away from the old dichotomies of static/dynamic, diachronic/synchronic, structure/function, individual/society. A resurgence of the *Annales* spirit is underway, but not this time spearheaded by historians, and not, this time, with imperialistic aims. History can offer to geography and sociology its invaluable variety and depth; its experience of social change, sometimes catastrophic; and its immense record of human activity, creativity, and achievement. And modern computing facilities provide a fertile field in which to nurture such interdisciplinary dialogue and collaboration. Through them we can begin to build systematic models explicitly informed by social theory and incorporating both the spatial and the temporal dimensions.

Notes

1.   *On The Education of Children.*

2.   Cf. A. M. Snodgrass, *Archaic Greece: the age of experiment*, Dent, 1980; R. Hagg (ed.), *The Greek Renaissance of the Eighth Century BC*, Swedish Institute at Athens, Stockholm, 1983.

3.   Cf. eg. P. Abrams, 'Towns and Economic Growth: Some theories and problems', in P. Abrams and E. A. Wrigley (eds.), *Towns in Societies*, Cambridge, 1979, pp. 9–33: R. Harris, 'The spatial approach to the urban question: a comment', *Environment and Planning*, D 1, 1983, pp. 101–5.

4.   Cf. eg. D. Harvey, *Social Justice and the City*, Arnold, 1973: A. Giddens, *The Constitution of Society*, Polity Press, 1984.

5.   On all of these points, see the various papers in J. Sabloff (ed.), *Simulations in Archaeology*, University of New Mexico Press, 1981.

6.   See Figure 1. This figure shows the topography of the area, and the model's general accuracy in this respect — only six of the 109 sites were weighted to reflect major topographic barriers: the three on the island of Euboia and the three on the Perakhora peninsual (just north of the Korinthia).

7.   For proper discussions and proofs see the works by Wilson cited *infra*.

8.   Cf. Wilson, *Entropy in Urban and Regional Modelling*, Pion, 1970; *Catastrophe Theory and Bifurcation: applications to urban and regional systems*, Croom Helm/University of California Press, 1981.

9.   Cf. Giddens, *Central Problems in Social Theory*, Macmillan, 1979; *A Contemporary Critique of Historical Materialism*, Macmillan, 1981; *Profiles and*

Critiques in Social Theory, Macmillan, 1982; *Constitution of Society*, Polity Press, 1984; *The Nation-State and Violence*, Polity Press, 1985.

10. Cf. esp. Giddens, *Constitution of Society*, pp. 143ff., 258–62; *idem*, *Central Problems*, p. 103.

11. Original version, J. D. Nystuen and M. F. Dacey, 'A graph theory interpretation of nodal regions', *Papers, Regional Science Association*, 7, 1961, pp. 29–42, as extended in T. E. Rihll and A. G. Wilson, *Settlement structures in Ancient Greece: model-based approaches to analysis*, Leeds School of Geography Working Paper 424, 1985.

12. Cf. *Archaiologika Analekta Athenon* 7, 1974, pp. 325–38; 10, 1977, pp. 273–86; *Archaeological Reports* 1974/5, p. 18; 1975/6, p. 16; 1980/81, p. 22.

13. There has been sporadic excavation of graves, the results of which are also illustrative: for instance, a three-day dig in 1938 produced nine poros sarcophagi, and one grave found in 1960 contained 26 vases dated *c*.560 BC. Cf. J. Wiseman, 'The Land of the Ancient Corinthians', *Studies in Mediterranean Archaeology* (L), Gothenburg, 1978, p. 66.

14. J. Salmon, *Wealthy Corinth*, Oxford, 1984, pp. 25, 35, 156.

15. Ay. Ionnis (no. 2), Akraiphnion (7), Hyria(?) (13), Koroneia (23), Thebes (25), Koropi (57), Athens (70), Kromna (78), Korinth (82), Argive Heraion (98), Argos (101), and Nauplia (106).

16. There is no need to be coy about this: people have used tools and techniques which work long before anybody understood precisely why and how they work. Computing is a fine example of this (witness the dearth of top-down design projects) and medicine is another (the recent re-establishment of some herbal treatment is, at least in part, due to scientific explanation, and justification, of 'traditional knowledge' that plant x is beneficial for the prevention and/or cure of problem y).

17. See M. S. Aldenderfer, 'Computer simulation for archaeology', in Sabloff (ed.), *op. cit*, 1981, pp. 11–49.

Mathematical Appendix

Spatial Interaction and location model

'Equal start' (or egalitarian) version

$$S_{ij} = A_i G_i W_j^\alpha e^{-\beta c_{ij}} \tag{1}$$

where

$$A_i = \frac{1}{\sum_j W_j^\alpha e^{-\beta c_{ij}}} \tag{2}$$

For notation see end.

Feedback version (Population = 'size' or resource availability).

$$S_{ij} = A_i W_i (W_j^F)^\alpha e^{-\beta c_{ij}} \tag{3}$$

where

$$A_i = \frac{1}{\sum_j (W_j^F)^\alpha e^{-\beta c_{ij}}} \tag{4}$$

Settlement 'size' or resource availability prediction

(Calculation of $\{W_j\}$ and $\{W_j^F\}$ used above). Calculate (1) using set of guessed starting values for W_j (for egalitarian situation, all values equal). Calculate

$$D_j = \sum_i S_{ij} \tag{5}$$

(D_j equals the total interaction flow attracted to j). If $D_j > W_j$, the calculated resource availability at j exceeds the original guess, and the hypothesis is that W_j should be increased. If D_j is less than W_j, then W_j should be decreased. At equilibrium, we require

$$D_j = W_j \tag{6}$$

So, substitute for D_j from (5)

$$\sum_i S_{ij} = W_j \tag{7}$$

and for S_{ij} from (1) and (2)

$$\sum_i \frac{G_i W_j^\alpha e^{-\beta c_{ij}}}{\sum_k W_k^\alpha e^{-\beta c_{ik}}} = W_j \tag{8}$$

These are non-linear simultaneous equations which can be solved for given values of α and β to give $\{W_j\}$, the spatial pattern of settlement resource availability (or 'size'). For feedback version, $\{W_j^F\}$, set G_i equal to W_i and rerun.

Notation

S_{ij}	=	interaction between i and j
G_i	=	population at i
W_j	=	resource availability or 'size' at j
c_{ij}	=	distance between i, the origin zone, and j, the destination zone
α	=	a parameter
β	=	a parameter
$e^{-\beta c_{ij}}$	=	a negative exponential function arising from entropy-maximising methods and acting as a distance-decay function.

The Hull Domesday Project

Domesday Book is, by any standards, a prime candidate for computer-
assisted research. It is a document of fundamental importance to the study of
early medieval English history and has attracted not a few devotees prepared
to spend a lifetime unravelling its secrets. Despite their efforts Domesday
remains, in many respects, an enigma: the mass of statistical information
concerning people and their economic resources is presented only on the level
of the individual landholding and its interpretation is hampered by formulae
fraught with difficulties. Overviews, aggregations and wholesale
rearrangements of the data into other more convenient formats were tasks
not undertaken in the past by historians lacking plentiful time and patience.
A computer, of course, can make light work of such operations. Fortunately
the regular structure and statistical content of Domesday lend themselves
well to computerisation. The text is composed of a sequence of entries and
these become the basic units of analysis. A typical entry has a varied range of
statistical data to which some at least of the standard analytical procedures
offered by computer software may be usefully applied.[1]

Concentrating on its statistics, one approach to computerising Domesday
involves the manual extraction of values from the text and analysis of huge
blocks of numbers using packages like SPSS or specially written
software.[2] Domesday is, however, a text not a data matrix. An
understanding of its vocabulary and its formulae lies at the heart of
Domesday scholarship: it is fundamental to studies of tenure, land units and
administrative structures, as well as to any worthwhile investigation of the
statistics embedded in the text. Moreover, for the student of early-medieval
place-names and personal names, Domesday is an unrivalled source; the first
documentary reference to most English settlements is to be found in its folios,
as well as a comprehensive record of landholders throughout the kingdom
both before and after the Conquest. Systematic study of these names, of the
'technical' vocabulary and the formulae of Domesday, can be undertaken
most efficiently if the entire text is computerised, and this is what has been
done at Hull. A machine-readable text of both the original Latin version of
Domesday and an English translation has been established, consisting in all
of about 2·25 million words. The raw text is, however, too large for data
retrieval to be efficient. To enable it to be analysed interactively, the text is
converted into a random-access text database, which is served by a multi-
purpose and 'user-friendly' editor.[3] This highly flexible tool allows the user to
search for words or phrases in specified contexts and to display on the screen
the pieces of text in which they appear, sorted according to predefined criteria
(for example, in village order within administrative units rather than in the
tenurial order of the Domesday text). The editor may then be employed

either to amend and supplement the selected text or to extract statistical values for analysis, displaying the results in tables, graphs or maps as required.

The regularity in the content and layout of Domesday entries can be discerned readily enough by the historian but not, unaided, by computer software. To make Domesday comprehensible to the database editor the text must be very carefully structured. The basic units of analysis, the individual entries, i.e. manors or lesser land units, are identified and the text divided up accordingly. The main classifiable features of the text are highlighted by the insertion of a framework of coded markers. Thus a certain sequence of characters (a word or larger portion of text) is delimited by a defined coded marker in order to identify it to the software as a value of a particular variable. The codebook is simple but flexible. Two broad categories of coded markers have been employed: those for names of people (classified according to their landholding status) and places (administrative and tenurial units) and those delimiting sections of text containing statistical information, with separate codes for tax assessment, ploughteams, population, manorial appurtenances and values. Refinements to the scheme of personal name codes enable us to look beyond tenurial classifications to distinguish, for instance, Anglo-Saxons holding land after the Conquest or women in Domesday. Whilst we may wish to lump together several different coding classifications for some purposes, so we must also have a means of splitting categories into their basic components, of identifying the individual landholder or village. This is achieved by allocating a unique reference number to each separate settlement (about 13,500 are recorded in Domesday) and to each distinguishable person, of uncertain number as yet. These reference numbers are also pointers to files containing further information on settlements (including OS co-ordinates to enable mapping) and people in Domesday.

Insertion of the framework of coded markers is achieved using the database editor, a function for which it is particularly well suited. In essence, the editing process involves the selection of words or formulae in context. With the text concerned displayed on the screen, the user is able to insert markers in a very flexible editing environment. The operator is, however, required to supervise the insertion of every marker; it is only a semi-automatic process. The structuring of a medium-sized Domesday county like Buckinghamshire requires about 4000 markers and takes several weeks from start to finish. For a very large county, like Lincolnshire, far more coded markers will be needed. It is likely that about 300,000 will be required for the whole of Domesday England.

In view of this huge editing task why did we opt for an interactive approach? The markers could be inserted automatically into a standard text file under program control or with a conventional line editor using repetitive edits. Variations in the formulae and layout of the Domesday text would, however, ensure an unacceptably high error-rate from such an approach; a lot of manual editing to correct mistakes would be needed. By contrast with line or context editors, which cannot handle large, complex text files very efficiently, the database editor allows us to dip into a large text at any point and move around randomly. The task is performed with great clarity as the text to be marked is always before us on the screen, with a moveable pointer indicating where insertions will be made. The editor has a number of features which significantly speed up the process of locating words and reduce the number of keystrokes required to mark them. In searching for text to be marked, 'offsets' can be employed which locate the required word or phrase in an entry by its relationship to another word. Thus names of Anglo-Saxon landholders can be found in the text very efficiently by selecting the word 'held' and directing the pointer to the words preceeding it, since the usual Domesday formula for pre-Conquest landholders is 'Alfred held . . . T.R.E.'. A facility for selecting all the words entirely in upper case enables the user to locate and delimit all placenames (all of which appear in capitals) in one serial sweep of the text. Our interactive database editor therefore provides us with an acceptable speed of performance combined with a high degree of accuracy.

The coded markers provide an essential framework within which analysis of the Domesday database can be conducted. Delimited information may be the subject of a particular textual search or it could define a context for investigation of other words; it may also provide the key to a complete restructuring of the text.

The capacity to search the text database for particular words or phrases, within contexts defined by the user, places an extraordinarily powerful research tool at the disposal of the historian. Pieces of text containing combinations of words, formulae or other textual features can be sought using standard Boolean operators; other normal database features such as wildcards, exclusion/inclusion lists may also be employed. The results of such searches appear on the screen instantly. The pieces of text may be displayed in the order in which they occur in Domesday but, based upon an inconvenient combination of geographical and tenurial criteria, this is not the most useful arrangement for the historian. The most obvious rearrangement is upon purely geographical principles, to reconstitute 'those villages and hundreds which the Norman clerks tore into shreds',[4] but the text could be restructured according to pre-conquest landholding conditions, or a combination of sorting criteria could be employed.

Analysis of the statistical values of Domesday will also usually be undertaken using a restructured text. The extraction of the often ambiguous values — for assessment, agrarian resources, population and annual revenue — and the compilation of totals is performed by the computer under software control. Applications programs are directed to the relevant points in the text by the coded markers; unhampered by human inconsistency, they interpret the statistical formulae in as many ways as predetermined and then produce a series of alternative sets of figures. Sub-totals and totals are provided at points determined by the order in which the data has been sorted (for example, for hundreds within a county, or for tenants holding from a particular tenant-in-chief on a national scale). Results may be presented in the form of tables, graphs or maps, the latter being a particularly powerful means of displaying data distributions arising from word-searches or statistical analysis.

The flexibility, speed and thoroughness with which Domesday can be studied using the Hull database tends to confirm David Bates' feeling that through the use of computers 'some major problems of Domesday interpretation may be close to solution'.[5] If the systematic tabulation of Domesday statistics on a national scale, called for so long ago by Maitland, is at last within the grasp of the historian, so it is now also far easier to trace the distribution of particular words and formulae throughout the whole text. The 51 appearances of the word 'bought' (*emit*) are spread fairly evenly throughout the folios of Great Domesday. By contrast the distribution of the word 'gave' (*dedit*) is far more uneven; nearly 100 of 266 occurrences are to be found in Hereford, Worcester and Gloucester, frequently in connection with lay gifts to the church. The subject of these purchases and 'gifts' is often a 'manor': a controversial term since the days of Maitland, it is now, however, a straightforward task to trace its distribution throughout the folios of Domesday. When investigated systematically, and the results mapped, the inconsistent usage of the word 'manor'[6] can be seen to be related to the extent of the seven 'circuits' of the Survey; it is used far more intensively in some groups of counties than others. Moreover, careful examination of the land unit terminology used in several of these circuits suggests that a consistent attempt was being made to distinguish between 'manors' and the other land units, apparently for the purposes of taxation. For example, in Circuit 3 (south-east Midlands) the term 'manor' is applied to only a proportion of the landholdings and these assume very significant patterns when the text is rearranged by hundred and village.[7] In circuits in which 'manor' is not such a common feature of the text, examination of those formulae which may have a manorial meaning could well provide equally revealing results.

*   *   *

One major problem facing anyone interested in the realities of the territorial settlement which followed the Norman conquest is that of the identification of the individual tenants who are recorded in Domesday Book as holding lands. Something is known of most of the tenants-in-chief holding land directly from the crown. The major problems arise with sub-infeudation, at the lower layers of the tenurial hierarchy; if, for example, the text of Domesday Book for Oxfordshire refers to a sub-tenant named simply Roger on 20 occasions, does this mean that we are dealing with 20 different men called Roger each holding some land, or a single tenant called Roger who holds 20 different pieces of land, or does the true picture lie somewhere in between these two extremes; can any of these Rogers be identified with Roger d'Ivry who held much land in the county? If one then extends this to the 35 counties covered by Domesday Book and the several thousand Christian names involved, the magnitude of the problem becomes clear. Yet before research can be done with any confidence on the nature and extent of the post-conquest Norman settlement in England this problem of identifications must be considered and, as far as is possible, a tenurial geography constructed.

'Identification' here means the linkage of individuals with the same or slightly different names who are in fact the same person. This is an unusual Nominal Record Linkage problem because it is impossible to design algorithms which will consistently link names. Much of this work must be done using standard historical methods of tracing the descents of the manors involved but manipulation of the computer database can aid the progress of identification in a number of ways. The first aid is found in the reconstitution of Domesday villages (vill lists). It is impossible to draw a hard and fast line between tenants-in-chief and sub-tenants; the two categories are not mutually exclusive, and even men who can be numbered among the greatest of the Conqueror's tenants-in-chief are found holding land from each other, perhaps to rationalise land already held in demesne or otherwise. The vill lists can be used to bring this easily to light. Longstanton in Cambridgeshire, for example, according to Domesday, was divided amongst four tenants-in-chief, one of whom was the sheriff of the county, Picot; the sub-tenant of William son of Ansculf in this vill, was called Picot, almost certainly the same man. It only takes a few minutes using vill lists to make such connections, whereas hitherto to check by hand whether any sub-tenants have the same name as the tenants in chief in the same village was an infinitely longer task. In addition, the vill lists bring together all the sub-tenants holding in a village, which suggest where it is likely that the same man was holding there from two different tenants-in-chief — for example, the Osmund who held Ludwell in Oxfordshire from Arnulf of Hesdin is almost certainly the same man as the Osmund who held there from Robert son of Thurstan.

This vill lists also provide a useful index of both the places and landholders of Domesday when using primary and secondary sources. This was not one of the reasons why they were produced originally but in fact it has become one of their most important uses. Checking through indices to charters or cartularies, for example, the relevance of particular entries can be seen at a glance. Employed in this way, the computer-produced listings speed up the process of searching printed sources considerably.

Information can be extracted from the database on a wider basis than that of the vill; for example, tenants can be listed and sorted by antecessor or by fief. This ability to restructure the information derived from the text is very valuable. Names can be extracted and listed according to their tenant-in-chief. While within an individual county many men held from a number of tenants-in-chief, perhaps to give some cohesion to otherwise scattered holdings, on a national level they may have held the bulk of their land from a single tenant in chief. Hugh of Bolbec, a landholder in his own right in Buckinghamshire and elsewhere, also held land from Walter Giffard. Domesday Book actually names him as Hugh of Bolbec when referring to his sub-tenancies in Buckinghamshire but in Oxfordshire a man named Hugh helds from Walter Giffard but is merely described as Hugh. A listing of Walter's sub-tenants, naming Hugh of Bolbec as important amongst them, is a pointer to the identity of the otherwise unsurnamed Hugh.

Searches through the text can be used to pick out men between whom there is some relationship. The Cartulary of Oseney Abbey records a tradition that Robert d'Oilly and Roger d'Ivry were sworn blood brothers.[8] They appear together in a number of entries in Domesday Book as joint sub-tenants — as in Arncott which they jointly held from Abingdon Abbey. Other places where land is held in common by men named Robert and Roger can be picked out from the computer database, their antecessors and immediate lords listed to see if it is this particular pair of Roger and Robert who are concerned. Similarly lands linked by family connections, perhaps through marriage, can be investigated and their tenancies and sub-tenancies considered closely to see whether likely identifications of individuals emerge. While this does not necessarily prove their identity, it does provide valuable information on the one hand towards making an educated guess, while on the other it is a pointer to the direction in which one should look next in attempting to trace manorial descents — for example to any available inquisitions *post mortem* for a particular family. Mapping information about the location of individuals' lands is yet another guide to identifications. Do the lands of a certain Edward, for example, lie near other portions of land which were held by Edward of Salisbury? This might help to identify the unknown Edward with the tenant-in-chief of that name.

Decisions remain the work of the historian — the computer provides information to enable work to be done speedily, efficiently and with great accuracy, saving the Domesday scholar a vast amount of clerical labour. Ideas can be confirmed and hunches followed up without the need to spend weary hours searching through the text of Domesday Book for the necessary information. One historian wrote of Domesday: 'portions of the tenurial map . . . are illegible in regard to the details of ownership at a manorial level'.[9] Yet application of the computer's abilities to manipulate information can be likened to the use of ultra-violet light to enhance illegible documents. Not everything may be rendered comprehensible but a substantial amount of additional information can be gleaned.

The information about the identifications of individual tenants is incorporated into our Domesday database. This is done by appending, to each occurrence of a personal name, a unique reference number which is also a pointer to a file storing, rather like footnotes, supportive evidence for identifications. If, for example, it is known that Ambrose who held of William Peverel in Nottinghamshire is the same Ambrose who held of Peverel in Buckinghamshire the same number will be appended to his name every time it appears. It will be a very straightforward matter to alter the numbers if further identifications are made or errors detected. As long as the names have the same number, however, in all extractions of information and calculations concerning them the software will treat them as the same person.

*   *   *

The final section of this paper will describe the development of mapping software which enables the presentation of results of interrogations of the database in a cartographic form. The mapping software forms an integral part of the database editor. Preparation for mapping begins with the production of a computer-readable map of the whole country, including the county boundaries, using a digitising programme developed in the Geography Department at Hull. An electronic cursor is used to trace the various boundaries. As this is done the OS co-ordinates for the line segments are recorded onto a floppy disc and provide the basis for the maps. The map has, of course, only to be digitised once; the transference of the OS references to the mainframe computer provide the framework for the drawing of maps.

A digitised map is the first of our mapping requirements; the second major task is the provision of OS co-ordinates for every identifiable place mentioned in Domesday Book. Like the unique numbers attached to the personal names in Domesday Book, every place-name also has a reference number appended to it which is linked to a file containing the OS references for each place. This is the basis for the drawing of point-data maps which show the location of selected vills. Thus for example, to map all references to land which was waste in 1086 in a particular county or counties, the information can be selected from the database, read into a file, linked up with the appropriate OS co-ordinates and produced as a point-data map showing the location of the land. An area infill map can also be used to display the results of interrogations of the database, especially for statistical material. The information about waste land referred to above could, for example, be extracted and displayed as a percentage of the total amount of land in the county, either in an individual county or across the country as a whole.

Maps are also being digitised for each county enabling information to be displayed down to a parish level. This is a particularly valuable option, since many modern parishes are co-terminous with Domesday villages.[10] Once the parishes have been digitised they can be selected in groups which across county boundaries. In this way maps can be produced displaying information about groups of parishes, perhaps those which lie along rivers or with regard to their height above sea level. Just as linked files exist which contain additional information about the identity of tenants and places, it will be possible to store topographical information about these settlements so that parishes displaying particular characteristics can be easily selected to link up with information drawn from the text of Domesday Book.

Mapping, like all the database operations, is carried out interactively at a terminal, directly connected to the University mainframe computer. A menu of options allows selection of the map outline or outlines required; point data or area infill can be chosen. Statistics or other information can be extracted from the database and any statistical calculations required can be carried out as an integral part of the mapping program. A finished map, with automatic key, will draw rapidly on the screen and can be produced in a hard copy form in colour or in black and white. To produce a map on the screen should take a few minutes, thus enabling initial results to be viewed quickly; if, for example, a researcher was interested in place-names and the incidence of certain types of names, the database could be interrogated to select and map all incidences of places ending in 'by' or 'thorpe'. If, on the other hand, the researcher was concerned with manors of over a certain value, again the information could be selected and analysed interactively at the terminal. Such an extraction of information alone could take weeks if done manually, and even so human error will mean that some places may be overlooked.

Demographers, place-name specialists, philologists, agrarian historians and those interested in eleventh century society, pre- and post-Conquest, as well as those concerned with studying the impact of the Norman Conquest and settlement on England will all find uses for the database. When complete, the Hull Domesday Database will allow and encourage proper exploitation, on both a national and a local level, of the most valuable source available for the history of England in the middle ages.

Notes

1.   On the inappropriateness of some statistical techniques for Domesday research, see J. D. Hamshere and M. D. Blakemore, 'Computerising Domesday Book', *Area*, 18, 1976, pp. 289–94 and J. D. Hamshere, 'A computer-assisted study of Domesday Worcestershire' in T. R. Slater & P. J. Jarvis (eds.), *Field and Forest: An Historical Geography of Warwickshire and Worcestershire*, Norwich, 1982, pp. 105–24.

2.   For the drawbacks of the approach see J. J. N. Palmer, 'Le Domesday Book', *Le Médiéviste et l'ordinateur*, XI, 1984, pp. 2–4, and *idem.*, 'Domesday Book and the Computer', in P. Sawyer (ed.), *Domesday Book: A Reassessment*, London, 1985, pp. 167–9.

3.   The database software has been written by Mr George Slater, of the Computer Centre, University of Hull. Director of the Domesday Project is Dr J. J. N. Palmer, Senior Lecturer, History Department, University of Hull.

4.   F. W. Maitland, *Domesday Book and Beyond*, Cambridge, 1897, p. 520.

5.   Review in *History and Archaeology Review*, 1, Summer 1986, pp. 60–1.

6.   'Manor' is very often abbreviated to 'M', both when used in the margin and in the body of the text.

7.   See J. J. N. Palmer, 'The Domesday Manor' in the forthcoming proceedings of the Royal Historical Society Domesday Conference, Winchester, 1986.

8.   *V.C.H. Oxfordshire* I, p. 383.

9.   R. Lennard, *Rural England: 1086–1135*, Oxford, 1959, p. 53.

10.   For more detail of the mapping aspects of the Domesday Project see J. J. N. Palmer, 'Computerising Domesday Book', *Transactions of the Institute of British Geographers*, n.s. 11, 1986, pp. 279–89.

4   *Harold W. Booton*

The Use of the Computer in the Study of the Economic and Social Structure of Late Medieval Aberdeen

The main aim of this paper is to outline briefly some of the more important social movements which took place within the urban society of later medieval Aberdeen. The very full and often detailed evidence from both the town council and burgh sasine (i.e. property) registers allows much detailed comment to be made on the social structure. The survival of a large amount of material for the medieval burgh justified the use of the mainframe Aberdeen University Computer (Honeywell 66/80) and the employment of the very flexible minitab package.[1] The minitab system is both easy to use and understand and is especially designed for researchers with only a limited prior knowledge of computing. This particular package and its simple statistical techniques point the way forward for the historian to be able to use the often copious evidence in urban historical studies both quickly and effectively.

In the context of the late medieval Aberdeen evidence all of the surviving material of burgh property transactions and the tax contributions of men and women from the town were placed on the memory of the computer. This data was stored in a 'worksheet' of various columns. In this particular study there are six columns of data called simply Cl, C2, C3, C4, C5 and C6. Cl is the code number created by the computer to place the data in the memory. C2 is all sellers of land, C3 all buyers of property, and C4 the named area in which a property was either sold or bought. C5 was used to record the prices paid for lands within the urban area and C6 contained taxation contributions made by the various buyers or sellers of property. It is important to note that the price and taxation evidence was converted from pounds and shillings Scots into decimal figures. For example 10 shillings became 0·50, 1 became 1·00 and so on. Having established a simple but effective framework for the evidence various commands were fed into the computer to analyse the data collected. The six columns of data contained evidence from between 1434 and 1520. In the case of Aberdeen this period saw over 2500 individuals make over 4000 transactions in urban property. Additionally column six contained over 4000 craftsmen and burgesses recorded on various taxation rolls between 1448 and 1472.

After this brief examination of the mechanics of the computing methods employed on the Aberdeen material we may now ask what does it reveal? There was an undoubtedly strong social current in favour of a small and exclusive merchant elite whose wealth and property became more concentrated between 1434 and 1520. For example, eleven families (namely Blinseil, Chalmer, Collison, Cullen, Fichet, Kintore, Mar, Menzies, Murray, Rutherford and Prat) accounted for 32% of property transactions between 1434 and 1520. They also paid by far the largest tax contributions. In the twenty-two years from 1448 to 1472 their average payment of taxation was 25 shillings, 9 shillings more than the general average contribution. The economic wealth of the 'eleven' was balanced by their political power. They enjoyed the office of burgh provost almost by turn and dominated the town council from one generation to the next. In the years from 1434 to 1524 an average of 45% of total council membership came from men of the eleven families. This Aberdeen social elite invested heavily in urban property and the Castlegate and Gallowgate were the most popular (and expensive) areas. Additionally the wealthiest families such as the Menzies acquired country estates in Aberdeenshire and Kincardineshire.

Using the tax roll evidence from the mid-fifteenth century allows the historian to pinpoint areas of affluence within the town. The burgh was divided into four quarters for the purpose of taxation and these were called the Even, the Crooked, the Green and the Futty. The Even and the Crooked, which included the Gallowgate, the Castlegate and the Upperkirkgate, had the greatest numbers of wealthy taxpayers.

The minitab system was used to print out the totals of property transactions for individuals from 1434 to 1483 and 1484 to 1520. This exercise
helped to reveal the activities of heiresses, craftsmen, notaries and landed
men.

Heiresses in Aberdeen between 1434 and 1520 accounted for over 7% of
total property transactions. Although this is a small percentage the group are
of great social interest because of the movement and change they helped
create within urban society. A woman who had outlived her husband was
usually married again if her husband had left much property — there was a
good premium on well dowered widows. The evidence for the Aberdeen
heiresses suggests that wealth tended to attract more wealth for the social
movement created by heiresses favoured the merchant elite. Over 56% of the
lands of heiresses in the period from 1434 to 1520 lay on the Castlegate,
Gallowgate and Croftlands of the burgh.

A small group of wealthy craftsmen prospered within late medieval
Aberdeen. Over 150 craftsmen were of sufficient wealth to be recorded as
making contributions towards the burgh tax assessments in the mid-fifteenth
century. Their average payment was 13 shillings in the period from 1448 to
1472. The craftsmen had a concentration of property dealings in the
Gallowgate and Shiprow of Aberdeen. Only 10% of their transactions were
in the expensive Castlegate.

Late medieval Aberdeen enjoyed enough economic prosperity to be able to
support nine or ten professional notaries over several generations between
1434 and 1534. They made a living from the demand for legal expertise from
both merchant burgesses and north east landed families. The primary
function of the notaries was the production of charters, sasines and other
legal documents for which they charged fees. The prosperity of the town
notaries is revealed in their investments in urban property. The Castlegate,
Shiprow and Green accounted for nearly half of their land investments in the
years from 1434 to 1534.

The rural hinterland of Aberdeen contained the estates of many great
landed families such as the Gordons, earls of Huntly, Hays, earls of Erroll,
Keith, earls Marischal, the earls of Mar, Lord Forbes and Lord Erskine.
Smallers barons and lairds such as the Irvines of Drum, Frasers of Philorth,
Setons of Meldrum and the Leslies were also of importance. These baronial
families played an important part in the political and economic life of late
medieval Aberdeen. A complementary part of these processes was their
investment in urban property. The more expensive areas of Aberdeen such as
the Castlegate and Gallowgate accounted for over 20% of the property
transactions of landed men between 1434 and 1530. It was a token of social
status for a nobleman to have a burgh townhouse and helped demonstrate to
both burgesses and fellow gentry a man's wealth and social standing within
medieval society.

Aside from revealing the urban land investments of various social groups
within medieval Aberdeen the minitab system allows the historian to probe
the evidence in other ways. It is possible to set out in the form of a histogram
the complete totals of property transactions from 1434 to 1524 by decadal
totals. This reveals that from 1464 to 1513 Aberdeen saw a slowly rising
number of property transactions. Part of this 'growth' is a statistical quirk

caused by the increased amount of evidence after 1484 when the burgh authorities began to keep a property register. At the same time there was a period of economic stability in late medieval Scotland[2] and this allowed some expansion within the urban economy of Aberdeen. This economic trend may help to account for the growing number of transactions over several decades.

Additionally the histogram of decadal totals helps to reveal the fragile nature of this prosperity. There was a very sharp fall in property transactions in Aberdeen from 1514 to 1523. The burgh in 1513 after the Scottish defeat at Flodden was in a state of panic and feared an English attack at any time. In the uncertain climate of war very few burgesses appear to have bought or sold property. Disease was the other factor which may have reduced land dealings. In 1514 the Aberdeen council made laws for 'keping of the toune fra strang seknes and . . . contageus pestilence'.[3] Although there is no direct proof of this fact the removal of the fear of English invasion and the disappearance of the plague may have helped property transactions rise by 78% between 1514 and 1515. The Aberdeen evidence indicates how the late medieval Scottish urban economy was influenced by outside circumstances such as war, or plague, which were beyond the control of both town and national authorities.

Some 26% of total property transactions between 1434 and 1520 were carried out by burgesses and craftsmen who accumulated or sold lands in just one generation and then vanished from the record sources This may suggest that the medieval burgh experienced a degree of turnover in the composition of the town population. Some caution must be exercised when using such figures for they are based on property holdings which might have changed hands only once, thereby by giving a false impression of a shortlived family. In theory the burgess could have founded a family of several generations but this is not recorded in the council or sasine registers because they bought and sold no further property and simply retained their original lands from one generation to the next. The Aberdeen elite families were themselves subject to social change. Of the eleven in existence during the early sixteenth century, only four had survived by the early seventeenth century. They were the Menzies, the Cullens, the Collisons, and the Rutherfords.[4]

Apart from the analysis of property and tax material from the fifteenth and early sixteenth centuries the minitab system was also used to investigate entry patterns for the elite burgesses of guild of Aberdeen from 1399 to 1510. This group are of particular social significance for they enjoyed considerable political and economic advantages in comparison with other sections of urban society. As such the guild attracted the wealthy and ambitious who were keen to join and gain the advantages of membership.

The guild material was broken down into the various means used to acquire entry. The fact that 64% of entrants between 1399 and 1510 inherited their status as guild members from their fathers suggests how strongly entrenched the older families were within the guild. Throughout the late medieval period inheritance remained the principal means of recruitment. Although it was of great significance there was some 'new' blood able to enter the guild. For example marriage of a non-burgess to the daughter of a burgess of guild accounted for 12% of total recruitment from 1399 to 1510. The Collison family are a spectacular example of such social climbing in the

1440s and this helped them to become one of the most important burgh families. Craftsmen entered the burgesses of guild from 1399 to 1510 and accounted for 13·5% of the total entry. They earned admission through the payment of the high entry fines levied by the burgh council. The town authorities were nearly always short of ready money and therefore encouraged such recruitment. There were periodic attempts by the burgh council to restrict entry but such legislation had a very limited impact. For example in 1496 it was ordered that no new burgesses were to be made for a period of three years. This was ignored with nineteen men being admitted to the guild from 1496 to 1498.

Late medieval Aberdeen acted as a catalyst in the creation of social interaction amongst landed men, burgesses, craftsmen and notaries. The activities of the various social groupings should be kept in perspective for both the property evidence and the guild material help reveal the dominance of a well established elite family structure within the town. The eleven elite families indicate that an oligarchic system prevailed in the late medieval burgh. The concept of an oligarchy suggests not just rule by a few, but selfish government by the minority. The medieval burgesses of Aberdeen would not have concurred with this modern judgment of their society. They considered' that town government by the elite men, who by their standards were the most prosperous and able, would therefore be good for them. There was in effect an 'aristocracy' amongst the burgess class of later medieval Aberdeen. The guild evidence and property material reveal it was an elite which the most ambitious might enter and some men successfully managed this.

Notes

1.   See T. Ryan, B. Joiner and B. Ryan, *Minitab Student Handbook*, Massachusetts, 1976.

2.   J. Wormald, *Court, Kirk and Community, Scotland 1470–1625*, London, 1981.

3.   J. Stuart (ed.), *Extracts from the Council Register of the Burgh of Aberdeen*, i, Spalding Club, Aberdeen, 1844, p. 90.

4.   D. MacNiven, 'Merchant and Trader in early seventeenth century Aberdeen', Unpublished M.Litt thesis, Aberdeen University, 1977, p. 104.

Thanks are due to Dr G. Simpson for reading this paper and to Mrs E. Riddell for typing it.

Historical Demography, Social Structure and the Computer

The Cambridge Group for the History of Population and Social Structure was established in 1964 to carry out research into long-term variations in demographic and social trends affecting the population of England.[1] The factors which lie behind the decision to use computer techniques in historical research may be many and varied: quantity of data, speed and consistency, complexity of analyses. In this paper a brief summary of four computer-based projects is described, each varying in both the nature of computer utilisation and demographic enquiry.

The prime source for obtaining population data are governmental censuses. Yet for England these have only been undertaken decennially since 1801. Prior to this date the historical demographer has chiefly to rely on the events recorded by ecclesiastical parish registers.[2] England is fortunate in that for 90 per cent of the 10,000 parishes these data are available with few interruptions from the 1610's, and for half of the parishes the data extend back to the 1560's. However, since the Cambridge Group has never been able to command either the financial or clerical resources that would be required to undertake the analysis of even a large sample of parishes, it was extremely fortunate that the Group was able to call upon the services of a large army of volunteers (what the French have termed 'le secret weapon anglais'), to collect information to form a wide regional sample of parishes.[3] The result of this effort was to produce annual and monthly totals of registration events for a period of three hundred years (1541–1840), for some five hundred parishes.

It was from this point that the computer entered the research arena. The decision to use electronic techniques in this case was made in part because of the sheer size of the resulting dataset, producing on average some four million monthly totals of events, yet more importantly, because of the complex manipulations of the data that were required. The initial consideration was to convert the collected sample totals of Church of England baptisms, marriages and burials into realistic national totals of births, marriages and deaths.[4] Once this had been undertaken, the major task was to produce age-specific population totals, and estimates of reproduction rates and mortality levels. This was achieved by using a path-breaking technique termed 'back-projection', so called because it proceeds from the demographic structure of a known population (in this case 1871), and, taking account of the recorded totals of births and deaths and establishing the level of net-migration, projects the known demographic structure backwards to the start of the data. This is achieved by matching the observed number of vital events to the changing demographic structure in which they were created.[5] The results of this research based on aggregative analysis (the counting of vital events), together with a discussion of demographic trends and their interaction with the socio-economic framework of the nation are detailed by Wrigley and Schofield, in *The Population History of England*, published in 1981.[6]

Since the publication of this volume the technique of back-projection has been generalised to take into consideration the findings of recent research on the formal relationships of population dynamics.[7] In the new model the levels of migration and mortality are estimated simultaneously, while under the previous model they were resolved in sequence. The new version has been renamed 'generalised-inverse projection' and can easily be modified to take account of additional historical information, such as census information at an earlier date.[8] This more flexible system for estimating past demographic structures from historical series of vital events not only underlined the findings of *The Population History of England*, but has also proved to be a valuable tool in checking the logical consistency of collected demographic data. The model was tested on Swedish population data since that country is fortunate in possessing a long-run of accurate historic censuses and registration data. The 'closeness-of-match' between the observed and the predicted series is illustrated in Figure 1, and it can be seen that the long-term trends are extremely similar, although sharp short-term fluctuations in net-migration figures are offset and evened-out.

Obviously, throughout this exercise of applying back-projection techniques to aggregated parish register data, a tailor-made program had to be written in a high-level computing language. However, where possible, extensive use was made of standard library mathematical sub-routines since there is no point in duplicating effort.[9] The input and storage of the data for this exercise proved to be no problem since these were simple rectangular matrices of integers. However, data structure proved to be a significant problem in the second demographic project, namely the analysis of family reconstitution records.

Family reconstitution is a technique of demographic analysis pioneered by the French demographer Louis Henry. Firstly, the events of baptism, marriage and burial, abstracted from parish registers, are linked into family records. Following from this demographic characteristics, such as age at marriage, birth intervals and completed family size (all unobtainable from aggregative analysis) can be calculated, subject to rules about observation.[10] In the late 1960's when work on this type of analysis was started, computer systems expected data to have a simple structure, a matrix of numbers, like the aggregative registration material. It was far from straightforward for computers to cope with complex hierarchical data structures with, for example, varying numbers of offspring per married couple as in the case of the family reconstitutions. For this reason a flexible system of record-handling was developed, the basis of which was to separate the logical structure of the input record, in this case a reconstituted family, from the physical structure of individual records stored by the computer.[11]

Consequently, data no longer had to be 'keyed' into the computer in a fixed rectangular form with each record having the same dimensions, padding out

Figure 1   *Sweden 1700–1980, observed and estimated population figures*

A. Total population

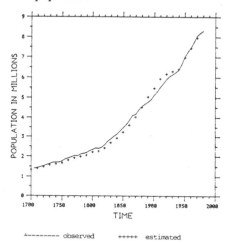

B. Net emigration

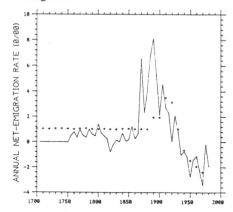

Information supplied by Jim Oeppen, Cambridge Group

missing values or unoccupied fields with blanks; instead only relevant, valid information needed to be keyed in a variable format. To produce the required demographic calculations from the family reconstitution studies, specific programs also had to be written in a high-level programming language.[12] Of course, much of this research, both input and analysis, could now be undertaken using a suitable statistical package providing facilities for hierarchical data manipulation.[13]

Initially all of the links which combined to make up a family reconstitution study were carried out by hand, first transcribing all of the baptism, burial and marriage information onto slips, sorting and linking them accordingly. This operation is not only extremely time-consuming, it is prone to a variety of human error. In reconstituting a population a large number of the links, say ninety per cent, are relatively easy to assign; the problem comes with the remaining ten per cent. For these difficult cases the manual linker invariably relies on historical judgement or intuition. Yet if these decisions are not consistent across the reconstitution, or across several reconstitutions carried out by several researchers, then comparative accuracy can be called into question. Equally, if an individual in the data has a number of different links that can plausibly be made, it is time-consuming and difficult for the researcher to carry each one through the resulting possibilities to discover which is the optimum link. For these reasons, efforts have recently been made to automate the process of reconstitution.[14]

The development of optical character reading machines has now enabled printed parish register volumes and transcripts to be read into the computer directly, once the machine has been 'trained' to read the type-set of a particular volume.[15] After the parish register entries have been entered into the computer they have to be formatted and input to a system file. If, as was usual in the English case, the incumbent or parish clerk made the entries in a standard or number of standard patterns, computer programs can be written to locate these patterns and read them into a system file. Non-standard entries detected by the program require individual formatting and input.[16] Upon completion of the system file, the process of reconstitution can start. The first obstacle to be crossed is the standardisation of all names, surnames and christian names, for all three documents, baptisms, marriages and burials. This is achieved by assigning a soundex code to each name, breaking the names down into their sound producing elements.[17] Thus the surnames Robbins, Robins, Robens and Robbyns would all be assigned the same code since, although spelt differently, they all sound the same. It is impossible to derive a foolproof algorithm that will cope with the immense variety of spelling habits in the past, so the computer-generated standardisation needs sometimes to be inspected and edited accordingly. Other string variables such as occupation and residence are also standardised and coded. Linking of the vital events is then carried out using the allocated codes, rather than the original strings. All possible links are made by the computer, allocating scores according to the 'likeness' of the match for the individuals involved. These scores are determined by a variety of factors: closeness of age, compatibility with other family members, matching features of occupation or birthplace, where given, and others. At this stage there may be several clusters of multiple links, of which only some will be true. The clusters are decomposed into separate and coherent sequences of links representing the events occurring throughout a single individual's life by finding the link in which one has the greatest confidence, (the link with the highest score), and deleting all links in the same cluster which are incompatible with it. The process is then repeated taking the link with the highest score in the set of remaining links until no multiple links remain. The various stages of this linking process are illustrated in Figure 2 using an example from the parish registers of Bletchingdon, Oxfordshire.[18] The linked families shown in the last panel of Figure 2 are written by the computer into a structured file, as in the case of family records that had been compiled manually and keyed into machine-readable form. This file is then used for statistical analysis, as described above.

Whereas the study of English historical demography is focussed around parish registers, research on historical social structure, the third application of computer techniques, is centered around the analysis of census documents and, on the rare occasions they exist, pre-census listings of inhabitants.[19] Like family reconstitution the computerisation of these documents was for a long time hampered by the complex logical and hierarchical structure of these records.[20] In some analyses the individual may

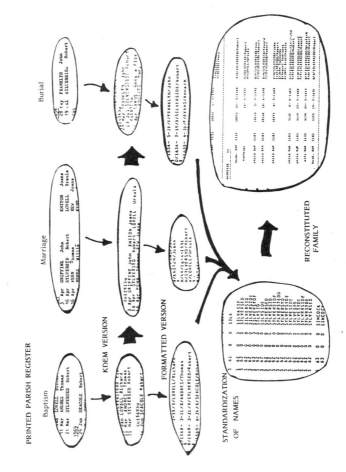

Figure 2   *The process of automated family reconstitution*

be the required level of observation, in others it may be the house or household, alternatively it may be what is termed the 'conjugal family unit', a unit of individuals linked either through marriage or a parent-child relationship.[21] The latter forms a particular problem since a conjugal unit may occur anywhere within a household, perhaps excluding the head, and there may be multiple numbers of conjugal units per household.

Since the application of computer techniques to household listings of inhabitants was developed much later than the analysis of parish registers, an entirely different strategy was adopted. It was decided to design a complete suite of input, checking and analytical programs entirely within a statistical software package that could freely manipulate hierarchical data structures.[22] Although this method may be inefficient in terms of computer processing and resources, in comparison to writing tailor-made programs in a high-level computer language, this disadvantage was seen to be out-weighed by the key advantage that researchers could amend and extend the analytical programs with a minimum of computer knowledge and training. To begin the operation census data are input to the computer in the same style adopted for the initial family reconstitution studies. Data are stored in a variable format with tags or pointers to indicate the logical structure of the document. Records are punched as in the original, with no standardisation of entries and no pre-coding of information.[23] This procedure is not only faster but makes for less error-prone transcription and data-entry. In addition, entering the data in full is the only way to ensure that the data has the potential to be utilised to the maximum. Ignoring, reducing or leaving out an item of information may prove to be disastrous for unforeseen future research, and may render the dataset useless to subsequent researchers. It would be both naive and foolish for a researcher to think that he can predict all possible future uses of a datasource.

Obviously, the grouping together of various items of census information by the use of codes is required to both aid computer efficiency and facilitate the analysis of the data.[24] This is achieved by the use of coding dictionaries. Such dictionaries not only save time; for example, for a census of a rural parish the occupation code for 'agricultural labourer' need only be entered once, rather than for some fifty percent of the male working population; but the process of post-coding, rather than pre-coding, enables the researcher to re-structure the codes, or allocate an entirely new coding schema, since the original values from which the codes are derived are retained within the data structure.[25]

A series of checking programs have been written which search the census data for logical inconsistencies, such as offspring having a recorded age which would have resulted in their mother conceiving at an unreasonably young or old age, usually the result of an error in data-punching or alternatively inaccurate enumeration. The computer also searches for cases requiring particular attention in the subsequent analysis, specifically the occurence of conjugal family units outside that of the head of the household. Some of these cases may require specific coding, primarily to ease the efficiency of subsequent analytical computing. In this respect it was necessary to develop a flexible coding scheme, to enable the researcher to cope with ambiguous situations within the census data. An example of this would be where a grandchild within a household may be the offspring of either a son or daughter also resident within the household. Such a system of coding allows the researcher to alternate strategies in later analyses rather than being restricted by decisions that were made, perhaps in error, during the initial stages of coding. This feature may be of particular importance if the information in the document is not very complete, as is the case with some pre-census listings, and consequently many inferences have to be made. An example of this flexibility can be seen in the case of identifying conjugal family units. As mentioned before, a conjugal unit is formed either by a husband-wife relationship, a parent-child relationship, or a combination of the two. In the case of a parent-child relationship, the parent may not only be married or widowed, but can be unmarried, i.e. the child in the conjugal unit can be illegitimate. Often conjugal units based on an illegitimate birth can not be assigned with a high degree of certainty. Consequently, if such relationships were critical to the research, a flexible system of analysis may have to be implemented. Table 1, for example, illustrates the differences in household structure by kin type, both maximising and minimising illegitimate relationships, and although, as one would expect in the British case, the numbers of extended and multiple households are small, the respective strategies produce a two-fold difference in the number of multiple households.

Once the data have been checked and coded satisfactorily the analysis of the census can begin. In this respect, research at the Cambridge Group has been directed to the development of some eighty-five standard analytical tables, the 'model tables' as they have come to be known.[26] These tables are divided into several thematic groups examining a variety of demographic and social structures: occupational structure, kin composition, the elderly, etc. The prime purpose of these tables is not to restrict analysis but rather to provide a broad framework for comparative studies of social structure, both chronologically and spatially. A suite of programs has been written to produce each of the model tables, with an added facility enabling the researcher to produce the tables for any specified sub-group of the population, perhaps an occupation or geographic sub-group, and, if required, produce similar tables yet with redefined categories. Perhaps the most well-known of the model tables is that which classifies residential kin within a household into the six family-type categories illustrated in Table 1, the Hammel-Laslett table of household classification.[27] This has become a benchmark by which historic global family structures are compared. However, it is wrong to judge historic household classification by this single table. This is one of the strengths of the model tables, since although two censuses separated by either time or space may display similar patterns in regard to the kin composition of the household, their social or demographic structure as measured by other characteristics, such as age-gap between spouses, age and sex of household heads, or occupational structure may differ sharply.

The model tables are designed to apply strictly to the 'static' analysis of census material, that is to say the analysis of a single place for a single time.[28] Although the analysis of this type of data is extremely fruitful, much can be gained by linking the individuals in successive censuses of a given

Table 1   *Household   structure: minimising   and   maximising*
                     *illegitimacy. Abergele, Denbighshire 1851**

Household Type				minimum		maximum	
				n	%	n	%
1)	Solitaries	a)	widowed	28	8.5	28	8.5
		b)	single	12	3.6	12	3.6
	Sub-total			40	12.1	40	12.1
2)	No family	a)	co-residence siblings	8	2.4	8	2.4
		b)	other co-residence relatives	9	2.7	10	3.0
		c)	siblings and relatives	–	–	–	–
		d)	no familial relationship given	1	0.3	1	0.3
	Sub-total			18	5.4	19	5.7
3)	Simple family	a)	married couples, no offspring	38	11.6	38	11.6
		b)	married couples, with offspring	147	44.7	147	44.7
		c)	widowers with offspring	12	3.7	11	3.3
		d)	widows with offspring	30	9.1	29	8.8
	Sub-total			227	69.1	225	68.4
4)	Extended family	a)	extension upwards	8	2.4	9	2.7
		b)	extension downwards	26	7.9	21	6.4
		c)	extension sideways	4	1.2	4	1.2
		d)	combination	1	0.3	1	0.3
	Sub-total			39	11.8	35	10.6
5)	Multiple family	a)	secondary units upwards	–	–	–	–
		b)	secondary units downwards	4	1.2	9	2.7
		c)	secondary units sideways	–	–	–	–
		d)	frérèches	1	0.3	1	0.3
		e)	combination	–	–	–	–
	Sub-total			5	1.5	10	3.0
6)	Indeterminate			–	–	–	–
	Total			329	99.9	329	99.8

* The machine-readable data used for the calculation of this table were collected and supplied by M.
Anderson, University of Edinburgh, as part of the ESRC funded two-percent 1851 census National
Sample Project.

community, providing a framework for dynamic analysis in which
individuals, families and households can be traced over time, witnessing the
departure of household members, either through migration or death, and the
arrival of new members.[29] Following basically the same technique and
method as the linking undertaken in family reconstitution studies, programs
have been written to merge two censuses together. The resulting linked
dataset provides a further dimension to the model tables, comparing the
characteristics of 'movers' and 'stayers' and the evolution of households.
Development continues and much more work is required since, as of yet, no

standard method has been devised for categorising household evolution over time.[30]

The evolution and dissolution of households and the interaction between demographic behaviour and family characteristics were the chief issues that prompted the establishment of the fourth computer-based research project, that of micro-simulation.[31] Using a set of demographic parameters defining mortality, fertility and nuptiality, and the probability of these various demographic events occurring at a specified time in an individual's life-span, a model 'population universe' is simulated through time, from which the kin relationships between all individuals can be derived.[32] From this theoretical population one can calculate the number and ages of living kin of different kinds that a person of a given age might be expected to have, for example the numbers of surviving children when a person is aged over 70 years. Moreover, by varying the demographic parameters independently of each other, the researcher can quantify the effect each parameter has on the 'population' as a whole. Consequently it can assist us to gain information in areas where the necessary historical data are lacking, as, for example, in Table 2, which shows the size and distribution of kin sets according to the demographic characteristics of the eighteenth-century pre-industrial and twentieth-century contemporary worlds. This illustrates a number of

Table 2   *Simulated kin sets: contemporary and pre-industrial England*

				Age of individual					
	0	11	22	33	44	55	66	77	88
Contemporary									
Ascending kin									
Mean number	8.15	7.39	6.18	4.43	2.94	1.43	0.26	0.01	—
Mean age	42.2	51.3	58.9	64.6	71.7	80.0	87.3	—	—
None (%)	0	0	0	0.3	5.0	28.3	77.9	99.3	100
Descending kin									
Mean number	—	—	0.48	3.07	4.21	5.63	7.33	7.88	7.62
Mean age	—	—	2.8	6.8	14.7	20.3	25.2	33.3	43.1
None (%)	100	100	71.3	10.3	5.3	4.0	4.0	4.0	4.7
Lateral kin									
Mean number	3.15	5.66	6.34	6.41	6.19	5.72	4.82	3.16	1.37
Mean age	7.7	13.2	22.2	32.6	43.2	53.6	63.3	71.6	78.4
None (%)	15.0	1.0	1.0	0.7	0.7	1.0	3.3	10.7	38.3
Pre-industrial									
Ascending kin									
Mean number	8.66	6.66	4.86	3.13	1.54	0.43	0.05	—	—
Mean age	37.5	45.6	53.2	61.1	68.6	75.4	75.0	—	—
None (%)	0	1.0	1.3	8.0	32.3	71.0	95.7	100	100
Descending kin									
Mean number	—	0.18	1.54	6.29	10.01	11.86	14.61	16.14	14.69
Mean age	—	3.14	4.50	7.0	12.7	19.3	22.8	27.5	35.0
None (%)	100	93.0	50.7	8.0	4.7	3.7	4.0		4.3
Lateral kin									
Mean number	10.14	15.75	17.04	15.92	13.49	10.56	7.26	3.80	1.35
Mean age	8.8	13.7	21.4	30.8	41.0	50.6	59.1	65.9	70.8
None (%)	6.0	0.7	0.3	0.3	0.3	1.7	4.7	14.0	49.0

*   Example taken from P. Laslett, 'The significance of the past in the study of ageing', p. 386.

important features relevant to the notion of kin support of the elderly.[33] Taking only descending kin (grandchildren, children, nephews and nieces), declines in mortality have outweighed declines in fertility to produce greater numbers of relatives, nearly twice as many now compared with two hundred years ago, yet despite this overall trend, the proportion of elderly persons (aged 55 +) with no descending kin at all remains broadly the same.

Unlike the other three projects described in this article, the micro-simulation project does not use historical data directly as an input, although it requires historical information to choose plausible demographic rates of births, marriage and deaths. The purpose of the simulation, rather, is to create data, in this case a theoretical population. Yet despite this obvious difference there are similarities of approach with the other projects. Due to the complex nature of the algorithms the simulation routines had to be written in a high-level computer language, yet the researcher specifies demographic parameters expressed in the form of a simply constructed macro, separate from the simulation programs. Also, the resulting simulated 'population universe' can be analysed according to the researcher's preferences using a standard software package. Thus, hopefully, a balance between flexibility, computer efficiency and 'user-friendliness' is maintained.

In each of the four projects outlined above the role which the computer plays is different, yet in each the computer is an indispensible aid to research. Although the reasons for using computing techniques are specific to each case, the advantages are clear, indeed all four of these projects could not have been undertaken in their existing form had it not been for automated techniques. The celebrated French historian Emmanuel Le Roy Ladurie once remarked that if the historian of tomorrow refused to learn computer techniques then he would cease to exist.[35] This is to overrate the computer, since in some branches of historical research little advantage would probably be gained via the use of a computer, if we except the use of word-processing. However, it is clear that the use of computer techniques has allowed major advances in our knowledge of the past: in particular it has enabled the construction of long-term demographic trends, and helped to place these trends within the socio-economics context that generated them.

Notes

1. A summary of the Cambridge Group's research activities can be found in the *SSRC Newsletter* (now ESRC), 44, Nov 1981, pp. 10–13.
2. For a summary of the main demographic sources and the problems associated with them see M. Drake, *Historical Demography: problems and projects*, The Open University, Milton Keynes, 1974.
3. The call for volunteers to abstract the required parish register data lead eventually to the publication of the bi-annual journal *Local Population Studies*.
4. This conversion process is fully described in E. A. Wrigley and R. S. Schofield, *The Population History of England, 1541–1871: a reconstruction*, London 1981, chapters 1–4.
5. The 'back-projection' technique is an expansion of the method initially proposed in R. D. Lee, 'Estimating series of vital rates and age structures from baptisms and burials: a new technique, with applications to pre-industrial England',

Population Studies, 28, 1974, pp. 495–512. It is detailed in Appendix 15 of Wrigley and Schofield, *Population History*, pp. 715–738. See also R. D. Lee, 'Inverse Projection and Back Projection: A Critical Appraisal, and Comparative Results for England, 1539–1871', *Population Studies*, 39, 1985, pp. 233–48.

6.   See footnote 4.

7.   See, for example, S. H. Preston and A. J. Coale, 'Age-Structure, Growth, Attrition and Accession: A New Synthesis', *Population Index*, 48(2), 1982, pp. 217–59, and W. B. Arthur and J. W. Vaupel, 'Some General Relationships in Population Dynamics', *Population Index*, 50(2), 1984, pp. 214–26.

8.   A description of the new model is provided in J. Oeppen, 'Inverse Projection and Back-Projection: Variants of a More General Constrained Projection Model', unpublished paper, Cambridge Group, 1985.

9.   For example, the NAG library of mathematical routines.

10.   M. Fleury and L. Henry, *Nouveau manuel de dépouillement et d'exploitation d'état civil ancien*, 3rd ed., INED, Paris, 1985, Chapter 5; and for an English example, E. A. Wrigley, 'Family Reconstitution', Chapter 4 in E. A. Wrigley, (ed.), *An Introduction to English Historical Demography*, London, 1966.

11.   The list-processor routines were developed originally by the Computing Laboratory of the University of Newcastle upon Tyne in IBM Assembler code, and re-implemented in Cambridge in ALGOL68C. R. S. Schofield and R. S. Davies, 'Towards a flexible data input and record management system', *Historical Methods Newsletter*, 7, 1974, pp. 115–24. See also M. Overton, 'Computer analysis of an inconsistent data source: the case of probate inventories', *Journal of Historical Geography*, 3(4), 1977, pp. 317–26.

12.   Originally in ALGOL60, then in ALGOL68.

13.   Such as SAS, or SPSS-x supported by SIR. See A. A. Ray (ed.), *SAS User's Guide Basics*, Cary, NC: SAS Institute Inc., 1982; Anon, *SPSS-x User's Guide*, Chicago, Il:SPSS Inc., 1983, and Anon, *SIR/DBMS: manual supplement*, Evanston, Il: SIR Inc., 1984.

14.   For a statement on the logic of record linkage see E. A. Wrigley and R. S. Schofield, 'Nominal record linkage by computer and the logic of family reconstitution', in E. A. Wrigley (ed.), *Identifying People in the Past*, London, 1973, pp. 64–101. Also see M. Skolnick, 'A computer program for linking records', *Historical Methods Newsletter*, 4(4), 1971, pp. 114–25; C. J. Jardine and A. D. J. Macfarlane, 'Computer input of historical records for multi-source record linkage', in M. W. Flinn (ed.), *Proceedings of the 7th International Economic History Congress*, Edinburgh 1978, pp. 71–78; and I. Winchester, 'Record Linkage in the Microcomputer Era: A Survey', *Demographic Data Base Newsletter*, 3, Umeå, 1985.

15.   In Cambridge a Kurzweil data entry machine (KDEM) has been used to read printed parish register transcripts.

16.   Since English parish registers usually contain little more than names and the date of the event the records are relatively easy to format. In the case of continental countries whose records are often more textual, although the general principal can be applied the exercise will of course be far less straightforward.

17.   For a description of Soundex codes see W. Phillips, 'Record linkage for a chronic disease register', in E. D. Acheson (ed.), *Record Linkage in Medicine*, Edinburgh, 1968, pp. 120–53; R. S. Schofield, 'The Standardisation of names and the Automatic Linking of Historical Records', *Annales de démographie historique*, 1972, pp. 359–64, and I. Winchester, 'The Linkage of historical records by man and computer: techniques and problems', *Journal of Interdisciplinary History*, 1, 1970, pp. 107–24. A computer program can be found in J. Hitchon, 'Russell Soundex Code: a BBC Basic Program', *Computers in Genealogy*, 1(5), 1983, pp. 122–3.

18.   The development of the automated family reconstitution programs has been undertaken by Ros Davies of the Cambridge Group. I would like to thank Bridget

Taylor for providing the Bletchingdon example.

19. For a summary of data input schemes see K. Schürer, 'Historical Research in the Age of the Computer: An Assessment of the Present Situation', *Historical Social Research*, 36, 1985, pp. 43–54.

20. A list of the parishes enumerated in pre-industrial times has appeared in successive issues of *Local Population Studies* starting in 1968. From issue 24, Spring 1980, the list has been repeated and expanded to include details on the range of information on individuals and household to be found in each document. For a review of research on household structure see R. Wall, 'The household, demographic and economic change in England, 1650–1970', in R. Wall, J. Robin, and P. Laslett (eds.), *Family Forms in Historic Europe*, Cambridge, 1983, pp. 493–512.

21. Definitions of the terms 'household' and 'conjugal family unit' appear in P. Laslett and R. Wall, (eds.), *Household and Family in Past Time*, Cambridge, 1972. See especially pp. 34–44.

22. The software package chosen for this project was SAS (see footnote 13). The suite of programs written to analyse census documents are collectively known as CAMTAB. This system is described more fully in R. Wall and K. Schürer, 'Computing the History of the Family: A Question of Standards', in F. Daelmans (ed.), *Sources et methodes de la démographie historique avant 1850*, Brussels, 1984, pp. 113–33.

23. Input formats for census data are discussed in K. Schürer, 'Methodology: recording data from original sources', *Historical Social Sciences Newsletter*, 2, 1984, pp. 8–11, and K. Schürer, 'Census enumerators' returns and the Computer', *Local Historian*, 16(6), 1985, pp. 335–42.

24. Details of coding historical material are given in K. H. Jarausch, 'Some Reflections on Coding', Paper submitted to the International Workshop on the Creation, Linkage and Usage of Large Scale Interdisciplinary Source Banks in this Historical Disciplines, Göttingen, July 1985; M. Thaller, 'A draft proposal for a standard for the coding of Machine Readable Sources', Paper submitted to the International Workshop on Standardisation and Exchange of Machine Readable Data in the Historical Disciplines, Graz, June 1986; and K. H. Jarausch, G. Arminger and M. Thaller, *Quantitative Methoden in der Geschichtswissenschaft: Eine Einfuhrung in die Forschung, Datenverarbeitung und Statistik*, Darmstadt, 1985.

25. This point is expanded in Schürer, 'Census enumerators' returns'.

26. The analysis of census documents is discussed in P. Laslett, 'The study of social structure from listings of inhabitants', in Wrigley (ed.), *An Introduction to English Historical Demography*, pp. 160–78, and P. Laslett, 'Mean household size over three centuries', in Laslett and Wall (eds.), *Household and Family*, pp. 123–58. A list of the model tables appears in the Appendix to P. Laslett, 'The family and household as work group and kin group: areas of traditional Europe compared', in Wall, Robin and Laslett, *Family Forms*, pp. 560–3.

27. The classification of households by residential kin is detailed in P. Laslett and E. Hammell, 'Comparing household structure over time and between cultures', *Comparative Studies in Society and History*, 16, 1974, pp. 73–111, and P. Laslett and R. Wall (eds.), *Household and Family*, pp. 23–32. See also J. Lee and J. Gjerde, 'Comparative household morphology of stem, joint and nuclear household systems: Norway, China and the United States', *Continuity and Change*, 1(1), 1986, pp. 89–111.

28. The static nature of census data has lead to various criticisms of census-based research; see especially L. Berkner, 'The stem family and the development cycle of the peasant household', *American Historical Review*, 77, 1972, pp. 398–418, and 'The use and misuse of census data for the historical analysis of family structure', *Journal of Interdisciplinary History*, 5, 1975, pp. 721–38. But see also M. Anderson, 'Some problems in the use of census type material for the study of family and kinship systems' in J. Sundin and E. Soderland (eds.), *Time, Space and Man*, Umeå, 1979, pp. 69–80.

29. For example see M. Segalen, 'The family cycle and household structure: Five

generations in a French Village', *Journal of Family History*, 2(3), 1977, pp. 223–36, and H. Smith, 'Family and Class: The Household Economy of Languedoc Winegrowers, 1830–1870', *Journal of Family History*, 9(1), 1984, pp. 67–87.

30.   This problem is expressed in E. A. Wrigley, 'Reflections on the History of the Family', *Daedalus, Proceedings of the American Academy of Arts and Sciences*, 106(2), 1977, pp. 71–85, and R. Sieder and M. Mitteraurer, 'The reconstruction of the family life course: theoretical problems and empirical results', in Wall, Robin and Laslett, *Family Forms*, pp. 309–45.

31.   Population simulation techniques are discussed in K. Wachter, E. Hammell and P. Laslett, *Statistical Studies of Historical Social Structure*, London, 1978, especially chapters 1–5.

32.   The simulation system developed in Cambridge is known as CAMSIM, this was originally devised on a mainframe computer using PL1 and has now been adapted to run on microcomputers using the 'C' language. CAMSIM is described in J. E. Smith, 'Computer simulation of kin sets and kin counts', in J. Bongaarts, K. Wachter and T. K. Burch (eds.), *Family Demography: Methods and their Application*, Oxford, forthcoming, 1987.

33.   This simulation example is taken from P. Laslett, 'The Significance of the Past in the Study of Ageing', *Ageing and Society*, 4(4), 1984, pp. 379–89.

34.   Using software packages such as SAS, SPSS or dBASE.

35.   E. Le Roy Ladurie, *Le territoire de l'historien*, Paris, 1973, p. 14.

I would like to thank Ms R Davies, J Oeppen, R Schofield and R Wall, all of the Cambridge Group, for their valuable comments on this paper.

6   *John Beckett and Trevor Foulds*

Reconstructing an English Village in the Eighteenth and Nineteenth Centuries using FAMULUS 77: Laxton, Nottinghamshire

Laxton, a few miles from Newark in Nottinghamshire, is nowadays one of England's most famous villages, visited annually by thousands of schoolchildren, by American tourists, and by large numbers of others who have heard its name since the Conservative government decided in 1979 to sell the property it owned in the village. It is an open field village still operating a manor court, the last such example in England. Unfortunately fame has not brought enlightenment. Laxton may have made the publications of the English Tourist Board, but though much talked about, and much lauded for its open fields — for which passing travellers are urged to leave the main highway — the village has not been greatly researched. In 1938 C. S. and C. S. Orwin published *The Open Fields*, part of which was devoted to the village and the working of the field system. But most of the book was concerned with the splendid survey drawn up by Mark Pierce in 1635 and now in the Bodleian Library. For later accounts of the village the intrepid researcher must depend on an unpublished doctoral thesis, and some brief articles published in the not especially well known *East Midlands Geographer*. Almost everything else written on Laxton in recent years — and there has been much of it — has been derivative.

What seemed to be needed was an answer to the obvious question, just how like its medieval predecessor is modern Laxton? We know that the physical structure has not changed greatly. The nuclear village is much the same today as in 1635. But what about the community? If, as the neo-Marxists have long held whatever the evidence to the contrary, the great enclosure movement of the eighteenth and nineteenth centuries ripped apart the old organic community of medieval England, expelled peasant smallholders from the land, and introduced capitalist class relationships in the countryside, what about Laxton? The village has excellent documentation; indeed in terms of English rural society and village studies it lacks only an enclosure award. So the evidence existed to ask questions about how far the community had changed through time. However, linking the enormous amount of data which can be culled from parish registers and censuses, estate surveys and rentals, is a time-consuming task even for a village of little more than 600 people. Moreover, the technique known as family reconstitution, which has been used for this kind of study, is seriously flawed in terms of what it can produce. If Laxton were to be examined in any detail, and if the project were to be completed within a decent time limit, computer facilities would obviously be required.

It was necessary from the beginning to think in terms of record linkage, and how information from one or more sources could be merged to provide information about landholding and social structure in the village through time. In addition, it was important to see the project as a model, rather than as a one-off piece of work. Village study is at the heart of local historical research, and any techniques developed in the course of examining Laxton might also have significant spin-offs for similar — and presumably enclosed — villages. With this twin aim in view — of asking how the Laxton community fared through time and of developing techniques which other researchers might be able to employ, the question arose of how the material could best be handled for the purposes of analysis.

For Laxton, as indeed for many other villages, the best material survives for the nineteenth century. A combination of the decennial census enumerators' book (1841–51), the tithe map (1839), and other private surveys, enables a clear picture to be drawn. From the census returns the village can be analysed according to sex, age, occupation, household structure and migration patterns, and by merging and comparing these through time it is possible to build up a picture of change in the community between 1841 and 1881. In addition, private census returns of 1831 and 1821 have provided valuable information for the earlier years of the century. By merging material from the tithe award of 1839 — which shows the number of farmers, the number of holdings, ownership and occupation — with the 1841 census returns a picture was developed of the community as it stood in *c.* 1840. The detail is sufficient to identify which people lived in particular houses, and what occupation villagers followed.

To push the picture backwards through time, and to develop an idea of property turnover and the extent to which families moved in and out of the village — quite apart from changing their holdings — the best available sources were estate surveys. Laxton has several of these, the majority with accompanying maps. These could be merged to compare property holdings through time. So far, material has been collated from a private survey undertaken for the major landowner, Earl Manvers, in 1862, the tithe map, and other surveys of 1820, 1812 and 1789. The 1789 and 1862 surveys only cover Manvers' property (i.e. *c.* ⅔ of the village). Other surveys, which we are intending to build in, exist for 1736, 1691 and 1635. To fill the longer gaps between surveys we are introducing material from Protestation and Hearth Tax returns, estate rentals and Land Tax Assessments. Finally, we shall superimpose upon this data information drawn from estate papers and letters, poor rate books, churchwardens' accounts and even school log books. For the relatively poorly documented post-1900 period some oral testimony will be required. In the end it should be possible to demonstrate — among other things — changes in land ownership, changes in tenure, family continuity, and village social structure.

With the rather exceptionally long run of evidence for Laxton from the early seventeenth century to the mid-nineteenth century, it was almost essential to include computer assistance, and it also seemed that the source material would be susceptible to computerisation. Here was the first problem. Neither of us had sufficient knowledge of what packages were available to cope with the vast amount of evidence provided by the source material. We wanted a package that could cope with text rather than figures. We would not particularly want vast amounts of meaningless statistical data. We required something that would be able to sift out personal names, field names, occupations, age and sex differences, and could cope with the text and figures and be as flexible as possible. But we are historians not experts in computer software. We presented our needs to the University of Nottingham's computer centre and they recommended FAMULUS 77 as being probably the package best able to cope with what we envisaged; it would handle vast amounts of textual data speedily and efficiently and an attractive part of the package, we were assured, was that it was simple to use. It did not require mind-bending acrobatics by the user to organise and collate the data. But the major attraction was that it possessed the capability of being able to merge similar or dissimilar databases and to us this was extremely important in evolving the picture of Laxton through time, for the source material to be used, censuses, field surveys, hearth tax returns, land tax returns, etc., was not all of the same evidentiary infrastructure.

It was therefore necessary to break down the infrastructure of the sources for the fields by which FAMULUS 77 deals with data to maximise efficiently the use of these fields and the information they were to contain. It was essential to get this right from the start otherwise time would be wasted in continually re-creating databases. This was so successful that in the last 13 months we have only had to re-name a field once, and this occurred sufficiently early in the project to cause little problem. Because of the speed at which FAMULUS 77 operates it is less than a days work to dump 10 databases and re-create them.

We have encountered very few real difficulties in using FAMULUS 77. There are certain problems of fitting in the evidence of the source material with the structure of the package but these have not been insuperable. The recognition of orthographic eccentricities is a perennial problem. This has been overcome not by reducing personal names to a series of numbers which produce additional eccentricities, but by retaining the given spelling and providing a preferred spelling for sorting procedures, so aiding collation. In this way the census material has been the easiest for FAMULUS 77 to handle. By merging the 5 censuses 1841–1881 we have been able to see patterns, individual and familial, of continuity and change.

However, merged databases are not as easy to handle or evaluate as a single database. The larger the merge (e.g. more than two databases) the greater the corresponding difficulties can be, though in the case of the censuses they were very few indeed. The field surveys are a different matter. Their structure, e.g. the way the information is put down on paper, appears to be largely the same. But when they are merged FAMULUS 77 has unintentionally revealed some embarrassing problems causing difficulty in sorting procedures to collate information. Some were foreseen but others were hidden until the package uncovered them. In short, the problem lies mostly with the source material — for very little of it remains constant from one survey to the next — and partly with FAMULUS 77 because it was not written with our type of needs in mind. Occupiers appear to be relatively stable and changes of tenure are superficially visible; but this can be deceptive, and tracking continuity and change by computer has become awkward. The plan numbers of individual strips of land are not constant; those of the surveys 1635 to 1812 are; thence the plan numbers for the 1820, 1839, and 1862 surveys change, so correlation between the first group of surveys and the remaining individual surveys in the second group becomes difficult. Sorting on individual acreages to provide another basis for determining continuity and change has revealed surprises. Unfortunately acreages change also. To the human eye these may seem minimal — a question of a few perches at times — but to FAMULUS 77 these are not easily recognisable, and without it being able to handle this type of problem easily, plotting rationalisation or change of holdings or tenures is difficult. Furthermore, the merged databases of surveys has introduced an unexpected change at this period: evidence for the change of furlong names within the open fields themselves! This might be expected with the enclosures but not necessarily with the furlongs. If whole furlongs alone changed their names this would be easier to detect. But the furlongs can be subject to division and re-naming, causing added difficulties for collation.

Conclusion

We have far to go, but already some interesting results are emerging and some awkward problems are being thrown up. On the positive side, it is clear that any idea that Laxton has somehow been caught in a time-warp needs to be abandoned. Families came and went with remarkable regularity. Nor did the fields remain unchanged. Our major problem has been to discover changes in tenure and in field names over time, since it seems clear that even over relatively short time spans parcels of land were swapped around, and, above all, strips were forever being enclosed to make larger farms and more compact holdings. All this we shall be documenting in detail when the research is completed. What we see in Laxton today is the result of generations of change and development, not a medieval village which somehow missed out on the march of history. We have just been involved in writing the text for a Visitor's Centre in the village to make this clear.

The computer techniques are both a help and a hindrance. They have enabled us to collate vast amounts of data very quickly. On the other hand they do not always answer our basic questions. The field name problems with the surveys would have taken much longer to discover without the computer, but at present we can see very little way in which it can help us to sort out the problems thrown up. Old-fashioned techniques of hand sorting and the roving eye of the fallible human brain may have to be used, although digitisation of the maps may prove to be the answer to some of our difficulties.

7   *Josef Smets*

South French Society and the French Revolution. The Creation of a Large Database with CLIO

Introduction

As I have been working for three years in Göttingen on CLIO in order to adapt it to several series of German, Dutch and French sources,[1] we decided with Manfred Thaller and the CNUSC (Centre National Universitaire Sud Calcul) to implement this program on the IBM machines of the CNUSC in Montpellier. As we needed an informatic structure in order to receive immediately the program CLIO from the Max-Planck-Institut für Geschichte, we founded the association IRHIS (Institut de Recherche

Historique par l'Informatique et la Statistique) in June 1985 which has been integrated as Electronic Data Preparation Unit in the 'Commission Régionale d'Histoire de la Révolution Française: Languedoc-Roussillon'.

The CNUSC of Montpellier began the transcription of CLIO in December 1985, and the responsible person (Francisco Acosta) working on CLIO since then thinks that the program can probably be operational at the CNUSC in September of 1986. At the same time IRHIS and the CNUSC have discussed a co-operative plan that determines the tasks of each of them in order to make this program accessible to further users in France, such as university sections in human sciences or other research units. The CNUSC contribution consists at first in the actual transcription of CLIO on its IBM machine and, afterwards, in the maintenance of this program at Montpellier. For its part, IRHIS would not only assume the translation of the user's guide (from German to French) but would also test, with the help of the CNUSC, the French version of CLIO on the IBM machine.

To attain these goals, it is evident that IRHIS has to create its own historical database before working on the CNUSC's mainframe. Having therefore proposed the general theme *La société languedocienne avant et après la Revolution Française, 1750–1850*, and realising that the input of long documentary series is very expensive in time, IRHIS attempted to gather a large number of partners in the whole region of Languedoc-Roussillon. After 1989 (bicentenary of the French Revolution) when we hope to have finished a certain number of our computing and statistical methods with CLIO and other programs (such SAS, or UNIRAS) our group will extend its investigation either in time — towards the seventeenth and even to the sixteenth century — or on the whole of France, in which case we would work together with EDP-interested partners of other French universities or laboratories.

The Geographical Area

Our research project concerns the Languedoc. In ancient France this province was the most extended administrative entity of the French kingdom, assembling rather various regions with changing physiognomies.

Figure 1   *The Languedoc-Rousillon during the Revolution*[2]

From the Rhone in the East to the Garonne in the West, from the rough mountains in the North — in fact Mont Lozère, Cévennes, Montagne Noire form an incurved line from the North to the South and, then, to the West — to the Mediterranean plain in the South, no other French province had the same great number of quite different and such characteristic landscapes as the Languedoc. Not only the relief but also the climate differentiates the western part (Haut-Languedoc) under oceanic influence from the south-eastern part (Bas-Languedoc) under Mediterranean influence and, finally, from the northern highlands (Massif Central) with continental climate. So there are many contrasts which we can group in the three main landscapes just mentioned.

The Haut-Languedoc, whose economic and demographic centre is undeniably Toulouse, has two faces, one agrarian, the other industrial. Its temperate climate and field structure facilitate an important cereal production monopolising the land of this part of the Languedoc. Besides this type of agriculture, an important textile production characterises such cities as Toulouse or Carcassonne.

The Mediterranean Bas-Languedoc is the most various of the three Languedocian regions. Not monoculture but polyculture reigns in its different landscapes so that the peasants try hard to produce wheat, wine and olives according to the quality of their rather unfertile ground. Those of the Garrigues possess great sheep flocks that furnish the necessary wool for the two royal factories founded by Colbert (Les Saptes, Villeneuvette) and four others (La Trivalle, Pennautier, Bize, Clermont) and, finally, to important drapery centres such Lodève, Bédarieux, St. Chinian, La Bastide and La Salvetat. Silk production was very important too, and it occupied a lot of sub-Cevenol villages and little towns (Ganges, Sauve, St. Hypolite, St. Martin-de-Londres) where Ganges took a key position in the trade with the rich and Calvinist silk merchants of Nîmes and these last with Lyon. The influential merchants of Montpellier sold the regional products on the greatest fair of the French kingdom (Beaucaire). They exported wine to Dutch and Germans and wool products to the Levant via the young port of Sète or the old, much more important port of Marseilles.

The third main landscape includes the most mountainous part of the province. It has certainly been the poorest because its rough and continental climate and its rather unfertile ground permitted only a scanty diet that was essentially based on chestnut and rye. These conditions pushed many mountain dwellers to look for work in the more fertile and richer South.

The whole province was divided at first in 22, and since 1694 (creation of the diocese of Alès), in 23 civil dioceses. Their extent could vary in a rather perceptible way between small ones — like Lodève or Agde — and quite large ones — like Montpellier, Narbonne or Toulouse.

Figure 2   *The civil dioceses of the Languedoc before 1789*[3]

——— border of the province   - - - border of the civil dioceses

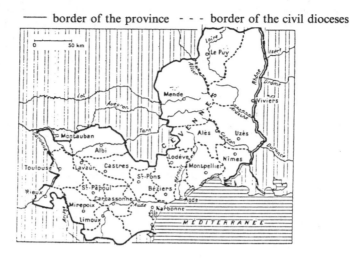

But the entire province has always lacked a truly chief city because the rivals Toulouse and Montpellier each concentrated on different political, juridical and economic powers. The sovereign juridical institution (Parlement) was sitting in Toulouse whereas the sovereign financial court (Cour des aides) or the royal administration (Intendant) worked within the walls of Montpellier. The annual meetings of the most famous diet of the kingdom (États de Languedoc) which was presided over by the archbishop of Narbonne, were held at first at Pézenas, and then at Montpellier as well.

The Toulousain economy was rather oriented to the Atlantic coast (via the Garonne to Bordeaux) and did not profit by the new channel (Canal du Midi) which connected Toulouse with the Mediterranean port of Sète. On the other hand, the commerce of Montpellier used exclusively the Mediterranean ports of Marseilles and Sète. At least, Catholicism and Calvinism were rending the Languedocian population, and divided it since the Revocation of the Edict of Nantes (1685) and the disastrous War of the Camisards (1702–1713).

As we all know, the French Revolution transformed French society. In 1790 (15 January), the old provinces, including Languedoc, were abolished and the constituents were rearranged into a new administrative chessboard with smaller departments, unit districts, cantons and parishes. From now on, eight departments covered the ancient province of the Languedoc: Aude (Carcassonne), Ardèche (Privas), Gard (Nîmes), a part of the Haute-Garonne (Toulouse), a part of the Haute-Loire (Le Puy), Hérault (Montellier) Lozère (Mende) and the Tarn (Castres).

Figure 3   *The division of the Languedoc*
            into departments, 1790[4]

The Demographic Area

After these general geographic and economic observations about the
Languedoc, it is not surprising that the human settlement in this contrasted
province distinguishes regions with more or less numerous people.

As we might expect, the mountainous landscapes — like those from
Lozère, Velay and Vivarais or the lower Garrigues which are situated just
between the southern plain and the northern highlands — were often
desperately underpopulated, whereas the Mediterranean urbanised coast
(Bas-Languedoc), except its swampy part, or the Aquitanian basin (Haut-
Languedoc) knew a real density of human settlement. Louis
Dermigny[5] gave, in his time, some examples: the demographic evolution of
45 parishes in the diocese of Montpellier seperates them into two nearly equal
groups. Obviously there exists a natural opposition between the suburban
zone just around Montpellier with fertile lands and the swampy border of the
Mediterranean which was regularly ravaged by all kinds of epidemic deseases
(fevers, malaria)[6] and also the very dry Garrigues with its rocky ground.[7]

In spite of a certain number of classic demographic studies (undertaken in
the 1960s) on communities of the Haut-Languedoc (at the university of
Toulouse under the direction of J. Godechot) and about those of the Bas-
Languedoc (at the university of Montpellier under the direction of L.
Dermigny), it is still rather difficult to estimate the population of the
Languedoc or to know exactly its demographic profile. Indeed these studies

did not cover the whole province and they have simply been too conventional because they dealt with only one village. Such problems as geographical mobility among the lower social classes necessarly qualified the results of those works which were unfortunately limited to one place. They were also limited in time because they did not go beyond the French Revolution. Nevertheless, some cautious estimates made by the top of the provincial administration, the intendants, provide us with a rough idea of the number of inhabitants of this important south-French province. The intendant Basville suggested 1,500,000 inhabitants at the end of the seventeenth century and, nearly one hundred years later, in 1788, his collegue Ballainvilliers counted about two million.[8] L. Dermigny, on the other hand, thinks that the Languedocian population first fell from 1,300,000 inhabitants around 1700 to 1,200,000 in 1715, and then grew to 1,700,000 in 1799,[8] a growth of 42% in 75 years which is confirmed by a number of the most important Languedocian towns. And according to the very important work of Raymond Dugrand[10] on the Bas-Languedoc — which covers mainly the two departments Hérault and Gard — it seems that this demographic growth has continued during the first half of the nineteenth century so that the population of the old province might have reached 2,200,000, perhaps 2,300,000 inhabitants at 1850. This population lived in 2500 communities or 2626 parishes whose most important towns, in 1789, were Toulouse with 52,860, Nîmes with 42,000 and Montpellier with 31,000 inhabitants.

Methods

At the beginning of this paper it was said that IRHIS intends to constitute a historical data base about the region of the Languedoc in using the program CLIO.[11] Its most important features have not changed since Manfred Thaller's article 'Automation on Parnassus. CLIO — A Databank oriented System for Historians'[12] because CLIO still permits
   —a flexible input system combining free field and tag/content representation of data that can be structured in very complex hierarchies
   —a retrieval system
   —a system for the interactive coding of historical sources
   —a system for nominative record linkage.
IRHIS does not intend to limit its investigation to classic demographic questions and complex family reconstitution. On the contrary, IRHIS aims to write a 'Histoire totale' (total history) of a whole region. To do so, practically all existing sources can be

linked together to form a kind of vastly expanded family reconstitution, reconstructing not only the biological families — as usually done in comparable studies which are primarily oriented towards the study of problems of historical demography — but also socioeconomic families.[13]

In the special case of our research, priority is given to the Languedocian registers of baptisms, marriages and burials which will be linked by means of the names of the people concerned. But considering the enormous number of all Languedocian communities (2500), and taking into account the birth, death and marriage rates, IRHIS would have to input, for just the period from 1750 to 1850, at least some thirteen million deeds![14]

Figure 4   *Immigration at Montpellier in the eighteenth century*[15]

It seems evident that IRHIS cannot undertake the input of such a large amount of this source material. In the beginning we confine our investigation to some precise areas which correspond to different typical landscapes and to characteristic demographic laws of the Languedoc. This implies nevertheless that we cannot exclude the rather important phenomenon of migration which characterised Languedocian society more than one might imagine. In the same time the migration guides us to follow the texture of the close human and social relationships existing among the multiple Languedocian landscapes. As we know that the main direction of migration has been from country to town and from mountains to plain, we will start our research with towns like Béziers, Montpellier and Nîmes and their surrounding villages — in fact, the urban and suburban zones with the highest density.[16] The different immigration rates will already point out the further villages and landscapes whose registers we should input in a second stage. In proceeding in this way, we ensure the recording of registers not only of single villages but also of their immediate neighbourhoods — indeed in our opinion each village is the centre of a human, social, economic, cultural, even linguistic micro-cosmos just composed of this village and its neighbouring communities. This method allows us to progress rapidly from the rich coast to the poor mountainous parts of the region, especially to the *garrigues* (of Montpellier and Nîmes) and to the high Cevennes or even to more distant highlands of the

Massif Central.

It is superfluous to mention that these registers will be used for a primary family reconstitution that will be connected further with another important Languedocian source: the old and more recent public registers of lands (*compoix* and cadastres). Indeed, they permit us to describe exactly not only the division of land property or of all cultures before and after the French Revolution but also the devolution of each patrimony within all the families studied. Nominal tax-registers like the *taille* and the *vingtième* will help us to complete our investigation about the economic and geographic cleavages within Languedocian society.

The third important series of documents will be several nominal census lists drawn up regularly since the beginning of the French Revolution and going beyond the Napoleonic Empire. Those concerning the revolutionary period in particular permit us to measure the number of active 'militants' and, therefore, the real role of the Languedocian people in the French Revolution, rather neglected until now. Including another nominal list from 1787, which mentions all people who want to return to the Calvinist confession, a first global approach of the Calvinist population persecuted during the whole eighteenth century would also be possible and inform us about the question of whether most pre-Revolution Calvinists became republicans.

Finally, it is not unimportant to underline that the input work will be done in the archives — and perhaps with the help of some of their personnel. Indeed CLIO releases us from manual transcription of the originals — and their coding too — so that we will transcribe literally all the sources mentioned above.

When IRHIS has finished inputting such a large amount of source material on a microcomputer, this material has to be worked upon by CLIO. Always with CLIO we perform linkages of files via names of persons mentioned therein in order to leave the restrained local (village) research and to create a vast regional databank. The way in which this databank will be classed is clear: it will contain at first two files where all informations will be classed behind each family in the first one and behind each individual in the second one. Thousands of popular biographies will complete, then, something like a regional family history.

But our regional databank allows us to create new files which treat precise aspects of Languedocian society:

a)   demographic attitudes
     —fertility, marriage and death rates
     —migratory movements on a regional scale
     —evolution and structure of the Languedocian population
b)   social structures
     —socioeconomic hierarchies: land possession, income, wealth and
        poverty . . .
     —social mobility through several generations
     —sociopolitical classes: profile of their recruitment, of their succession
     —marginal groups: beggars, shepherds, soldiers
     —professional classes: structures, functions, evolution, geographical

division

— social classes: nobility, clergy, middle-class, peasants . . .

c) geographical and economic structures:

— agriculture, industries, commerce . . .

— landscapes: swampy coast, *garrigues*, Cévennes, Aquitanian basin, highlands (Larzac . . .)

d) cultural structures

— religion: Catholicism against Calvinism

— school: from primary school to university, who can read and write?

e) medical and biological structures

— medicine: from barber to doctor (*barbier, charlatan, rebouteux, sage-femme, practicien, chirurgien, docteur*)

— disease: cause of death, epidemic

— genetics: hereditary diseases

The number of files representing a precise theme can increase in proportion to the nature and the quality of the sources we will use. The list of research themes mentioned above gives only a little idea about the great number of subjects which a regional databank can help us to realise in the coming years.

Notes

1. For my post-doctoral thesis, *Paysans des garrigues montpelliéraines, paysans des marais rhénans, 1715–1840. Deux sociétés traditionnelles traitées par ordinateur.*

2. See Henri Michel, 'Le Languedoc moderne', in G. Cholvy (ed.), *Le Languedoc et le Roussillon*, Roanne, 1982, p. 198.

3. See E. le Roy Ladurie, *Histoire du Languedoc*, Paris, 1974, p. 90.

4. From J. Godechot, *Les institutions de la France sous la Révolution et l'Empire*, Paris, P.U.F., 1951 (map 1).

5. L. Dermigny, 'De la Révocation à la Révolution', in P. Wolff (ed.), *Histoire du Languedoc*, Toulouse, 1968, p. 384.

6. See Y. Maurin, 'Le problème de la mortalité dans les communes des étangs à la fin di 18e siècle et au début du 19e siècle', *Études sur l'Hérault*, 15, 1984. The death rate in the coastal villages was very high, reaching, for children under the age of ten, 50·4% at Vic and 48·3% at Villeneuve. But Ganges, the most important silk production centre of the Cévennes, shows a picture of child mortality no less sad: in the years 1685–1792, 2337 (59·2%) of the 3944 deaths were under five years of age. See R. Dugrand, *Villes et campagnes en Bas-Languedoc*, Paris, 1963, p.433.

7. See J. Smets, 'Écologie, habitat et santé: la mutation lente et difficile de deux sociétés traditionnelles (XVIII-XIXe siècles)', communication presented at the 110e Congrès National des Sociétés Savantes, Montpellier, 1–5 April 1985.

8. See H. Michel, *op. cit.*, p. 221.

9. See L. Dermigny, *op. cit.*, p. 381.

10. See R. Dugrand, *Villes et campagnes en Bas-Languedoc*, Paris, 1963. On demographic evolution in the eighteenth century pp. 431–7, and in the nineteenth century pp. 438–64. Beetween 1801 and 1851 the author has calculated a growth of 35·2%.

11. Its research can be compared to a Canadian project combining regional and social history about a precise landscape: the Saguenay (1842–1941). See G. Bouchard, 'Un essai d'anthropologie régionale: l'histoire sociale du Saguenay aux XIXe et XXe

siècles', in *Annales, E.S.C.*, 1979, pp. 106–25. During this period the registers of baptisms, marriages and burials contain 340,000 deeds.

12.   Manfred Thaller, 'Automation on Parnassus. CLIO — A Databank Oriented System for Historians', in *Historical Social Research/Historische Sozialforschung*, 15, July 1980, pp. 40–65.

13.   Thaller, *op. cit.*, p. 40.

14.   The birth rate is estimated at 45·6% for 1700–10, 42·9% for 1740–50, 40·1% at 1770, 39·6% at 1790, and at least 32·5% and 26·8% for 1821–31 and 1851–61 respectively. The death rate seems to fall from 42·5% at 1700 to 31·6% at 1750 and nearly 26% at 1790, and remains at this level until 1861–71. (26% in 1821–31 and 26·7% in 1851–61). See L. Dermigny, *op. cit.*, pp. 387–9 and R. Dugrand, *op. cit.*, pp. 432–3. The annual number of births could be about 57,000 at 1750, about 68,000 at 1820 and 61,500 at 1850, and that of deaths about 44,500, 54,500 and 60,000 at the same dates. This gives nearly 6,500,000 births, 4,900,000 deaths and 1,600,000 marriages.

15.   See L. Dermigny, *op. cit.*, p. 386.

16.   See the immigration to Nîmes. Leslie Page Moch, *Paths to the city. Regional Migration in Nineteenth-Century France*, Beverley Hills/London/New Delhi, 1983.

8 *Gun Stenflo and Jan Sundin*

Using a Large Historical Database. An Example from the Demographic Database in Umeå

1. History and Content of the Database

The Demographic Database at Umeå University was started in 1973 as a labour market project. Its purpose was twofold: to give researchers access to data more easily than before, and to provide work for unemployed people in northern Sweden. The project became a permanent university department in 1978 and today the staff consists of about twenty people in Umeå working with the system and the output questions and another fifty persons in Haparanda on the Finnish border in the north doing the registration. In addition three groups of about fifteen persons each are financed by Swedish Board of Labour in three different places in northern Sweden.

Today the primary database of parish records contains six parishes situated in different parts of Sweden and two regions in northern Sweden. The first region consists of the town of Sundsvall and about fifteen parishes around it, an area which experienced a rapid industrialisation of the forest industry during the last decades of the nineteenth century. The second region consists of the town of Skellefteå and its surroundings, with a somewhat different history from that of the first region. A third region will be added to the database in the near future, the town of Linköping and about thirty small parishes outside it on a plain in southern Sweden.

The period of registration is mainly the nineteenth century, although some extensions have been made. The data from the Skellefteå region starts already during the first half of the eighteenth century, and for one parish in the south data has been registered until the middle of the 1920's.

At the request of research other sources than parish records have been registered in order to be linked with the former: in data on land use and landscape, taxation poll registers, school records, age lists of workers at iron foundries and records of patients at the hospitals in the same region, etc.

Some years ago a successful test was performed on the aggregated, previously unprinted, statistics made by parish priests. It will therefore be followed by an almost complete registration of this material for the years 1749–1890, a unique set of information on such aspects as marriage, fertility, mortality, population growth and social change in Sweden.

2. The Content of the Sources

Most attention has been paid to the parish records, owing to their richness of information. As well as records of births, marriages and deaths the Swedish priests had to keep a so called 'examination register' from the seventeenth century and onwards.

These registers have in some parishes been preserved from the first half of the seventeenth century. The geographical coverage improves with time, and after 1800 they are to be found in almost every Swedish parish. Information increases over time until we have a very detailed, continuous picture of each individual and household after 1800.

It should be noted that this 'system of information' gives the researcher the possibility of establishing the exact population living in a parish each year, the 'population at risk'. Secondly, it will usually be possible to find any individual before he/she was entered on the page or after being crossed out. The life histories of people moving from one parish to another within a region of registration are automatically linked in the database. Later on, as mentioned above, certain selected model cohorts of migrants will be collected and registered regardless of their origin and destination. Full life histories has been constructed for about 10% of the registered population. This percentage will rise considerably in the regions as fewer persons are lost due to migration.

The sources are very rich and have been used for research in many different subjects; demography, history, linguistics, human geography and religion. The paper *History on Data*, obtainable from the authors, contains further information about the Demographic Database.

Figure 1   *Summary of the information in the parish records*

INFORMATION TABLE   SOURCES

i = Individual data
s = Aggregated parish data

		A	H	B	C	D	E	F	G	MTL
Identity	Name, sex	i	i	i	i	i	i	i	s	i
	Birth date (age)	i	i	i	i		i	i	s	i
	Birth place	i	i		i					
	Legitimate birth	i	i	i	i			i	s	
	Number among children	i			i					
Village/ occupation	Department, village, house	i	i	i	i	i	i	i		i
	Assessment unit of land	i								i
	Occupation/title	i	i	i			i	i	s	i
	Household position	i	i	i					s	i
Family	Family position	i	i	i					s	i
	Parents/children	i	i	i	i			i		i
	Husband/wife	i	i	i	i		i	i	s	i
	Civil status/marriage	i	i	i	i		i	i	s	i
	Dissolving of marriage	i						i	s	i
Migration	Volume, page, line	i	i	i	i	i	i	i		i
	In- and out-registration	i	i	i					s	
	In- and out-migration time	i	i	i					s	
	In- and out-migration place	i	i	i						
Examination/ and others	Catechism knowledge	i	i	i						
	Comprehension, intelligence	i	i	i						
	Behaviour, morals	i	i							
	Church exam (every year)	i	i	i						
	Date of Holy Com (every year)	i	i	i		i				
Other infor- mation	Vaccination	i	i							
	Priest observations	i	i	i	i	i	i	i		i
	Date and parish of baptism	i	i		i					
	Godfathers/godmothers				i					
	Dates of marriage and bann	i	i				i			
	Death, burial	i						i		
	Cause of death							i		

A = Catecethical examination register   D = Holy Communion register
H = Certificate of change of address   E = Marriage register
B = Migration register   F = Death and burial register
C = Birth/baptism register   G = Parish statistics
MTL = Registers of assessment units of land (taxation poll registers) and other sources

3. Understanding the Information

The projection of the world mirrored in the historical records is of course the theoretical limit of inference which the user must be well aware of. Our experience is that the greatest danger for the user lies in lack of deeper understanding of how the information system created by the ministers actually functioned, and what consequences this has for his analysis. The more the researcher knows about the intentions of the information system when originally created, and about the socio-economic content, the better. Uncritical use of data can lead to misinterpretations or, at worst, incorrect calculations of rates and correlations. It will be one of the most important tasks of the Demographic Database and its staff to inform users about such problems, but in the end the primary responsibility has to rest with the researcher, who is the only one who can match his intentions with the data.

Simple data errors can usually be kept within control, the size being documented for the researcher, as long as the source of information is well structured. The responsibility for the builder of the database is to transfer the data from source to computer in a way that will not limit research possibilities further. In many cases it is possible to generate new information and discover mistakes in the sources when different items of information are put together and thus improve the research possibilities. Such opportunities must of course be explored. It is also very important to consider what different kinds of research the sources could be used for, and to consider all the different research demands when the system is designed.

The documentation of the system is very important and must be constructed in a way that makes it possible for the user to understand the process and what implications it might have for the results. The

Figure 2 *Church examination register from Timrå parish. Volume AI:8. 1884–1893.*

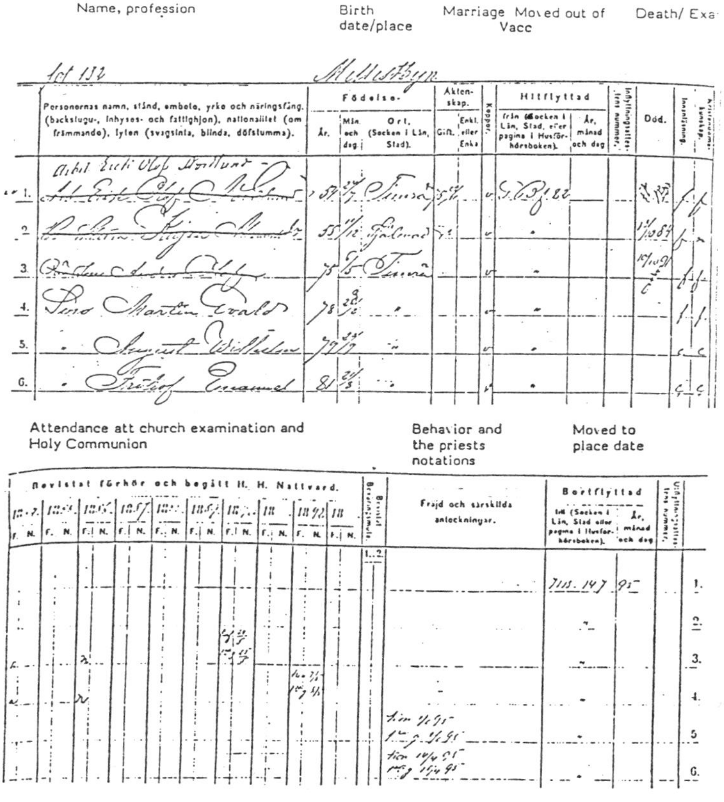
Name, profession
Birth date/place
Marriage
Moved out of Vacc
Death/ Exa
Födelse-
Hitflyttad
Död.
Attendance att church examination and Holy Communion
Behavior and the priests notations
Moved to place date
Bortflyttad
Frejd och särskilda anteckningar.

documentation must be built in modules, making it possible for the user to read only those parts relating to the problem in question.

4. Conclusions

The conclusions so far are the following:

1. Only well structured sources with a limited amount of textual information should normally be used for large-scale, well structured databases. This will make it possible to develop simple rules for the data transfer process and facilitate the production of simple documentation.
2. The researcher and the constructor of the information system must agree on their responsibilities when they cooperate. The constructor must provide the user with all the relevant documentation about how the processing has been performed. The constructor might also provide information about the sources. The responsibility of understanding the impact the primary source and processing have on a certain problem must, however, belong to the researcher.
3. Provide the user with tools for selection and transfer of data to analysis packages. This will make the user of the information system independent.

Individuals

9 *Hélène Millet*

From Sources to Data: the Construction of a Prosopographical Data-Bank

As prosopography deals with individual biographies in order to study a part of the social body, it cannot be reduced to the making of biographical dictionaries.[1] The accumulation of particular notices is indeed unable by itself to inform us about groups and social intricacy. On the other hand, the best way to understand how links, attractions or antipathies help to create micro-societies is to consider personal lives. Some of them are exceptional. Most are made up of similar features, similar, that is, in that they can be compared. And, with comparisons, we are entering into a new world, that of measures and mathematics[2] which is now widely open to historians thanks to computing.

To carry out prosopographical investigations, computers need to be used by historians not only as gigantic memories, but also as tools to solve problems of identity or non-identity; and it depends upon the researcher's skill in defining adequate standard units of measure. In this sense, we cannot say there are any prosopographical data; what is given and cannot be altered is biographic. As to prosopography, it creates variables and algorithms and calculates results.

However, the preliminary biographical investigations are so long and require the analysis of such wide and numerous sources, that it would be a pity not to preserve the results of this patient industry. That is why the group of historians[3] which has formed in order to study how cathedral canons contributed to the building of medieval states, decided to connect this prosopographical work about canons with the creation of a biographical data-bank.

While studying the canons of Laon,[4] I realised that this type of clerk, being often officers or royal counsellors, was closely integrated into the establishment of political power; his own clerical status made him a sort of 'hinge' between Church and State. As the whole of Europe is covered by diocesan organisation, with cathedral chapters alongside bishops, it can be established whether this statement is appropriate only to fourteenth-century France or can be extended to each kind of medieval developing state. But to test this hypothesis requires a wide prosopographical comparative study: in the course of the plan of researches of the C.N.R.S. about the growth of the modern State,[5] several historians, whose main interests lie in Church history, decided to unite their efforts. So each of us chose one peculiar chapter for whose members he had already gathered biographical information.[6] From this starting point, we intend to draw comparisons between lands and times, by means of a common inquiry, in order to see if the sharing of canons in management of states can be related to peculiar dynasties or popes, what were the respective influences of social position and of scholarly attainments on the canon's destinies, whether clerical careers were prior to or consequent upon political services, how nationalism could coexist with the catholic, international ideal.

During a meeting at Paris, which had been a kind of brainstorming, we made an inventory of pertinent and available information concerning our problem. But we did not have enough time to plan and draw up a common form which must be filled for each canon by everyone. So this work was only performed by two of us, Elisabeth Mornet and myself, who bear the entire responsibility for its deficiencies.

Two ideas underpinned our approach: first, we had to organise items in order to solve the problem about the sharing of canons in public offices, but, second, these items had to be input in a suitable way to make them serve as a biographical data-bank. To some extent there are tensions between these two activities, for they suppose quite different solutions as to relations between sources and data. When one is holding an inquiry one can organise information by following a logical pattern, which is a product of one's mind, and insert in it deductive notions coming both from precise sources and general learning. Since the whole is intended for private use there is no difficulty in this method. By contrast, a data-bank is obviously designed for public use; and the best way to satisfy people's appetite for biographical information is to deliver them the exact source of the information. Everybody knows indeed how frustrating it is to read in a biographical dictionary a sentence such as : 'he was born about 1343' without knowing how the author of the notice had been led to that conclusion.

So, for our project, if we had no other ambition than to offer a lot of biographical information about canons, arguably the best solution would have been to store pure extracts of records and index them with some descriptive key-words of the content. But such a method was, of course, inefficient for us because we needed to handle clearly expressed data in order to get results for our inquiry in the next future. So we devised a kind of composition, trying to frame questions which could be answered by information directly picked up from records or indicating when such questions could not be directly inferred from the sources.

As to the extraction of data from sources, the problem we had to solve is in fact well-known to historians who store series of repetitive sources: their structure is to be drawn out so that they can be closely followed during input.[7] Besides, this formal structure can also be considered as the most efficient tool of understanding. But our canons appear in numerous and varied types of documents, so that it multiplies problems. However, in most of them, a distinction can be drawn between standard and unique information. A typical example is given by petitions presented to Popes in which we find a kind of identity card and indications concerning ecclesiastical career: *talis, clericus Parisiensis, consiliarius regis, canonicus prebendatus Laudunensis* and so on, are conventional words which can be found in other sources in the same stereotyped manner, so that they can be considered as pure data. Moreover, the interest of such information widely overflows the frame of the petition which conveys them, so that it would be a nonsense to link them to their appearance into a papal register: consequently, we did not retain the cohesion of this type of source and split the information into elements which can be inserted into a logical plan depending on the problem under study. There is only one objection to this option: with regard to the petition, the gathering of such indications might have an influence on its reception by the Pope. But this real loss of information can be corrected by the mention, in the part of the form devoted to benefits, that there existed a petition for obtaining such or such a prebend.

The logical plan we defined is therefore not inspired by sources, but it is made of questions which are moulded to the indications as they are to be found in records. For instance, with regard to ecclesiastical residence, it is uncommon to find a document where a canon is said to be a resident, but signs exist which must not be neglected: the acquisition of a house or frequent mentions of presence to capitular meetings. There are places in the form where these testimonies regarding a residence can be located. In the same way, we carefully distinguished types of exemption: capitular from papal and, in this second case, exemptions that were granted to persons from those linked to an office. But a canon could also choose to be a *foraneus* or even be penalised for contravening residential rules. All these possibilities are inventoried in the form, so that the problem of residence will be balanced according to the genuine medieval expression of facts.

Sometimes it may be interesting to notify the existence of sources without even referring to the details they give. Consider the register of a confraternity: if one finds the name of a canon in it, the interest lies in the evidence of his membership of the association rather than the sum he paid as a subscription. So some questions in our form, particularly those devoted to networks, deal only with the presence of a canon in one particular type of source.

More generally speaking, details about the preservation of records have their right place in biographical notices. We must not forget that the extent to which we can know individuals depends on it. Consequently, we managed a systematic possibility to give explanations about missing information: default of records, partial failing inside a series, lack of examination of the source by the researcher, uncertain understanding are reasons which can be notified by the use of coefficients.

On the other hand, for the inquiry, we could not avoid asking questions which have no expressed responses into sources. In order to make the distinction they are written on the form in smaller typographic characters. Some of them refer to general historical knowledge. They mainly concern assumptions about offices: whether certain individuals should be considered as being in the service of the state or as having some other kind of career.

We had also to point out information which can be deduced from sources. A good instance is that of geographical origin. As there was no civil register, several types of information can be gathered: the exact place of birth, the church where baptism was celebrated, the diocese where the boy entered into the Church or even the villages where his family had properties. As to biography, when we are lucky enough to know these datas, they must be kept. But when one is dealing with prosopography, they must be reduced to their highest common factor, that is the mentioned of diocese, so that comparisons can be made.

We are quite conscious that the record form which has resulted from this approach is just a kind of patchwork where rough data extracted from records are mixed with responses to elaborate questions. But in the way they are drawn up, they are almost ready to be submitted to a statistical package because each one is reduced to an elementary bit of information. The complexity of reality has been transmitted to the logical and structured plan. Questions to the data-bank will of course be limited to the kind of information entered in the form; but exclusion of details will be corrected, we would hope, by the final insertion of source-references. This last operation is submitted to the solution of problems of ownership of data. Researchers are rightly jealous of their information till the publication of the results; and computing, as far as it admits uncontrolled copies and corrections or additions which cannot be detected, may sometimes appear as an insecure anonymous assistant!

Notes

1. Cf. H. Millet, 'Notice biographique et enquête prosopograhique', forthcoming in *Prosopographie, Actes de la Table ronde, Rome, 1985.*

2. Cf. J.-P. Genet, 'Histoire, informatique, mesure', *Histoire & Mesure*, 1, 1986, pp. 7–18.

3. This group includes historians from Great-Britain (I. Cowan, B. Dobson, D. Lepine, D. Smith), Western Germany (G. Fouquet, R. Holbach), Italy (R. Bizzochi, G. Chittolini, T. Montecchi), Norway (S. Bagge), Poland (M. Koczerska), Spain (M. Santamaria-Lancho), Belgique (J. Pycke) and France (P. Lorentz, H. Millet, R. Montel, E. Mornet, F. Rapp, J. Verger et C. Vulliez).

4. H. Millet, *Les chanoines du chapitre cathédral de Laon (1272–1412)*, Rome, 1982.

5. The Action Thématique Programmée 'Genèse de l'État moderne' of the Centre National de la Recherche Scientifique began in 1985.

6. The canons submitted to the study are to be from York, Glasgow, Lincoln, Exeter, Roskilde, Bergen, Krakow, Speier, Trier, Strasbourg, Tournai, Laon, Orléans, South of France, Segovia, Lombardy, Tuscany, Rome and Pope Boniface VIII's curia.

7. See, for instance, B. Guillemain, 'Une operation en cours. Le traitement informatique des suppliques d'Urbain V', in *L'Archivio Segreto Vaticano e le ricerche*

storiche. Città del Vaticano, 1981, Rome, 1983, pp. 193–205, and J. Williamson, 'Land and Family in Pre-Black Death England', in H. Millet (ed.), *Informatique et Prosopographie. Actes de la Table ronde Paris, 1984*, Paris, 1985, pp. 13–17.

10 *Michelle Magdelaine*

'Le Refuge', a project to study the Huguenot exodus, *c*. 1680–1700

For the past few years, the I.H.M.C. of the C.N.R.S. has undertaken a vast enquiry on the second Protestant Refuge: the aim is to reconstruct the first generation of 'religious fugitives' who left France between the 1680's and the 1700's. It is obvious that French Calvinists left the kingdom well before — the movement, even if it slowed down, hardly stopped between the sixteenth and the end of the seventeenth century — and continued to do so during a good part of the eighteenth century.

It is equally true that between 1684–85 and 1700 we witness a true exodus, and that all provinces of the kingdom were affected. From the estimates which seem most valid at the moment, those of the pastor Samuel Mours, it would appear that there were in France, for a population of 20 million, a little less than one million Protestants of which some 200,000 left. The Protestants are more numerous south of the Loire than north, but the latter are the provinces which provide the proportionally greater number of refugees, even if, in absolute numbers, the southern provinces take the lead.

In order to reconstruct this first generation, it was therefore necessary to make an inventory of the quantitative sources in France, state registers, lists of fugitives, official tax lists of their possessions, enquiries into the new converts who emigrated, etc. It was necessary too to carry out this work in the countries of the Refuge, Switzerland (where many Huguenots established themselves but which many more simply passed through), Germany, the Netherlands, Great Britain, Ireland, to mention but the most important. In these different countries there exist abundant and varied sources: distribution or charity lists, indicating, apart from the surnames, first names, profession, geographic origin of the fugitives, the help given to them in the form of money or goods, lists of establishment in the colonies, state registers, legal sources, reparation registers for those who had renounced protestantism in France, etc.

The creation of a computerised database bringing together this first generation first necessitated a single method for going through them, so as to create an homogenous secondary source. It also involved the use of a computer program which would permit the data being entered 'clearly', in order that it would be immediately readable. For this it was necessary not to make an *a priori* choice among the information available in the manuscript sources because this data base is created, not with a single aim for the genealogy, but as an historical object, to be used for demographic, political, economic, socio-professional, religious or cultural history. Above all, thanks to the computer, it is possible to follow the refugees from their point of departure to their establishment abroad, through their peregrinations, and thus to draw a complete history of this migration, the most important of modern times.

The setting up of this database is now a European project in which France, Switzerland, the Netherlands, Federal Germany and Ireland collaborate. All those working on it, from universities or otherwise, have accepted the constraints of a single method, seeing beyond it the desired aim.

Treatment

The most important problem, when faced with such a mass of documents, is to set up a strict method for going through them, which does not betray the texts but which, at the same time, is supple enough to ensure that nothing is left aside.

This is what the CLEO programme of the I.R.H.T. permits. Once the zones introduced by a code have been set up the text is clearly presented and is thus accessible to all. Each document is made up of entries concerning one or more persons. Once it has been computerised it is possible to make sortings or counts

Finally, working on files from different areas, although far from all the existing sources have been studied, one can already follow certain individuals from their village to Berlin, between 1686 and 1698, through the various stages of their journey through Switzerland and Germany.

11   *P. J. Corfield*

Computerising Urban Occupations ·

Almost 2,000 separately-identified occupations for 30,000 individuals, living in British towns in the 1770s and 1780s, have now been computerised, forming the core of a databank for analysis and record linkage. The information was derived from urban *Directories*, which listed names and addresses of the local business community. Merchants were ubiquitous, as were grocers and dealers. Inn-keepers and alehouse-keepers also thrived. The central functions of towns as market- and meeting-places were emphatically signalled.

Very noticeably, however, these sources also listed a great array of specialist practitioners, including some rare avocations unknown to the *Oxford English Dictionary*. The most mysterious were the two women 'grutt-makers', living in Bristol in 1775. It now seems that they were oatmeal-makers, the term being a regional variant of 'groats', albeit unlisted in eighteenth-century dictionaries and handbooks. A great many other manufacturing occupations were identified, demonstrating the remarkable array of goods made in towns well before the spread of the modern factory system.

Analysis of this material was not at all complex in computer terms, but the project required a heavy allocation of disk space, and, above all, needed skilled consideration at the stage of inputting data. That was because, while names and addresses were recorded as in the original sources, each occupation had to be given a specially-devised threefold classification. In many cases, that entailed research into the nature of eighteenth-century work processes. But, as a result, each occupation was identified individually, as well as within an appropriate economic sector and sub-sector.

Detailed pictures can then be established, showing the economic profile of the commercial and business leadership within the different urban centres. Contrasts between manufacturing and service towns were apparent, although all places had a core of both service industries and staple producers. These *Directories* were primarily concerned with men, as they usually formed the business elites. Yet, interestingly, 8% of these listings referred to women. They were not engaged in quite the same range of occupations as were the men, but they shared in the prevalent variety. There were, for example, female knife- and scissors-makers in Sheffield (1787), as well as a female blacksmith in Southampton (1784), a female funeral undertaker in Dublin (1784), and a female pilot in Liverpool (1774), among many others.

Space was also allocated on file for additional information about multiple occupations. In fact, it proved unusual for people in these sources to name more than one line of business, which was interesting in itself. Only just over 11% of all *Directory* men and women listed more than one job, and a tiny fraction (0·6%) had three or more. But these included some startling combinations of occupation. In Norwich (1783), a mathematics teacher was also a silk throwster. Not to be outdone, in Glasgow (1784) a language teacher was convivially also a vintner. Meanwhile, in Edinburgh (1773) a lodgings-keeper was sombrely employed as a manufacturer of grave-cloths.

A few notable individuals additionally listed their social status in the urban *Directories*. Again, they constituted a minority: approximately 12% of the total. Of these, one third had no formal occupation and were listed simply for their social importance, while two-thirds were also in business of some sort. Most status titles were very simple, as in 'Mr', 'Mrs', and 'Miss'. But there was a scattering of grander personages. They included a variety of gentlemen, ladies, knights, esquires, earls and countesses. And, nestling humbly among the list of Aldermen at Winchester in 1784, was the name of James, Duke of Chandos.

Clearly, it was not strictly true that all of urban life was contained within the early commercial *Directories*. Pimps and prostitutes did not appear (although there were some semi-spoof published listings of the names and addresses of the latter). But a sufficient variety of trades were listed to offer significant insights into the organisation of urban economic life. For example, the distribution of occupations can be studied on a street-by-street basis. The main shopping and manufacturing areas are thus revealed.

Computer-mapping provides an excellent visual representation of the data. An exercise in this technique was undertaken for the town of Shrewsbury, a relatively compact urban centre for which a good eighteenth-century street map was available (the more contemporaneous the sources, the better the 'match' of street names). Occupational data from the local *Directory* of 1786 were already on file. Using a digitising table, the Shrewsbury street pattern was manually transcribed to form a street file, incorporating in addition the looping course of the River Severn, as it elegantly defines the town centre.

A software package (ARC/INFO) was then kindly made available by Birkbeck College, London. It is a commercially-produced information system, designed to handle geographical data. Within INFO, new files were created, linking the digitised streets to those recorded in the *Directory*. Symbols were established to indicate the local density of any given occupational group. Then, once graphic requirements had been determined, a sequence of maps were provided. These could be analysed interactively on the terminal, or sent to the plotter to produce a hard copy.

The results were at once handsome and informative. On the original maps, the occupational data were drawn in orange and black, the river in blue. For reproduction purposes, black-and-white proved quite satisfactory. Shrewsbury's urban fusion of occupations could then be analysed closely. Its crowded shopping streets contrasted with the more spartan suburbs, while hostelries were located both in the centre and on the main routes from town. 'Here we have smoke, noise, scandal, affectation, and pretension', cried Farquhar's heroine (1706) in mock-salute to Shrewsbury as a provincial capital. These maps confirm and locate its urban and commercial diversity.

Reports

The early *Directories* are analysed in detail in an article in *Urban History Yearbook* (1984) and a brief account of occupational specialisms has been published in the *Times Higher Educational Supplement* 671, 13 September 1985.

Funding

This research was funded by the Economic and Social Research Council

(1983–85), with additional financial support from Bedford College, University of London. Assistance with computer-mapping was provided by the Geography Department, Birkbeck College, University of London.

Successful completion of the project was aided by the Computer Centre at Royal Holloway and Bedford New College, and, above all, by the indefatigable industry and good cheer of research assistant, Serena Kelly.

Future Plans

Current work is concerned with computerising early professional listings, and there are plans for additional work on commercial *Directories*. Full information is available from Dr P.J. Corfield, Dept. of History, Royal Holloway and Bedford New College, University of London, Egham, Surrey.

* This report has also appeared in *Humanities Communication Newsletter*, no. 7, 1986.

12 *David Marshall, David Cairns and Shaun Richards*

PIRELI: a Research Tool for the Humanities and Social Sciences

Interdisciplinary research in history and literature is a prominent feature of the overall research profile of the Humanities Department, North Staffordshire Polytechnic and feeds directly into, and from, the teaching of the Department's degrees, particularly the B.A. Literature and History. Naturally therefore, a central concern here is the examination of the situation, conditions of production, and reception of texts and the 'reading formation' of readers. From this has developed a research project linking these theoretical concerns with the general area of Irish cultural politics in the later nineteenth and early twentieth centuries and using the PIRELI[1] database as its central tool for recording the vital parameters of the texts examined and permitting subsequent serendipitous research upon those texts.

This particular research project proceeds by the collection and analysis of information on the amount and nature of the fictional, factual and periodical reading materials available to the Irish reading public in the period 1840–1914 (with particular reference to the Dublin conurbation). In the course of the project we intend to examine the content of representative samples of the most widely circulating items in terms of their ideological and political elements, and thus to assess the contribution of these sources to the development of various forms of Irish national consciousness in this crucial period for the development of Irish separatism, together with the linked phenomenon of the Irish Literary Revival.

The theoretical framework which we are elaborating and testing was, as we have indicated, initially produced in the course of developing and running a final year interdisciplinary paper which deals with the inter-relationship of literature and ideology in late nineteenth and early twentieth century Ireland. In preparing teaching materials we were faced with the necessity of hypothesising how it was that Irish readers and audiences came to react in particular ways to individual texts and dramatic performances. This has been necessary because in several significant and well documented cases the extreme reactions of the audiences and/or readerships of performances and texts appears, on the face of it, not to have been foreseen by the author or playwright involved (e.g *The Playboy Riots* of 1907). Such reactions demand investigation and explication via an adequately formulated methodology.

Subsequently the procedure adopted has been subjected to further development in papers given to a number of conferences and in publications in which we have elaborated a coherent and active theory of textual reception which, in part drawing upon the work of a number of theorists, details how, and under what conditions, a text is differentially interpreted by particular readers and groups of readers.

The concept of 'reception theory' is not a novel one;, however, current reception theory (e.g. H.R.Jauss, *Towards an Aesthetic of Reception*, 1982) operates within a framework which is almost entirely text-centred — hypothesising the essential features of a reader's response by interpreting elements of the text in a particular way. Thus the reader in current reception theory is seen as a passive creation of the text. We propose to substitute for this framework one which is historically grounded and in which the text is seen as being dialectically produced in the continuing act of reception according to the reader's own, socially determined, reading of the text. The elaboration and testing of such a framework demands the cataloguing, description and analysis of a substantial sample of those texts which from 1840 contributed to shaping the consciousness of Irish readers (and Dublin readers in particular) so that we can sophisticate, and enhance, our present ability to explain the reactions of audiences and readerships.

Our previous examinations of the Irish Literary Revival, and in particular those of our studies which have dealt with Synge's plays, have confirmed in novel, and theoretically coherent ways, the often repeated (but untheorised) assertions that the reading and performance of literary and dramatic texts had observable political and social consequences. Our approach represents an advance on what has hitherto been mainstream critical practice in Anglo-Irish literature in that we have been able to pinpoint those particular elements in texts and dramatic performances which produced reactions — and in some cases riots.

The concept of 'shaping' the consciousness of the reader in our approach is derived from theories of the 'subject' and the production of consciousness as developed by Jacques Lacan and Louis Althusser. Rather than assume the determination of response to texts as being produced by ideological dissonance, as is currently the case in Anglo-Irish literature, we propose to analyse the ideological determinants predominating in the reading materials available — in order to test the notion that these produce a 'horizon of expectations' which leads to the acceptance or rejection of texts according to their confirmation or denial of pre-existing nationalist 'norms'.

The project which is now under way at the Polytechnic is intended to widen the base of empirical materials upon which we have already been drawing (memoirs, contemporary journals and newspapers etc.), in order to cover a wider range of materials than is currently available for the contextual investigation of the Literary Revival. It includes school readers, texts and associated materials, together with a selection of the more significant (in circulation terms) of contemporary journals and periodicals, and lastly the most widely published and circulating literary, dramatic and historical texts.

The cataloguing and categorising of journals, school readers and so on is being carried out by constructing a PIRELI data-base which we intend ultimately to make generally available to researchers. The database is rather more than a simple catalogue of title, author, date and place of publication for in addition to this information this particular database, PIRELI, makes provision for the recording of a large number key-word descriptors by means of which salient features of the content of the item can be listed. The software of PIRELI then makes it possible for the enquirer to search the entire database for particular descriptors either singly or in combination as well as to provide lists of author, title etc. holdings for general bibliographic and cataloguing purposes.

The database is designed for online interactive use so that it is possible to start an enquiry using very general terms and then to refine the topic by subsequent more focussed definition of the terms of reference. The philosophy which underpins PIRELI makes it particularly suited to interdisciplinary research, for rather than profiling individual items the procedure for compiling the database requires the compilation of as complete a series of entries as is possible and impels the persons entering the data to cover not merely their particular areas of interest but to record the full range of issues etc., mentioned or discussed. In this way a PIRELI abstract prepared by a legal theorist can be utilised by a literature or history researcher — and vice-versa.

In the case of the project described above, it is our intention, once we have entered a significant number of records concerning materials from the period in question onto the database, that we shall use it as a flexible means of testing hypotheses, developed via the theoretical framework described earlier. It is our contention that in this way we will be able to approach far more nearly to an accurate description of the particular forms of consciousness shared by writers, audiences and readers of the period than has previously proved possible, and that we shall thus be enabled to move towards explaining how the common denominators of those forms of consciousness were produced and reproduced in specific instances.

Note

1. PIRELI is the acronym for *P*olytechnic *I*nformation *RE*trieval of *L*egal *I*nformation. As it suggests, the system was initially designed by D. V. Marshall of the Department of Law, North Staffordshire Polytechnic for recording information on cases, articles and texts for lawyers, but has since been modified to deal with the needs of disciplines generally in the Arts, Humanities and Social Sciences. It is currently being substantially extended in the general areas of history and literature.

13 *Harold Mytum*

Recording Graveyards on the BBC Micro ·

Introduction

Graveyard memorials provide an important source of historical information. The most obvious is that of the inscription, but there is also much that is of value in the form, decoration, and location of the monuments. In order that valid generalisations can be made it is essential that a large body of data is collected and analysed, and it is for this reason that a computer is required. The particular study for which the programs are being produced is conducted in Pembrokeshire, south-west Wales. Welsh is the predominant language in the north of the county, with English having this role in the south. The boundary between these two linguistic areas is called the Landsker, and this has been surprisingly static and clearly defined since at least the seventeenth century. Contrasts in the languages used can be easily detected, but other less obvious trends relating to wider aspects of culture and social organisation can be recognised only through computerised manipulation of the data. Although the initial impetus for the development of the micro computer for graveyard recording and analysis was the Welsh study, the programs produced can be used elsewhere.

The BBC micro has been selected for use in this project because of its ready availability in schools and homes in Britain. Using a micro with limited capacity does cause complications with processing large numbers of records, but by careful sorting and merging useful results can be obtained. The programs developed will be made available to schools and local history and archaeology groups, and it is hoped that the data collected by others can all be stored at the University of York, forming a national database.

Recording the data

Special A4 forms have been designed for the recording of the memorials. The form has room for a full free format copy of the inscription, an individual black-and-white photograph of the stone, and a section for comments, but because of the limited memory in the micro and on discs, the only data fed into the computer is coded. The data to be input is placed on the right hand side of the form, with the boxes clearly marked out for easy recording in the field. The data can be considered under three headings; background information, the memorial as an artefact, and the content of the inscription.

Background information

The background information records the dedication of the church, its denomination and its location (in relation to the Landsker for this study, as well as the place and grid reference). Also noted is the recorder and the date when the record was made. Normally each file consists of all the records from one graveyard, but large graveyards fill more than one side of disc and so need more than one file.

The memorial as an artefact

Every memorial is numbered and its location within the graveyard recorded using a site grid on the same principal as the national grid. Its orientation, measured with a compass, is also noted. The condition of the memorial and the inscription is noted, particularly with reference to the legibility of the text and whether the monument is still *in situ*. This is important because for some sorting and counting certain categories of monument should be excluded because they are not a relevant part of the database for that analysis. For example one gravestone may be perfectly preserved but have been moved to facilitate mechanical cutting of the grass. As a document recording the deaths of individuals this monument is perfectly valid. However, its site grid reference would be inappropriate in the study of the distribution of burials in the churchyard because it would no longer mark the grave plot. For the latter analysis, therefore, the memorial could be excluded from the count. Details of the size, form and materials used in the monument are also recorded, together with the technique of the inscription, the style of the letters and any motifs or symbols used.

The content of the inscription

Much information can be derived from the inscription itself. The languages used are of particular importance in this study, but a range of other categories of information is also obtained. Quotations often occur on the stones below the details of the deceased, and many are Biblical, though others also occur. Most gravestones begin with a phrase which is standardised, such as 'In loving memory' or 'Er cof am', but these are not constant though time or space, and reflect differing attitudes to death.

Some aspects of social structure can be obtained from the anthropological terms used to describe the deceased. The position of women in society, viewed as wives or mothers, can be contrasted with men who usually are given greater prominence and have a fuller description — even if they are not buried there, but are being mentioned on their dead spouse's memorial. Only men have more than familial relationships stated, and mariners in particular record profession, rank, and often the ship on which they served. Many memorials give the farm or address of the deceased as well as their name. This may be because of the numerous individuals of the same name in the area, and identification needed to be clarified; alternatively it suggests a great sense of identity with place, and this is supported by ethnographic and linguistic material from elsewhere. The use of placenames is more common in the Welsh than English parts of Pembrokeshire.

The demographic information from the stones is recorded in a form that consists of sex, age at death in years, month and year of death. This is recorded for each individual commemorated; the number of others mentioned on the stone (such as surviving spouses or children who erected the stone) is also recorded in the computer. The location of the body is also of importance; sometimes memorials are set up but the individual is not buried on the site. This may be because the body has been lost, such as at sea, or buried elsewhere, as in a war grave. If comparison is being made between burial registers and gravestone data then such individuals need to be excluded.

The forms can be filled in partly in the field, and partly back at base. It is a relatively quick and easy matter to train volunteers to use the forms, and with a group of 12 a graveyard of 150–200 memorials can be completed in a day. It has been found essential that forms are checked on site and again at base to ensure that all fields have been filled correctly and legibly. Every volunteer must have a fully annotated code list and can record memorials very efficiently. Schools and local history groups can easily use the forms, and if necessary some of the categories can be altered or extended to fit with local conditions, provided a full record is made of what these are and care is taken to ensure that the changes have been consistently made. An obvious example would be the materials used for the memorials; local stones were used in other parts of the country that were not available in Pembrokeshire and so have not been given a code. The location of the graveyard in relation to the Landsker would not be relevant outside south-west Wales, but the same field could be used to denote urban or rural, or the county in which a graveyard was located.

The provision of a measured graveyard plan with all the stones marked is necessary for the study of graveyard development, but for many aspects of the work would not be essential. However, even when a detailed plan is not required or practicable, it is vital that a sketch plan is made with all the memorials marked and numbered. This should also show graveyard boundaries, paths, major trees and other notable features. The sketch plan forms an important part of the record in case any memorial needs to be visited again to check information or to obtain more if, for example, one of the coded categories subsequently requires subdivision. Searching for memorials without any plan can be a long and frustrating business even in a graveyard of only 100 stones.

The programs

The data has been entered onto disc using Clare's Betabase database package. This in itself provides a measure of flexibility with its editing and sorting routines, but it is the menu of special programs for the analysis of the graveyard data which is of particular interest here. Special emphasis has been placed on graphical output because this is an easier medium by which to recognise trends, and excites the imagination more than large tables of figures. Two main forms of graphical output have been developed — the demographic information shown on line graphs, and the changes in style demonstrated on a form of bar chart known as a 'battleship curve'.

The demographic curves

The package that has been developed is deliberately designed to be user-friendly and menu-driven. After various parameters for the search have been set, the computer finds the relevant data from the file requested. Further files can then be searched, so that large graveyards on more than one side of disc can be combined, or any number of graveyards can be added together to provide regional samples. Once all files have been searched, the computer automatically prints out a table.

For mortality, the search covers the sex, age, month and year of death. Search strings can be for males, females or both, and though there are default values, these can be changed for the ages, months and years of death that are to be included. Up to six search strings can be entered at once, and each produces a separate table showing the number of deaths per decade with the average age, and number of deaths per month, and average age. The infinite choice available with the flexible form of the search strings enables, for example, child mortality (however defined) to be excluded when required, and male and female mortality to be compared.

For births, the program calculates the year of birth of each individual commemorated where his year of death and age is stated; the numbers per decade can then be printed out. Clearly, these births would not necessarily relate to births and baptisms in the parish where burial took place, but for wider surveys the figures may be of considerable value.

Once the tables have been printed out,the researcher can either carry out different searches, or can chose to display some of the already sorted data graphically. The scale of the graph is chosen by the default to fill the screen, but the researcher can alter this, for example if direct comparison between two different graphs is anticipated. In that case, identical scales would be wanted, even if one graph only filled a small part of the screen.

The graph is previewed on the screen, and can be printed or abandoned. The same search string could then be displayed at another scale, or a different search string chosen. Whenever a graph is to be printed, a title can be typed in and which appears at the top of the graph. Certain set information is automatically printed, but a particular comment can be most valuable if many graphs are being produced (Figure 1). By using the tables to see which sets of data may be most usefully portrayed graphically, and by previewing the graphs on the screen, the relatively slow printing of hard copy on the dot printer can be kept to the minimum.

Figure 1   *Average age at death of females — Nevern*

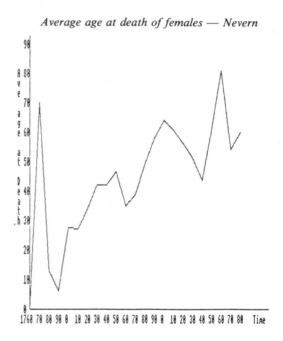

The 'battleship curves'

A second suite of programs allow stylistic changes through time to be plotted on 'battleship curves'. These are bar charts where the bars are placed horizontally, and are centrally placed (Figure 2). The effect is an aesthetically pleasing one which allows quick assessment of trends in popularity. It is also possible to mount various battleship curves on the same large sheet and see how the falling popularity of one attribute may be compensated by the rise of another.

Figure 2   *Rudbaxton white marble*

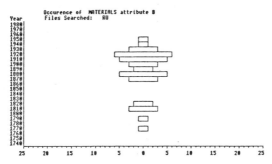

One of ten fields from the records can be selected from a menu and searched. As with the demographic curves, more than one file can be combined for this procedure. This can be particularly important in the study of some stylistic elements because they may be relatively rare and no significant conclusions can be drawn until many files are searched. Once all the searching has been completed, a table is printed out with all the attribute states along the x axis, and decades along the y axis. From this table it is easy to select which attribute states should be graphically represented by the 'battleship curves'. For example, the attribute state 'white marble' might be selected from the field 'material' (Figure 2). Some graveyards contain burials covering too long a period for all to appear on the screen at once, and if this is the case a choice has to be made as to whether to ignore the earliest or latest decades. This is no great hindrance because the printed table can indicate which part would be most suitable, and of course two different graphs could be printed if required.

The curves are previewed on the screen and if satisfactory a heading can be added prior to printing. All the curves are at present to a standard scale, and as a result it is not possible to print graphs where any attribute state has a value greater than twenty-five for any one decade. This is only a severe limitation if groups of graveyards need to be combined for analysis; very rarely would a single graveyard contain such common attribute states.

Conclusions

Graveyard memorials contain a large amount of data of interest to historians as well as archaeologists, linguists, art historians and ethnologists. To answer most questions of general interest, large quantities of memorials from one or more graveyards have to be manipulated and without a computer the sheer quantity of complex information makes this impossible, slow and prone to error.

The programs developed for use on the BBC micro allow groups such as schools and local history societies to collect and analyse graveyard data, producing meaningful patterns without long periods of sorting and counting.

The results can be output as tables or in graphical form. Graveyards contain more than genealogical data, and should be treated as a precious resource to be cherished, recorded and protected.

* This research has been funded by the Center for Field Research of Belmont, Massachusetts, U.S.A. and the University of York.

Economy

14 *Michael Gervers*

The DEEDS Project and a Survey of the Essex Textile Industry in the Twelfth and Thirteenth Centuries

In 1968 I undertook to transcribe and edit the content of a section of the Cartulary of the Order of the Hospital of St John of Jerusalem in England. This section contains 967 entries dating from *c.* 1120 to the end of the fourteenth century; nearly all of them pertain to the County of Essex. The majority of these reflect the growth of the Order's landed estate in the north central part of the county.

It soon became evident that no significant historical evaluation could be made of the charter sources unless they were dated and most of them were not. For those unfamiliar with medieval English sources I should point out that, unlike continental examples, English private charters are rarely dated prior to the passage of the *Statute of Mortmain* in 1279 and that the custom does not become general until about 1300. As a result, published charters of the period have regularly been assigned such dates by their editors as 'early', 'middle' or 'late' twelfth or thirteenth century. More precise methods of dating can be applied, but, based as they are on internal evidence, the process is devastatingly time consuming. The transcription of the charters took less than eight months, while the dating of the undated examples took about fifteen months.

A second stumbling block in the edition was determining the topographical identity of charters, particularly twelfth-century ones, in which no parish or hamlet names were given. As in the dating of undated documents, a solution could only be derived from a comparison of information internal to the document with other entries in the cartulary, or with external sources. That internal information consists largely of personal names, which must be identified with similar names occurring in dated documents or in documents containing place names. Obviously, comprehensive indices become essential at this stage, both in the edition in progress and in the comparative sources. Prior to assigning dates and places to the charters, therefore, I spent another fifteen months preparing a 40,000-card index of persons, places and things.

From start to finish the process took nearly four years. At the end of this period and about the time I started to prepare my manuscript for publication, I began to consider computers as a means in future work of reducing time spent on dating, identifying places, building indices and clerical work. I devised a plan to locate and obtain copies of all extant medieval charters for Essex from 1066 to 1300, an estimated 25,000, and to computerize their content. I explained my objectives to the University of Toronto Computing Services, who recommended that I break the content of the sources into fields which could then be entered into a hierarchical database called Mark IV. It is they who designed the database. It is divided into 40 segments containing 142 subfields. Over the years, the content of the 967 charters in the Hospitaller Cartulary was coded comprehensively, and entered into the hierarchical Mark IV format designed for it. Part of the project led to the preparation of a microfiche concordance of those charters, which is available at a nominal fee for interested parties.[1]

The next priority was to add the content of dated sources to the corpus. We began with the Feet of Fines for Essex, of which there are over 2,600 for our period in the calendered edition prepared by R. E. C. Kirk and published by the Essex Archaeological Society between 1899 and 1949. The Fines are now also included in the corpus, although the coding is less comprehensive as it was taken from Kirk's calendar rather than from the originals. More recently, we have also coded the thirteenth-century Inquisitions Post Mortem for Essex. Once they have been incorporated the corpus will consist of nearly 4,000 records. We are still a long way from our final objective of combining all pre-fourteenth-century Essex charters into a single database, but we can begin to use what we have to situate undated conveyances in place and time. An article by Dr Lesley Kordecki in a recent issue of the *Journal of the Society of Archivists*[2] describes the dating process and how, with a database of 1800 charter records, it was possible to attribute a date to a document which was within a quarter century of its actual date of issue. This attribution is far from satisfactory, but we expect that the accuracy will improve as the number of records in the corpus grows.

Despite the increasing number of colleagues in the Humanities at the University of Toronto who are using computers in their work, there has been very little interest in obtaining mainframe software which can handle large data bases. There are only a few of us using Mark IV and as a consequence the system's days are clearly numbered. I decided, therefore, in January 1986 to transfer as much computing as possible to a personal computer. The transfer would also incorporate a change from a hierarchical to a relational database for the organization of the data.

We acquired a COMPAQ 286 Deskpro, an AT clone which far out-performs its model, with 640K RAM, a 1·2 megabyte floppy drive, a 70 megabyte hard disk drive, a 60 megabyte Tall Grass external tape backup and an Epson FX 185 wide carriage printer. The PC is connected to the IBM mainframe by a dedicated telephone line and a Gandalf modem which enables us to manipulate data there at a rate of 4800 baud. Downloading and uploading of files is accomplished by the software KERMIT, which takes about an hour to transfer a megabyte of data.

We are still, unfortunately, dependent on the mainframe as that is where the majority of our data is stored. We anticipate that we have some 35 megabytes of information in Mark IV, but since the hierarchical format does not lend itself to a straightforward measurement of content, we shall only be able to determine the size of the DEEDS database when the files have been extracted from Mark IV and flattened out. We are familiar with the process as we have been preparing flat files for years prior to analysing data from the corpus by means of the widely used statistical package SAS.

The recent introduction of a PC version of SAS assisted us in our decision to transfer data manipulation to a personal computer. The producers of SAS-PC have provided a site-licence to the University of Toronto and member users can obtain personal copies of the complete software for $50·00 Canadian a year. The PC version is more versatile even than its mainframe counterpart, and because of the compatibility of both makes a viable reality of mixed-mode computing.

The relational database into which we plan to put the DEEDS corpus is called ORACLE. It is available both for the mainframe and the PC. Our objective in the original plan was to code the content of charter sources such that information could be extracted from the database for questions which had not been formulated at the time the data was entered. One such query derives from the large number of occupational names occurring in our sources. In recent months we have extracted from our Mark IV database all references to such names and, after preliminary analysis, are making our way towards some interesting conclusions. In view of the large number of occupations, we decided first to exclude all ecclesiastics and nobles from the file, secondly to exclude all but the artisans and finally to concentrate on textile workers and the textile industry. Out of 3500 records we have been able to distinguish 92 different people involved in various aspects of the trade from *c.* 1175 to *c.* 1300. Textile workers are not the first to appear, but those who precede them, namely metal and wood workers, do so by only a quarter century. We do not know, therefore, whether our sample reflects industrial beginnings, or whether it reflects merely the entry of artisans to the ranks 1) of those holding or exchanging property, 2) of those considered eligible to append their names as witnesses to property exchange documents or 3) of those who considered it necessary, and who could afford, to record an exchange in writing.

Eleven trades are mentioned, including chaloners or blanket makers, coif makers, drapers, dyers, fullers, hatters, hose makers, loom makers (possibly), a napper, tailors and weavers. All appear among the largely rural evidence of the private charters from the Hospitaller Cartulary. Only half of this list is to be found in the names occurring in the royal Feet of Fines, that is to say chaloners, drapers, dyers, fullers, tailors and weavers. This difference leaves some doubt as to the nature of the occupations of coif makers, hatters, hose

Figure 1   *Frequency and distribution of textile workers, 1125–1300*

a

OCCUP	FREQUENCY	CUM FREQ	PERCENT	CUM PERCENT
TAIL	33	33	35.870	35.870
DRAP	14	47	15.217	51.087
WEVR	12	59	13.043	64.130
FULL	10	69	10.870	75.000
DYER	7	76	7.609	82.609
HUDE	4	80	4.348	86.957
HOSE	4	84	4.348	91.304
CHAL	3	87	3.261	94.565
LOOM	2	89	2.174	96.739
COIF	2	91	2.174	98.913
NAPR	1	92	1.087	100.000

b

HUNDRED	FREQUENCY	CUM FREQ	PERCENT	CUM PERCENT
HINCKFRD	33	33	35.870	35.870
LEXDEN	9	42	9.783	45.652
DENGIE	7	49	7.609	53.261
SUFFOLK	6	55	6.522	59.783
CHELMSFD	6	61	6.522	66.304
BECONTRE	6	67	6.522	72.826
WALTHAM	5	72	5.435	78.261
ONGAR	4	76	4.348	82.609
UTTLESFD	3	79	3.261	85.870
FRESHWEL	3	82	3.261	89.130
CHAFFORD	3	85	3.261	92.391
ROCHFORD	2	87	2.174	94.565
DUNMOW	2	89	2.174	96.739
BARSTABL	2	91	2.174	98.913
WITHAM	1	92	1.087	100.000

and loom makers and the napper. Figure 1 shows that the core of the industry, in terms of the frequency of occurrence, is made up of those appearing in both of our major sources, that is, tailors, drapers, weavers, fullers and dyers. Of this group, the tailors are by far the most numerous (Figure 2). They are also among the first to appear historically. They are preceded by hatters and hosiers but, taken together, the three suggest that in the late twelfth century, textile activity revolved more around the production of finished clothing than around the manufacture and sale of cloth.

More striking still is the almost complete absence of references to textile workers in charters dating from the first quarter of the thirteenth century. The period coincides exactly with the reign of King John and the minority of Henry III. One might have thought that during a period of such political instability there would have been a reluctance to transfer property, thus leading to a smaller proportion of written records in which occupational names would occur. In fact, however, as many charters in our sample are issued in this quarter century as in the previous one. Furthermore, other groups of artisans appear at this time while textile workers do not.

Equally remarkable is that, starting *c.* 1225, almost as though reflecting the confidence inspired by Henry III's confirmation of Magna Carta, there is a sudden explosion of textile workers into the sources. Between *c.* 1225 and *c.* 1240, all but one of the eleven occupations are mentioned. Foremost among these are the tailors, drapers and weavers, making it seem, that a trade industry in textile manufacture had begun.

There is an apparent decline in the second half of the century, but this merely reflects a reduction in the number of surviving documents in our sources. In real terms, the proportion of references to textile workers compared to the number of documents in the Cartulary shows an increase of 30% of the third over the second quarter, but a 37% decline of the fourth

Figure 2   *Occupations over 25-year spans*

OCCUP   SPAN25YR

Cell contents: FREQUENCY / PERCENT / ROW PCT / COL PCT

OCCUP	1175–99	1200–24	1225–49	1250–74	1275–00	TOTAL
CHAL	0 / 0.00 / 0.00 / 0.00	0 / 0.00 / 0.00 / 0.00	1 / 1.09 / 33.33 / 2.44	1 / 1.09 / 33.33 / 3.57	1 / 1.09 / 33.33 / 5.56	3 / 3.26
COIF	0 / 0.00 / 0.00 / 0.00	0 / 0.00 / 0.00 / 0.00	2 / 2.17 / 100.00 / 4.88	0 / 0.00 / 0.00 / 0.00	0 / 0.00 / 0.00 / 0.00	2 / 2.17
DRAP	0 / 0.00 / 0.00 / 0.00	0 / 0.00 / 0.00 / 0.00	7 / 7.61 / 50.00 / 17.07	6 / 6.52 / 42.86 / 21.43	1 / 1.09 / 7.14 / 5.56	14 / 15.22
DYER	0 / 0.00 / 0.00 / 0.00	0 / 0.00 / 0.00 / 0.00	2 / 2.17 / 28.57 / 4.88	4 / 4.35 / 57.14 / 14.29	1 / 1.09 / 14.29 / 5.56	7 / 7.61
FULL	0 / 0.00 / 0.00 / 0.00	0 / 0.00 / 0.00 / 0.00	4 / 4.35 / 40.00 / 9.76	4 / 4.35 / 40.00 / 14.29	2 / 2.17 / 20.00 / 11.11	10 / 10.87
HOSE	1 / 1.09 / 25.00 / 25.00	0 / 0.00 / 0.00 / 0.00	0 / 0.00 / 0.00 / 0.00	2 / 2.17 / 50.00 / 7.14	1 / 1.09 / 25.00 / 5.56	4 / 4.35
HUDE	1 / 1.09 / 25.00 / 25.00	0 / 0.00 / 0.00 / 0.00	1 / 1.09 / 25.00 / 2.44	1 / 1.09 / 25.00 / 3.57	1 / 1.09 / 25.00 / 5.56	4 / 4.35
LOOM	0 / 0.00 / 0.00 / 0.00	0 / 0.00 / 0.00 / 0.00	1 / 1.09 / 50.00 / 2.44	1 / 1.09 / 50.00 / 3.57	0 / 0.00 / 0.00 / 0.00	2 / 2.17
NAPR	0 / 0.00 / 0.00 / 0.00	0 / 0.00 / 0.00 / 0.00	1 / 1.09 / 100.00 / 2.44	0 / 0.00 / 0.00 / 0.00	0 / 0.00 / 0.00 / 0.00	1 / 1.09
TAIL	1 / 1.09 / 3.03 / 25.00	1 / 1.09 / 3.03 / 100.00	16 / 17.39 / 48.48 / 39.02	5 / 5.43 / 15.15 / 17.86	10 / 10.87 / 30.30 / 55.56	33 / 35.87
WEVR	1 / 1.09 / 8.33 / 25.00	0 / 0.00 / 0.00 / 0.00	6 / 6.52 / 50.00 / 14.63	4 / 4.35 / 33.33 / 14.29	1 / 1.09 / 8.33 / 5.56	12 / 13.04
TOTAL	4 / 4.35	1 / 1.09	41 / 44.57	28 / 30.43	18 / 19.57	92 / 100.00

over the third. The Fines show a 25% decline of the third over the second quarter, but no further decline in the fourth quarter. In actual fact, therefore, the apex of economic activity and growth may have been in the second quarter, when it all began. If the charters suggest an increase in the third quarter while the Fines indicate a reduction, the explanation may be in the county-wide coverage of the latter and the regional concentration of the former in north central Essex where most of the production was taking place. Both sources reflect decline in the last quarter when compared with the second. This decline may correspond to the depression in the English textile industry which, it is argued, began in 1270.[3]

Figure 1b gives some indication of the topographical distribution of the industry. Excluding 'Suffolk', which represents the county rather than a hundred, the greatest concentrations of workers are to be found in the hundreds of Hinckford, Lexden, Dengie, Chelmsford and Becontree. If we separate references in the Fines from those in the Cartulary we find that the parishes of concentration in the Fines are exactly the same as those for both groups taken together, but in a different order. Cartulary sources point to Hinckford, Lexden and Chelmsford too, but exchange Freshwell and Waltham Hundreds for Dengie and Becontree in the Fines. The reason for this differentiation is that the Cartulary contains very few charters from the southern part of Essex, while the Fines cover the entire county. The disproportionately large number of references to Hinckford Hundred arises from the concentration of transactions from the region preserved in the Cartulary. Of the 33 occurrences there of textile workers, 28 are from the Cartulary.

When considered in conjunction with actual occupations, we find that textile production involving weaving, dying, and fulling is concentrated in Hinckford and Lexden Hundreds and to a lesser extent in Chelmsford Hundred. Activity in Dengie and Becontree is of a very different order. There we find only tailors and drapers, suggesting that while textiles were manufactured in north and central Essex, work in the south was confined largely to cutting the cloth and trading in it. Such activities are quite in keeping with what one might expect to find in port towns along the Thames, where the emphasis was on trade rather than on manufacture.

Another approach to the computerized file on textile workers can be made through a consideration of the roles these men filled in the charters. In this case, the number of references increases from 92 to 138, as some of the workers appear more than once in the sources, participating in different transactions and performing different roles. Roles have been reduced to five categories: 1) agent, meaning someone acting for another party, 2) donors or grantors, 3) recipients of property transferred, 4) spectators, including tenants and neighbours and 5) witnesses. These witnesses, who represent 36% of all roles held by textile workers, derive entirely from the entries in the Cartulary for the Fines were never witnessed.

Donors and recipients are nearly equal in number. There are half as many spectators as witnesses and a small group of 5 agents. The latter group is actually composed of only two tailors. The percentage breakdown of roles is somewhat compromised by the fact that no witnesses occur in the Fines. If they did, we can hardly doubt that the total number of individual textile workers would be increased in proportion to the ratio of entries in the Cartulary compared to those in the Fines, that is to say by a multiple of 4.

More germane to our present study is the relationship of occupations to roles (Figure 3). We have already noted that the role of agent is only filled by tailor. Only six of the eleven occupations are found in the role of donor. These are, in descending order, tailors, drapers, weavers, chaloners, dyers and hatters. Five of the eleven occur as recipients, but 90% of the recipients are drapers and tailors. The remaining 10% are filled equally, that is to say on one occasion each, by a chaloner, a dyer and a fuller. Seven of our eleven trades occur in the inactive, spectator role of neighbour or tenant. 71% of these are fullers, tailors and weavers. The remainder include a coifmaker, 2

Figure 3   *Occupations by role group*

OCCUP   ROLEGRP

FREQUENCY
PERCENT
ROW PCT
COL PCT

OCCUP		AGENT	DONOR	RECEIVER	SPECTATR	WITNESS	TOTAL
CHAL	0	0	3	1	0	0	4
	.	0.00	2.17	0.72	0.00	0.00	2.90
	.	0.00	75.00	25.00	0.00	0.00	
	.	0.00	10.34	3.33	0.00	0.00	
COIF	0	0	0	0	1	1	2
	.	0.00	0.00	0.00	0.72	0.72	1.45
	−.	0.00	0.00	0.00	50.00	50.00	
	.	0.00	0.00	0.00	4.17	2.00	
DRAP	0	0	7	14	2	4	27
	.	0.00	5.07	10.14	1.45	2.90	19.57
	.	0.00	25.93	51.85	7.41	14.81	
	.	0.00	24.14	46.67	8.33	8.00	
DYER	1	0	3	1	3	1	8
	.	0.00	2.17	0.72	2.17	0.72	5.80
	.	0.00	37.50	12.50	37.50	12.50	
	.	0.00	10.34	3.33	12.50	2.00	
FULL	0	0	0	1	5	6	12
	.	0.00	0.00	0.72	3.62	4.35	8.70
	.	0.00	0.00	8.33	41.67	50.00	
	.	0.00	0.00	3.33	20.83	12.00	
HOSE	0	0	0	0	0	12	12
	.	0.00	0.00	0.00	0.00	8.70	8.70
	.	0.00	0.00	0.00	0.00	100.00	
	.	0.00	0.00	0.00	0.00	24.00	
HUDE	0	0	1	0	1	4	6
	.	0.00	0.72	0.00	0.72	2.90	4.35
	.	0.00	16.67	0.00	16.67	66.67	
	.	0.00	3.45	0.00	4.17	8.00	
LOOM	0	0	0	0	0	5	5
	.	0.00	0.00	0.00	0.00	3.62	3.62
	.	0.00	0.00	0.00	0.00	100.00	
	.	0.00	0.00	0.00	0.00	10.00	
NAPR	0	0	0	0	0	1	1
	.	0.00	0.00	0.00	0.00	0.72	0.72
	.	0.00	0.00	0.00	0.00	100.00	
	.	0.00	0.00	0.00	0.00	2.00	
TAIL	0	5	11	13	6	12	47
	.	3.62	7.97	9.42	4.35	8.70	34.06
	.	10.64	23.40	27.66	12.77	25.53	
	.	100.00	37.93	43.33	25.00	24.00	
WEVR	1	0	4	0	6	4	14
	.	0.00	2.90	0.00	4.35	2.90	10.14
	.	0.00	28.57	0.00	42.86	28.57	
	.	0.00	13.79	0.00	25.00	8.00	
TOTAL	.	5	29	30	24	50	138
		3.62	21.01	21.74	17.39	36.23	100.00

drapers, 3 dyers and a hatter.

Anybody could be a witness, although the chaloners are never found as such. Coif, hose and loom makers, and nappers, only occur as witnesses. In descending percentages of the witness role from 67% to 26% we have hatters, fullers, weavers and tailors. Least frequent of all in the role of witness are drapers and dyers, at 15% and 13% respectively.

We can pursue this avenue of inquiry to best advantage if we distinguish between the active roles of donor and recipient and the inactive ones of spectator and witness. Agents may be excluded from this consideration. Our thesis will be that, in general terms, those filling the active roles probably have a higher economic and social standing than those who occupy a proportionately greater percentage of the inactive ones. The role distribution of the chaloners compares most similarly to that of the drapers and so we feel justified in combining the two. A simple calculation provides us with the following breakdown with respect to the active roles.

Chaloners & Drapers	81%
Tailors	57%
Dyers	50%
Weavers	29%
Hatters	17%
Fullers	8%
Coif, hose and loom makers, and nappers, only occur in the inactive roles	

We propose that these percentages reflect broadly the social and economic distinctions between members of the Essex textile industry in the thirteenth century. The drapers and chaloners are at the top of the list and have the highest percentage of recipients (45%) with respect to the total number of roles. They are followed in the role of recipient by the tailors with 31% and the dyers with 13%. Weavers, hatters and fullers follow at a noticeable distance and in that order. The correlation between the capacity to give or receive property on the one hand and social and economic status on the other seems from this small example to be self evident.

Dividing the analysis between the Cartulary and the Fines reveals an interesting feature. The four occupations which are only represented by inactive roles are entirely absent from the Fines. Either they were too low on the economic scale to be mentioned in such a source, or we have misidentified the occupation. In view of the absence of any textile workers in the charters of the Cartulary prior to *c.* 1175, at a time when tailors at least must have been active, we venture to suggest from the evidence of these charters and the Fines that the possibility of an individual's appearing in the historical record is to a large extent determined by his ability to hold property, and more particularly, to grant or receive it.

• There is already more information in the database than a single researcher could analyse in a lifetime, yet a good deal more must still be added before the corpus can be used to meet our original objective: to date as precisely as possible undated twelfth and thirteenth-century Essex charters and to assign accurate place names to charters in which no such names appear. With the necessary means at hand, the DEEDS project can be expected to grow for some time to come.

Notes

1. Inquiries may be addressed to the DEEDS project, Division of Humanities, Scarborough Campus, University of Toronto, 1265 Military Trail, Scarborough, Ontario, Canada M1C 1AH.
2. 7:5, April, 1984, pp. 299–311.
3. Andrew Woodger, 'The Eclipse of the Burel Weaver: Some Technological Develpments in the Thirteenth Century', *Textile History*, 12, 1981, pp. 59–76 (p. 59 & n. 2).

15 *Hans Jørgen Marker*

Danish Prices and Wages and the Microcomputer

The Objective and the Problems Involved in Reaching it

The sources of Danish history are comparatively scarce until the Reformation in 1536. After that date a large part of the central administrative material is preserved. From the late sixteenth century the sources become so numerous that few scholars have dealt with them from the statistical point of view. The history of prices and wages usually starts in the age of Absolutism from 1660, when normative sources become available in a reasonable number.

This paper will present some suggestions on how to deal with the numerous but yet sporadic quantitative historical sources of the late sixteenth and early seventeenth century. Danish price and wage data will serve as an example. Data like this represents complex data structures, as both kinds of materials may be divided according to two criteria, time and sort, leaving a number of cells of which some have none and others have many observations.

No single Danish source contains a basis for the production of a series of prices and wages before 1660.[1] That means that a series of data has to be collected from several different sources. In an unpublished paper at the University of Århus[2] I have approached the problem in a couple of ways. This study serves as a pilot study for my ongoing research project which deals with additional price and wage observations from the same period and territory. The pilot study dealt with 'The influence of the development in prices, wages an taxes on the cash outcome from an estate in eastern Jutland owned by great nobles in the period 1619 to 1655'.

The Data

One of the problems in this sort of material is to distinguish whether a 'price' or 'wage' represents an amount which was in fact to be paid, or an amount which somebody thought should be paid. In order to cope with that problem I use only genuine transactions as observations in the analysis. The term 'genuine transaction' refers to a situation where some goods changed hands and some money was paid. If the genuine transaction is to be of use in the investigation, the price as well as the quantity must be recorded.

The Available Sources

Three kinds of sources of price and wage data remain from the time before 1660. They are the official records, the ledgers of the estates of the nobility, and occasional occurrences of data in sources concerned with other things, for example in private letters.

Among the official records the most important are the ledgers from the fiefs. Many of these are preserved from the late sixteenth century to 1660, when the fiefs were replaced by the 'amt's. Some data are found in the letters from the Central Administration. Another (semi-)official source is the personal diaries of the King (Christian IV's *skrivekalendere*). Quite a substantial part of the national economy was considered the personal resources of the King (at least by the King himself). The personal diaries of the King contain information on the way in which some of the money was spent or invested. Some ledgers from noblemen's estates are preserved from the first half of the seventeenth century. These are Eske Brok's diaries, the ledger of Sophie Brahe, the ledgers of the county of Løvenholm (earlier the estate Gjesingholm), the ledgers of Herlufsholm and Sorø, which were primarily educational institutions, of Vallø-Lellinge, Skinnerup and Kjærstrupgård, which belonged to members of the royal family, and of Selsø, Cortfitz Ulfeldt's Torup and of Kay Lykke's estates in Jutland and Funen.[3] The first three estates mentioned were situated close to one another in and around the district ('herred') of Sønderhald north of Århus.

Of letters there are the personal letters of the King himself[4] and of some noblemen, for instance Kristoffer Gøje.[5] In the pilot study I chose to use written material from noblemen owning estates in and around the district of Sønderhald in central eastern Jutland just north of Århus. This choice was made for several reasons. Firstly such material existed, and nowhere else in the kingdom was such a concentration of private ledgers remaining. Secondly this material was printed and as such readily at hand. Thirdly the concentration in time, geography and social provenance minimized some methodological problems in combining the materials. The decision to use private and not official material was made in order to minimize the problem with valuations appearing as prices, i.e. official valuations forced on the other party in a transaction by the power of state. The materials were the diaries of Eske Brok, the ledger of Christian Rantzau's estates in Nørrejylland (Jutland north of the Duchy of Slesvig) and the ledger made by Sophie Brahe.

Collection of Data

For the pilot study the data collected was written on index cards, each card carrying the relevant information for one genuine transaction. The cards were then sorted, first by the commodity or labour output which was the subject of the transaction, and then by time. The cards have now been transformed into a machine readable form. The dataset contains 2,380 prices and 192 wages.

The data from the fief of Kalø has now been collected. The result was 2,475 prices and 360 wages. We have access to the ledgers in the form of microfilms, which are read on a reader/printer. A hard copy is taken of each page contaning price or wage information. This is done for two reasons. First, if the data had been keyed in directly, I would have had to look from one screen to another and back again which would be most tiring. And secondly, the hard copies are needed for later reference purposes.

The data is then keyed into a microcomputer. Currently a HP125 is used for that purpose, but we are applying for funds for the purchase of a more sophisticated device. The data entry system used is our own product; it is a fairly simple program allowing different setups.

We use two different data entry setups, one for prices and one for wages. The price form contains: Date, Designation, Unit price, Units, Price, Purchaser, Purchaser's domicile, Vendor, Vendor's Domicile, Comment, Source. The wage form contains: Date, Occupation, Working place, Name, Period, Wage, Wage per time unit, Payment in kind, Commentary, Source. Some of the information to be entered into the forms can be found in the sources, some have to be calculated. If the description of a transaction contains insufficient information for analysis, the observation has to be discarded.

Transformation of Data to a Uniform Appearance

The observations as given in the sources are far from homogeneous as regards monetary units as well as quantity. The monetary system in the major part of Northern Europe in the seventeenth century was based on silver coins. The main unit was the 'daler', (Thaler). The 'daler' was divided into 'marks', which were divided into 'skilling', (Schilling, shilling), which were again divided into 'hvid' (album) and 'penninge', (Pfennig, pence). The number of each unit to one another differed considerably in the different countries and in time.

In Denmark several systems were used. After 1625, for example, we had 1 rigsdaler = 4 rigsmark (or ortsdaler) = 96 skilling = 288 hvid = 1152 penninge, and I sletdaler = 4 sletmark = 64 skilling, and 1 kurantdaler = 4 kurantmark = 80 skilling. At the same time German money from the Hanseatic town of Lübeck was used with 1 Reichsthaler (lybsk) = 2 Mark (lybsk) = 48 Schilling (lybsk) where 1 skilling (lybsk) = 2 skilling (dansk, Danish). Often the words used about the monetary units involved in a transaction are ambiguous. It may be daler sometimes meaning rigsdaler and at other times sletdaler or even kurantdaler. In such cases the only way to decide the currency involved may be to recalculate the total price from the total quantity and price per unit when available.[6]

The units of measurement for commodities are even more complex. Often individual measurement systems were used for each commodity. And we find several different systems with local variations all over the country. In order to cope with these problems it is necessary to have precise knowledge of the different systems used. This I had to acquire when I made the first investigation. The information is not readily available, but has to be gathered from many sources of which some contain false information as well.

The state of the ongoing investigation is as outlined above. We are now waiting for the microfilms containing the ledger of the fief of Dronningborg. When the data entry of that dataset has been completed the analysis can start.

Statistical data handling

The statistical data handling will take place on a mainframe computer. The plan is to use SAS for this purpose. In the pilot study a programmable calculator was used, as a computer was not available. But the technical means used for the statistical data handling are of less importance than the methods involved. Investigations based on these old materials are rare and on Danish materials practically unknown. This means that we have no knowledge of the kinds of statistical distributions involved other than what can be derived from the material itself. In other words, extreme caution has to be exercised in connection with the conclusions.

The data may be organized in two arrays, one containing prices and one containing wages and each having as column index the years covered and as row index the various commodities/labour outputs involved. These arrays have several observations in a few of the cells, one observation in some and none in many. Consequently more data are missing than available. The right

Figure 1   *The development of wages*

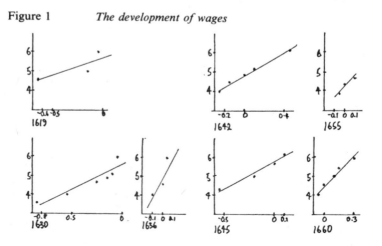

way in which to treat such material will probably always be a matter of discussion. One way might be to discard it immediately. That procedure would be defensible, but very little knowledge would be gained by it.

In my first investigation on prices and wages I treated the two arrays in different ways. In the price array I computed the average price for each cell based on weighted average. The prices assigned to the empty cells were then computed by linear interpolation between the prices in the nearest non-empty cells on both sides. When an empty cell had no non-empty cell on one of its sides, no price was assigned to it. In this way I obtained prices in most of the cells from 1619 to 1655. By a total count in the ledger of Sophie Brahe I found the average total quantity bought or sold at the Rosenkrantz estates in the years 1630–40. These quantities I then used as weights for the computation of indices of the development in the purchase and selling prices of the estates belonging to the high nobility in eastern Jutland (Figure 2). In a similar way I calculated an index on the development of food prices (Figure 3) (prisudviklingen) based on a contemporary table for the estimation of the quantity of food to be used for feeding the employees of a manor.[7]

Figure 2　　　　*Price index*

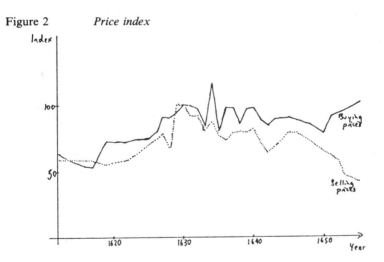

The wages would not allow such a procedure. Here the empty cells outnumbered the non-empty by about 5·5 to 1. Instead, I separated 72 wages given to people with a permanent appointment to the manors investigated, and who were paid on a yearly basis. For these wages I made the assumption that all the wages involved participated in a common trend. All the wage observations concerned people with a permanent appointment to the manors investigated, and paid on a yearly basis. In order to be able to test the development and not the actual size of the wages I divided all the wages in each category by the average value for that category, thereby obtaining observations with distributions of the same type as the original observations

Figure 3   *The development of wages and of the prices of food*

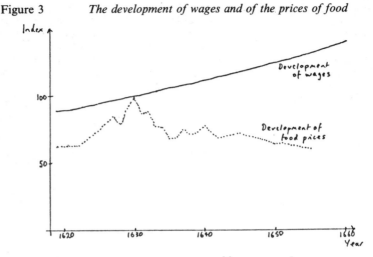

but with average 1 in all categories. These new observations I called relative wages. I grouped the relative wages by year. I then took the Napirian logarithms of the relative wages obtaining what I called the relative wage logarithms. Further, I made the assumption that the relative wage logarithms were Gauss distributed. This assumption cannot be proved within the material itself, but I find it generally acceptable to describe prices and wages as logarithmically Gauss distributed, and trial diagrams which I made for each cell with sufficient information did not contradict the assumption (Figure 1).

The next step was to test whether there was a linear development of the relative wage logarithms. To do so I had to test for homogeneity of variance. For this purpose I used Bartlett's test for homogeneity of variance. The hypothesis was accepted with a probability of 41%. I then proceeded with testing for linear regression. This was accepted with 8·4%.

This accepted hypothesis of a linear development of the logarithms of the wages is equivalent to an exponential development of the wages themselves. The maximum likelihood estimator for the slope of the logarithms of the wages was 0·01602 giving an antilogarithm of 1·01067 or an average increase in the wages of about 1·07%. The possible procedures for the material I am gathering now will probably be similar to the procedures outlined above.

Control of Results

Results like those outlined above are in themselves not very meaningful. They may be significant statements about the past, or they may be mere arithmetical exercises. It is not easy for the reader to decide which situation pertains. Therefore it is the responsibility of the author to provide a comparison of the results with the information we have of similar conditions in the past. In the pilot study I computed the development of the yield of an estate belonging to the nobility in eastern Jutland. For this I used the results outlined above and from a totally traditional historical investigation I have made of the development of the taxation of the nobility. And I used the result of Bennike Madsen's investigation of the development of the taxation of the farmers.[8] By using as weight the average amount spent in the ledger of Sophie Brahe I was then able to compute indices showing the development in the major incomes and expenses of an estate belonging to the nobility, and from those an index of the development of the yield of the estate (Figure 4).

Figure 4   *Development of net yield of a noble estate*

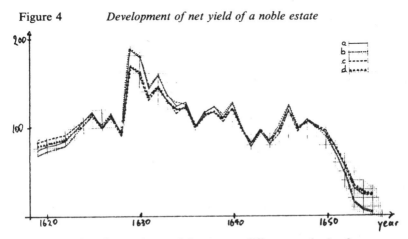

The four lines a, b, c and d represent different methods of calculation.

The development of the economy of the nobility in the time before 1660 has been the subject of much discussion (the remaining sources are quite good for that purpose), so that the results of my investigation could be compared with statements on that subject. It turned out that my index confirmed and refined the accepted view, the conclusion being that the result of the investigation was probable.

For the investigation in progress I have two means of control. First, to compute the development of the yield of a fief and to confront that with the debate on that subject. And secondly, to confront the development of prices and wages found in this investigation directly with the results of the pilot study. The outcome of the latter comparison will, I hope, be that the two materials show the same development in prices and wages. If that turns out to be the case, they can (and will) be combined into one.

Notes

1. Astrid Friis and Kristof Glamann, *A History of Prices and Wages in Denmark 1660–1800*, I, London, New York and Toronto, 1958, p. viii.

2. H. J. Marker, *En modelanalyse til belysning af den indflydelse, som udviklingen i priser, lønninger og skatter udøvede på pengeafkastet af en østjysk højadelig godsbesiddelse i perioden fra kornprisfaldet 1618–20 frem til årene forud for Karl-Gustav-krigene 1657–60*, unpublished manuscript, Arhus, 1982.

3. E. Ladewig Petersen, *Adelige Herregårdsregnskaber fra 1600-tallet*, Hilsen til Hæstrup 9. aug 1969, Odense 1969, pp. 91–2.

4. C. F. Bricka and J. A. Fridericia, *Kong Christian den Fjerdes Egenhaendige Breve*, Copenhagen, 1878–91, and Johanne Skovgaard, same title, Copenhagen, 1970.

5. G. Bang, *Breve til og fra Kristoffer Gøje og Birgitte Bolle*, Copenhagen, 1898–99.

6. Further information can be found in H. J. Marker, 'Sletdalerbegrebet i første fjerdedel af 17. århundrede', *Historie*, XV, 4, 1985, p. 633 *et seq.*

7. Arent Berntsen, *Danmarckis og Norgis Fructbar Herlighed*, Copenhagen, 1656.

8. H. Bennike Madsen, *Det danske skattevæsen. Kategorier og klasser. Sketter på landbefolkningen 1530–1660*, Odènse, 1978.

16 *Mark Overton*

Computer Analysis of Probate Inventories: from Portable to Mainframe

Probate inventories are a well-known historical source and several studies using them have resorted to computer techniques. In all cases however, data has been abstracted from inventories before being stored in a computer so that quite substantial processing by hand is usually necessary before advantage can be taken of computer analysis. This is not surprising since the documents are neither standardised nor consistent so they do not readily conform to the format of the regular data matrix required by many standard statistical packages, or to the fixed number of fields per record and the fixed record length which many database packages demand. This paper presents a methodology for processing complete inventories that starts with the recording of inventories directly into a portable microcomputer and finishes with data that can be input to orthodox statistical packages or database programs. The pre-processing of inventories by hand is thus replaced by computer processing that is both more flexible and more rapid.

Probate inventories are familiar to most economic and social historians and there are now more than a dozen introductions to them. Inventories list and value the moveable goods and chattels of deceased persons and were drawn up to assist the process of granting probate. They survive for most parts of England and Wales and in total over a million are extant for the period from the mid-sixteenth to the mid-eighteenth centuries. The documents itemise all moveable goods and chattels and so list domestic and household items, clothes, money, debts, fuel, crops, livestock, agricultural implements, the tools and stock-in-trade of craftsmen: indeed any object that was literally moveable. Virtually any commodity may be found in an inventory, although some inventories (referring to such people as mercers, chapmen and apothecaries for example) list a much wider and more esoteric range of goods than others. Since their main purpose was to value the deceased's goods inventories invariably give valuations for items (or groups of items) but quantities are not always given.

It should be apparent from this brief description that information in inventories cannot be entered into a database or data matrix in a straightforward way. Computer programs, particularly package programs, demand data that has no ambiguities and is consistent and standardised between cases so that one set of instructions can deal with all possible eventualities, yet both the items recorded and the ways in which they are recorded vary from inventory to inventory. The difficulties with inventories are of two kinds; those stemming from their open-ended descriptions, and those resulting from the form in which information is expressed. As the appraisers of an inventory had no pre-defined categories to follow, they concocted their own, resulting in a bewildering range and variety of descriptions. There is no limit to the number of items that may be listed and the level of detail at which objects are described varies considerably. Descriptions of cattle for example, range from a detailed description of age, colour, size, and even name, to a generic term like 'neat' or 'cattle'. Information in inventories is presented according the basic format of 'Quantity — Item — Value'. Table 1 lists the possible variations on this formula. Four variants are possible when only one item is mentioned in a line (termed a group in Table 1) since either quantity or value may be missing, and when more than one item is mentioned per line (a compound group) six basic forms are possible. The variations arise because data on quantities or values may be missing and because two or more items may be combined together. A third problem is that an item may be repeated in an inventory so that multiple entries occur for a particular commodity.

The variety of descriptions and the form of information necessarily complicate analysis. For example, using inventories to derive an acreage of wheat does not simply involve searching for the mention of wheat in conjunction with an acreage (say, '2 Acres of Wheat 6li'). Before the figure of 2 acres could be used it would be necessary to check that growing wheat was not combined with some other crop in another entry (say, '4 acres of wheat and rye'), that wheat was not recorded without an acreage (say 'all the wheat on the ground 10li'), and that there was no generic description that could include wheat (say 'corn growing upon the ground 23li 13s 4d'). In all but the last case it would, however, be possible to note the fact that wheat was present on the farm even though the exact quantity was uncertain.

Table 1   *The Form of Information in Probate Inventories*

Q = Quantity   I = Item   V = Value

A. Simple Groups

1	2	3	4
Q I V	Q I	I V	I

B. Compound Groups

1	2	3
Q_1 I_1 Q_2 I_2 V_{1+2}	Q_{1+2} I_1 I_2 V_{1+2}	I_1 I_2 V_{1+2}

4	5	6
Q_{1+2} I_1 I_2	Q_1 I_1 I_2 V_{1+2}	Q_{1+2} I_1 I_2 Q_{3+4} I_3 I_4 $V_{1+2+3+4}$

C. Other groups reduce to simple groups

e.g. Q_1 I_1 Q_2 I_2 = Q_1 I_1, Q_2 I_2

                     Q_1 I_1 I_2 = Q_1 I_1, I_2

The solution to the problem of open-ended descriptions is to define categories into which information is placed that can accommodate varying levels of detail and can cope with descriptions for which no category has been pre-defined. One such categorisation for the analysis of the agricultural content of inventories has been outlined in a previous paper describing a method for analysing inventories which was devised in the early 1970s.[1] The most common items were assigned pre-defined categories arranged in a hierarchy of decreasing detail so that information could be recorded at an appropriate level of detail. Categories were also available for dealing with the situations where items were combined together and for descriptions for which no predefined category was available. Numeric codes were used to define these additional items and to denote which categories of information were combined together. The categories formed a data matrix of 176 variables (in addition to the standard heading information for each inventory). The problem with this matrix is that many elements are empty, since the number of items mentioned varies from inventory to inventory and quantities are frequently missing, so that an average of only 15 columns out of the possible 176 are used for the average inventory. The matrix was compacted to economise on storage and data were entered using the IBM FORTRAN IV NAMELIST facility, which tags each data element with an alphanumeric label locating its position in the matrix, rather than the more conventional format of fixed fields. Table 2 gives examples of the input of inventory information to this matrix using fixed fields (Table 2a) and NAMELIST formats (Table 2b).

This strategy proved successful in overcoming the two problems in inventories of varied descriptions and the format of information, and was used to analyse the agricultural content of some 4000 inventories from Norfolk and Suffolk. Ten years later however, it appears time consuming and inflexible. The agricultural content from inventories was first transcribed in the record office and then had to be translated into NAMELIST format for

Table 2 *The Input of Inventory Data*

A. Fixed Field

```
9001    3628134006DENTON    NBENNETT    J288627 73      1           1
9002 5      1       1
9003                1                                               2700
9004                                                                20   125
9005                            225                 11038
9006                                    2  15
90078   120
9011 5  3628134007YELVERTONNDENNYE      R302629 53      1       9660
9012        1       1               3    55 1300
9013 3      6       1       1200   165 3
9014            8                                   24                   12
9015                            300                         440
9016    16
90178   600
```

B. NAMELIST

```
900     3628134006DENTON    NBENNETT    J288627 73      1           1
&V MCN=5,HEN=1,BSN=1,HN=1,LCV=27,BB=20,BBV=1.25,CCAV=2.25,CCBV=1.1,CCBC=38,
PEB=2,PEBV=.15,HAV=1.2,&END
901  5  3628134007YELVERTONNDENNYE      R302629 53      1       9660
&V HEN=1,BSN=1,OCN=3,OCC=55,CCV=13,OHM=3,OHC=6,YHN=1,HCV=12,PN=3,PV=1.65,
WB=8,MB=24,BB=12,MAB=16,CCBV2=4.4,CCAV=3,HAV=6,&END
```

C. Free Form

```
900/134006/BENNETT/J//DENTON/N/0/3/1628/W/288627/
    1 HORSE + 5 MILKCOWS + 1 HEIFER + 1 BUDBULL 27,ACORN ;45,
    20 BARLEY;25, 2 PEAS ;3,1CART, HAY ;24, WHEAT+MASLIN+MALT ;22/
901/134007/DENNYE/R//YELVERTON/N/5/3/1628//302629/
    3WORKING HORSES +1 COLT 12,HAY 6, 3COWS+1BUDBULL+1BUD HEIFER 13,
    3HOGS1;13,SUM96;12,8 WHEAT+24 MASLIN+12 MALT 3;6,
    12 BARLEY+4 MALT 1;2,1 CART, ACORN 3/
```

D. Output from Data Entry Program

```
/1.34.6/BENNETT/J//DENTON/N/////Q1I2Q5I3Q1I4Q1I5V27,I6V2.25,Q2OI7V1.25,Q2I8V.15,
Q1I9,I10V5,I11I12I13V1.1,/1.34.7/DENNYE/R//YELVERTON/N/5/3/1628//Q3I14Q1I15V12,I
10V6,Q3I16Q1I5Q1I17V13,Q3I18,I1V96.6,Q8I11Q24I12Q12I13V3.3,Q12I7Q4I13V1.1,Q1I9,I
6V3,/
```

key punching. This was straightforward enough but time consuming since values were converted from shillings and old pence into pence, duplicate entries for a single entry had to be added together, and for most inventories numeric codes had to be assigned to combined categories and to descriptions with no pre-assigned category.[2]

Although categorisation of the data from inventories is essential it is best done after the data have been gathered rather than before. Moreover, if inventories are being used to investigate several topics several categorisations may be more appropriate than a single one. Further, storing information from inventories in a matrix is unwieldy since so many elements are missing and the original structure of the data (as shown in Table 1) is so different. Thus the new techniques for analysing inventories categorise the information after it has been stored by the computer so that many alternative categorisations may be carried out quickly and easily by computer programs. The complete inventory may be recorded almost verbatim and information is stored in a form that closely resembles its structure in the document. Once information has been categorised and processed it can emerge in the form of a regular data matrix suitable for further analysis by standard package programs.

The structure of the analysis is shown in Figure 1. The first stage simply involves entering the information from inventories into a computer. This can

Figure 1   *A Computer Analysis of Probate Inventories*

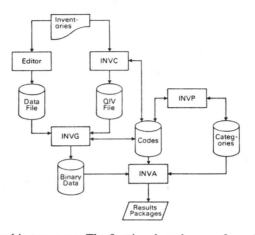

be achieved in two ways. The first involves the use of an editor on a micro, mini or mainframe computer to enter the data into a data file.The format of the information is such a file is shown in Table 2c. The first line for each inventory lists basic information that is usually present in all inventories — reference numbers, name, initial, place, county, date, whether the inventory has an associated will, grid reference,and comments. Following this are the groups as defined in Table 1 which are entered directly, from copies of the original documents or from transcripts, according to certain rules. These are that items must consist of alphabetic characters; quantities (if present) must precede items; values (if present) must follow items; pounds, shillings and pence must be separated by the characters ';' or ':'; each group is terminated by a comma; the inventory must be terminated by a slash, and combined items are indicated by the character ' + '. Although the example shows only agricultural information (the information is the same as that in Tables 2a and 2b) the method is applicable to all items recorded in inventories. The format of the groups in Table 2c matches the theoretical formats in Table 1.

The second way of getting inventory information into a computer file involves using a data entry program (INVC in Figure 1) which prompts for the basic information and then for each group. Groups are entered according to the rules already described except that the terminator is not required. The program also maintains a dictionary of each unique item encountered (stored in a code file) and each item is checked with the dictionary as it is entered. Items not in the dictionary are queried so that most spelling mistakes are trapped as they are made. The output from the input program goes into a QIV file, so called because of its structure as Table 2d demonstrates. In order to save space the program assigns each unique item a numeric code that is also stored in the code file, which in effect, performs the function of a codebook. The user of the program does not need to know what the codes are since all subsequent interaction with the data involves referring to items by name, although internal processing uses numeric codes. The input program also converts shillings and pence to decimal fractions of a pound. The input program runs on a variety of microcomputers but is most effective when used with portable microcomputer. A small battery powered computer can be taken into a record office and inventories recorded directly into it without the necessity of xeroxing or transcribing the documents first. Data from the portable computer can be transferred to other computers for subsequent analysis by tape or disc, but most conveniently by direct transmission, either via a direct link or through the public telephone network using an acoustic coupler. Whether the data are entered directly to a disc file using an editor, or via the data entry program, no coding or pre-formatting is done by hand.

The remainder of the analysis is carried out on a mainframe computer. The program INVG in Figure 1 processes the data put into a data file using an editor or the output from the data entry program. The main function of the program is to assign codes to items (unless they have already been assigned by the data entry program) but it also assigns numeric codes to items which are combined together. The output from the program consists of a revised code file and a file of binary data and an optional listing of the data. An example of a code file is given in Table 3 showing a selection of items and their numerical codes and the codes indicating which items are combined together. The data in the binary file are structured according to the format shown in Table 4 which is similar to the format of inventory information shown in Table 1 and illustrated in Table 2d, but the groups are expanded so that subsequent analysis is simplified. Each simple group has three data elements; the code for the item, a number for the quantity and a number for the value. A negative number indicates that a quantity or value is missing and a zero that the quantity or value is combined with that of another item. Compound groups can have up to 9 data elements so that each item is recorded once with a quantity or value that applies uniquely to it, and then again if it is combined with another item. Expanding the groups in this way makes it fairly simple matter to analyse the new binary data file. The steps involved in calculating

Table 3   *An Inventory Codefile*

```
83 52
    7        BARLEY
    5        BUDBULL
   17        BUDHEIFER
   48        BULL
   55        BULLOCKS
   70        BURLINGS
   79        CALF
                .
                .

   76        VETCHES
   73        WEANEDPIGS
   46        WEANINGCALVES
   11        WHEAT
   14        WORKINGHORSES
   33        YEARLINGBULLOCKS
   72        YEARLINGS
        2    1    1    2    0    0    0    0    0    0    0    0    0    0
        4    2    2    3    4    5    0    0    0    0    0    0    0    0
        2   30    2   22    0    0    0    0    0    0    0    0    0    0
        3   21    3   32   55    0    0    0    0    0    0    0    0    0
        3   41    3   38   70    0    0    0    0    0    0    0    0    0
```

Table 4 — *The Storage of Information in Probate Inventories*

Q = Quantity   I = Item   V = Value

-1 = Missing   0 = Combined

A. Simple Groups

1	2	3	4
Q I V	Q I	I V	I

$Q : I : V$ $Q : I : -1$ $-1 : I : V$ $-1 : I : -1$

B. Compound Groups

1	2	3
$Q_1\ I_1\ Q_2\ I_2\ V_{1+2}$	$Q_{1+2}\ I_1\ I_2\ V_{1+2}$	$I_1\ I_2\ V_{1+2}$
$Q_1 : I_1 : 0$ $Q_2 : I_2 : 0$ $0 : I_1+I_2 : V_{1+2}$	$Q_{1+2} : I_1+I_2 : V_{1+2}$	$-1 : I_1+I_2 : V_{1+2}$

4	5	6
$Q_{1+2}\ I_1\ I_2$	$Q_1\ I_1\ I_2\ V_{1+2}$	$Q_{1+2}\ I_1\ I_2\ Q_{3+4}\ I_3\ I_4\ V_{1+2+3+4}$
$Q_{1+2} : I_1+I_2 : -1$	$Q_1 : I_1 : 0$ $-1 : I_2 : 0$ $-1 : I_1+I_2 : V_{1+2}$	$Q_{1+2} : I_1+I_2 : 0$ $Q_{3+4} : I_3+I_4 : 0$ $0 : I_1+I_2+I_3+I_4 : V_{1+2+3+4}$

Table 5 — *The Storage of Inventory Information: an Example*

```
900/134006/BENNETT/J
 1.00     2    0.0   :   5.00     3    0.0   :   1.00     4    0.0
 1.00     5    0.0   :   0.0   20002   27.00  :  -1.00     6    2.25
20.00     7    1.25  :   2.00     8    0.15  :   1.00     9   -1.00
-1.00    10    1.20  :  -1.00   20003   1.10  :
901/134007/DENNYE/R/
 3.00    84    0.0   :   1.00    15    0.0   :   0.0   20053   12.00
-1.00    10    6.00  :   3.00    16    0.0   :   1.00     5    0.0
 1.00    17    0.0   :   0.0   20005   13.00  :   3.00    18    1.65
-1.00     1   96.60  :   8.00    11    0.0   :  24.00    12    0.0
12.00    13    0.0   :   0.0   20003   3.30  :  12.00     7    0.0
 4.00    13    0.0   :   0.0   20006   1.10  :   1.00     9   -1.00
-1.00     6    3.00  :
```

an acreage of wheat discussed above for example simply involve searching for the code for wheat and determining whether a quantity is given (in either a simple or compound group), whether the quantity is missing or the item combined, and then searching for the codes for generic descriptions like 'wintercorn', 'corn', or 'crops'. An example of a listing output from this coding program is shown in Table 5; the integer numbers are codes, the numbers preceding them are quantities and the numbers following are the values. Codes with 20,000 added to them refer to combined items. The structure of the data follows the rules in Table 4 and once again the data are from the inventories shown in Table 2.

The remaining programs are concerned with the analysis of the inventory data rather than with its coding and storage. Analysis can take many forms, but the stages described here assume that the data are to be categorised in some way with the output consisting of a rectangular matrix with one row per

Table 6   *A Category File*

```
   15  3
   CATTLE    LSK
   HORSES    LSK
   SHEEP     LSK
   POULTRY   LSK
   PIGS      LSK
   AWCORN    ACORN      ACROPS
   WCORN     CORN       CROPS
   ASCORN    ACORN      ACROPS
   SCORN     CORN       CROPS
   APULSES   AFODDER    ACROPS
   PULSES    FODDER     CROPS
   AGRASS    AFODDER    ACROPS
   GRASS     FODDER     CROPS
   AROOTS    AFODDER    ACROPS
   ROOTS     FODDER     CROPS
```

inventory and one column per category of information. There are many possible categorisations. Some examples include the acreages and values of crops, the number and values of livestock types, the presence or absence of particular household items, the valuations of particular commodities, and the total values assigned to particular types of commodity. These categories are set up using the program INVP which uses two files, once containing the codes and the other the categories. Table 6 indicates how a category file is structured. The two numbers indicate that the categorisation involves a hierarchy with a maximum of three levels with 15 categories at the lowest level. The column of names on the left describe these categories (for livestock and for stored and growing crops in this case), the names in the middle column those at the second level, and the names on the right refer to the third level (which only consist of growing crops, ACROPS, and stored crops, CROPS). The program works interactively by writing each unique item from the code file on a VDU screen and prompting for the category (at the first level in the hierarchy) with which it is to be associated. Each item in the code file is then tagged with its category code. Once the code file has been modified in this way the inventory data can be analysed using the particular categorisation. Table 6 gives an example this analysis using the program INVA. Three numbers are given for each category; a 1 or 0 to indicate presence or absence, a quantity, and a value. Negative numbers indicate a missing quantity or value, or that the category could be present since an item is described with a generic term which could embrace other categories. Thus for the first inventory growing corn (ACORN) is mentioned with a value of £2·25 which could include wintercorn (AWCORN), or summercorn (ASCORN), or both. Both stored summercorn and wintercorn are present (WCORN and SCORN) but cannot provide a quantity or a value since they are combined together (in the entry WHEAT + MASLIN + MALT ;22 in Table 1c). The data would not normally be output in the form shown in Table 7 but would form the input for some other program or package.

Despite the advances being made in the development of computer software, due partly to the opportunities offered by spectacular developments in hardware, but also to more imaginative programming, standard package programs, whether for statistical analysis or for database management, still make quite strict demands on the data they use. Many data sources do not readily conform to these constraints so it seems likely that there will continue to be a need for programs especially written for specific

Table 7   *Categorised Inventory Data*

```
900/134006/BENNETT/J//DENTON/N/0/3/1628/W/288627/
  CATTLE       1      7.00     -1.00
  HORSES       1      1.00     -1.00
  SHEEP        0      0.0       0.0
  POULTRY      0      0.0       0.0
  PIGS         0      0.0       0.0
  AWCORN      -1     -1.00     -1.00
  WCORN        1     -1.00     -1.00
  ASCORN      -1     -1.00     -1.00
  SCORN        1     -1.00     -1.00
  APULSES      0      0.0       0.0
  PULSES       1      2.00      0.15
  AGRASS       0      0.0       0.0
  GRASS        1     -1.00      1.20
  AROOTS       0      0.0       0.0
  ROOTS        0      0.0       0.0
  LSK          1      8.00     27.00
  ACORN        1     -1.00      2.25
  CORN         1     -1.00      2.35
  AFODDER      0      0.0       0.0
  FODDER       1     -1.00      1.35
  ACROPS       1     -1.00      2.25
  CROPS        1     -1.00      3.70
901/134007/DENNYE/R//YELVERTON/N/5/3/1628//302629/
  CATTLE       1      5.00     13.00
  HORSES       1      4.00     12.00
  SHEEP        0      0.0       0.0
  POULTRY      0      0.0       0.0
  PIGS         1      3.00      1.65
  AWCORN      -1     -1.00     -1.00
  WCORN        1     32.00     -1.00
  ASCORN      -1     -1.00     -1.00
  SCORN        1     28.00     -1.00
  APULSES      0      0.0       0.0
  PULSES       0      0.0       0.0
  AGRASS       0      0.0       0.0
  GRASS        1     -1.00      6.00
  AROOTS       0      0.0       0.0
  ROOTS        0      0.0       0.0
  LSK          1     12.00     26.65
  ACORN        1     -1.00      3.00
  CORN         1     60.00      4.40
  AFODDER      0      0.0       0.0
  FODDER       1     -1.00      6.00
  ACROPS       1     -1.00      3.00
  CROPS        1     -1.00     10.40
```

sources, if only to convert the information in them to a form that is more amenable to standard packages. Without such programs much unnecessary time and effort will continue to be wasted in preparing data by hand. This paper has provided one example of a suite of programs for the processing of probate inventories. The object is to make the procedures for analysing inventories as rapid as possible while maintaining flexibility. To this end data is stored in a form which closely mirrors the way information is structured in the documents so that input is very straightforward and the stored information can be categorised in a number of ways. Computers have opened up exciting possibilties in historical research but there is still some way to go in eliminating the unnecessary drudgery they have brought with them.

Notes

1. Mark Overton, 'Computer analysis of an inconsistent data source: the case of probate inventories', *Journal of Historical Geography*, 3, 1977, pp. 317–26.
2. See Mark Overton, 'The diffusion of agricultural innovations in early modern England: turnips and clover in Norfolk and Suffolk, 1580–1740', *Transactions of the Institute of British Geographers*, new series, 10, 1984, pp. 205–21.

Historical Archiving with dBASE: a Solicitor's Accounts, 1716–44

The Catholic solicitor Mannock Strickland (1683–1744) died intestate with no immediate successor to his practice; his complete business papers have therefore survived and were taken in 1753 by his son-in-law Michael Blount to Mapledurham House, Oxfordshire, where they still are. In studying his career for a higher degree thesis at Birkbeck College London it became almost immediately apparent that the only satisfactory key to his professional activities lay in an attempt to analyse his account books and then to attempt to relate them to his other office papers. With help from Edward James, Education Consultant at Imperial College London, we devised a simple computerised means of handling the problems which offers a satisfactory and advantageous means of handling any historical source text which can be broken down into sections. What follows is the text of the display which accompanied the demonstrations given at the conference.

The Problem

How to discern the pattern of clientage of an eighteenth-century solicitor. Initial sources available (among complete office papers):

Deeds - random survival, since many clearly returned to owners; not usually informative about lawyer's part in their creation.

Letters — plenty *to* him, only 41 *from* him. Surely no solicitor writes only 1·5 letters a year!

Administration papers (he died intestate in mid-career) — voluminous, disorganised. Highly promising, but *not* the first (or only) port of call.

Household bills — lovely if you want to know *how* he lived and what he ate.

Account books - Eureka! But what a daunting lot of them!

Sources

A series of 4 cash day books (1726–1744), 4 more with sections devoted to individual clients (1716–1744), a fee account book and 'small conveyance book'. Average size 200 pages, 12–15 entries per page (*c.*25,000 entries in all). Manual analysis either hit-and-miss or downright impossible.

Solution

Abandon hope altogether or try a computer. Choice dictated by need to be able to input data and do searches at home, so it had to be a micro. *Advantages*: total control of material, own choice of place of work (does wonders for your typing, too). *Disadvantages*: takes ages, especially if you're also running a full-time job; you do your own inputting (unless you have an angel of a keyboarder who can read the writing); searching may have to be done in a number of sections. It works!

Input and Output

The first attempt aimed at simplifying and reducing the task by using tabulated forms:

```
list
00001  1  226/03/09Dividend   S.S.Stock  $1500              45.0.0.
00002  1  226/03/16Receipt    Wright     William            50.0.0.
00003  1  226/03/17Interest   Petre      Mr,Senior  $442    11.0.0.
00004  1  227/03/30Receipt    Valette    Mr.                9.18.0.
00005  1  227/04/03Receipt    Petre      Lady               60.0.0.
00006  1  227/04/03Agent      Dicconson  Mr.                5.5.0.     Strickland  Mother              Money returned
00007  1  227/04/13Receipt    Thybaud    Mr.                14.10.0.
00008  1  227/04/13Receipt    You        Mrs.               10.16.0.
00009  1  227/04/14Sale       S.S.Stock  $1500              1561.5.6.
00010  1  227/04/22Receipt    Penson     Mr.    Eyre,Henry  57.15.9.   Brailsford  Radclyffe  Eyre,John  Bond exchange
00011  1  227/04/26Receipt    Smalley    Mrs.               20.0.0.
00012  1  227/04/29Receipt    Bradley                       4.4.0.     Strickland  Franck  Hodgson,Mr. Loan repayment
```

It didn't work — the nature of the data precludes tight specification of content of columns, and precise relationship of one to another cannot be made clear. It is impossible to read back the sense of the original.

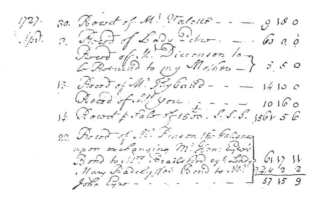

dBASE was chosen because of the need for a powerful program flexible enough to accommodate not only this

but also this

and this

The obvious turns out to be the best. Each entry contains the *full text*. There are two interlocking files: the *database* and the *keyfile*. Although dBASE permits a search on the database itself, various features in this case made additional use of a keyfile essential — this would not always be necessary. Text is useable for publication if required.

Record structure

Each entry consists of: *Book (archive) no.*, *Page reference*, *Date (year/month/day)*, *Transaction type*, *Cash amount*, *Text of entry* (up to 6 lines at 80 characters). Any number of keywords may then be appended after completion of entry (28 characters each); degree of indexing can be as great or small as judged appropriate or necessary. This format can be varied and set to specific requirements.

Text file

Line	Vol	Page	Date	Amount	Transaction type
10	E49	2	27/03/30	9.18. 0.	Receipt
11	Reced of Mr. Valette				
12	E49	2	27/04/03	60. 0. 0.	Receipt
13	Reced of Lady Petre				
14	E49	2	27/04/03	5. 5. 0.	Agent
15	Reced of Mr. Dicconson to be Returned to my Mother				
16	E49	2	27/04/13	14.10. 0.	Receipt
17	Reced of Mr. Thybaud				
18	E49	2	27/04/13	10.16. 0.	Receipt
19	Reced of Mrs. You				
20	E49	2	27/04/14	1561. 5. 6.	Stock sale
21	Reced pr Sale of $.1500. S.S.S.				
22	E49	2	27/04/22	57.15. 9.	Bond exchange
23	Reced of Mr. Penson the ballance upon exchanging Mr. Hen: Eyre´s Bond to Mrs.				
24	Brailsford agt. Lady Mary Radclyffe´s Bond to Mr. John Eyre				
25				61:17:11	
26				Repd. 4: 2: 2	

Keyword file

Line	Keyword	Between lines	
12	Receipt	10	11
13	Valette,Mr.	10	11
14	Receipt	12	13
15	Petre,Lady	12	13
16	Agent	14	15
17	Dicconson,Mr.	14	15
18	Strickland,Mother	14	15
19	Receipt	16	17
20	Thybaud,Mr.	16	17
21	Receipt	18	19
22	You,Mrs.	18	19
23	Stock	20	21
24	Sale	20	21
25	South Sea Stock	20	21
26	£1500	20	21
27	Bond exchange	22	26
28	Penson,Mr.	22	26

Searching

Keywords do not have signifiers attached — they could have but were not felt necessary. Searches can be undertaken as needed on an inter-related pair of keywords by creation of a sub-file to be searched again with additional keys.

```
Search for the keyword cause on text file a:mannock and key file a:mankey

CAUSE
```

Book: E49   Page: 8   Date: 27/07/19   Amount: 21. 0. 0.
Transaction type: Cause

Reced of Mr. Shimell on Account of Mrs. Marshes Cause

Book: E49   Page: 22   Date: 27/02/23   Amount: 56.18. 0.
Transaction type: Costs in cause

Reced of Mr. Shimell the Costs I pd Mr. Moore upon Ld. Petre's Nonsuit in
Mrs. Marshes Cause

Book: E49   Page: 34   Date: 28/07/27   Amount: 50. 0. 0.
Transaction type: Cause

Reced of Mr. Shimell on Account in Mr. Marshes Cause

Other applications

The format has been successfully used for indexing archival data and in calendaring archives. Processing of other forms of text is possible — some examples were shown at Westfield, which included entries in a law precedent book and diary or journal entries; the format, is, however, best suited to text which naturally falls into sections. Recent developments make it easier still to handle text where the sections vary greatly in length. It is not really suitable for continuous text work. It has, however, successfully provided the means of tackling a problem not otherwise tractable, and the system devised for this purpose has now been investigated as a means of handling seventeenth century building accounts and also the documentation of the work of George Romney.

Comprehensive Computerisation of a Very Large Documentary Source: the Portbooks Project at Wolverhampton Polytechnic

When working from a new documentary source every historian has to decide how information should be extracted. Usually, a small and carefully defined part of the information is noted down for subsequent analysis. In other cases, when there are doubts about the interpretation of the documents or the questions which they may be required to answer, the conventional approach is to make a thorough precis or a transcript of the evidence. When the source demands cautious treatment but is too large for transcription to be practicable, however, it has often been disregarded by researchers who know that life is short and their time may be spent more fruitfully on other things. The Port Books, detailed records of cargoes carried in and out of English ports from the sixteenth to the eighteenth centuries, are a classic example of such a source, being generally considered impenetrable because of their sheer volume and the uncertainty of their interpretation. A few historians, notably Willan, Stephens and Hinton, have made pioneering attempts to exploit the Port Books; but using conventional methods they have been able only to scratch the surface, leaving many questions of interpretation unanswered and much of the potential of the source unexplored.[1]

Computers have been used for many years to analyse evidence abstracted from one or more sources, mainly in quantitative ways.[2] With recent advances in software, however, exciting possibilities are beginning to be revealed for more wide-ranging research from large and complex documentary series. Because they are able to deal quickly with enormous quantities of information, computers have made feasible even the treatment of sources like the Port Books in a comprehensive manner similar to traditional transcription. This allows the evidence to be tested and evaluated as research continues and to be applied readily to questions which arise only during or after the completion of the investigation. While the effort of transcribing voluminous records in full is not reduced by the computer, the rewards are immeasurably increased, radically altering the costs and benefits of their use.

The Portbooks Project at Wolverhampton Polytechnic takes such a comprehensive approach to computerising and analysing the Coastal Port Books for Gloucester between *c.*1580 and 1765 and illustrates some of the problems and advantages it entails. The Project was initiated by two members of the Polytechnic staff, Dr Jeff Cox and Dr Malcolm Wanklyn[3] in 1982, and continues under the direction of a Research Assistant, Peter Wakelin, and a programmer, Michael Griffiths. Although the primary interest was in data about the river trade of Shropshire in the seventeenth and eighteenth centuries, a source-oriented approach was adopted from the beginning because it was realised that the potential for studies using other information was considerable, and that thorough computerisation would aid interpretation of the records as a whole.

The Coastal Port Books for Gloucester consist of about 160 volumes of parchment and vellum held at the Public Record Office. They were kept in conjunction with Overseas Port Books as part of the system of collecting duties on foreign trade. Their role was to record and cross-check the movements and cargoes of boats travelling through Gloucester to and from other British ports, thereby ensuring that they did not carry foreign trade and evade duties under the pretence of coastal movement. Cargoes being carried along the coast were listed in the books and on a certificate, or 'coquet', which was given to the master of the ship. The cargo was listed again at the next port and checked against the coquet to ensure that none had gone astray. Similar records exist for scores of British ports in the same period.

The books typically contain information concerning the names of the boats and their 'home' ports, the names of people involved in the trade, the dates on which coquets were issued, the cargoes carried on each vessel, and the ports to and from which traffic was moving. A typical entry for a boat passing out of Gloucester was that for the Prosperity in October 1725 (see Figure 1). Well over 50,000 voyages are included in the 160 volumes which have survived, and these touch upon the activities of more than two thousand merchants and ship's masters and hundreds of different boats, mainly from the river-side towns between Welshpool and the Bristol Channel. Over a thousand different types of goods are mentioned, from fundamental producer goods such as coal, iron, clay and wool to consumables such as earthenware, cider, 'elephants' teeth' and more mysterious items which are only gradually being identified.

The potential of the records for shedding light on the economy of the Severn Valley in the period before the Industrial Revolution is vast. The information is capable of suggesting answers to questions about not only the state of trade, but also its organisation and the people involved in it, the nature of the river and estuary as transport routes, and the production and

Figure 1   *A page from the Gloucester Coastal Port Books recording outward voyages in October 1725.*

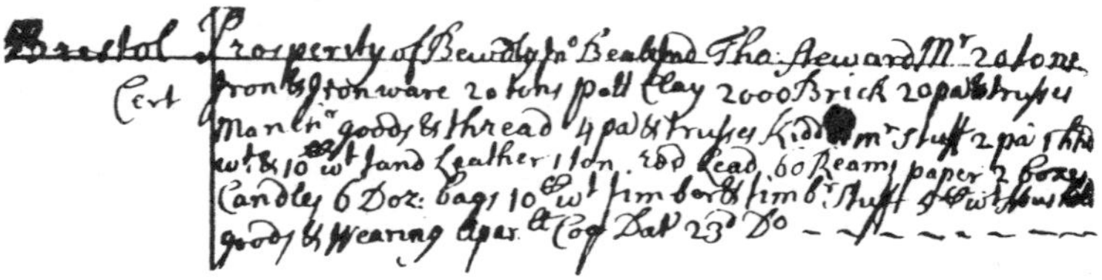

Public Record Office, Chancery Lane, London, E190/1261/1 folio 10. Crown Copyright, reproduced by permission of the Controller of Her Majesty's Stationery Office.

consumption of diverse economic sectors. The enquiries that may be made of the data will be almost endless when the computerisation is complete; yet access to the information would be impossibly time-consuming by traditional manual methods. Indeed, though some historians have had strong reservations about the accuracy of the Port Books,[5] it is probably this inaccessibility, and the ensuing difficulty of testing their veracity, which have caused them to be used so little.

Comprehensive computerisation is undoubtedly the best way to make the information readily available; but it has presented many practical difficulties. The most formidable concern the logistics of entering so large a quantity of data into a computer, and finding ways of storing the information which allow the computer to manipulate it without departing too far from the original documents.

In order to accommodate the records in a regular and convenient format some re-ordering of the data has been permitted, and in a few instances their expression has been simplified or abbreviated. However, no part of the written details has been excluded from computerisation, and modification of the data has been considered acceptable only if it does not make analysis dependent on judgements which might have to be revised at a later stage. Each entry in the Port Books is broken down logically into 20 field types, some of which are repeated to accommodate more than one item, so that an average record contains about 40 fields. The data are stored using a commercial database package called *Information* on Wolverhampton Polytechnic's PRIME mainframe system.

The greatest faithfulness to the manuscripts would have been achieved by transcribing them in a word-processed form, but this would have made analysis much more difficult in return for very modest benefits in the interpretation of manuscript entries that are themselves generally logical and clearly ordered.[6] One reason for compartmentalising the data in fields is to facilitate numerical calculation and alphabetical sorting. Another is that identical character strings may relate to different facts by reason of their precise positions. The names of ports, for instance, appear in three fields, but have different meanings in each: in one field they refer to the boat's home port, in another to its port of departure, and in another to its destination.

The proliferation of fields in each record seems unwieldy, especially given that some are usually empty, but this is necessary if the information is to be accessible. Positions have had to be found for several classes of data which do not appear in all of the Port Books. Second and third merchants are named, for instance, in only one or two decades between 1630 and 1760, but the information is potentially of considerable value and needs to be stored separately for ready sorting and selection. The same is true of dates other than that on which the coquet was issued, which appear in only about five percent of the records but are the sole evidence for journey times of vessels.

The policy of comprehensive computerisation also results in some data being included whose meaning is unknown. Some of the marks in the margins of the documents, for instance, are not yet properly understood and may prove to be of no value, or, alternatively, of great significance. A similar problem exists with regard to the second dates given in some records, which probably do not have a consistent meaning. Thus, the second date field may contain facts which differ fundamentally but are not apparently differentiated. Until the variations in their meaning are appreciated, these can only be put in the same field. They can be separated automatically once their relationship to other variables, such as the particular book in which they were written, is understood.

Two policies have been followed with regard to the transliteration of words from the Port Books: standardising spellings (by modernisation or abbreviation) where the meaning is certain, and accurately transcribing words about which there is some doubt. Thus, boat names, units of measure, commodities, and Christian names mostly have been standardised, while surnames have been spelled exactly as in the original. None of the data have been simplified in ways which would prevent the analysis of their most detailed meanings. The temptation has been resisted, for instance, to record cargoes by a regular classification instead of their original descriptions (recording battery wares simply as metal manufactures, or Kidderminster stuffs as textiles), though this would speed analysis for many purposes.

Faithful computerisation in this way has proved valuable in many instances. If cargoes had been classified, for example, words whose meaning was not known could not have been included, and decisions about the classification of commodities could not have been changed. The temptation to standardise spellings of surnames was even greater, given that the name of a single boatman could be spelled as variously as Uxley, Uxly, Huxley or Huxly. To record all of these as Huxley would have grouped the records relating to one boatman, but would have failed to distinguish other individuals whose names may have been spelled consistently as Uxley or Uxly. Surnames have therefore been spelled as in the original document so that premature judgements of 'who's who' do not affect the stored data. The problem of sorting and selecting names which are spelled erratically has been solved by creating a separate file which lists standardised equivalents of surnames. The database can be interrogated by reference to the standard surnames which apply, or by the original spelling if that is preferred in particular cases. Judgements about surnames can be reversed at any time by editing the file of standard spellings.

The comprehensive approach to computerising the Port Books has been taken not only in selecting all the data from each entry, but also in aiming to include all of the volumes which survive. Sampling was rejected for several reasons. Systematic sampling of particular periods or volumes was dismissed because large and irregular fluctuations of trade apparent in the books suggested that none would on its own be representative. Also, both random and systematic sampling would have omitted much of the fine detail which the documents illustrate so well, such as the rare occurrences of important industrialists as named merchants, or the consecutive pattern of voyages of a particular vessel during its lifetime. Finally, it was considered that as much information as possible should be included if the precise nature of the Port Books as historical evidence was to be understood.

Taken together, the extent of the material and the painstaking way it has to be tackled throw up the greatest problem inherent in the comprehensive approach: the logistical challenge of doing so much work. To transcribe 55,000 records with an average of 40 fields from difficult manuscripts onto computer forms, to enter them into the computer, and to check the information contained, would be impossible within the constraints of most historical research, which is done on low budgets, usually by single researchers. The development time alone, in designing the format of the database, formulating methods of entry, and writing programmes for its operation, has been a major commitment.

The main solution has been to divide the work of transcription between a large number of people who have agreed to take part in the project on a voluntary basis. By advertising through local history newsletters and adult education tutors, a network of about thirty amateur historians has been established in the Severn Valley who work from copies of the Port Books at home or in local history research classes. Microfilms of the documents have been purchased from the Public Record Office, and these are copied and bound into volumes resembling the originals. Volunteers transcribe onto printed forms the entries for boats from the place or places in which they are interested and then pass the book to subsequent volunteers or Polytechnic staff until all the entries have been transcribed. In return, they can receive print-outs of the information in a sorted and analysed form. Invaluable assistance is also given by Data Preparation staff at the Polytechnic, who undertake the task of typing the transcribed data into the computer.

The contribution made by volunteers to the project has proved very productive. It does, however, make additional demands in terms of practical organisation and data management. Organising the work is time-consuming, with the need to keep geographically dispersed volunteers supplied with materials, and to plan and control the work they do. Because the volunteers are sometimes working from poor quality copies and may not be experienced at transcribing similar documents, care also has to be taken to ensure the accuracy and consistency of data entered.

It is of obvious importance that data should be accurate in relation to the original documents. If volunteers have doubts about the transcription of a word, therefore, they write three crosses in its place. Regular print-outs of these blank items can then be checked against the microfilms or the original documents by members of the Polytechnic research team. However, data must also be consistent within the database. Severe problems could arise, for instance, if the names of commodities were misspelled, since searching for them in the computer file is based upon the character strings they contain. Mistakes over some standardised terms are very likely with a large number of volunteers transcribing unfamiliar words like 'fustic', 'horse nail stubs' or 'raddle'. All field contents liable to errors are therefore checked automatically against a separate file of allowed character strings: in the case of commodities nearly a thousand items. If the strings entered do not agree with these spellings, the discrepancy is notified in a print-out and the word is corrected or added to the reference file as a new term.

Compiling a database of the size envisaged by the Portbooks Project is a slow business. Since its inception about one fifth of the entries (12,000 in all) have been transcribed, and more are being added at an accelerating rate. All voyages of boats from Shropshire ports between 1616 and 1725 have been transcribed by Nancy Cox and Malcolm Wanklyn at the Polytechnic, and a large proportion of the voyages from Bewdley have been added by Mavis

Barrett and other volunteers in the Bewdley Research Group. Research from this material has already provided evidence for an article on the river trade of Shrewsbury in the seventeenth century, a book about Bewdley, and an article about the early work of Abraham Darby at Coalbrookdale. The work of research classes in Evesham, Worcester and Gloucester, and other individual volunteers, is gradually extending research to the trade of other ports and periods.

The possibilities for further analysis of the Portbooks Database are varied and numerous. It will make available information about the navigation of the river, the inter-regional exchanges of western England, and the production and consumption of commodities as diverse as agricultural produce, textiles, coal, and imported luxury goods. The greatest use of the computer in this analysis will not be in performing calculations or applying inferential statistics to the material so much as providing sorted and selected data from the 55,000 voyages described. Print-outs can be made of the vessels carrying iron, for example, the voyages of particular masters, or the boats operating from particular ports, so that they can be analysed separately. This is perhaps the computer's most vital contribution to the use of very large historical sources.

It is hoped that more sophisticated methods will be developed for other enquiries. For example, a range of cross-reference files will gradually be compiled to allow the extraction of data according to externally imposed classifications. The file of standard surnames already exists for this purpose and a file of commodity types will be instituted to extract cargoes according to the raw materials they include or the industrial sectors to which they were related. There is considerable scope for more complex reference files of this sort, for instance to identify records relating to specific persons according to their Christian and surnames, their dates of activity and the names of the boats in which they traded. It is hoped that data will also be automatically correlated with other sources, for example to compare periods of inactivity in trade with the dates of wars or known floods and droughts, to convert cargo descriptions into tonnage equivalents so that trade may be quantified in aggregate, or to compare the activity recorded at Gloucester with that at other ports.

The fact that the records have been computerised so comprehensively will endow the Portbooks Database with great flexibility. It is anticipated that it will not only be used for research and teaching at Wolverhampton Polytechnic, but will become a standard reference source for local historians and scholars from other institutions making a very wide range of enquiries. Interpretations of the data are bound to change as research reveals more about the nature of the documents, but this process will not be hindered by any narrow assumptions behind the original collection of the information. In this instance, therefore, the comprehensive approach will have had important advantages over more circumscribed research.

To work in such a way is, nevertheless, a long and difficult undertaking which depends on the co-operation of numerous contributors, on the availiability of facilities to co-ordinate them, and on successful compromises being found between textual accuracy and logical structure. It is to be hoped that the Portbooks Project has largely satisfied these requirements and will provide a model for the computerisation of books for other ports. Perhaps the time may come when the coastal trade of all England can be analysed at the touch of a button.

Notes

1. T. S. Willan, *The English Coasting Trade 1600–1750*, Manchester, 1938, 1967; W. B. Stephens 'The Cloth Exports of the Provincial Ports 1600–40', *Economic History Review*, 2nd Series, XXII, 1969, pp. 228–48; R. K. Hinton (ed.), *The Port Books of Boston 1601–1640*, Lincoln Record Society, 1956.

2. One computer project was undertaken by G. Alan Metters to compile a database of simplified and selected information from the Lynn Port Books 1604–14 for his doctoral thesis at the University of East Anglia, 1982, 'The Rulers and Merchants of Kings Lynn in the Early Seventeenth Century'.

3. With advice from Punna Athwall and Beatrice Hammond of the Wolverhampton Polytechnic Computer Centre.

4. G. N. Clarke, *Guide to English Commercial Statistics 1696–1782*, London, 1938, pp. 52–6; J. H. Andrews, 'Two Problems in the Interpretation of the Port Books', *Economic History Review*, 2nd Series, IX, 1956, pp. 119–22.

5. By contrast the Domesday Book contains far more irregular and controversial entries which have benefitted from literal transcription in the Hull University database. See J. J. N. Palmer 'Computerising Domesday Book', *Transactions of the Institute of British Geographers*, 11, No. 3, 1986, pp. 279–89, and Andrew Ayton and Virginia Davis, 'The Hull Domesday Project', ch. 3 of this volume.

The author wishes to thank Jeff and Nancy Cox, Michael Trueman, Malcolm Wanklyn and Harvey Woolf for their comments on drafts of this paper.

19   *Charles Harvey and Peter Taylor*

Computer Modelling and Analysis of the Individual and Aggregate Capital Stocks, Cash Flows and Performance of British Mining Companies in Spain, 1851–1913

Foreign capital and economic development

This research has been concerned with foreign direct investment in Spain in the period 1851–1913. During these years the country emerged as one of the world's leading mining nations, with a booming export trade in lead, copper, iron and sulphur. A large part of the capital and enterprise promoting the boom came from overseas, mainly from Britain, and allied to the fact that national economic growth was very limited, this has since led to the charge that the Spanish economy was 'dominated' by foreigners and 'exploited in true colonial fashion'. As a result, Spain is seen by many scholars to have missed a glorious opportunity for generalised economic development, and the Spanish case is often cited by critics as a prime example of the damaging effects of foreign control of natural resource development.

There are, however, good reasons for doubting the accuracy of the 'standard story' of foreign involvement in Spanish mining. In particular, the facts used to demonstrate that Spain was a land of rich and easy pickings for foreign companies relate to just a handful of cases, and then only for selected periods. Acceptable tests of major propositions generally have not been forthcoming. What has been lacking most is the systematic consideration of foreign investment and profitability at the sectoral level, based on the financial records of the majority of foreign mining companies operating in Spain. The aim of the project detailed below has been to rectify this situation.

Two major aspects of the 'standard story' have been examined to date.

1. The idea that a large and rising number of firms established themselves with ease due to the abundance of Spanish mineral deposits.
2. The proposition that very high profits were earned by foreigners; so bleeding the country of capital which might have funded national economic growth.

The results obtained show neither proposition to be tenable. Mining in Spain was in fact a high risk business in which most companies failed. When account is taken of failed companies as well as successful ones, and allowance is made for the risks involved, profits were not of an exceptionally high order. Together with other materials, these findings lead to a view of foreign direct investment quite different from the orthodox representation. The results of the research are presented in a forthcoming article in the *Economic History Review*, 'Mineral Wealth and Economic Development: Foreign Direct Investment in Spain, 1851–1913'. The remainder of this paper can be thought of, in part at least, as the methodological counterpart to the *Review* article.

Data series and data entry

Four major computer analyses have been conducted, one with several sub-analyses, and all broken down by mineral and sometimes by company. These are:

1. Capital and earnings series and internal rates of return of six leading companies in Spanish mining.
2. The same for 174 British companies on an aggregated, disaggregated and individual basis.
3. The birth, life and death characteristics of the 174 British companies for which data are available.

4. The output, employment and productivity of the individual Spanish and foreign mining concerns listed in the Spanish Mining Survey of 1891.

The first three analyses all used the same intermediate data file, while the latter used a completely independent file. The first two analyses used specially written programs to create and analyse the individual company series, while the latter two analyses were undertaken using SPSS, the Statistical Package for the Social Sciences. The latter analyses were therefore very easily executed, although for the fourth, several programs had to be written to combine cases which together constituted different branches of the same firms, and to arrange the mining survey data before the SPSS analysis could take place.

The major difficulty with the capital stocks and income flows for the 174 companies was the potentially large number of items of data. Each firm had seven series of data, each of which fell within the sixty-three years under consideration. Thus for each company there was a possible $7 \times 63 = 441$ items, and so for the whole 174 firms there would be 76,734 items. This would have been a substantial amount of data to input in its raw form, especially as many items were six digits and over. However as many firms had comparatively short lives, and as some of the series, especially the capital series, had the same values for several years in succession, alternative approaches for inputting data were possible. The data for each company could be considered to occupy a 63 by 7 matrix in which each row represented a year and each column a series, and which would completely describe its financial stocks and flows. The matrices for most firms would be extremely 'sparse', containing a large number of zeros, because their lives were much shorter than the 63 year period covered by the study. Even within the rows representing periods for which the companies were operating there could often be a lot of zero values in certain columns; for example, some companies had no bonds, interest payments or dividends. Thus instead of each firm's matrix being input as a whole, row by row, it was decided that the matrix would be packed series by series with date codes to indicate where values appeared in the matrix. Further, as the series often had constant values for successive periods, the date codes could be used to indicate the start and the end of a period for which values were constant. In this way only one value and the two date codes had to be input to describe a constant value for many years in a particular series. Packing the data also reduced the amount of coding from the summary sheets (derived from the original sources) on to the computer coding sheets ready for punching into the computer file. The programs analysing the data therefore had to unpack the data to create the matrix for each company in the computer's memory before the analysis itself could take place.

The total data occupied nearly 1600 records in the file, each record being an 80 column card image, with many records containing just one code or only a few items in addition to the check and continuation codes. If the data had been put in raw it would have filled more than 11,000 such records. Although there was thus a very considerable saving of effort, the approach did involve the necessity of writing a fairly complicated 'unpacking' program. A simpler and probably quicker approach would have been to have input the data row by row just for the years in which a company was in existence. This would have increased the amount of data input; subsequent calculations revealing that it would have taken up 2004 fully filled records. But this would have greatly reduced the amount of time and effort required to write and test the unpacking program.

Computational methods

Once each company's matrix has been created in memory, several analyses and aggregations followed. These could, in theory, have all been done in one big run of the program. However, because of the need to iron out errors in the data and programs, each analysis and aggregation was done in a separate run. There were thus over twenty final program runs, excluding the development and test runs.

The only analysis carried out at the individual company level, other than for the six leading companies, was the calculation of internal rates of return for those companies that had positive cumulative net cash flows during their lives. Surprisingly, this was only about two dozen companies. Of the 174 companies, 51 had missing values in certain series and so their computer records contained a missing values code to flag the programs to exclude them from any analysis which utilised that particular series. A further 70 or so companies paid no dividends or interest, and another couple of dozen, although paying interest and dividends, absorbed more cash during their existence than they repatriated to Britain.

The internal rate of return was calculated on the basis the net annual flow of resources between Spain and Britain. The annual flow from Spain to Britain was simply the sum of the company's dividends, interest payments and repayment of bond finance. The annual flow from Britain to Spain was more difficult to calculate. This was the change in the annual value of the company's stock of capital in Spain, but only if this change was positive as any reduction in the capital stock represented depreciation of book value and not a flow back to Britain. The annual net values of these two flows for the whole of the period formed the net flow series.

The net flow series was contained in a 63 cell array, though most company's lives were much shorter than 63 years. The array was then used as the basis for the calculation of the Internal Rate of Return (IRR) — the discount rate (i.e. compound interest rate) that reduces the sum of the series to zero. Further details of the method can be found in any text on investment appraisal. The relevant subroutine first calculated the Net Present Value, which is the sum of a series at a particular discount rate, for every 10% point between 0% and 100%, in order to show the general form of the Present Value curve over a reasonably sensible range, and to find the 10% range in which the IRR was located. The subroutine then found the IRR to three places of decimals using the method of bisection. Essentially, this successively splits the range in which the IRR is located into two in order to locate it within a smaller and smaller range.

The number of sign changes in the flow series was calculated in the program to show the number of roots (i.e. IRR values) that mathematically existed for the series. Although there were usually multiple roots, the Present Value curves were well behaved over the range 0% to 100%, thus:

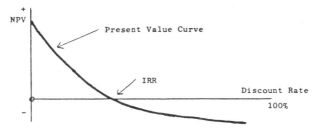

Although multiple roots existed, the root found in this range made economic sense both as regards the research and as regards the decision-making of investors at the time. The firms that had absorbed more cash than they had repatriated to Britain all showed a present value curve that asyptotically reached zero, thus:

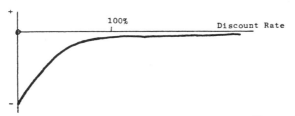

Some of these cases were checked to 1000% and were still negative even though imperceptibly close to zero as they had been since 100–200%.

The net flow series for each of the 123 companies without missing values were aggregated to form a net flow series for the majority of the industry. It was important to calculate the individual net flow series for each company and then to aggregate them, rather than aggregate the raw series and then derive overall net flow series, as the latter method would understate the flows from Britain. This was because increases in some capital series would be offset by reductions, due to bankruptcy etc., in others. The aggregated flow series was graphed to show the pattern of net flows between the two countries over the period. The series was also used to calculate an IRR figure for the majority of the industry for which there was reliable data, and so show an Internal Rate of Return to Britain. Aggregations were also carried out by mineral grouping, so that a net flow series and IRR were calculated for iron, copper, lead and other activities. All subsequent analyses were also aggregated in total and by each of the mineral sub-groups, but were not performed for each company.

As 26 companies were still in existence in 1913 and continued to be so for many years, the IRR calculations obviously understated true rates of return. To overcome this, the analyses were all run again employing terminal values for these companies. Stock market valuation was used wherever possible, but otherwise a terminal value was calculated according to the following formula:

$$\text{Terminal value} = A\left[\frac{1-(\frac{1}{1+r})^n}{r}\right]$$

Where: r: discount rate expressed as a decimal (7% used)

n: number of years in existence after 1913

A: expected average annual dividend flow based on trend average in the years preceding 1913

Other analyses included the calculation of annual dividends and interest payments as a percentage of capital employed, averaged over five year periods, first by book value of capital and second by sunk capital from Britain. The analyses by book value were intended to show the annual commercial returns of the companies in existence as perceived by contemporary investors. The analyses by sunk capital were intended to show the annual percentage returns on all the capital that had flowed from Britain to date, even though some had already been 'used up' by failed companies. This therefore represented the overall return to Britain. The sunk capital was calculated by creating a cumulative series of the annual capital flow series used in the creation of the net flow series.

The analysis of the six leading companies used the same data packing and IRR programs as the above analyses. The SPSS analyses produced frequency tables, cross tabulations, means and variances, ratios and breakdowns according to various criteria. SPSS was also used for the preliminary estimation of production functions based on the 1891 survey data to compare the relative efficiency of foreign and Spanish firms.

Conclusion

One general conclusion that can be drawn with regard to the computing aspects of our research, is that simple and fairly unsophisticated methods of data entry and calculation may often be more efficient in terms of total time and effort used than more sophisticated approaches. This can be stated even though the project could not have been undertaken without the power of the computer. The IRR was calculated very successfully using a simple algorithm, while the data was input using an over-sophisticated technique. However, if the data had been input in the most obvious manner this would probably have been even more time consuming. The most efficient approach of only inputting the relevant rows complete with zeros, could have been recognised if we had been more fully conversant with the raw data at the outset and had undertaken a few simple calculations of the work involved. The key is to have a good knowledge of the overall form and extent of the data before deciding on the best way of entering it, rather than to choose elegance of method for its own sake.

Computer Databases at the Department of Economic History, University of Exeter

Building on the excellent hardware and programming facilities offered by the University Computer Unit and the Faculty of Social Studies' own Data Processing Unit, the department of economic history has initiated a number of different database projects. Three have already been substantially developed and have been instrumental in producing a range of published and forthcoming material. They are: *The Mineral Statistics of the United Kingdom: Metalliferous and Associated Minerals 1845–1913* by Dr Roger Burt, *Poaching and Social Conflict in Rural Devon* and the *Devon Business Records Data Base* by Dr J. H. Porter, *Soviet Science-Production Associations* by Dr R. A. Lewis.

I. Mineral Statistics of the United Kingdom — Dr R. Burt.

The economic history department at Exeter has for many years been interested in the traditional metal mining industries of the south west and other parts of the U.K. They played a strategic role in the early stages of industrialisation and dominated the regional economies of the south west, central and north eastern Wales and the central Pennines, from Derbyshire to Northumberland. However, the history of the industries has received comparatively little attention in most conventional studies of economic growth in the eighteenth and nineteenth centuries. This is not because of any lack of information on these industries. Indeed, from the mid-nineteenth century the detail of production, ownership and employment in metal mining was probably more systematically recorded than in any other industry. Unlike the better known textile, engineering and coal mining industries, the record of activity at every single metal mine was meticulously recorded and published in every year from the mid-1840s to the First World War. However, the sheer volume of this material long militated against its effective use. It needed the facility of new computer database systems to analyse and interpret it effectively. Like so many other projects discussed in this volume, our venture was entirely dependent on a fundamental change in the 'academic production function' created by modern computer technology.

The idea of creating a database of mixed statistical and alphabetic information relating to ferrous and non-ferrous mining in the U.K. was first developed in the mid-1970s and initiated in 1976 with the aid of a grant from the Social Science Research Council. The material was to be derived from *The Mineral Statistics of the United Kingdom*, an annual series published between 1855 and 1882 by the Mining Record of the Geological Survey and

Museum and thereafter by Her Majesty's Inspectors of Mines. These volumes contain details of the output, ownership, management and employment at mines operating, or recently suspended, in all parts of the British Isles. They also contain details of domestic and overseas trade in minerals, market prices and a range of other miscellaneous information. It should be noticed that coal mining was not included in this study because detailed mine-by-mine returns were never published in these returns or elsewhere.

Wherever it was possible to tabulate the material in time series, it was extracted and entered into a specially written database system on an ICL System 4 machine. This Cobol programme has been transferred recently to the University of Exeter's new mainframe Prime machines and continues in use, though there are currently discussions about converting to a version of the standard *INFORMATION* database. Although the material requires a substantial storage space of over 3000K there is also a possibility of moving it from the Prime machine to an IBM compatible micro with increased disk facilities. Storage of the material in independent county files facilitates ease of use for detailed regional studies but creates some difficulty for nationwide analysis of extensively occurring minerals, such as iron and lead. Compatible material for mining in some other countries, particularly the major mining districts of the United States, is currently being assembled and it is hoped eventually to establish a framework for a fully international database. This would greatly facilitate the study of both national and international aspects of mining development during the critical years of change in the late nineteenth and early twentieth centuries.

The existing database has two principal types of use. Firstly to facilitate the writing of general books, articles and dissertations on various aspects of British mining. This includes already published work on lead, manganese, tin, and rare minerals as well as important forthcoming studies of arsenic and iron. Secondly, we have embarked on a program of publishing the contents of the data bank itself. From the original annual returns, the material has been reassembled on a mine-by-mine basis, listing all available information for the period 1845–1913 under each mine name. Seven separate county volumes have already appeared, covering all of the Pennine mining districts, the Isle of Man, and parts of Wales and the south west. A further five volumes are planned to complete the coverage of the UK and two of these should appear before the end of 1987. Originally declined by commercial publishers, this project was initiated as a private enterprise venture between the Department of Economic History and the Northern Mine Research Society. High quality photo-ready copy was produced from the computer; it was printed and bound by commercial printers; and marketed directly through the auspices of local mining history societies. The volume sold well, found commercial outlets and recovered costs, producing a small additional capital for further ventures. Over 2000 copies of this and later volumes have already been sold, mainly to local historians who find them an invaluable research text. The University of Exeter has taken on the publication of the Devon, Somerset and Cornwall volumes and found good sales through all of its normal local and national commercial outlets. Figure 1 shows a specimen of the range and format of the material produced in these volumes, which appear with an

Figure 1

```
CAEGYNON                      RHEIDOL VALLEY                    SN 717784 0047

Production: Lead & Silver    Ore(tons)  Lead(tons)  Silver(ozs)    Value(£)
            1853               23.90       19.50        0.00          0.00
            1854               52.00       37.00        0.00          0.00
            1855               45.00       40.00        0.00          0.00
            1856               38.00       28.30        0.00          0.00
            1857        No detailed return
            1858               56.00       39.00        0.00          0.00
            1859               10.50        7.50        0.00          0.00
            1860-1861 No detailed return
            1871               55.00       40.00        0.00          0.00
            1872               42.90       31.50        0.00          0.00
            1873        No detailed return
            1874               35.00       25.50        0.00        455.00
            1875               12.60        9.40        0.00          0.00
            Comment 1857-1858 CAEGYON; 1874 FOR SILVER SEE CWMYSTWYTH
            Zinc             Ore(tons)  Metal(tons)    Value(£)
            1854               33.10        0.00         0.00
            1855                9.50        0.00         0.00
            1858               10.00        0.00        27.50
            1859-1861 No detailed return
            1870               25.00        0.00        75.00
            1871              134.00        0.00       402.00
            1872              322.00        0.00      1416.00
            1873               60.00        0.00       264.00
            1874              127.80        0.00       370.00
            1875                6.20        0.00        18.50
            Comment 1854 CAE GIRON
Ownership:  1863-1865 W.H.PUNCHARD & CO.; 1866-1868 CARDIGAN CONSOLIDATED
            MINING CO.; 1869-1870 CAEGYNON; 1871-1877 CAEGYNON LEAD
            MINING CO.; 1897-1898 H.R.MERTON & CO.; 1911-1912 LERI MINING
            CO.LTD.; 1913 LERY MINING CO.LTD.
            Comment 1859-1860 ABANDONED; 1864-1865 SUSPENDED; 1866-1877
            OR GLANRHEIDOL UNITED; 1912-1913 IDLE
Management: Chief Agent 1863 GEO.WILLIAMS, 1866-1867 S.PEARCE; 1868-1869
            E.PEARCE; 1870-1877 THOS.HODGE; 1897 JOHN OWEN
            Secretary 1871-1877 F.REED WILSON
Employment:             Underground    Surface      Total
            1897              1                        1
            1898             20             5          25
            1911             10                        10
            1912                            1           1
```

introduction summarising the principal aspects of mining in the county during the period.

In the future it is hoped to expand the range of material held in the data banks to include second order reference information to archival and other sources relating to the mines. This would include the availability of plans, sections, geological data and all indications of the location of underground reserves and size and yield of remaining ore deposits. The ESRC has proved resistant to funding such 'practically useful' research but we hope to expand existing contacts with commercial mining companies, local and central government and others concerned with the redevelopment of all mining property. If mining history can be shown to be of current commercial value, we are optimistic of success.

II. Dr J. H. Porter has three principal files on the Prime and at SWURCC.

1. Offences against the game laws in Devon 1860–1900
This comprises 6,298 prosecutions before the Devonshire petty sessions and assize. The source of the data is the *Devon Weekly Times* newspaper. The basic information comprises (where known) the date of the offence by year and month, name of the offender, occupation, place of residence, petty session division and chairman of the sessions, offence, place of offence and

the penalty in shillings or term of imprisonment with or without hard labour.

The analysis comprises (1) seasonality by each quarter of the year, in total and for each petty session division (2) frequency of cases per year for all offences and per year for each offence (3) occupation, known for 51 per cent of the prosecutions (4) penalty bands for those convicted; in total, for each division and for each offence. (5) An analysis of the number of cases taken by each named chairman of each division and their penalty pattern. This last proved to be disappointing because the results were inconclusive.

2. Prostitution in Devon 1860–1900

A file of 615 prosecutions (Source *DWT* as above) of named prostitutes, brothel keepers and disorderly houses. The offences of the prostitutes are (1) soliciting (2) theft (3) assault and (4) drunk and/or disorderly. The basic data is a chronological list by name and year, by offence and by petty session division. Analysis shows (1) the location of offences by division (2) penalties and (3) repeaters.

3. Devon Business Records Data Base

This is a survey of business records held in Devon in the Devon Record Office and in private hands. It was originally compiled in 1977 and has been updated in 1985 and 1986. The organisation of the database is at present in progress. The original survey amounted to 120 A4 pages. The update has produced a further 1500 entries. It is intended to make this file available to *bona fide* researchers.

Each entry lists the nature and data of the records (e.g. ledger, letter books, maps and plans) as listed in the DRO accession lists. The organisation is by Minimum List Heading and by name of the organisation/person and place. (Copies of the original survey are held in the Devon Record Offices at Exeter and Plymouth).

III. A Database of Science-Production Association in the USSR — Dr R. A. Lewis

This database has been established in connection with research into the development and role of science-production associations in Soviet industry. These bodies were first established in some number as part of a key series of reforms in the Soviet industrial R & D system which was introduced in 1968. The science-production associations were seen as organisations which would improve the technological performance of Soviet industry by fostering closer links between Research and Development and industrial production. This goal was to be achieved through the administrative union of R & D facilities and production plants. The particular characteristic of the science-production associations was that the production function was to be subordinate to the R & D function. The top-level of management was to be provided by the chief R & D establishment in the new organisation.

Varying degrees of priority have been given to the science-production associations over the succeeding years. At present there are over 200 in Soviet industry, and they are seen as an integral part of the Gorbachev package for technological modernisation.

As part of the research into these associations, information was accumulated on the history, size and structure of individual associations. This information concerned not only those in industry but also those which were being established in other sectors of the economy. It soon became apparent that there would be considerable advantages in holding this material in the form of a computerised database rather than on file cards. When held on the computer, the data could be more easily amended, added to and sorted. In particular, since the extent of the information about each association varied considerably, the use of the computer would enable the swift identification of those associations for which a particular piece of information was available.

The establishment of a computer database has also made it possible to consider the possibility of pooling the information on science-production associations which has been gathered by various researchers, with members of a consortium accessing the database via JANET or PSS.

The database was set up using software written within the University of Exeter's Social Studies Data Processing Unit, but it is shortly to be transferred to the INFORMATION data management system which has recently become available on Exeter's network of Prime computers.

The database now contains details of over 300 science-production associations in all parts of the Soviet economy. The amount of information on each varies considerably. In the case of some which are in the military-related sector it may be, for example, only that there is an unnamed science-production association working in aviation in a particular city. In addition to the basic name and place, the fields within each record of the file are set up to contain information on:
—ministerial subordination
—area of activity
—date of foundation (and closure where relevant)
—name of the director (and previous directors)
—the constituent organisations
—its R & D activity, in terms of the numbers of its R & D workforce and the size of its R & D expenditure.
Individual data entries are referenced and the last field in the record for each association contains the sources which provided the information. Generally, these are included in an abbreviated form, as a separate sources file has been established to contain the full bibliographical details.

IV. As well as these established projects, several new databases are also under construction by other members of the department. Michael Havinden is accumulating material on nineteenth century colonial trade. Dr David Starkey, Research Fellow in maritime history, is developing databases on privateering and the shipping of Devon ports. Ena Cumming has assembled material on population in the parish of Morchard Bishop.

As part of the department's project on deindustralisation in the South West, the initial work is at present being undertaken in order to establish a database of the population census material relating to Devon and Cornwall.

Politics

21   *David Rheubottom*

Computers and the Political Structure of a Fifteenth-Century City-State (Ragusa)

The Ragusa (Dubrovnik) Project attempts an anthropological investigation of political and economic careers in the entire ruling patrician class of a fifteenth century city-state.[1] In this paper I concentrate on the structure and content of some of the data sets constructed during this project, and on ways in which both mainframe and personal computer are being used to process this information. As a report on research methodology, I largely ignore the theoretical issues these data are being used to address and, perhaps more unhappily, I also ignore substantive results achieved so far.

Several features of Ragusa (Dubrovnik of the fifteenth century) make it especially suitable for this type of study. First, the city-state was small. With a patrician population of about 400 adult males alive at one time, it was about the size of a community that an anthropologist would study in the field. Second, the archival sources are incredibly rich. As Braudel has observed,

the Ragusan Archives are far and away the most valuable for our knowledge of the Mediterranean . . . To anyone with the time and patience to study the voluminous *Acta Consiliorum*, they afford an opportunity to observe the extraordinarily well-preserved spectacle of a medieval town in action.[2]

Not only are these series very extensive for the mid-fifteenth century, but the fact that there are so many different series about almost all aspects of political and economic life makes it possible to study this community 'as a whole'. These two features, very rich sources on a small but important community, makes Ragusa an excellent subject for anthropological study. Ragusa also had an additional advantage for me. Having already done anthropological fieldwork in a traditional Yugoslav village, I was already familiar with features of Slav social structure.

From the outset it was my intention to use the computer for data processing. Heavy duty processing is done on the mainframe at the University of Manchester Regional Computer Centre (UMRCC) using SPSS and some PASCAL programs.[3] But most work is done at home on an Apricot micro using dBase II and several homebrew programs written in 'C'.[4] Somewhat paradoxically, the database being used at home on the micro is more sophisticated and I begin with it. The structure of this relational database and the contents of the data files are outlined first, and I then go on to discuss the 'flat files' being processed on the mainframe and describe how the materials on office-holding are being processed.[5]

At the heart of the project are several large data files of kinship and marriage. The first of these, called GEN, is an eight-field database (Figure 1). It includes given name,[6] sex, status (as patrician, illegitimate offspring, or otherwise), and date of death of any individual mentioned in the documents. Since dates of birth are unknown and can only be estimated, no special field is set aside for this information. GEN also includes a field called 'Hack'

Figure 1   *Data Fields in GEN*

ID	Identification Number
HACK	Hackenberg Number
NAM	Christian Name
SEX	Gender
DEAD	Date of Death (Yr/Month/Day)
STAT	Status
MUMID	Mother's Identification Number
COMMENT	Pointer to Comment Text File

Figure 2   *Hackenberg Numbers*

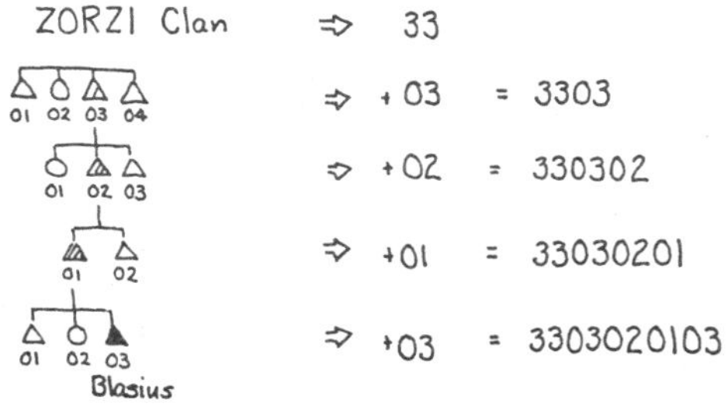

ZORZI Clan   ⇒   33

⇒ + 03   = 3303

⇒ + 02   = 330302

⇒ + 01   = 33030201

⇒ + 03   = 3303020103

Blasius

containing genealogical information.[7] This field, the 'Hack number', consists of a series of two digit numbers. The first two code the individual's clan affiliation (Figure 2). There were thirty-five agnatic patricians clans at the beginning of the fifteenth century although several of these disappeared in the following decades. The following pairs of digits encode generation level and birth order. Blasius, reading upwards from the bottom of the genealogy, is the third child of the first child of the second child of the third child in the Zorzi clan. Thus, Blasius' genealogical code would be (moving from the top of the genealogy down): 3303020103. Since the genealogy field encodes a person's agnatic antecedents, the Hack numbers for paternal kinsmen can be extracted from the code using various string functions.

In addition, GEN also includes a unique four-digit identification number for each individual. This ID serves two purposes. It allows us to include individuals in the fields whose precise genealogical position may be unknown. It also gives a unique identifier which can be used to link GEN to other files in a relational database.[8] There is an additional field in GEN which includes the individuals' mothers' ID. The ID for mother enables us to locate her GEN file and, through her Hack number, various maternal or affinal relatives. Finally, there is a comment field which contains a pointer to a comment file on the individual. Since files are terse by design, much textual material and additional information is kept in text files 'pointed at' and located by the entry in the comment field. At present GEN contains information on about 3000 individuals.

Some important information on marriages is contained in two files. One, called PAC, contains skeletal details of the matrimonial contract (*Pacta Matrimonialia*). This contract formally committed the couple to marriage, specified the time when the marriage would be consummated, indicated whether papal dispensation had been applied for if the marriage transgressed the Church's limits on intermarriage, details of the dowry, and so forth. Like GEN in being a terse and highly structured data file, PAC contains critical information on the matrimonial contract and pointers to files were more verbose and elaborate information are stored (Figure 3). PAC also contains the ID numbers of bride and groom. These ID numbers point back to GEN or on to the second marriage file. If either party had guardians or tutors, PAC also contains pointers to files containing their names and other information. The second marriage file is called CAR (*Carta Dotalis*). It records skeletal details of the eventual dowry settlement (Figure 4). The often very elaborate incidental information on the various loans, sales, and other arrangements that were required for paying the dowry are once again pointed at by a comment field. The linking of ID numbers and dates between GEN, PAC, CAR, and other files makes it possible to reconstruct marital careers, the offspring of a particular unions, and so forth (Figure 5).

The task of linking files and extracting particular types of information is accomplished through a set of purpose-built command files. At present these constitute a set of primitive genealogical utilities, but they are written so that they can be combined into more powerful search and analysis tools. Using GSX (Graphics System Extension) I am working out routines for interactive display and manipulation of genealogical data.[9] At present, however, this latter effort has resulted in a few paltry successes and a couple of hopeful

Figure 3   *Data Fields in PAC*

GID	Groom's ID
BID	Bride's ID
CONS	Period Until Consummation
DOTE	Dotal Amount
VEST	Amount for Vestments
CAR	Carta Dotalis Date
BEGIN	Date of Contract
END	Date at End of Contract
REND	Reason for End of Contract
COMMENT	Pointer to Comment Text File

Figure 4   *Data Fields in CAR*

HID	Husband's ID
WID	Wife's ID
DOTE	Dotal Amount
EXAG	Amount in Gold
BEGIN	Date of Contract
END	Date at End of Contract
REND	Reason for End of Contract
COMMENT	Pointer to Comment Text File

Figure 5   *Links Between Records*

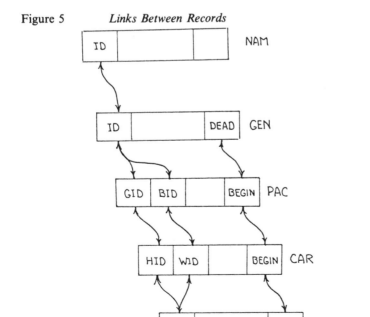

failures.

The database on kinship and marriage has been developed by breaking down some rather large and cumbersome flat files. The information contained in these files was abstracted from archival sources, coded onto code sheets, punched onto cards, and then loaded. This was a very time-consuming and laborious process. The development of the database system has been a further time-consuming and laborious process. In future work I would like to use a system which will allow direct entry of free text. Then, running a database program as a background activity, it would be possible to move through text files placing blocks of text, or data abstracted from the text, directly into the database.

Moving from files on kinship and marriage to political data, there are two major files. These are both flat files on mainframe (with copies on floppy disk) and they have not as yet been converted into a more useful relational database. The first, OFFHOLD, contains information on state offices and their incumbents between 1440 and 1460 (Figure 6). Its fields include date of election, the office, name of the newly elected office-holder, the name of the previous incumbent, and (where known) the reason the previous incumbent vacated office. Since approximately 50 offices had to be filled each year, and since many offices had multiple incumbents, this data set is very extensive. It includes over 3500 records.

In addition to information on office holding, it was also possible to collect information on elections to these offices. Election data includes the names of all candidates nominated for a particular office, the number of votes cast for each candidate, and the outcome of the ballot (Figure 7). Since the material on elections is particularly voluminous, it was decided to sample this material at intervals of five years. All the various elections held in 1440, 1445, 1450,

Figure 6   *Data Fields in OFFHOLD*

REF	–	Source of Information
BEGIN	–	Date of Election
OFFICE	–	Office
SUR	–	Surname of Office-Holder
NAM	–	Christian Name of Office-Holder
FNAM	–	Father's Christian Name of Office-Holder
REPSUR	–	Surname of Person Replaced
REPNAM	–	Christian Name of Person Replaced
REPFNAM	–	Father's Christian Name of Person Replaced
REASON	–	Reason Person Replaced Vacated Office

Figure 7   *Data Fields in ELECT*

REF	–	Source of Information
BEGIN	–	Date of Election
ACTION	–	Type of Council Action
OFFICE	–	Office
CANDI	–	Status of Candidate
SUR	–	Surname of Candidate
NAM	–	Christian Name of Candidate
FNAM	–	Father's Christian Name of Candidate
FFNAM	–	Father's Father's Christian Name of Candidate
PRO	–	Votes Pro
CON	–	Votes Con
ABS	–	Votes Abstaining
BALLOT	–	Number of Members Balloting
AGENDA	–	Number of Item on Agenda

1455 and 1460 were collected for analysis. I hope that analysis will reveal patterns in competition for office and the relative standing of various candidates. These five sets, called ELEC40, ELEC45, and so forth, occupy over 4400 records.

To date only OFFHOLD has been analysed. Almost all of this work has been on the mainframes at UMRCC. First, a series of indexes have been prepared which list the data by (a) name of office-holder, (b) by office, and (c) by date of election. While they have proved very useful in some small analytical tasks, they were prepared initially to use as reference aids in the Dubrovnik Archives. I will find out just how useful they are when I next return to the archives.

OFFHOLD has been used to chart political careers. First, I analysed career structure looking for the sequence of offices that the 'typical' patrician might hold. It was known how these offices ranked in terms of relative status from other sources, but it has been very useful and illuminating to work out the normative pattern. Simple statistical techniques were used to determine which offices were most likely to preceed, or follow, any particular office. I also determined the number of offices, and the number of years, which were likely to intervene between any two given offices. From this analysis the normative order of office-holding has been worked out and also the pattern of several different career structures.

Moving on from this, individual careers are being examined against the backdrop of typical career structure. While the work is not very advanced, I am particularly interested in seeing individual careers in the context of particular events in a person's life. The same materials, seen in the context of significant events in the political life of this most interesting city-state, is a long-term goal of this research. More immediately, I shall be juxtaposing several different individuals' political careers in order to work out patterns of alliance and opposition in Ragusan politics. This is where the election materials (ELEC40, etc.) will become critical. By looking at people who opposed one another for office, and by examining the outcome of the balloting, it should be possible to determine the relative strength of various contenders and to see how these changed over time and circumstance.

Finally, OFFHOLD will be used to chart the flow of various individuals through state offices and governing councils. From these data it should be possible to see if certain sets of individuals monopolised various sectors of government and to relate these sets to ties of kinship and marriage. From this outline it will be seen that the Ragusan research is a long-range project. While the major databases are now in place, the processes of expanding and amending them will continue. One of the principal advantages of the relational database is the ease with which they can be revised and amended. They also permit items of information to be brought together in new ways in order to address questions which were not anticipated when the database was first established. As I have indicated, they are being used to address problems in kinship and marriage. They are also being used to study politics in an Early Modern European city-state. from these beginnings I intend to bring together kinship and politics and, in the long term, economics as well.

Notes

1. This project began in 1978 with a grant from the E.S.R.C. Subsequent work has been supported by a Staff Travel Grant from the University of Manchester. I am grateful to both bodies for their support.
2. Fernand Braudel, *The Mediterranean and the Mediterranean World in the Age of Philip II*, 2nd. ed., London, Collins, 1973, pp. 1258–9.
3. The latter were written in the Data Preparation Section of the Faculty of Economic and Social Studies specifically for this study. I am very grateful to Margaret Irvine who wrote the programs and undertook the processing.
4. I wish to acknowledge the training and the inspiration I received at the RAI-UKC Winter School in Computing for Anthropologists from John Davis, Michael Fischer, and Nick Ryan.
5. E. F. Codd, 'A Relational Model of Data for Large Shared Data Banks', *Communications of the ACM*, 13, 1979, p. 6: James Martin, *Computer Data-Base Organization*, Englewood Cliffs, Prentice-Hall, 1977.
6. There is a separate file on NAMZ, as well as other files, which are not discussed. The process of identifying particular individuals is too complex a topic to be dealt with in any detail here. Suffice it to report that NAMZ contains all patrician names and a personal identification number, where the latter can be determined. There is a separate glossary of names and a command file which checks for equivalents. Unknown or problematic names are 'dumped' for manual checking.
7. Named after Robert Hackenberg who first outlined the system (Robert A. Hackenberg, 'Parameters of an Ethnic Group: a Method for Studying the Total Tribe', *American Anthropologist*, 69, 1967, pp. 478–92.).
8. A third purpose is that is permits more compact files. A four digit ID number takes up much less total space than the thirty digit Hackenburg number or about forty digits for given names and surnames.
9. Nick Ryan, 'Gtree: A System for Interactive Display and Manipulation of Genealogical Data', *Bulletin of Information on Computing in Anthropology*, 3, 1985, pp. 6–20.

22 *Valerie Cromwell*

House of Commons' Voting, 1861–1926: a Computer-Eye View

This paper describes a large-scale E.S.R.C. funded project (£51,000) to analyse British parliamentary voting. Such work has only proved possible with that level of funding if it was to be completed in reasonable time. Also it was only possible with the level of statistical tools and fast and big computers currently available.

The challenge of the project is the size of the data involved and the associated analytical problems. The following table gives an indication of the scale of the data and the pattern of voting participation.

Figure 1   *Table of voting participation by M.P.s in individual sessions*

Session	Total no. divisi- ons	High- est no. of votes by an M.P	Total no. of indivi- dual M.P.s voting	M.P.s voting over 50% of total no. of divisions	% of M.P.s voting who vote in 50% or less than 50% of total no. of divisions
1861	187	182	654 (662)	71	89.14
1871	270	269	648	127	80.40
1876	242	241	651	125	80.79
1881	411	408	648	153	76.39
1886	143	139	676 (680)	166	75.44
1891	416	415	675	136	79.85
1896	419	418	670	205	69.40
1901	482	481	670	246	62.83
1906	501 (2)*	500	680	421	38.09
1911	451	443	690	335	51.44
1916	67	65	609	121	80.13
1921	370	356	641	180	71.92
1926	563	560	615	362	41.14

(Table derived from research funded by the Economic and Social Research Council, Research Grant E 00 23 0051)

* One unnumbered division included.
  Total given in brackets includes M.P.s who did not vote.

The main purpose and justification for the grant

1. The analysis of House of Commons' voting at 5-yearly intervals, 1861–1936: in order to use the evidence of that voting to test the long-held assumptions about trends in party loyalty and cohesion from mid-nineteenth century to the 1930's and political behaviour.
2. The creation of valuable machine-readable source for others.
3. The development of analytical and data handling tools.

The background to the Project

Much work on roll-call analysis had been done in the U.S.A. and more recently elsewhere which encouraged work on British parliamentary voting: usually such work has been done with groups with significantly fewer participants or voting divisions than are to be found in any British peacetime parliamentary session since the early nineteenth century. The total number of members voting in any Commons' session never fell far short of 700: the number of divisions in a session rose from 187 in 1861 to 270 in 1871, 411 in 1881, 482 in 1901, 563 in 1926. The scale of the data remained and remains a barrier to such work. It is even more difficult with studies of electoral voting and attempts to link-up voting with census material.

My early work on the 1860's showed the volatility of voting behaviour and the impracticality of embarking on large-scale analysis. The development of new statistical techniques in the 1970's looked hopeful in that they were being successfully applied to voting. Large scale analysis became possible because of association with Professor Robin Sibson's Spatial Data Project (University of Bath). A method was needed which would permit analysis of all divisions in a parliamentary session in a way which would distinguish similar and dissimilar patterns of individual voting behaviour. The happy coincidence of advances in computer technology and pioneering work in multivariate data analysis at Bath offered the opportunity to experiment.

In 1980 the S.S.R.C. funded a pilot project to apply multidimensional scaling and other computer techniques to all the divisions in 1861, thereby testing suitability of methods. The aim was to analyse the M.P.s' voting behaviour in such a way that as full and as unbiased a *picture* of voting behaviour could be drawn. Coloured computer maps were drawn. The maps produced showed M.P.s as points in such a way that the distances between them are in good agreement with the similarity values. Similarity values = ratio

$$\frac{\text{No. of divs. in which voted identically}}{\text{No. of divs. in which both voted}}$$

Thus, M.P.s voting similarly are close
      M.P.s voting differently are distant

M.P.s had to vote in at least 5 divisions in common to be included in the analysis. A league table of voting was created. The M.P.s were then divided into overlapping sets of 100 down the league table. Each set was analysed for behaviour in all divisions and in 8 selected categories of divisions. The pilot project was written up in 'Mapping the Political World of 1861: a Multidimensional Analysis of House of Commons' Division Lists', *Legislative Studies Quarterly*, VII, 1982, pp. 281–97. This analysis resulted in the E.S.R.S. grant for the major project begun in October 1983.

The research project

All divisions in the chosen sessions are being analysed at 5-yearly intervals — a distance close enough for individual behaviour and distant enough for group behaviour over time to be analysed. All divisions in each session are being analysed: Why? The value of significant votes is obvious at moments of high political tension, for example at times of large or hairsbreadth majorities. By looking at *all* divisions it is hoped to provide an indicator of discrimination and resource. Work in the pilot project on different categories of division demonstrated the usefulness of the methods tried.

Limitations of voting analysis

i)   What does a vote in a Commons' division imply? It is very positive evidence — 'clear cut and reliable' as recently described: it is a very public statement of, for example, political sympathy, a personal tie, local loyalty, desire to please a party leader, obedience to the party whip in order to keep the party's support at next election, a desire to postpone an issue or to shake a minister — in fact a payment for services rendered or an investment in the future. It is 'hard' evidence of a public political action — for whatever reason. But it is only one element of analysis of political behaviour.

ii) The problem of abstention is an analytical minefield. Apart from the problems of identifying explanations such as illness or holidays, it is well known that abstention could have political uses, as with Disraeli in 1861 (56 votes in total of 187). There was often mileage in avoiding voting.

When Prime Minister in 1876 Disraeli still only voted 106 times in a total of 241 — though he became an Earl on 12 August. To put Disraeli's voting record in perspective, it should be noted that Gladstone only voted in 28 divisions in a total of 143 in 1886; Harcourt, his Chancellor of the Exchequer in 60 and Childers, his Home Secretary in 71 divisions. Even more surprising, in 1911, Asquith only voted 150 times in a total of 451 divisions, Lloyd George 190, Balfour 132 and Bonar Law 165, while John Clynes and George Lansbury voted 282 and 283 times respectively. This pattern of voting by leading politicians must be set against the steadily increasing level of voting in the 50 years before 1914.

Even with the obvious limitations of using the Commons' votes for the analysis of political behaviour, it is hoped that it will be possible to chart with some sensitivity the changes in British parliamentary behaviour in the period of the emergence of the mass party. The large variations of voting participation inevitably limits the analysis. At a crude level, the number of times a member votes against his party of nominal allegiance must always be set against the number of times he voted in the session: in 1861 John Maguire and Wilfrid Lawson both voted 45 times against their supposed party: for Maguire it was 45 out of 80, over half — while for Lawson, it was 45 out of 133 — about a third. The analysis should take care of that. In the initial stages of the analysis, all divisions are being considered equally in identifying similarity of behaviour: the purpose is to distinguish similarity or dissimilarity of voting behaviour. For this, the difficulties of low participation present a challenge, but not a serious obstacle. The increasing rate of cohesion within the major parties in the Commons can be easily and quickly demonstrated: in 1883, in 194 divisions, the Conservative voted the same way, with less than 10% of them dissenting, in 68% of the votes, the Liberals 58%. In 1894, in 214 divisions the same figures were 94% and 89%:

in 1903, in 225 divisions, the figures were 91% and 90%. The experience of our pilot project encourages us to believe that even with such cohesion it will be possible to trace groupings and allegiances within as well as across parties.

Throughout the period cabinet politics remained crucial in the making of policy: certainly until 1914 individual ministers retained a high level of independence in the preparation of legislation. What must remain surprising is the continued domination of the national party organisations by the parliamentary organisations of the parliamentary parties in an age of a mass electorate: . . . this project will only help in a limited way to explain some of these phenomena.

Parliamentary voting is only a very small part of the evidence for the history of the functioning of British political parties, but, thanks to the computer, it can now be analysed in a fairly sophisticated way.

23   *John Turner*

The Labour Vote and the Franchise After 1918: an Investigation of the English Evidence

The problem addressed in this study was first raised by Matthew, McKibbin, and Kay in a pioneering article in 1976.[1] They suggested that the rise of the Labour Party in twentieth-century Britain had been universally misunderstood. Historians had been obsessed by the results of the First World War: the destruction of the historic Liberal party, the apparent growth of class consciousness, and the upsurge of trade union activity. This, the three maintained, was mostly irrelevant: the true explanation lay in the terms of the 1918 Representation of the People Act, which enfranchised all men over 21 and most women over 30. Before 1914 the franchise had been biassed against the working class, and Labour had therefore been unable to realise its true strength. Once the bias had been corrected, Labour could live up to its potential and replace the Liberals as the major party of opposition.

Two lines of criticism were immediately apparent. The allegations of bias in the pre-war electorate were contested by Duncan Tanner, and the claim that pre-war Liberal voters did not form the majority of post-war Labour voters was challenged by Michael Hart.[2] No critic has directly addressed the central question of how the 'new' electors actually voted in the immediate post-war elections. This is what is attempted in the present study, which uses regression techniques to analyse the social correlates of voting in the 1918 and 1922 elections.

It is not easy to study historical electoral behaviour in Britain. Since the enactment of the secret ballot in 1872, voting has been recorded at a constituency level, but never for smaller units. Furthermore, Parliamentary boundaries do not coincide with the administrative units used for the Census enumeration. In other countries historians have been able to correlate the social characteristics of constituencies with their voting behaviour, and even to determine the voting patterns of different ethnic groups and classes.[3] In Britain very little of this is possible. Nor is sample survey data available for Britain before the late 1930s. To make matters especially awkward, the 1918 Representation of the People Act changed most constituency boundaries, so it is not even possible to calculate 'swing' between pre-war and post-war

Table 1   *Data and Variables used in the Analysis*

A. Source and scope of data

UNITS OF ANALYSIS	DATA AVAILABLE
Administrative counties N = 40	Electorate Totals before and after 1918 (After - Before = New Voters) Totals for male, female and service electors 1918.
Boroughs, County Remainders (W.L. Miller's Constant Units) N = 119	Social and economic variables from the 1921 and 1931 Censuses (Occupations, housing density, religion, age structure, immigrants)
Constituencies N = 475	Party Votes Distribution of the Coupon Candidate allegiances Male Electors) From Female Electors) 1918 Service Electors) Reg'r Occupation Electors)

B. Variables used in analyses

LABPROP	Labour proportion of total votes cast
LIBLEAD	Labour lead over uncouponed Liberal as proportion of votes cast
NOLIBCON	Dummy variable: 1 = No Liberal or Conservative standing
COUPON	Dummy variable: 1 = Couponed Liberal or Conservative standing
LABCAND	Dummy variable: 1 = Constituency previously contested by a Labour candidate
FEMPROP	Female electors as proportion of total electorate
NEWV	Estimated new male electors as proportion of total electorate
OCCUPROP	Occupation voters as proportion of total electorate
NOPR31	Non-operatives as proportion of occupied males
MINERS	Miners as proportion of occupied males
AGRI21	Males employed in agriculture as proportion of occupied males
PRS21	Roman Catholic Priests per capita
ANG21	Anglican clergymen per capita
MIN21	Nonconformist ministers per capita

elections.

Ingenuity is therefore essential. The main types of data used here are described in Table 1. The registers of electors provide miscellaneous data about parliamentary constituencies. The last register taken under the old legislation was prepared in 1915 in readiness for a wartime election which never happened. It is the best available guide to the size and distribution of the pre-war electorate. The 1918 Register, prepared in haste for the post-war Election, gives totals for the new constituencies, and also breaks down the electorate into men, women, plural voters, and those eligible for the service franchise. This last statistic was a valuable indirect measure of the age and occupational structure of constituencies, as explained below.

Other measures were derived from the 1921 census, which provides data at the level of boroughs and counties. Here I have followed the methods used by W. L. Miller.[4] Miller grouped all constituencies into 'constant units' which were either counties or administrative boroughs, and therefore it was possible to attribute census data to them. Lastly, party sources and parliamentary division lists gave information about the candidates in the 1918 election and the distribution of the notorious 'Coupon' letter sent to government approved candidates.[5] The analysis reported here used English data alone, because of the difficulty of recovering information about the 'new' electorate in Scotland, and the peculiar cultural and political significance of religious allegiance and rurality in both Scotland and Wales.

The first goal was to estimate how the 'new' electorate was distributed among the constituencies. In aggregate the English electorate grew between 1915 and 1918 from about 6·28m to 16·02m. Of the 1918 electorate 6·49m (just over 40%) were women, newly enfranchised. About the same number would have been men enfranchised under the old system, and thus about 20% of the 1918 electorate were men who would probably not have been enfranchised under the old system. Constituencies varied widely in the proportion of women among their electors; the proportion of new voters among the male electorate was also presumed to vary. Both Matthew *et al.* and their opponents agree that enfranchisement levels before 1918 varied according to the social and demographic characteristics of constituencies, though they cannot agree on which characteristics were salient.

Two approaches were possible. The first was to construct constant units in which it would be possible to count the electors in the 1915 Register and subtract this number from the male electors on the 1918 register to give an estimate of the new male electors. The second was to find some characteristic of the 1918 constituencies which could stand proxy for the proportion of new male voters in the electorate. In the end both were used, in tandem. The only constant units untouched by the 1918 Act were the administrative counties and a handful of boroughs: 76 units in all, varying in size and population from the borough of Lincoln to the whole of the LCC area north of the Thames. It would clearly be absurd to assume that the proportion of new electors was the same in all North London constituencies. But by using a characteristic separately measurable for each constituency the measure could be refined. The registers give the number of voters in each constituency entitled to the service franchise because they were serving overseas during the election. It happened that the criteria for inclusion in the armed forces were markedly similar to the known criteria for exclusion from the pre-1918 franchise. The Military Service Acts took young men before older married men, and unskilled men before skilled men. The work of Peter Dewey and Ian Beckett has shown that the composition of the Army by age and occupational origin was, by the end of the war, largely what had been intended by the governments which had passed these measures.[6] For their part, the antagonists in the franchise debate allege that the pre-war franchise discriminated against the less affluent working class and against the young unmarried man.

There is, moreover, a strong observed correlation between the proportions of service voters and 'new' voters at the level of the administrative counties, for which both measures can be derived. A good fit to the data is obtained by dividing the counties into two groups, an industrial group and a rural/suburban group. The very strong correlations obtained — ($R2 = 0.82$ for the rural and suburban counties, $R2 = 0.87$ for industrial counties) are inflated by the aggregation, but even so they confirm a linear relationship between the two figures. The service vote can therefore be used as the basis of an estimate of the 'new' vote. It is not satisfactory on its own, because the fit is not perfect. But it may be assumed that the particular economic structure of each county affected the impact of the military service acts on its underlying age and income structure: agricultural labourers, for example, being much less likely to enlist than clerks.[7] Taking this into account by using the county ratio between service voters and new voters as an index by which to multiply the service vote in each constituency, one can get an estimate of the 'new' vote from the observed service vote. This estimate was used throughout the analyses.

The next goal was to relate the Labour vote in each constituency in 1918 to the characteristics of the electorate. The first step used only constituency level data. The Labour proportion of votes cast was taken as the dependent variable in a number of multiple linear regression equations. The independent variables used included the proportion of women in the electorate, the estimated proportion of new voters, the proportion of plural voters, and a number of variables to express the different structures of electoral contests. In 1918 most Labour candidates were opposed by a 'couponed' candidate. In a number of cases no coupon was issued: some Labour candidates in this position had only minor-party opposition, while in other cases local Conservatives or Liberals stood without the coupon. The voters therefore had very different messages from the parties, and this was reflected both in the turnout and the voters' willingness to vote Labour. Two dummy variables were used to indicate the constituencies where Labour faced a couponed candidate, and at the other extreme the constituencies with no major-party opposition at all. On the assumption that a history of political organisation would help the Labour candidate, whatever the other characteristics of the seat, a variable was introduced to represent the proportion of the vote received by a Labour candidate (if any) at the 1910 elections.

One of the equations used in this step is shown in Table 2. As Matthew *et al.* would predict, it did make a difference if there were more new voters in a constituency: but the difference was in the wrong direction. The more new

Table 2　　　*The Labour Vote with Constituency Variables*

A. Equation tested

Dependent Variable: LABPROP

Independent Variables	Regression Coeff.	T	Sig. T
NOLIBCON	0.442	11.516	.0000
OLDLAB	0.0016	5.135	.0000
COUPON	-0.107	-5.449	.0000
FEMPROP	-1.419	-5.295	.0000
OCCUPROP	-1.33	-2.780	.0058
NEWV	-0.348	-2.423	.0160
(Constant)	1.039	9.396	.0000

R^2 (adjusted) = 0.597

N of Cases = 312

B. Residual Breakdown [mean, (n of cases)]

	MIDDLE CLASS	MIXED CLASS	WORKING CLASS	URBAN/ RURAL	RURAL	MINING	ROW TOTAL
LONDON	-.060 (4)	-.057 (12)	-.043 (18)	.00 (0)	.00 (0)	.00 (0)	-.050 (34)
S.E.	-.020 (15)	-.050 (13)	-.002 (8)	-.028 (12)	.062 (6)	.00 (0)	-.017 (54)
E.ANGLIA	-.014 (1)	-.017 (2)	.00 (0)	.00 (0)	.119 (3)	.00 (0)	.051 (6)
CENTRAL	.047 (1)	.071 (1)	.084 (3)	.031 (1)	.100 (3)	.00 (0)	.078 (9)
WESSEX	-.061 (1)	-.050 (4)	.00 (0)	.052 (2)	.032 (2)	.00 (0)	-.010 (9)
BRISTOL	.134 (2)	.025 (3)	.151 (1)	.132 (2)	.070 (7)	.00 (0)	.083 (15)
DEVON/ CORNWALL	-.010 (1)	-.009 (1)	-.050 (1)	.141 (2)	-.128 (1)	.00 (0)	.014 (6)
WEST MIDLANDS	.00 (0)	.035 (6)	-.024 (13)	.012 (6)	.057 (3)	.00 (0)	.005 (28)
EAST MIDLANDS	.00 (0)	-.053 (5)	.044 (4)	.032 (4)	.020 (3)	.047 (6)	.017 (22)
LANCS	.007 (2)	.006 (12)	-.001 (31)	-.021 (7)	.00 (0)	.113 (3)	.005 (55)
YORKS	-.111 (1)	-.047 (11)	.025 (18)	-.081 (3)	-.169 (2)	.084 (9)	-.00007 (44)
NORTH	.00 (0)	-.070 (11)	-.005 (3)	.082 (4)	-.029 (1)	.009 (11)	-.013 (30)
COLUMN TOTAL	-.014 (28)	-.033 (81)	-.002 (100)	.011 (43)	.042 (31)	.051 (29)	.0000 (312)

voters, the less the constituency tended towards the Labour party. Moreover, the female vote, newly introduced by the 1918 Act, also clearly moved against the Labour party. On these figures the Representation of the People Act, far from being an opportunity for Labour, was a double hindrance.

The tabulated residuals from this equation[8] suggested that London and South-Eastern constituencies in each category were less friendly to Labour than the franchise and electoral structure variables would predict. Mining constituencies as a whole were even more strongly Labour than predicted.

Table 3   *The Labour Vote with Constituency and Constant Unit Variables*

A. Equation tested

Dependent Variable: LABPROP

Independent Variables	Regression Coeff.	T	Sig. T
NOLIBCON	0.454	12.16	.0000
OLDLAB	0.0016	5.10	.0000
COUPON	-0.101	-5.31	.0000
FEMPROP	-1.237	-4.21	.0000
NOPR21	-0.364	-2.89	.0041
RPP	0.0015	3.89	.0001
MINERS	0.133	2.42	.0159
NEWV	-0.301	-2.12	.0346
(Constant)	0.824	7.12	.0000

$R^2 = 0.623$

N of Cases = 308

B. Residual Breakdown [mean, (n of cases)]

	MIDDLE CLASS	MIXED CLASS	WORKING CLASS	URBAN/ RURAL	RURAL	MINING	ROW TOTAL
LONDON	-.027 (4)	-.008 (12)	.006 (18)	.00 (0)	.00 (0)	.00 (0)	-.003 (34)
S.E.	-.002 (15)	-.027 (13)	.035 (8)	-.013 (12)	.064 (6)	.00 (0)	.003 (54)
E.ANGLIA	-.013 (1)	-.043 (2)	.00 (0)	.00 (0)	.083 (3)	.00 (0)	.025 (6)
CENTRAL	.038 (1)	.064 (1)	.061 (3)	-.004 (1)	.070 (3)	.00 (0)	.055 (9)
WESSEX	-.074 (1)	-.066 (4)	.00 (0)	.026 (2)	.025 (2)	.00 (0)	-.026 (9)
BRISTOL	.114 (2)	.013 (3)	.156 (1)	.099 (2)	.032 (7)	.00 (0)	.056 (15)
DEVON/ CORNWALL	-.034 (1)	-.033 (1)	-.068 (1)	.107 (2)	-.143 (1)	.00 (0)	-.011 (6)
WEST MIDLANDS	.00 (0)	.029 (6)	-.024 (13)	-.004 (6)	.044 (3)	.00 (0)	-.001 (28)
EAST MIDLANDS	.00 (0)	-.083 (5)	.006 (4)	.001 (4)	-.009 (3)	.010 (6)	-.016 (22)
LANCS	.009 (2)	.014 (12)	-.002 (30)	-.034 (7)	.00 (0)	.100 (2)	.002 (53)
YORKS	-.103 (1)	-.045 (10)	.017 (17)	-.102 (3)	-.188 (2)	.066 (9)	-.008 (42)
NORTH	.00 (0)	-.062 (11)	-.014 (3)	.063 (4)	-.041 (1)	-.005 (11)	-.019 (30)
COLUMN TOTAL	-.003 (28)	-.024 (80)	.006 (98)	-.0002 (43)	.022 (31)	.028 (28)	.000 (308)

Middle class constituencies were less Labour-inclined than working-class constituencies, and the more rural the constituency the stronger its Labour vote, after all the other variables had been taken into account.

The next step was to incorporate this information into new analyses, using census data. Each constituency was assigned the values for the Miller constant unit in which it was found. There are great drawbacks to this approach. For technical reasons, the coefficients obtained in 'split-level' regressions like these are certain to be lower than they would be if the data were collected for the smaller unit.[9] Moreover, the use of constant unit data conceals interesting variations within the unit. Nevertheless it is a useful exercise, with typical results shown in Table 3. The fit is slightly better than in the previous equation, and once again the constituencies with more women and more new voters were found to be more hostile to Labour. Tabulation of residuals confirms that the class and and mining effects in the table are reduced, though not eliminated, by the inclusion of explicit measures.

The Matthew, McKibbin and Kay hypothesis is not supported by these analyses. Labour did not gain, but rather suffered, from the effects of the 1918 Representation of the people Act. Women and new male voters were more reluctant than established voters to support Labour. Further confirmation of this comes from an analysis carried out on the same data, which tried to test directly the proposition that Labour's lead over the Liberals would be greatest in constituencies with the largest number of new voters, who had not had the opportunity to form a Liberal allegiance. By regressing the difference between Labour and non-couponed Liberal proportions of the vote in the few constituencies where the two stood together, it was found that Labour's lead was inversely related to the proportion of new voters. Labour's strength seems to have lain very much with the male working-class voters, enfranchised before 1918, whose unionisation and economic security was probably the key to their allegiance.[10]

It is clear that the socio-economic variables used in this study are not the only determinants of voting patterns. The use of analytic methods such as those reported here can refine our view of more purely 'political' causation. For example, the conventional wisdom is that 'pacifism' was very bad for Labour candidates. This, like other 'qualitative' suggestions, can be checked by listing the constituencies in the order of their residuals from an equation with good predictive power. These residuals, rather than the raw figures of the Labour vote, represent the extent to which voting diverged from what a socio-economic model would predict. Take Leicester West, where Ramsay Macdonald was vilified for his anti-war views. His vote was lower than predicted by the equations, but his experience hardly differed from other working-class candidates in the East Midlands. In Bradford East, F. W. Jowett, an outspoken pacifist and ILP member, won more than half again as many votes as predicted, far ahead of his neighbours in the West Riding, though other Bradford Labour candidates did quite well.

Another important suggestion has been made by Tanner, who tried to refute the suggestion that strike activity during the war was conducive to Labour voting at the end. He contrasted the behaviour of Coventry with that of the working-class constituencies in nearby Birmingham, whose strike record was less but whose Labour vote was higher. The residuals show that in fact Coventry performed better in relation to its predicted outcome than any of the Birmingham working-class constituencies except Aston. Another benefit of the ordered list of residuals is that it makes it possible to see clusters of constituencies whose performance was similar: all the Sheffield constituencies in 1918 are rather down, while much of the Gloucestershire area is unaccountably up. This is enough to fire the imagination to further questions.

It is in observations like these, where the particular quality of different areas and constituencies is highlighted by the contrast with a general quantitative model explaining some but not all of the variation between them, that the future of quantitative, computer-aided investigation of electoral history must lie. In a classic article in 1954 Tukey and Wilk remarked that 'one of the truly incisive tools of exposure is the computation and adequate examination of residuals'.[11] Powerful and interesting techniques have been developed for this under the general label of Exploratory Data Analysis, but this study has perhaps shown that it is possible to use the tried warhorse of conventional statistical analysis — Good Old SPSS — to much the same end.

Notes

1. H. C. G. Matthew, R. I. McKibbin and J. A. Kay, 'The franchise factor in the rise of the Labour Party', *English Historical Review*, xci, 1976.

2. Duncan Tanner, 'The Parliamentary Electoral System, the "Fourth" Reform Act and the Rise of Labour in England and Wales', *Bulletin of the Institute of Historical Research*, lvi, 134 (Nov. 1983), pp. 205–19; M. Hart, 'The Liberals, the war, and the franchise', *E. H. R.* , xcvii, 1982.

3. E. Terrence Jones, 'Ecological inference and electoral analysis', *Journal of Interdisciplinary History*, ii, 1972, pp. 249–62; J. Morgan Kousser, 'Ecological regression and the analysis of past politics', *ibid.*, iv, 1974, pp. 237–62; Alan J. Lichtman, 'Correlation, regression, and the ecological fallacy', *ibid.*, iv, 1974, pp. 417–33.

4. William L. Miller, *Electoral Dynamics in Britain since 1918*, London, Macmillan, 1977. I am greatly indebted to Professor Miller for allowing me to use his data in machine-readable form.

5. Roy Douglas, 'A Classification of the Members of Parliament elected in 1918', *Bulletin of the Institute of Historical Research*, 1974, pp. 74–94.

6. P. E. Dewey, 'Military recruiting and the British labour force during the First World War', *Historical Journal*, xxvii, 1984, pp. 199–223; Ian Beckett, 'The British Army, 1914–1918: the illusion of change', in John Turner (ed.), *The British Experience in the First World War*, London, Allen & Unwin, 1987.

7. Dewey, pp. 216–17.

8. Constituency typology as in Neal Blewett, *The Peers, the Parties and the People: the General Election of 1910*, London, Macmillan, 1972, pp. 488–94. Geographical areas as used by Henry Pelling, *Social Geography of British Elections*, London, Macmillan, 1967.

9. See Miller, p. 106.

10. C. Chamberlain, 'The growth of support for the Labour Party in Britain', *British Journal of Sociology*, xxiv, 1973.

11. J. W. Tukey and M. B. Wilk, 'Data analysis and statistics: techniques and approaches', in Edward R. Tufte (ed.), *The Quantitative Analysis of Social Problems*, London, Addison Wesley, 1969, pp. 370–90.

PART II

Methodology

Database

24 *Manfred Thaller*

Methods and Techniques of Historical Computation

Computers have no inbuilt prejudice favouring science; indeed, they crunch numbers which deal with the fluctuation of sun spots as happily as those describing the income of medieval landlords. So what is historical about the uses a historian makes of these machines? Is there indeed a difference between what we are asking them to do and what everybody else is doing?

Software specific for a genuinely historical application has been declared to be necessary a number of times already;[1] as has software for the Humanities in general.[2] The author has been engaged since 1978 in an effort to provide an integrated database-oriented system, known as CLIO, which should be able to handle as many types of historical sources as possible and apply to them as many methodologies as feasible.[3] He is trying right now to re-implement an improved and machine independent version, which is also able to run on at least the larger type of microcomputer.[4]

Precisely because he is permanently engaged in the minutiae of implementing a software concept on a machine, he thinks, however, that the concept is more important than the actual commands to be given by the user to the final software product. We will, therefore, not try to describe the command language we have implemented, nor of the version we are trying to develop right now, but return to the original question we raised: what makes computing specifically historical?[5] We will do so by formulating a catalogue of general theses, which we have been using when designing our own developments, what — in our opinion — constitutes state-of-the-art historical software.

General, by the way, seems to be one of terms requiring most urgently a specific description: our considerations have been drawn from work on database-oriented software and, general as they are, they reflect this.

1. General Considerations

Historical software deals with problems (a) not appearing in other disciplines, (b) on hardware as available to a typical historian and can (c) be controlled with a level of skills a historian can be expected to acquire without re-focussing his main research interests.

It is therefore controlled by a command language which is *object oriented*, as opposed to *procedural*. The user can access the data objects that shall be processed by specifying their symbolic names, without knowing what steps the system has to perform to do so — and without having to learn about the abstract data model[6] of the files being used.

It is furthermore *source-oriented* as opposed to being *method-oriented*. Data is being input as closely to the original source as possible, keeping, for example the original spelling in all cases where there can be any doubt about the meaning of a word or passage of text. The software is responsible for bringing it from this representation to the one required by other (not necessarily historical) programs used to apply a specific methodology to the information contained in the original source.

As far as these aims allow, it is *efficient*: efficiency being tentatively assumed to mean that a corpus of at least 100,000 lines of input data can (a) be administrated in dialogue on equipment typically available to historical researchers and (b) be processed quickly enough in batch applications to guarantee a turn-around of 24 hours or less in a typical academic environment.

There are, as a rule, as few limitations as possible which are not imposed by the capacity of the hardware used. Specifically, variable length and/or frequent absence of any field in the data do not influence efficiency.

2. Data Structure

Data is administrated as collections of pieces of text, without any assumptions about its meaning. All such assumptions (the social status to be derived from a given occupation; the chronological meaning of a date based on a Saint assigned different days in the calendar of various dioceses; the exchange rate of two currencies) are administrated in tables which are completely independent from the data as such.

The data structure that is used to administrate source material is *context-sensitive*: (a) the order of entries within a specific source remains available when it is turned to the computer and (b) every information can be connected to a specific frame in time and space.[7]

The data structure is *fuzzy*.[8] This means (a), that vagueness of terminology is handled as such: a person known to be 'approximately fifty' is treated differently from a person known to be (assumably precisely) 'fifty'. It means (b) furthermore, that the fact that a given string of characters could be a surname as well as a place of origin can be considered by the software, as well as the fact that a person in a census list could belong to two different families with equal probability. It means (c) finally, that there is nothing like 'every variable has a value'; indeed the system does not support any entity which completely represents the classical concept of a variable, but structures of interrelated items of information. If a person has five different occupations, the variable 'occupation' has five equivalent values.

The data structure that is used internally by the machine is independent of the input conventions[9] used: such input conventions allow the historian to choose between free field formats, descriptor-descriptum logic (also known as 'tag-content' or name list), as well as systems of logical bracketing.

The data structure that is used to describe a source during input can be augmented by the user by specifying inference rules: the system is, for example, able to learn that in all cases, where the 'date of birth' of a person has not been specified, the 'date of baptism' shall be used instead. Another user does not need to know of this mechanism to take advantage of it.

3. Retrieval of Data

Retrieval can be performed by accessing (a) all items of the data which have a specific symbolic name ('process all fields "surname" and the field "first name" being related to it'), (b) all items of data with a specific structural location ('process all fields "first name of a child" and the field "surname of the head of household" structurally related to this child'),(c) all items of data which have a certain content ('process all fields, which contain the string "Aberystwyth", irrespective of the name or structural location this field has') and (d) all items of data which are related to another item via common content ('process all fields "surname" and connect to them all fields "place of origin" which are related to a person having the same "surname" as the one mentioned previously'). If a user specifies any such request, the system is itself responsible for translating it into the most efficient access path.

This implies that for retrieval purposes the system behaves as a hybrid between a structured DBMS, a full-text retrieval system and a document retrieval system. The dividing lines between these parts are transparent; it has, for example, to be possible to ask for all documents containing a word starting with 'murd'(a typical full-text-retrieval function), restrict one's interest to those sources addressed by that, which contain a particular pattern of thesaurus items within a free-text field of one 'document' (a typical document retrieval function) and plot for all those documents the distribution of the monetary values contained within the field 'fine' (a typical function of a structured data bank).

All data items selected by any access method available can be (a) displayed, (b) printed, (c) sorted and (d) passed further on to files in a number of formats preparing later stages of processing this information.

In all these cases it is possible to combine into one unit of output items of information which come from arbitrary positions in the underlying structure of the administrated data.

4. Preparation of Statistical Analysis

While a software system of the kind described above has to be able to perform a core of statistical functions — particularly aggregating across various possible logical paths in the data — statistics as such can not be considered to be specifically historical. Specific, however, is the need to transform all the properties of the data structure presented as section two of this paper into data which can be analysed by commercially available software.[10] This implies particularly two classes of functions:

(a)   The system has to have the ability to use the tables mentioned to translate the original vocabulary of the source into statistical codes and figures ('code'occupations, convert the notations of monetary units into a figure representing the local purchasing value of them, represent days given by the feast of a Saint by the number that has passed on that day since a common starting date for all calendar calculations).

(b)   The system has to have the ability to project the complex structures, which can be administrated by it, into flat cases or a system of such, which are acceptable to available statistical software. As far as control variables are necessary to use such a structure of flat cases — as the 'record types' of SPSS-X[11] or the 'linking variables'of P-STAT[12] — they should as default be created automatically out of the knowledge stored in the data dictionary, which is such an obvious precondition for a system as the one we just describe, that we have not mentioned it explicitly so far.

5. Nominative Record Linkage

An encompassing system of historical software has to have the basic ability to overcome differences in spelling. As the precise method to do so is dependent on the local conditions under which the source has been created (and on a whole array of phonetic properties of the various languages), we do not think it very wise that historical software, intended to be general, should be implemented incorporating the precise rules applicable to a given area and/or time. Instead the methods used for Soundex[13] codes — or alternative methods for name comparison, as described, for example, by Guth[14], Oldervoll[15] and Portmann[16] — should be implemented as a general framework for a multi-purpose algorithm of name comparison which can than be augmented by specifying all local peculiarities via the command language of the system.

While overcoming spelling differences in surnames is certainly that aspect of nominative record linkage[17] which gets most attention, one might almost say it deserves it least: many methods have been published and bring results of a quality which is usually quite acceptable. Indeed the two problems of selecting pocket variables and of allowing the historian to react to proposals of who might be identical with whom, seem to be much more crucial for the final outcome.

This is also the area where the experiences of about twelve projects using our software[18] have more than generally influenced decisions to make major changes in the design of the new implementation where our theses are derived from. We will therefore more explicitly than hitherto in this paper differentiate between what we have done and what we intend to do.

So far, the basic philosophy of record linkage with our software worked like this:

(a) a user starts with two databases representing two sources,
(b) from both databases files containing the information that might be used for identification are derived,
(c) the cases (usually persons) in these files are compared, according to rules laid down by the user.
(d) A set of proposals made by the machine — who might be identical with whom — is presented to the user on a printout, containing not only the information that let the computer think this to be a potential identity, but also all other information derived from the original databases.
(e) The user creates a file containing a list of the numbers of the proposals he or she thinks acceptable.
(f) The machine uses this list to strike out of the auxiliary files all persons which have been identified already.
(g) The user refines — or simply softens — the rules for identity and steps c to g are repeated as often as necessary to reduce the auxiliary files to a number of cases which can more easily be linked by hand.
(h) The two databases — which all the time remained unchanged — are combined into a new composite one, re-using for this purpose the files with accepted proposals.

This model worked well with three or four of our projects, and quite acceptably with almost all of the remaining ones, the exception being a dissertation project, where no agreement between the user and our staff could be reached on the level of knowledge a historian using a software system can be expected to acquire about it.

   Three problem areas could be identified:

*   True to the philosophy 'there's no limit but the size of the machine', some users tended to pack a great deal of information into the auxiliary files, which in some cases contained forty or more fields ('variables') for the visual inspection of the proposal. Besides contributing to the destruction of German forests this behaviour did anything but speed up the process of reviewing the proposals.
*   Almost all projects found about 80% of all theoretically possible identities within a pretty short time, flipping rapidly through lists of easily decidable proposals with three, in some cases two, passes of the logic described above. It is certainly also reasonable that all the projects spent about the same time (and number of passes) to bring this percentage to 90%. It is open to doubt, however, whether the constant temptation to try 'just another set of rules', which almost all projects were vitiated by, and which made for many more passes and much

longer time-scales, was so very productive, since additional linkages were found at a rapidly diminishing rate.
* The most serious shortcoming turned out to be that in many cases researchers wanted to have at their disposal at a later pass information collected at an earlier one (additional information about the couple in a given marriage, as collected from children accredited to the marriage record already, being the most prominent example).

These experiences lead us to the following theses about the way a 'best of possible worlds' system should handle the situation:

* The auxiliary files — which turned out to be very useful for their potential of being relieved of unwanted cases without having to bother about the integrity of the data bank — should contain the pocket variable only. The user should have the choice between:
  — Inspecting the proposals interactively (with the help of a split screen) using the standard display commands of the retrieval system, to select any combination of information available in the database to illustrate the quality of the proposal, adapting the amount of information to the complexity of each case.
  — The batch-oriented listing of a user defined amount of information, as in the current system.
* The user should have the option to merge, already at the time a proposal is accepted interactively, the relevant parts of the two system files in question.

6. Merging of Files

It has to be possible to merge any two subsets of two databases. The initial considerations about the data structure imply the following abilities for the relevant modules:

If any two fields of data which are selected by a global merge command share the same full name, they should be merged. That is, if a 'person' in file 'a' should be merged with an 'heir' in source 'b' the directive: 'Merge "person" and "heir"' should imply, among others, the following rules:

* 'Merge "name of person" and "name of heir"'.
* 'Merge "son of person" and "son of heir"'.
* and, by recursion, 'Merge "name of son of person" and "name of son of heir"'.

If any two items of information are marked in the data dictionary as being related to any user defined table (e.g. a field 'price' to a table 'currency system'), an explicit or implicit command to merge these two fields should imply a check of the consistency of these two tables. If they can be merged logically themselves (a somewhat complex condition, being beyond the scope of this paper) that should be done and the items of information should be merged too. If they cannot be merged, the names of the two items should be permutated until they are different and then be treated as names which are present in only one of the two databases (which have their data dictionaries updated automatically during that process, of course). If two items of information, that have to be merged, contain different information within two databases, the user should be able to control formal rules, dealing with such conflicts. Examples are:

* 'If two files contain two "date of birth" items, which should be merged, but are not identical, the should become *terminus post quem* and *terminus ante quem* of a fuzzy representation of "date of birth"'.
* 'If two files contain two "military rank" items, which should be merged, but are not identical, the should be turned into logically equivalent but successive entries into an item "military career", being ordered according to the content of the item "date" in both files.'

7. Text Processing

Text processing proper — as well as computer supported typesetting — are right now areas where so much commercial development is taking place that it is hard to see why historical software would have to be developed for these purposes. Historical software *will*, however, aim at the following goals:

* Humanists are used to seeing printed material, where typographical properties of a text carry meaning. (Emendations appearing in another font, for example.) As soon as appropriate printers are available, historical software should have the quality to implement this concept, being built around a definition of strings, which includes a string handling library allowing for things like 'sensitivity for font' or 'sensitivity for differences in print size above "n" printing points', in much the same way that current software handles optional case sensitivity.
* There *are* a few symbols which are pretty frequent in historical material, while virtually absent from modern text processing — the venerable Chrismon of medieval charters, superscripted 'v' and the like. Historical software should therefore have the ability to handle strings out of an expendable character set accessible for redefinition.

8. Processing of Running Texts

This author has many doubts as to whether, at a time when full-text retrieval systems become easily available on micros, there still is much point in the publication of printed concordances. He even doubts that there is much more point in producing them as printouts or micro fiches. (You *can* tell even the most primitive full-text retrieval system to look for all quotations where 'monk' and 'king' appear within 'n' words of context. Even the most cleverly printed concordance can not arrange anything but the context of *one* word on a line.) Such full-text capabilities have been built into the very definition of what we consider 'historical software'.

There are a number of services regarding running texts, however, which definitely have to be provided: particularly a whole range of (in the broadest possible meaning) content analytical measures, describing flexibly proportions between various classes of words, which should be available within a system of historical software. And for some time to come, at least some of the less trivial kinds of word lists will be more economically provided by batch-oriented functions, rather than their use being simulated by functions of a full-text retrieval system.

9. Utopian rather than Historical Software?

Many readers may have the impression that what we described in this paper is not so much a catalogue of theses of what historical software should do, but just a daydream too costly ever to materialize.

The first answer that comes to the mind of the author would be: well, we did it. As mentioned previously: a prototype of a system like the one presented has been developed at our institute between 1978 and 1983. It adheres to what today we consider a record linkage design with deficiencies clearly to be stressed. Conceived in the pre-micro days of computing, it does not support the advanced string handling logic we have described. In many details it is much less elegant than we would like to have it. But it has been used and continues to be so; used in a number of student projects without funding, too.

So we do not see why we should not repeat this performance, when we reimplement it to be available on as many machines as possible and specifically on microcomputers which have a hard disk. Indeed right now (November 1986) a functional core system of the new version has been implemented and is being debugged and tested.

Still, one should close with another thesis about what historical software is: underfunded. If we need specific software, we will have to create it. And it seems unlikely that the market for computer programs which are able to evaluate whether the church calendars of two dioceses are equivalent, will ever become so large that industry will invest in it. The solution, we think, for problems specific for the discipline can be found only within it. Historians have for centuries considered the edition of historical sources, to make them available to their colleagues, as a legitimate activity of an historian. They have developed common standards how such editions should be done and to make the intellectual labour of one historian into the building blocks of another's study. This model we try to follow, by creating out of a general scheme, such as the one we present here, some hard technical definitions, that allow us to share the burden of development among a number of historical research institutions. Given a well-defined general concept of interfaces between various parts of the system, we believe that a researcher contributing to a general system a module tailored to the specific needs of her or his research, may in turn receive the whole system for his purposes, and benefit from similar efforts of other colleagues.

Notes

1. E.g. Ian Winchester, 'Priorities for Record Linkage: A Theoretical and Practical Checklist', in Jerome M. Clubb and Erwin K. Scheuch (eds.), *Historical Social Research*, Stuttgart, 1980 (= Historisch-Sozialwissenschaftliche Forschungen 6), pp. 414–30, particularly 429–30.

2. E.g. Richard W. Bailey (ed.), *Computing in the Humanities*, Amsterdam, 1982. The Editor's introduction, p. 5 is very instructive about the development that has been taking place when compared with the evaluations of the first wave of computer enthusiasm, e.g. Edmund A. Bowles, 'Toward a Research of New Dimensions', *Computers in Humanistic Research*, Englewood Cliffs, 1967, pp. 12–13.

3. The manuals are available on request. Short overviews in English are Manfred Thaller, 'Beyond Collecting. The Design and Implementation of CLIO, a DBMS for the Social Historical Sciences', in Robert F. Allen (ed.), *Data Bases in the Humanities and Social Sciences*, 2, Osprey, Florida, 1985, pp. 328–34, and — outdated in *every* detail, but with many examples — Manfred Thaller, 'Automation on Parnassus. CLIO — A Databank Oriented System for Historians', in *Historical Social Research/Historische Sozialforschung*, 15, July 1980, pp. 40–65.

4. This zero version currently being implemented consists of a superset of the data structure available in the 'old' version, is however restricted to one data type, textual data; it allows batch-oriented as well as dialogue-oriented retrieval, but none of the more advanced commands of the 'old' systems. The zero version, to be installed at a number of selected test sites in January 1987 for field tests, will be available for XENIX and MS-DOS for the PC/XT/AT family plus VAXes running under VMS in January; at least one other UNIX type of system will also be the aim of an early portable version of the system; the availability for IBM CMS/VM mainframes and CDC machines under NOS/VE is not guaranteed but highly probable.

5. For another answer to this question see: Andrew A. Beveridges and George V. Sweeting: 'Running Records and the Automated Reconstruction of Historical Narrative', *Historical Social Research/Historische Sozialforschung*, 35, July 1985, pp. 31–44.

6. We do not share the unconditional admiration for the relational data model, currently in vogue. To discuss this disagreement with a prevailing opinion, we would have to go very much into technical detail. Three points, however, should be raised: (a) the relational data model is *not* the only one presently discussed in information science. For a more general treatment of alternatives see Dionysios C. Tsichritzis and Frederick H. Lochovsky, *Data Models*, Englewood Cliffs, 1982; (b) any electronic treatment of data implies a certain model of the reality (cf. William Kent, *Data and Reality*, Amsterdam etc., 1978). Historical data require models which are sensitive for the context within which they occur — the relational model is not very useful for describing high level contexts; (c) even if the relational model would rightfully reign supreme, a historian using the computer is a historian, not a computer specialist: interesting for him (or her) should be the properties and usefulness of a given command language, not the properties of an abstract data model.

7. Manfred Thaller, 'Ungefähre Exaktheit. Theoretische Grundlagen und praktische Möglichkeiten einer Formulierung historischer Quellen als Produkte "unscharfer" Systeme', in Herta Nagl und Franz Wimmer (ed.), *Neue Ansätze in der Geschichtswissenschaft. Eine philosophisch-historische Tagung*, Vienna, 1984 (= Conceptus Studien 1).

8. On our interpretation of fuzzyness see the quotation in the last footnote. On the current meaning of fuzzyness in computational theory see: Lotfi A. Zadeh: 'The concept of a Linguistic Variable and its Application to Approximate Reasoning', *Information Sciences*, 8, 1975, pp. 199–249, 301–57 and 9, 1976, pp. 43–80.

9. On input methods for Historical Data see: Manfred Thaller, 'A Proposal for a

Standard for the Coding of Machine Readable Sources', in *Historical Social Research/Historische Sozialforschung*, 40, 1987.

10. On data preparation software see 'Empfehlungen für ein integriertes Datenaufbereitungspaket für die historische Sozialforschung' in *Historical Social Research/ Historische Sozialforschung* 19 (July 1981), 83–92. For a non-trivial example see Manfred Thaller, 'Zur Formalisierbarkeit hermeneutischen Verstehens in der Historie', in *Mentalitäten und Lebensverhältnisse*, Göttingen, 1982, pp. 439–54.

11. *SPSS X User's Guide*, New York, 1983, pp. 161–88.

12. Shirell Buhler *et al.*, *P-STAT Users Manual*, Princeton, 1983, pp. 274–91.

13. See already H. B. Newcombe, 'Record Linking. The design of efficient systems for linking records into individual and family histories', *American Journal for Human Genetics*, 19, 1967, pp. 335–59.

14. Gloria Guth, 'Surname Spellings and Computerized Record Linkage', *Historical Methods Newsletter*, 10, 1976/77, pp. 10–16.

15. Jan Oldervoll, 'Automatic Record Linkage of 18th Century Nominal Records', in Robert F. Allen (ed.), *Data Bases in the Humanities and Social Sciences*, 2, Osprey, Florida, 1985.

16. Urs Portmann, 'The Identification of Persons in the Middle Ages: Results from the First "Freiburger Bürgerbuch" (1341–1416)' in *Historical Social Research/Historische Sozialforschung*, 18, April 1981, pp. 11–26.

17. For the basics see E. A. Wrigley (ed.), *Identifying People in the Past*, London, 1973.

18. Cf. At an earlier stage for the nine projects supported at that time, Manfred Thaller, 'Can we afford to use the Computer; can we afford not to use it?', in Helen Millet (ed.), *Informatique et Prosopographie*, Paris, 1986, pp. 339–51.

25   *Michael Greenhalgh*

Databases for Art Historians: Problems and Possibilities

Introduction

It is important to realise that there is no more a 'typical' art historian than there is a 'typical' museum collection, and that the purposes to which computerised databases of art works may be put are equally various. It is irrelevant to argue that many collections of art works are in the process of computerisation for administrative rather than for strictly art historical purposes, as the spin-off for the discipline is the same.

This paper tries to define the special needs of some art historians when they use computers, especially in the areas of complicated and irregular record structures and the storage of images; it goes on to suggest ways in which some of these needs are addressed by developing technology. Furthermore, it shows how certain needs may be circumvented by adopting a more down-to-earth approach to problems. The videodisk and networking are presented as two advances of importance, and the paper ends with a discussion of the importance of standards.

Inevitably, because of the 'neutral' nature of many data, the paper's main points and conclusions are applicable to *any* database project — and not just to those concerned with the history of art. The problems we face in the storage, structuring and manipulation of any historical data are similar: art history is often exceptional only because of a standing need for images and ways to describe and hence retrieve them.

Peculiarities of Art Historical Databases

Although, to a computer, all data may look the same when transformed into binary form, the ways in which different types of user require their data organising and manipulating vary greatly. Some art historians would claim that their needs are special, because the complicated structure of their data must be reflected in that of the database which will represent it.

Some may need:

1. Indexed items and free text in the same document or record;
2. Some form of indexing on the free text itself;
3. An irregular (and changeable) record length and hence structure, depending upon the entity/object being recorded. This might involve the repetition of fields or groups of fields (e.g. to record suite of paintings or furniture, or other collections which belong together for some reason);
4. A way of coping with different kinds of entities needing diverse treatment — artists cannot be handled in the same way as paintings, nor patrons in the same way as prints.

Of course, it may be that these are features of any 'humanities' database: although it could be argued that, given the 'pictorial dimension', in no other field are the possibilities for complicated record structure so rich. And if structures are to be complicated (in order to reflect the state of the real world, which is the task of any database), then the retrieval of the same in whole and (especially) in part can be very tricky.

But where art history does differ from 'straight' history is in having to deal with series of objects which have survived (plus some for which there is only documentary evidence) and which, stored in collections public and private, have been the object of more or less intense cataloguing activity. These form a natural focus for the work of art historians, being their most important 'primary documents'. There can now be few local and especially national collections which have no basic catalogue of their art-works; and most have in hand the computerisation of those catalogues. In other words, art historians and museum personnel deal in images, the 'useful' description of which in words can present problems as difficult as those of determining a structure for complicated records.

A second difference, perhaps, lies in the potential variety of the primary documents with which an art historian might have to deal in a wide-ranging database. For a study of art at Versailles, for instance, one might need printed books and their illustrations, individual prints and drawings, maps, project designs accepted and rejected, building plans, paintings, furniture, legal documents of various kinds, quotations from journals — all perhaps set within a framework of dates. Evidently, the task of collecting together even parts of such material in computerised form will be a major task, calling on individual museums and collections from the Chateau de Versailles itself to the Bibliothèque Nationale, the Cabinet des Estampes and the Musée du Louvre.

The Problems

1. How does one 'computerise' an image?

The aim of most art historical databases is to arrive at the images sought via a structured, written description of them. This is quickly said, but not easily effected, some of the problems being:

1. How does one describe an image in a fashion regular enough for a database record? The language used must be normalised; and this entails some kind of thesaurus, whether on-line or in book form.
2. In what detail does one describe it? If the finished database cannot respond to reasonable questions, the product is just as useless as if it does things in great detail (and perfectly) but never gets finished.
3. How does one deal with uncertainty, given that a computer likes precision? Works must be attributed to a person, group or area; and dated with a precision which depends on the nature of the sources. Strict conventions are needed if the records containing uncertainties are to be accurately retrieved.
4. If the database does store various files on various types of entity, how does one relate files together? That is, how does one answer realistic questions such as 'Give me all painters of French origin who worked in Rome between years X and Y, with a list of the works they produced there'?

2. Complicated record structures

Some art historians would claim that, since a database is a reflection of the real world, then it should model complexity as closely as it can. A big problem in art history is the modelling of groups of objects which, for some reason, belong together: how, indeed, do you relate the parts to the whole?

Tricky examples might include:

1. Different states of an engraving, some perhaps retouched by different artists or pulled in different centuries;

2. Sets of paintings by different artists which somehow belong together, perhaps because they were intended for the same room;
3. Works of different kinds which belong somehow together — such as table settings including porcelain and siiver — which must be capable of interrogation from either end of the 'hierarchical tree' (if that is the database structure to be used).

There is an overwhelming processing problem associated with what is (to some of us) an overwhelming logical one as well: namely that in order to retrieve, for example, a coffee-spoon from our table settings, the numbers of files brought into play, and the complication of the queries posed, might well bring all but the largest machines to a halt.

Is there not a simpler way of dealing with such groups?

3. Dealing with text

I question the approach to the storage of information which allows large quantities of text to be stored and interrogated. The end product may eventually be perfect, but the overheads in terms of data entry, machine size, and time to complete any project are very great. I suggest that the advantages of a type of package which actually restricts what can be input may prove to be overwhelming. Indeed, using a modern database package (and not a document retrieval package) might avoid some of the tedious thesaurus problems which seem to take such a long time to resolve.

4. The potential breadth of the subject

Without getting into a semantic dog-fight, it is evident that the interests of some art historians, desirous as they are of explaining the how, the why and the what of art and its production, cast their net very wide indeed, involving themselves now in statistics or politics, now in economics or military history. And while some might stick to their artistic last and deal with just one artist or one restricted period, others treat a theme through time.

5. Vagueness

Problems arise when the objects on which most art historians focus lack the usual semi-solid 'hooks' by which the Rembrandts and the Davids can be identified — artist, date, accepted title, provenance. The more vaguely an object has been catalogued, the more difficult it is to manipulate successfully in a machine. This would apply to large areas of mediaeval art, to some art of the classical period, and perhaps to much of non-European art as well. Either insufficient survives to create a 'chain', or it has been insufficiently studied — or perhaps there is simply too much of it (too many votive statuettes, coins, pottery lamps).

Their Solution

Database work is as much an exercise in careful planning and administration as it is in actually manipulating data in a package, but the acknowledged rules for successful work are much easier to enunciate than they are to follow. I repeat them here because (as a glance at some current projects makes clear) some of the elementary rules tend to be ignored — perhaps in the rush to get the data entered:

1. Requirements Analysis, which will help determine feasibility, is the essential first stage in any project, for here are taken the fundamental decisions which will control all remaining stages of the process. Unfortunately, Requirements Analysis is often overlooked, because a decision to use a computer has already been made (perhaps for reasons which have nothing to do with its inherent suitability), and there is an urge to start programming immediately. Answers will be needed in the following areas:

   a. The scale of the problem. Is it a small one? Or is it both large and complicated?
   b. If a small problem, will it change as the requirements change? How is it envisaged to cope with such changes?
   c. The financial implications of a computer solution. Are the expense and the time to implement the solution affordable?
   d. Possibility of a manual solution. Contrary to the belief of some computer buffs, not everything can be done better on a computer.
   e. Have similar problems already been solved in a similar fashion? That is, does suitable software exist which performed the task?
   f. Is the project, perhaps, a pioneer in the type or extent of the problem being tackled? Pioneering is often an uncomfortable position to be in, unless one really knows what one is doing, and has funds and time to match.

   To sum up: why is the system required? It needs to be *justified*.
2. A Formal Specification is now needed, of what the database system is to do in terms of input, manipulation and output. Who will use it for data entry and/or querying? What level of skill do they possess, and how is this to be catered for? Making a list of the kinds of likely queries will give some indication of what the database should contain.
3. Now consider the future — that is, the question of the maintenance of the database as something which continues to respond to user requirements: this aspect of the problem is so often overlooked. A small, personal database project can well be abandoned once its narrow purpose has been fulfilled; but larger, funded projects must have built into them the means of easy maintenance and upgrading.
4. Concentrate on the data, which are the point of the exercise, and not on the software and the machine, which are no more than transient tools.

Of course, all these worthy processes will not cause complicated record structures to turn into simple ones; but it is possible that, once the scope of the project is matched to the likely audience, it will be seen that simplification is called for if the work is ever to be finished.

The Relational Model

I take this opportunity to emphasise the direction of modern database work, which is towards relational databases, and this on *all* sizes of machines. Relational databases, which organise their material in a series of flat tables, are the way of the future: hierarchical systems which, like the network systems which are a more complicated version of the same animal, have a built-in structure to reflect that of the data, are now part of the past.

This fact is recognised even by companies who need to manipulate massive quantities of data: many of them, as a stop-gap, are using interfaces to their (old hierarchical) systems which provide a relational view of their data. Since some relational systems allow large amounts of free text, they may suit even those amongst us who believe that the more text one can cram into a record, the better!

This is therefore a plea for the adoption of relational systems wherever possible. And if this sounds as religious in its zeal as the beatitudinous general advice for establishing a database already given, consider the advantages of the relational against the hierarchical model. In the former, the data are stored completely separately from the programs which manipulate them; whereas in the latter, the data get mixed up with the programs because this is the only way to express hierarchy. In the former, no user view is imposed upon the data, because every entity is normalised into its simplest form; in the latter, the very concept of hierarchy invites the designer to build structure into a database — a structure which may not be valid in a few years time. In the former, powerful and easy-to-use DMLs (Data Manipulation Languages) such as Sequel and Query-by-Example allow anyone to manipulate the data; in the latter, programs have to be specially written to cater for *every* intricate retrieval.

All these factors add up to the clinching argument in favour of a relational approach, that surrounding the independence of the data from the programs: no relational tables are dependent upon any package, for they can be exported and imported at will. A relational approach is therefore easier to update and to maintain — both factors which account for a considerable part of the expense of large database operations.

The Possibilities

These depend on the directions we might expect database work in art history to take, most of which are dependent upon:

1. The continuing compilation of computerised catalogues of the great local and national collections of art works, presumably to be made available to all via networks.
2. The broadening availability of machines and packages to individual researchers for small projects.
3. The development of group research (as is common in subjects like archaeology), and of funding for this.
4. The development of protocols for accessing remote databases and

interchanging information between systems large and small.
5. Developments in graphics and the videodisk — on which see below.
6. The widespread adoption of the relational model.

One problem we face might be called the 'weight of the past'. We should recognise that art history, precisely because of the cataloguing needs of public collections great and small, has been one of the first non-science disciplines to benefit from pioneering schemes. Although it would be over-dramatic to suggest that all these are either direct failures, or still woefully incomplete, it nevertheless does still seem that some institutional schemes are propelled by delusions of grandeur: the motto is not 'Keep it Simple', but 'Make it Complicated' — presumably on the assumption that a computer can deal with anything thrown at it. Several institutions have learned from the burdens they have already incurred (of time, effort and money), and we can hope that future launches will be informed by a more realistic appreciation of the possible fruits to be derived from the time-scales available.

The Videodisk

The videodisk field is undoubtedly a most exciting one, and not just for art historians with their need for images. There exist several types of videodisk:

1. Images recorded in analog form, 54,000 per side. The images can take any form — pages of text, drawings, pictures, etc. These can be read by a TV monitor, but not displayed on a VDU at the same time as digital information from the computer. Using such a disk requires selection of the required image, perhaps via a database, and transmitting the number to the player using an interface.
2. Images recorded in digital form — that is, as a sequence of bits which, together, can be displayed in their appropriate place on a VDU. Each image might require 125Kb of store for black and white, and perhaps 375Kb for a colour image (i.e. 3x the black and white one). To a computer, then, there is no difference between images, data and programs, for all are represented in digital form. At present, there are two kinds of laser disk: CD-ROM, where the information is written at the factory (used for on-line dictionaries, encyclopaedias, and the like); and WORM — standing for Write Once, Read Many times. This can be done by the user.
3. For the future, we can expect an optical disk which can be erased and re-written under computer control — just like today's floppies and Winchesters.

We can take it as read that the eventual form of the digital disk will be used for all data and programs, and so can discuss the medium here under the headings of analog and digital.

1. The Optical Analog Disk
I can see no problems — beyond those of quality, colour, standardisation, expense, time, copyright and transmission — in the linking of art-historical

databases to the relevant images: a unique reference number forms a field in the record, and is bar-coded on a photograph of the image (where available). With a videodisc reader attached (plus its own high-quality screen), the image can be called to the screen; with a photograph to hand, the bar-code could be stripped, which would bring up the textual record for perusal on the VDU.

Quality: The quality of the videodisk image depends not only on that of the original image, but also on that of the viewing screen. With good originals and a good screen, very acceptable results are obtained: cf. the Warburg/Hertziana link-up demonstrated at Pisa.

Colour: Having persuaded nearly everyone in the art-historical world that colour slides are preferable to monochrome ones, it would seem perverse not to hope for colour images on videodisk — just as perverse as it might appear in ten years time to have finished an enregistration programme of monochrome images! The problem is that colour videodisk images are generally of poorer definition than their monochrome counterparts.

Standardisation: As far as I am aware, no single recognised standard for videodisc machines has yet emerged.

Expense and time: Collecting 108,000 images for enregistering onto a videodisc will be very expensive of time and personnel, especially since many of the images might need to be photographed section by section to attain sufficient quality.

Copyright: A problem we can perhaps duck at this conference, but which will not go away, for to the notion of legal copyright is added that of academic property — especially when networking becomes an everyday fact of life (on which, see below). Who owns data — especially in a database built up of pieces of data collected here and there as a bee collects pollen?

Transmission: Assuming that video-databanks would be held centrally, and accessed over lines, the problem of transmitting the data to the user appears: 'painting the screen' with monochrome data can be very slow over telephone lines; with colour data, it is even slower, because extra data must be transmitted to build up the colour image.

Nevertheless, and in spite of these stumbling blocks, it is not difficult to envisage the databases of the future with text linked to visual data, and the latter available in videodisk-packs, ten or twenty platters to a pack: speed of access to any image in the pack would be very fast (but NB transmission: above). It is worth underlining that such disk-packs would mean that the images would not necessarily have to be collected together 'physically' (e.g. all works by Poussin on one disk), because indexes to the data would maintain logical access to them.

2. The Optical Digital Disk
However, the digital disk is clearly the way of the future — although some of the analog problems (copyright, transmission, cost of equipment) remain with us.

The advantages of the optical digital disk are clear:

1. Images become simply information, stored in digital form on the same disk as programs and other data.
2. Storage problems are greatly reduced, because of the massive

capacities of optical disks.
3. Display problems (quality, re-sizing, selecting details from different images if desired, mixing with text and other data) are eliminated, for all of these can now be handled under software control.

However, one problem which has not yet been solved is the transmission of images over a network. The deed itself is simple, but not at the speeds that will be required. The more bits are to be transmitted, the longer it will take: a file of 375Kb, for example, representing one colour image, would take the same time to transmit as perhaps 100 pages of text.

Videodisks: a Summary
At the moment, the videodisk in whatever form is a 1:1 operation: one user will need some way of controlling the disk (usually a computer with its own VDU) as well as a disk player and monitor. Ten users will need ten sets of kit. If we think to the future, and to transmission, then it is conceivable to have a central computer with large optical disks serving any number of VDUs over a network.

But what should we do now? There is no one accepted standard for the analog disk, and the costs in terms of administration, scholarship and money of enregistering even one videodisk are high — although there is of course no need to fill one completely. Perhaps art historians need an institution like the Getty to take on the task of a videodisk of 'Renaissance Art', 'Baroque Art', etc — but the cataloguing of the objects would be a huge task.

However, there is one undeniable advantage of the analog videodisk which the digital version does not and cannot possess — an advantage which may ensure its longevity. This is that, although it may well be generated by a computer (simply to assemble the huge numbers of images to fill it), it does not require to be computer controlled thereafter: a series of (computer-generated) indexes could be stored on the disk (and cross-indexed up to several thousand pages if required). The user would then refer to the disk as he would to a picture book, finding the required image via the indexes. Nor is this all: the sound track on such a disk could be used to carry textual information; and a section of the disk could carry some 'software logic' — perhaps in the form of a series of menus whereby the user could be directed toward relevant indexes or groups of images.

Basic Desirable Standards

As computing becomes more widespread, so standards of various kinds become the more desirable. The snag is that there are different kinds of standards. Some of those I suggest below might help ensure the success of particular projects, while others should help ensure easy access to the data they store.

The aim of all standards is the preservation of the data. If projects in whatever fields are to to share data, then some standards are unavoidable. Naturally, they apply to all projects, and not just to those in the History of Art.

Note also that very few of what I suggest below as ground rules or requirements relate to specific machines or packages. However, careful attention to rules such as these will allow us to dismiss a considerable number of packages precisely because they run on only one type of machine; hence, by choosing more popular configurations, we can make data potentially accessible to a wider number of users. If account is not taken of the desire of future users to access useful databases remotely, and perhaps to download data, then whatever package is selected may not ultimately be suitable.

Requirements: Hardware and Operating System
Advice on these matters is easy to give, but apparently difficult to follow, because many projects are already committed in one way or another to certain kinds of hardware, software or operating system. What follows is therefore ideal — for projects which are free to follow reason rather than custom:

1. If the project is to be restricted to one machine (although I doubt that it can be), then use a popular machine, which is well established, well thought of, and with plenty of software other than database software.
2. Use a machine which is easily upgradable — or, for preference, one which runs the same Operating System on several sizes of the same machine.
3. Use a popular operating system. There are arguments in favour of UNIX, not only because of the tools and facilities it offers, but also because the computing community is working towards a standard, based on UNIX Sys-V, which will shortly subsume ULTRIX (the DEC offering) as well as the very popular Berkeley 4·2. Similarly XENIX (the IBM-PC micro O/S) will also soon be brought to conform with Sys-V. Hence UNIX Sys-V may turn out to be the nearest the computing world has yet approached to a standard operating system.
4. If the projects are sufficiently large or elaborate, we should consider using several machines of different sizes, to cater for institutions large and small, and also for individuals. If we do this, then it follows that our database software must run across a range of machines, and allow all the data, or sub-sets of it, to be freely interchanged across the whole range of machines.

Requirements: Database Software

1. The database should use the relational model. Any attempt to structure a database hierarchically will produce a monolith which is difficult to manage and almost impossible to change.

   On the other hand, a relational database may be thought of as a collection of separate files which are only brought together when one particular user wishes to interrogate one or more of them. Hence different interests can be catered for, and different suites of files developed by different groups of people. The place for rigour is in deciding which package to use: relational software is user-friendly enough to ensure that all tastes can be catered for.

2. The package must run on more than one make of machine; and, perhaps, be available over more than one operating system.
3. The package must come complete with a set of easy-to-use tools which will allow the amateur to create, run and maintain his own database.
4. The query language should be non-procedural, rather than procedural (i.e. of the SQL variety).
5. No specially commissioned software should be needed to make the database system work, as this would tend to introduce non-standard elements into the system.

Data Standards

I have made no mention in the above of data standards. But there is, of course, little point in trying to preserve data long-term without them, at least in networking environments where information can be interchanged freely. In comparison with data standards, it can be argued that all others — machine, operating system and software — are unimportant preciely because they are simply short-term solutions to the basic problem of the preservation of data.

After all, one point of computerisation is to get the data into a form suitable for potential use by many people; and because the data are so much more important than the hardware or software involved at any one moment, the real target of any standardisation must be the preservation of the data. This might sound very obvious: but the point should help clarify the reasons for not tying the data structures into any specific hardware/software configuration — at least without the possibility of easily disentangling them.

Networking

Networking (in its widest sense) is the key to success in large database projects. Indeed, although structuring of the data may well present some problems which we might need to discuss with software producers, the matter of getting the information to those who wish to use it is absolutely crucial.

Luckily, the computing world needs networking more and more, just as it requires software that is easy to use: more and more, the ordinary user can manipulate his own (and remote) data thanks to the ease of use of such 'software tools'.

Requirements for Data Interchange (Networking)

1. As already stated, versions of the software package should be available on more than one size of machine.
2. Networking software should be readily available which allows communication between mainframe, mini and micro computers. In other words, the mainframe running the big database must be accessible without trouble to common terminal protocols. Note that plenty of terminal emulation packages are now available.
3. Following on from (2), but at a greater level of sophistication, a

package should be chosen which either runs across a series of machine sizes (thereby allowing the transfer of sets or sub-sets of the data), or which is accessible to one of the stand-alone products which interfaces micro database packages with their mainframe big brothers. It is possible, for example, to send a query in dBASEII language from a micro to a mainframe, where it will be submitted in batch mode to a mainframe database; the necessary data is then extracted, sent back down the line, and used to populate dBASEII files. The process is transparent to the user.

Both these are trends which everyone interested in the flexible use of remote databases must take into account, as they are bound to develop quickly and to become widespread within five years.

4. Note that, properly exploited, networking software can abolish the need for any large, central and monolithic database: whole sets of files can be created, stored and maintained in different locations (with relevant specialisms), to be accessed, manipulated and even downloaded by users onto their own machine for further processing. Of course, this can be done only if the relational model of database is followed.

Conclusion

If this paper has dealt more with problems than with achievements, and more of possibilities than of actualities, this reflects the endemic state of the computer industry — and the excitement which is one of its attractions. More is always on offer than is delivered (at least at an affordable price); and it is the misfortune of Art History that it needs graphics for its computerisation projects to function effectively and efficiently.

Two questions arise naturally from this state of affairs:

—is a decision on standards to be taken following rational discussion, or will one be imposed by the *de facto* success of a certain group of protocols or (perhaps) projects?

—although we must all agree that transmission standards are paramount if any sense is to be made of networks, is it really the case that we can look forward to orchestration of projects at the level we would need for adequate data standards?

Whatever we do today, the important things are the data: if they can be gathered and preserved with as few structuring decisions as possible, then succeeding generations can do what they will with them. But if we impose our view and hence our structure on them, we will tend to tie the data to specific systems of computer software so closely that disentangling them will prove difficult. We will thereby reduce room for manoeuvre in the future.

Using a Computer to Analyse Late Sixteenth-Century Household Accounts

Part 1: Historical Aspects (Nesta Evans)

This is a brief report of a project generously funded by the ESRC, and forms part of a wider study by Dr A. Hassell Smith of the University of East Anglia of a north Norfolk community in the late sixteenth and early seventeenth centuries.

*   *   *

Nathaniel Bacon was the second son of Sir Nicholas, Lord Keeper to Elizabeth I. In 1569, when he was about 25 years old, he married Anne Gresham, the illegitimate daughter of Sir Thomas. The two fathers jointly provided the couple with an estate on the north Norfolk coast, mainly in the parishes of Langham, Morston and Stiffkey. In 1575 Nathaniel began the building of Stiffkey Hall and moved into the still unfinished house two years later. The account books discussed in this paper all fall within the decade 1587–97, although not all span the entire ten years. They are the household steward's expenditure book and his receipts, an estate yard account and lastly a book kept by the acaterer or kitchen steward. The accounts kept by the bailiff of the estate yard deal with building work and estate maintenance, but not with agriculture. Nathaniel Bacon farmed a large part of his estate and it seems that the farm bailiff's accounts are missing; so also, it would appear, are a wages book kept by the acaterer and Nathaniel's own private accounts.

The papers of Nathaniel Bacon of Stiffkey form a large and varied collection, some of which are suitable for computerisation. In particular this is true of his household and estate accounts, which offer the opportunity of an in-depth study not only of the household which lived at Stiffkey Hall but also of the community of which this house was the centre for a period of some thirty years. This is not the place for a survey of Bacon's complex accounting system, but suffice it to say that although some departmental accounts are missing there is sufficient material for what is probably a unique portrayal and understanding of a squire-dominated rural estate.

The first three figures printed here are: an example of the final form of the data in a print-out with each field labelled; parts of three sections of the classification codes, of which more later; and a brief illustration of the activities of one individual — Thomas Crumlin, Nathaniel's horsekeeper.

The very length and richness of these documents presented problems which it seemed only a computer could solve. The process of inputting the data almost certainly took considerably longer than writing the entries on

Figure 1 *Printout of data in final form*

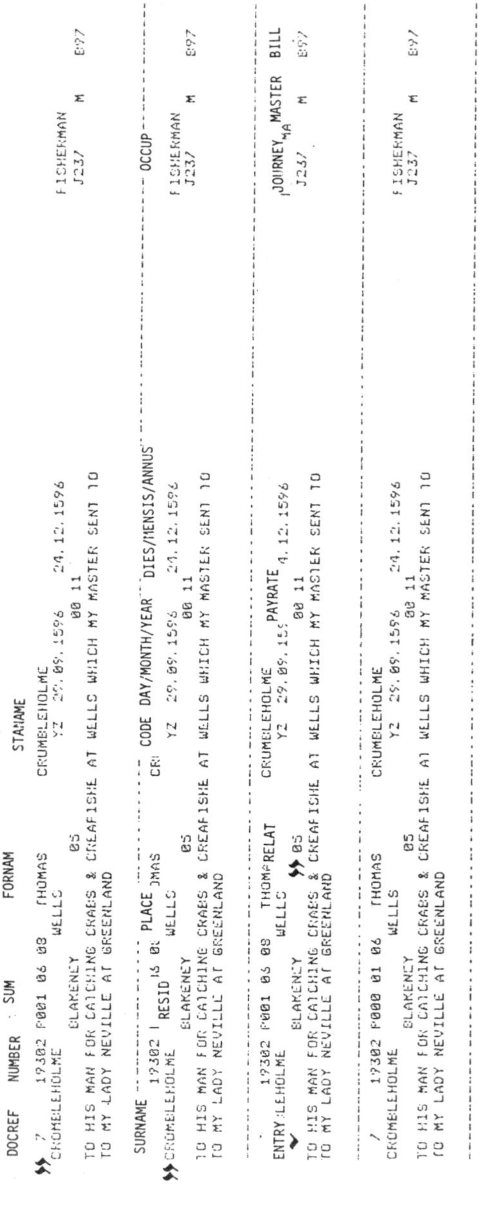

```
DOCREF    NUMBER   SUM          FORNAM              STANAME
 7        19302 P001 06 08   THOMAS          CRUMBLEHOLME
CROMBLEHOLME              WELLS               YZ  29.09.1596    24.12.1596           FISHERMAN
                BLAKENEY            05                          00 11                  J237    M    B97
TO HIS MAN FOR CATCHING CRABS & CREAFISHE AT WELLS WHICH MY MASTER SENT TO
TO MY LADY NEVILLE AT GREENLAND

SURNAME ------------- PLACE ------------- CODE DAY/MONTH/YEAR  DIES/MENSIS/ANNUS ------------- OCCUP ------------
          19302 P RESID 06 08  THOMAS          CRUMBLEHOLME
CROMBLEHOLME              WELLS               YZ  29.09.1596    24.12.1596           FISHERMAN
                BLAKENEY            05                          00 11                  J237    M    B97
TO HIS MAN FOR CATCHING CRABS & CREAFISHE AT WELLS WHICH MY MASTER SENT TO
TO MY LADY NEVILLE AT GREENLAND
-------------------------------------------------------------------------------------------------------------
          19302 P001 06 08   THOMA RELAT     CRUMBLEHOLME
ENTRY LEHOLME             WELLS               YZ  29.09.159 PAYRATE 4.12.1596        JOURNEY MA MASTER  BILL
                BLAKENEY            05                          00 11                  J237    M    B97
TO HIS MAN FOR CATCHING CRABS & CREAFISHE AT WELLS WHICH MY MASTER SENT TO
TO MY LADY NEVILLE AT GREENLAND
-------------------------------------------------------------------------------------------------------------
 7        19302 P000 01 06   THOMAS          CRUMBLEHOLME
CROMBLEHOLME              WELLS               YZ  29.09.1596    24.12.1596           FISHERMAN
                BLAKENEY            05                          00 11                  J237    M    B97
TO HIS MAN FOR CATCHING CRABS & CREAFISHE AT WELLS WHICH MY MASTER SENT TO
TO MY LADY NEVILLE AT GREENLAND
-------------------------------------------------------------------------------------------------------------
```

Figure 2   *Classification codes*

CODE		SUBJECT SECTION
FA	Dairy and Cheese chamber, expenses, equipment, etc.	Household: Service Court
FB	Floor coverings; buying/cutting materials, e.g. marram, grass, reeds, rushes; rush mats	Household: Furniture and Furnishings
FC	Carting/carrying, non-agricultural	Travel and Transport
FD	Cutting and maintenance of the river	Agriculture: Estate Maintenance
FE	Lawer (laver), planting hedges, making fences	" "
FH	Hopyard work	Agriculture: Activities
FJ	Haymaking, including contract mowing, all activities and if context indicates though work is unspecified	Agriculture: Activities
FK	Labourer, agricultural and building, undefined	Agriculture: Activities and Building: Work
HA	Household expenses for rented house and lodgings in Norwich	Household: General
HB	Brewery and bakehouse	Household: Utensils, etc.
HC	Cheese, butter, cream, purchases (see LG, sales)	Household: Provisions
HD	Chickens,. hens, capons (see HT below) purchases	Household: Provisions
HE	Fresh Fruit and Vegetables, nuts, etc.	Household: Provisions
HF	Wildfowl	Household: Provisions
HG	Pigs	Household: Provisions
HI	Fresh fish	Household: Provisions
JA	Assizes, quarter sessions, Sheriff's turn	Administration: Public
JC	Customs payments	Administration: Public
JD	Duchy of Lancaster, business and expenses	Administration: Public
JH	Estate administration, eg. surveying	Administration: Personal
JL	Legal Affairs	Administration: Personal
JM	Manor court business	Administration: Personal
JN	Militia rates/administration, impressing	Administration: Public
JO	Law and order	Administration: Public
JP	Privy seal business, loan collecting	Administration: Public
JR	Commissions, special and unspecified, Kirk's patent, meetings of JP's	Administration: Public

Figure 3   *The activities of Thomas Crumlin*

```
TO THE HORSEKEEPER FOR SHOEINGE OF THE HORSES WHEN THE CHYLDREN WENT HOME
-------------------------------------------------------------------------
    4    5590 POUD HO 10  +THOMAS      +CRUMLIN
CRUMLINN       +NORWICH             8R  29.09.1587   24.12.1587    HORSE KEEPER
                                                                 +  J005
TO HIM FOR 2.5 FOOTE OF PAVEING TYLE
-------------------------------------------------------------------------
    4    5591 POUD HO 06  +THOMAS      +CRUMLIN
CRUMLINN       +NORWICH             2W  29.09.1587   24.12.1587    HORSE KEEPER
                                                                 +  J005     L
TO HIM FOR A NOOKYH FOR MY MISTRESS
-------------------------------------------------------------------------
    4    5592 POUD H6 HO  +THOMAS      +CRUMLIN
CRUMLINN       +NORWICH             CL  29.09.1587   24.12.1587    HORSE KEEPER
                                                                 +  J005
TO HIM FOR 6 TRUSSES OF HAYE FOR THE HORSES
-------------------------------------------------------------------------
    4    5643 PODO 13 04   THOMAS      CRUMLIN
CRUMLINN                            8R  25.12.1587   24.03.1588   +HORSE KELPER IN NB'S HM
TO THOMAS CRUMLINN FOR HIS QUARTERS WAGES
-------------------------------------------------------------------------
    4    5918 PODO H3 HO   THOMAS      +CRUMLIN
CRUMLINN       +NORWICH             JA  25.12.1587   24.03.1588
                                                                   J011
TO MARTYN & HIM FOR THERE DYET 3 MEALES AT NORWICH WEEKE AFORE LENT SESSIONS
-------------------------------------------------------------------------
    4    5868 PODO H7 04  +THOMAS      CRUMLIN
CRUMLINN       BRANDON FERRY         EH  14.01.1588   14.01.1588   HORSE KEEPER
                                                                   J010      803
FOR HORSEMEAT AT BRANDEN FERDYE GOEINGE TO LONDON
-------------------------------------------------------------------------
    4    5869 PODO HO 08  +THOMAS      CRUMLIN
CRUMLINN       BRANDON FERRY         EH  14.01.1588   14.01.1588   HORSE KEEPER
                                                                   J010      803
FOR FROSTINGE THE HORSES THERE +AT BRANDON
-------------------------------------------------------------------------
    4    5870 PUDO H2 03  +THOMAS      CRUMLIN
CRUMLINN       NEWMARKET             EH  15.01.1588   15.01.1588   HORSE KEEPER
                                                                   J010      803
FOR HORSEMEAT AT NEWMARKET
-------------------------------------------------------------------------
    4    5871 PUDO H5 03  +THOMAS      CRUMLIN
CRUMLINN       BARKWAY              EH  15.01.1588   15.01.1588   HORSE KEEPER
                                                                   J010      803
```

index cards would have done, but the gain in speed of information retrieval was so enormous that the extra time spent on the earlier stage was fully justified. The time taken to search thousands of index cards for the answer to a simple query would have made the whole project impracticable; once the data was in a computer answers could be found in a matter of seconds. It also became possible to embark on more complex enquiries and relationships than would have been feasible with a card index. There is not space to illustrate fully the wealth of information that can be extracted from this very large database, and only a few examples can be given here. It is possible to discover which of the household servants travelled with their master or on their own and where they went to; social connections can be traced through visits and the giving and receiving of presents; and by analysing the pattern of shopping economic relationships can be established.

On the advice of my university's computer centre, a package called DATATRIEVE was chosen as best suited to the purpose by its flexibility and ease of use by a non-specialist. The inputting process was simplified because the data did not have to be placed in fixed fields at this stage; editing was also straightforward. An added advantage of DATATRIEVE is that it is possible to modify data after it has been converted into fixed field format.

In addition to converting the accounts into a form suitable for sorting and selection by computer, it seemed desirable to retain the original wording of the manuscripts. By so doing anyone using the database can refer to the account book entries as they appear in the documents. By sorting on the field NUMBER (each entry in the account book has an individual number) it is also possible to reconstitute the manuscripts.

Data preparation was relatively simple as coding was avoided as far as possible; names of persons, places and occupations were not coded. The most important code is a two-letter one used to classify the account book entries, and this is the principal means of sorting and selecting the data. There are a total of 230 two-letter codes and they are divided into 12 subject sections. It may well be felt that this is too many, but with such an enormous variety of subject matter in very long documents there was really no alternative. Figure 2 shows some of the codes in the sections dealing with the household, farming and administration and this gives a good idea of the way in which coding has been used. All the surnames were given a standard form to facilitate sorting, but each name was also entered as spelt in the manuscripts to avoid either splitting one person into two or conflating two or more individuals.

Undoubtedly the project has made easily available a wide range of information not only about the Bacon household and its neighbourhood, but also concerning a considerable variety of topics such as farming, the laying out of a garden, money lending, and travelling by Nathaniel and his servants. One of the most important results of the analysis is the interdependence of a gentry household, its immediate estate and its wider neighbourhood. For this we have to thank the meticulous detail with which the Bacon accounts were kept, as much as the powerful tool provided by a computer database.

The ESRC grant was only half what was requested, but nevertheless the result has been a manageable finite project, although there was no time to computerise other classes of documents in the Bacon collection, and the account books were selected just because they most easily lent themselves to this treatment. Documents, such as manorial court rolls, which do not have such a consistent format present far greater problems, but there are two other manuscript sources which could well lend themselves to computer analysis. These are the recognisance books recording Nathaniel Bacon's work as an active J.P., and the numerous field books or surveys of Stiffkey and of Langham and Morston, the two neighbouring parishes in which much of Bacon's estate lay. This raises the problem of trying to compare and amalgamate data from different sources. The format used for the account books would not be suitable as it stands for any other class of document, although it might be possible at least to ensure nominal linkage. Had the original intention been to create a database containing different types of manuscripts, then a different approach would have been necessary and the whole project would have been much more complex. Having regard to the limitations imposed by the time available to complete the project, it seemed best to concentrate on what appeared to be the most rewarding and unusual set of documents, which fortunately most easily lent themselves to computerisation.

Finally, historians using computers learn by their mistakes and the data they use can present intractable problems. If I were about to embark on this project again I think it would be possible to devise a more flexible scheme, but on the other hand this project has achieved what it set out to accomplish: a sophisticated means of analysis in preparation for a study of an early modern community through the account books of its resident gentleman. In about two years' time the database will be available to others. Enquiries should be addressed to Dr A. Hassell Smith, Centre of East Anglian Studies, University of East Anglia, Norwich, NR4 7TJ.

Part 2: Computing aspects (P. Anstey)

The University of East Anglia computing service has assisted with the computational side of the project. The reason for this involvement is that major projects of this nature can absorb embarrassingly large amounts of cpu in complicated retrieval searches, whilst the data itself may well occupy many times more disk space than that allowed for the vast majority of projects, university wide. There is, then, a special onus on such projects to make *responsible* and *economical* use of the resources made available through the central computing service.

Although the computing service at UEA keeps a watching brief on every large computing project, it has not the manpower resources for direct practical involvement in them all. However, since this was the first major computer based project to be undertaken by members of this part of the university, it was felt important to be involved not only to ensure sensible use of resources but also because a certain amount of specific practical guidance in computing was clearly appropriate whilst expertise was acquired. The amount of direct assistance was initially substantial, but has been slowly reduced as the project has proceeded. Those involved have been encouraged to become self-sufficient, and now receive support comparable to that available to any other members of the university research community.

When considering the use of resources, the error in looking only to cpu and disk resources must be emphasised. Regrettably, UK academic computing services often tend to do so because these are the resources for which they actually pay, and which they have to distribute equitably amongst their user community — usually with no expectation of income from the projects concerned. But there is a third valuable resource to take into account, that of human endeavour: labour and time expended in developing and using the computing systems. Clearly, a right balance has to be struck between *all* the resources involved, and the role of the computing service in this project was, amongst other things, to help achieve the appropriate balance for our situation.

The approach adopted in this project can be best described by considering first the data itself, then the software used to ask questions of it, and finally by describing the overall scheme used.

First, the data — or rather the nature of the data. The source material, as indicated in Part 1 of this paper, is in a series of account books, and the requirement was to set up the equivalent material in a computer-held file. However, the computer based version was to include additional information . . . a reference number for each entry, and explicit data relating to that entry. This could come from the entry itself, or from external evidence. The overall form is illustrated by Figure 4, where each line represents a single account book record.

The tabular form of the data immediately suggests the use of a database; but a resource problem arises because the account book entries vary enormously in length. Whilst within a fixed field length arrangement small amounts of wasted space in some fields can be tolerated (e.g. because of the variation in lengths of surnames in a surname field), the waste of space if the ENTRY field was set to the maximum length of text (650 characters) would

Figure 4   *The basic form of the data*

Entry ref. no.	32 entry related fields	Account book text (up to 650 chars.)
	xxxxxxx xxxx... ...xxx	xxxxxxxx
(a)	xxxxxxx xxxx... ...xxx	xxxxxxxxxxxxxxxxxxxxxxxxxxxxx
	xxxxxxx xxxx... ...xxx	xxxxx
(b)	xxxxxxx xxxx... ...xxx	xxxxxxxxxxxxxxxxx
	xxxxxxx xxxx... ...xxx	xxxxxxxxxxx
	xxxxxxx xxxx... ...xxx	xxxxxxx

Figure 5   *Use of database and overflow files to accommodate the data represented in Figure 4*

Database file:

	Entry ref. no.	32 entry related fields	Text field, called ENTRY (first 80 chars. only)	Cont. marker
	xxxxxxx	xxxx... ...xxx	xxxxxxxx	
(a)	xxxxxxx	xxxx... ...xxx	xxxxxxxxxxxx	+
	xxxxxxx	xxxx... ...xxx	xxxxx	
(b)	xxxxxxx	xxxx... ...xxx	xxxxxxxxxxxx	+
	xxxxxxx	xxxx... ...xxx	xxxxxxxxxxx	
	xxxxxxx	xxxx... ...xxx	xxxxxxx	

Overflow file:

	Entry ref. no.	Rest of the text (char. 81 onwards)
(a)	xxxxxxx	xxxxxxxxxxxxxx
(b)	xxxxxxx	xxxx

be enormous since the text for most entries was substantially shorter.

An alternative approach would have been to use variable length records. However, for rapid access to particular records — which is clearly important when interrogating data — use of an indexed file is required. Since indexed files are based on fixed field lengths, the use of fixed length records was inescapable.

The solution adopted is illustrated in Figure 5. A fixed field length of 80 characters was set for the ENTRY field so that it would accommodate the full text in a majority of the cases, and the bulk of the text in many other cases. This length was determined by inspection, and the data entry system arranged so that the ENTRY field was automatically chopped if necessary at that length. In such cases (represented by lines (a) and (b) in Figures 4 and 5) the software continues by entering a marker in an additional single character field on the end of the database file record, and putting that record's reference number and the remainder of the text for that entry into an 'overflow' file. The overflow file contains only records associated with long entries, and so is a fraction of the size of the main database file.

Having discussed the data itself, the means of interrogating it must now be considered. When the project started, there was the choice between writing project specific programs (as had been done in a much smaller, earlier project), or using FAMULUS (which has become a fairly standard academic information retrieval system), or using DATATRIEVE, an information retrieval system marketed by DEC and which was already available on the VAX computer at UEA. For ease of use and potential system efficiency DATATRIEVE was chosen, although in fact only a subset of its facilities have been used.

DATATRIEVE can work in conjunction with DEC's database management systems, or directly with 'ordinary' system files. Such a database management system was not available at UEA at the time, so to speed up data access an indexed or 'keyed' file was used, as described earlier. Initially, in view of the uncertainty in the range of questions to be asked of the data, a highly keyed database file was set up to give a wide variety of moderately fast access paths. However, because file size increases substantially with the number of keys, the final specification of three keys was a compromise giving rapid access for the most likely types of question, whilst keeping the file to an acceptable size.

The foregoing gave rise to a complete software system, as follows:

The data entry procedure consists of several basic steps (see Figure 6). The set of data to be added is entered into a simple serial file, with the contents of the various fields in a record separated by slashes. Then follows a somewhat limited computer-based validation. If this proves satisfactory then the next stage expands the fields to their required lengths and creates files ready to add into the database and overflow files. Upon the satisfactory completion of that stage, the new data is actually added in. This multi-stage procedure might seem complicated, but apart from the unavoidable labour of the entry of the raw data, it is a question only of issuing a command for each stage and checking the outcome.

This approach is simple to use and both faster and more resource efficient than using DATATRIEVE's prompted entry mode, which, in common with standard forms input programs, would not in any case have directly coped with the overflow data in the case of long account book entries.

Having entered some data, questions can be asked of it. In DATATRIEVE this is a simple task using a stylised form of English, as illustrated in Figure 7, where the example query extracts all database entries where the standardized surname (STANAME) field contains CRUMLIN and the YEAR field contains 1596. With a little practice, the user can work out how to form even

Figure 6   *The data entry procedure*

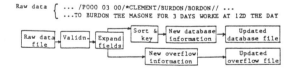

Figure 7   *Querying the database*

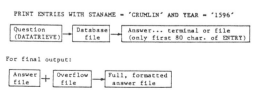

quite complicated queries and be fairly certain of being correct. This is important, because it leaves the user to think about the history rather than the niceties of computing. The simpler questions could be asked of the data online, but larger or more complicated requests were run in the batch stream. This has been perfectly acceptable to the project.

The answers produced have in some cases revealed further information relating to other records in the database; in such cases, the values of the appropriate fields have been modified accordingly, using DATATRIEVE directly.

As also illustrated in Figure 7, the querying using DATATRIEVE produces answers based only on the database file, without reference to the overflow file containing the ends of the (relatively few) long account book texts. This is usually satisfactory for day-to-day working, but when final outputs are required, the results of the relevant DATATRIEVE query must be stored in a file and then read by a simple post-processing program which incorporates the overflow file data as appropriate, and formats the output in a style suitable for listing on a 132 column line printer.

Although the above description of the overall system might make it seem rather complicated, in practice the system has served the project well. It is moderately efficient with respect to cpu and disk resource, and so satisfies the computing service, without sacrificing much in terms of ease of use — which is clearly important if the computer is to *serve* the project, as opposed to being the major focus of attention.

In conclusion, the question should be asked: 'would the computational aspects of the project be tackled in exactly the same way again?' Since the project started, the UEA computing service has acquired a relational database system, which could be used in its own right or in conjunction with DATATRIEVE. Also, the computing service has explored more of DATATRIEVE itself, and other possibilities arise. So the answer is 'probably not'. However, the aim of this paper is not primarily to give a description of 'the ideal system' because 'ideal' is relative to the cost of the various resources to hand. Rather, it is to leave a consciousness of computer and human resource, and a plea to use all of these responsibly, based on the fullest knowledge available at the time, as in this study of late sixteenth century household accounts.

Using the Data Base Management System SIR to Link Political Data from Viana de Castelo, Minho, Portugal, 1827–95

1. Introduction

In the last 500 years migration has had a major influence on the demographic structure of Portugal. During this time it has been subject to large fluctuations. Starting initially as an integral part of colonisation of Portugal's overseas territories,[1] migration escalated in the nineteenth century as it did in most European societies. Estimates from the evidence provided by Ferenczi and Wilcox (1929) suggest that between 1855 and 1895 over 550,000 people (of a population which increased from 3·5 to 4·5 million during the same period), left Portugal for America — usually Brazil.

As the nineteenth century progressed return migration became an increasingly important phenomenon throughout Europe. Remittances from emigrants had always had an influence on the economy of Portugal but in the late nineteenth century the economy of northern Portugal in particular was influenced by the *Brasileiros*, native born Portuguese who emigrated to Brazil to make their fortune and returned to Portugal displaying their success. Popular thought was that every peasant family produced at least one *Brasileiro*.[2]

Return migration among the elite has not been studied extensively, in particular with respect to its levels, its impact on the economy, and the demographic structure of the migrants. This paper considers population change in the city of Viana do Castelo, which is situated on the banks of the river Lima in the province of Minho in north-west Portugal, to examine levels and trends in nineteenth-century migration, particularly among the elite. The centre of Viana consisted of the two parishes of Santa Maria Maior da Matriz and Nossa Senhora de Monserrate. A prosperous trading community existed in Santa Maria Maior, the larger of the two, while fishing activities were housed in Monserrate. Data are examined from three sources; militia listings drawn up between 1827 and 1833, electoral rolls compiled annually from 1834 to 1895 and census data from the Portuguese censuses of 1864 and 1878. Each of these sources has some drawbacks and a specific aim of the paper is to examine the use of electoral rolls and militia lists in the reconstruction of demographic patterns in a historical society.

2. Data

This section will describe the data on which this paper is based, and the methods and software that have been used in their storage, coding, and subsequent retrieval. These data are drawn from three sources; the militia listing of 1827–1833, the electoral rolls of 1834 to 1895 and the censuses of 1864 and 1878.

2·1 The militia lists

Militia lists have been drawn up in Portugal since the seventeenth century. The lists drawn up between 1827 and 1833 under the influence of Dom Miguel were governed by the precise militia legislation of 1812. They are household listings, each covering one Company of a District; a purely military division of the land. Where more than one hearth existed in a house, each was distinguished by a letter of the alphabet.

The military District of Viana comprised twelve Companies: four in the town itself, one including one road of Santa Maria Maior and the whole of the parish of Meadella (about 1km to the east of the town, up the Lima valley), and the rest covering other surrounding parishes also to the north of the river. The First Company covered the commercial centre of the Santa Maria Maior; an area enclosed by the old town walls, the Third Company covered the area of Monserrate bordering the river; including the fishing community, and the Second and Fourth Companies covered most of the rest of the town.

First, the militia listings include all males. Second, females who could affect a male's liability for recruitment (wives, and single or widowed mothers) are included. Third, since every household had to be registered, female heads of households where no males resided are also recorded. Thus, only single and widowed females who were not heads of households and did not have male children do not appear. Name, marital status, date of birth (or age in years), place of birth, and father's name are consistently recorded for each male inhabitant, whereas, only name and marital status are generally recorded for females. Any further information relevant to potential military service could be entered at a later date by the scribe in an observations column. Such information typically included changes of address within and between military divisions, departure elsewhere, and death.

These extra observations, together with information on individuals entering the list after its initial creation were written in different inks by clerks with different styles of handwriting, often making it possible to distinguish between them.

The quality of reporting varies greatly from one list to another. For example, the lists for Santa Maria Maior and Monserrate have very different formats and record different data. Also, whereas as many as 6 different inks and styles of handwriting are discernible on the Santa Maria Maior listings, there are only 3 on those of Monserrate.

2·2 The electoral rolls

Between 1834 and 1895, electoral rolls were drawn up in most years. This paper considers 43 rolls drawn up in the years 1834–36, 1840, 1842–47,

1849–67, 1870–78, 1880–81, 1883, 1894–95.

In order to have appeared on a particular electoral roll, an individual must have both met the criteria stipulated in the electoral legislation pertaining to that year, and have been recognised to have met those criteria by the body drawing up the roll. In other words, inclusion in electoral rolls will have been subject not only to the legislation, but also to an individual's circumstances.

The information recorded varies from roll to roll, according to the legislation. Name, age, marital status and occupation are recorded on every roll (except that marital status was not recorded in 1840), together with one or more indicators of income (either direct or indirect). Road of residence is recorded on the first three rolls. A number of other observations such as literacy, whether the elector is the head of a household, whether he is eligible to be elected, whether he has performed jury service, etc., appear at various times during the period.

This paper uses only the 5 most important items of information for each individual electoral entry; name, age, marital status, occupation and place of birth.

2·3 Problems arising with the manuscript sources

In this section, the problems arising in the use of data from manuscript sources are illustrated and discussed, focusing on the discriminatory power available for Record Linkage.

First, the orthography of Portuguese had not yet been standardised in the nineteenth century, names were often abbreviated, and certain characters were interchangeable at certain times. At the same time, it was not uncommon for someone to change his own name, either by dropping a name, adding a name, or even swapping two names around. As an example, consider the following three names, which all refer to the same individual; Antonio Jose de Sousa Basto:

> Ant.º J.ᵉ de Sz.ᵃ B.º
> Antonio Jose de Sousa
> Antonio de Sousa Basto

Occupation and place of birth data suffered the same problems as the recording of names, and, in addition, were often ambiguously abbreviated.

Second, age recording was very inaccurate in the early electoral rolls, where a discrepancy between the ages recorded for one person in adjacent years of up to 10 or 12 years was not unusual. By the 1870's, however, the rolls were being 'updated' from the previous year, reducing the problem enormously.

Third, the clerk drawing up an electoral roll often used ditto marks where a number of persons appearing together in the roll had the same marital status. This obviously led to many errors, and care was taken to allow for this in the record linkage, and the analyses of the linked data.

Fourth, a rather more subtle problem arises in that a person may be recorded as having different occupations or places of birth in two years, whereupon closer examination of the data reveal that the two descriptions are not contradictory. As a trivial example, someone born in the parish of Santa Maior was also born in the town of Viana.

2·4 Data Entry and Storage

In order to retain the data in its original form without altering the structure of the manuscript sources, and to allow any item of information to be traced back to its source document, each set of information relating to one individual on a particular document (individual-entry) was given a unique identifier (the number of the individual entry; NID), coded according to the nature of the document, the year in which it was drawn up, the parish to which it related, and the position of the information within the document. This coding is such that if data are sorted by NID, they will automatically be sorted first within a document, then by parish, next in time, and, finally by type of document.

Initial experiments used a BASIC input program, run on the BBC, which could be used by someone with little computer experience. However, with limited resources, it was found to be far more efficient for an experienced researcher to enter the data one variable at a time. In general, textual data were entered into the WORDWISE word processing package available on the BBC, and later transferred to the mainframe, while numerical data was entered directly onto mainframe computer files. Only information on marital status was coded, and then in such a way as to be able to distinguish, for example, between persons explicitly recorded as married and those who were not.

Currently, there are 2407 militia records, and 19,582 electoral records stored on the mainframe, with offline backup files, each of which uses about 37 Mbytes of space.

2·5 The Software Requirements for Record Linkage

In order to enable records to be linked both within and between documents for subsequent analyses, several operations must be possible. First, and foremost, the data should be easily accessible for editing and, later, analysis. Second, it must be possible to transform or code the data in order to eliminate the simpler types of variation, such as spelling. Third, the comparison of one or more variables from each record should be a simple process, in order to allow concentration on the more complicated aspects of record linkage. Finally, it must be possible to store the links produced so that the linked data can be efficiently retrieved for subsequent analysis. One way to satisfy these requirements is to store the data in a database. In the rest of this section, the reasons for choosing the Scientific Information Retrieval (SIR) Data Base Management System (DBMS) for the storage, linkage, and retrieval of the Portuguese data will be discussed.

2·6 The Data Base Management System SIR

SIR is a hierarchical database system in its physical form; each record is stored following the record to which it relates. Thus, the unique identifier (NID) for the one individual-entry (a CASE in SIR) will point to several RECORDs concerning that entry, each of which, in turn, may contain several FIELDs (or VARIABLEs). For example, to retrieve the place of birth of the first individual recorded on the 1842 electoral roll of Santa Maria Maior, the CASE 28421001 would be located, then the electoral RECORD it refers to, and finally the place of birth VARIABLE would be extracted.

A major advantage of SIR is that, although it has a hierarchical physical model, one is not restricted to hierarchical access, the logical model of the database allows Hierarchical, Relational and Network access. It is the network facility that is most useful for record linkage; since from any position in the hierarchical physical model, it is possible to re-enter the hierarchy at any other whilst retaining the original position for subsequent continued search.

2·7 Standardisation and Data Coding using SIR

The biggest problem in the computer analysis of manuscript sources is that the bulk of them contain textual variables. It soon becomes apparent that, with each name, occupation, place of birth, etc., appearing many times on various documents, the space saved by coding each variable would be enormous. 'Look-up' tables can be created in SIR by constructing dummy CASEs (with negative NIDs) containing the standardisation tables for names, occupations, and places of birth.

Although this standardisation and coding of data is simply an extension of the way in which marital status is often recorded (ie. Single = 1, Married = 2, Widowed = 3), it simultaneously enables the frequencies of occurrence of each variable to be stored for use in record linkage programs, and allows the data to be processed more efficiently because numerical values for variables are available.

When a name, for example, was read into the database from a raw data file, it was split up into individual words, which were each indexed (for subsequent ease of data retrieval) and their frequencies of occurrence recorded. The individual names were coded and these codes were stored along with their position in the original name. Each word was then 'standardised' using a look-up table, and, finally, the whole name was recreated in its standardised form and given a standardised name code. This code was also indexed such that, on entering a person's name, his individual-entries can be quickly re-located. The result of this procedure is that each case stores one 7 digit number (taking up the space of only 4 characters in its binary form) instead of up to 50 characters.

Essentially similar procedures have been used to store the textual information on occupation, and place of birth.

3. Record Linkage

Much work has now been done on record linkage in historical demography. Although several general approaches and methodologies for efficient record linkage exist, each new study will always have its own peculiarities, and will require its own particular set of priorities in identifying two separate records as pertaining to the same individual. The type of data recorded, the frequency of recording, and the way in which these data were recorded will influence the researcher's choice of algorithm to resolve ambiguities in record linkage while maximising the accuracy of the constructed links. For example, in the electoral rolls of Santa Maria Maior, where age is very inaccurately recorded, it would be senseless to place too much emphasis on age discrepancies, even between rolls drawn up in adjacent years.

3·1 Record Linkage using SIR

The number uniquely identifying each individual-entry (or CASE), the NID, can be used to generate links which are stored in a subordinate record for each case. This record contains the NID of the next individual-entry (LID), and the first individual-entry (FID), of each person. The LID of the last individual-entry of one person is set to equal the FID, so that a chain is formed for each person, the end of which points back to its beginning; thus facilitating data processing. Subsequent identification of some relationship between different individuals can then be achieved by linking two or more chains together.

The FID serves several purposes. First, it enables a chain to be followed from its beginning even if it was entered at some other point. Second, it is possible to determine when the end of a chain has been reached. Third, when processing all the cases in the data base sequentially, and following the chain for each individual at the same time, it enables SIR to determine whether the information on one person has already been processed. Finally, the FID is the identifier used for linking different chains, for example a father's case will point to a record which contains the FID of his eldest son.

Generating links within SIR is a relatively simple task achieved using the report writer, which processes records that have been extracted from the database. The report writer can perform specific actions depending on whether the value of a certain variable remains the same, or changes.

A control variable is created from the variables available in the records to be linked. These variables will have the same value in records to be linked; they can be actual fields in the record or variables computed from the available fields. Numbers, stored in binary, can be converted to character strings. Several variables can then be combined by concatenating them with a delimiter between each one to form a string of up to 251 characters in length. These variables must of course appear in the same order for each record to be linked.

Once the control variable has been chosen on which to perform a linkage, the data to be linked are sorted by that variable, and then by NID in order to ensure that individual-entries are ordered in time within a value of the control variable. The links can then be generated using the following simple algorithm:

a)   When a new value of the control variable is encountered, write the NID and store the value for use as the FID.

b)   For each subsequent record with the same value of the control variable, write the NID and FID, followed by the NID alone on the next line.

c)   When the value of the control variable changes again, write the FID twice.

This process will write to a file in the following format, which can then be read back into SIR to form the link records for each individual entry:

a)	NID1	
b)	NID2	FID
	NID2	
b)	NID3	FID
	NID3	
b)	::::	
	::::	
b)	NIDn	FID
	NIDn	
c)	FID	FID

3·2 Approaches to Record Linkage

The major problem in most record linkage exercises is to determine a set of linkage criteria, or a control variable which will maximise the accuracy of the links generated. The choice of control variable will depend primarily on whether the researcher chooses an agglomerative or a divisive approach to record linkage. Then the components of the control variable must be chosen (or created) to be the most 'reliable' variables of the records to be linked.

The agglomerative method involves a gradual reduction of the number of variables contributing to the control variable, and thus relaxing the constraints under which a link is made. This approach is particularly applicable when there is a limit to the number of each type of record for one person, and is therefore being used in the linkage of birth, marriage, and death records. it is possible to control the generation of links when they are read back into the database, so that previous links, generated under more powerful constraints, are not overwritten.

The divisive method begins with just one variable, usually the name, which has been standardised and coded. this code is then used for the first stage of the linkage process. The resultant links are then followed, and any records which are inconsistent under a specified set of criteria, are removed and placed into another chain with a slightly altered standardised name code to allow subsequent linkage by code if necessary.

The operation of joining and separating different chains are fairly complex procedures. In order to join two chains which are non-overlapping, the end of the first can simply be made to point to the beginning of the second, and the FIDs of the second adjusted, otherwise however, one of the chains has to be completely dismantled, and its individual members inserted into the other chain. Similarly, to divide a chain into two non-overlapping sub-chains is quite straightforward, whereas to extract selected members from one chain to form a new chain is more complicated.

3·3 Record Linkage of the Militia Lists

On the one hand, the militia lists for Viana contain some people with more than one entry, who at some point in the period have moved from one household to another within the town (these movements are usually recorded on the list as observations such as 'Passou para Rua Nova de Santa Anna N. 7', although most moves are within the same street, in which case only the new number of the house was recorded). On the other hand, however, the lists include a large number of people (particularly women and young children) who have exactly the same name, and for whom little other information was recorded.

In order to avoid the incorrect linkage of many people therefore, an agglomerative approach was adopted within the militia lists. Links were created manually with the aid of SIR-produced alphabetically sorted lists of individuals and their personal details. As a result, some correct links may not have been made because of the adoption of this approach.

3·4 Record Linkage of the Electoral Rolls
Since the electorate of Viana was drawn from the political elite of the town (about 10% of the population, or 40% of adult males), and the conditions which an individual had to meet in order to become an elector concerned various measures of social and economic status, the information recorded for each person in each year is extensive. At the same time, two electors rarely shared the same name, and when they did, the other available information proved very powerful in differentiating between them. Consequently, a divisive approach was adopted within the electoral rolls.

4. Summary

This paper has addressed a number of methodological issues. It remains for this section to link some of the more important.

Within this context the extent of movement demonstrated amongst a group of society traditionally thought to be less mobile than the poor is considerable. In all periods there was a high level of movement as shown by the militia lists and absence from the electoral rolls. Evidence on permanent migration from electoral rolls must always be scanty as it is not possible to discriminate definitively between migrants, deaths and newly unqualified electors from this source alone. Such discrimination will require the use of ancillary information such as passport lists and death registration.

However, within these constraints the electoral rolls have proved to be useful sources for examining movement. They have the advantage of being a continuous population listing and the quality of collection in Viana permits careful analysis of the characteristics of the electorate over time.

As with all studies of this type the major problem is that of record linkage. The use of SIR, a highly versatile database management system, to store, manipulate, link, and subsequently retrieve data for analysis, thus easing the linkage of militia listings and electoral rolls, has proved very successful.

Notes

1. Joel Serrão, *A Emigração Portuguesa*, Lisbon, 1972.
2. C. B. Brettel, "'Emigrar para Voltar': A Portuguese ideology of return migration", *Papers in Anthropology*, 20, 1979, pp. 1–20.

Manuscript Sources
Lista Geral da Primeira Companhia de Ordenanças do Distrito de Vianna da Terçeira Brigada. Arquivo Municipal, Viana.

Lista Geral Da Terçeira Companhia de Ordenanças do Distrito de Vianna da Terçeira Brigada. Arquivo Municipal, Viana.

Registro da Lista Geral dos individuos do Concelho de Viana para votar na Eleiçao da Camara Municipal; Santa Maria Maior: 1834–1895. Arquivo Municipal e Biblioteca Municipal, Viana.

Bibliography

C. B. Brettel, '"Emigrar para Voltar": A Portuguese ideology of return migration', *Papers in Anthropology*, 20, 1979, pp. 1–20. Manuel Villaverde Cabral, *O desenvolvimento de capitalismo em Portugal no seculo XIX*, Lisbon, 1981, p. 137.

J. Caldas, *Historia de um Fogo Morto*, Porto: Renascença Portuguesa, 1981.

José Crespo, *Monografia de Viana do Castelo*, Câmara Municipal, Viana do Castelo, 1957.

Rui Feijó, 'Liberal Revolution, Social Change and Economic Development in the Region of Viana (Northwestern Portugal) in the First Three Quarters of the Nineteenth Century'. Unpublished Ph.D. thesis, St Antony's College, Oxford.

Imre Ferenczi and W. Wilcox, *National Bureau of Economic Research N14. Internal Migration*, Vol 1, WBER NY, 1929.

Alexandre Herculano, *Opúsculos*, I, Lisbon, 1978, p. 73.

M. A. F. Moreira, *O Porto de Viana do Castelo na Época dos Descobrimentos*, Câmara Municipal, Viana do Castelo, 1984.

M. H. Pereira, *A Política Portuguesa de Emigração (1850–1930)*, Lisbon, 1981.

E. Reis, I. Diamond, D. Doulton and A. Kitts, 'Population Dynamics in Viana do Castelo: the Evidence on Migration from the 1864 and 1878 censuses', presented at the conference on European Port Cities, Liverpool, 1985.

Robert Rowland, 'Âncora E Montaria, 1827: Duas freguesias do Noroeste segundo os livros de registo das Companhias de Ordenanças', in *Estudos Contemporâneos*, 2/3, *Perspectivas sobre o Norte de Portugal*, Porto, 1981.

Joel Serrão, *A Emigração Portuguesa*, Lisbon, 1972.

Abel Viana, *Viana do Castelo, Escorço Monografico*, Viana do Castelo: Aurora do Lima, 1953.

K. W. Wachter, E. A. Hammel and P. Laslett, *Statistical Studies of Historical Social Structure*, Academic Press, 1978.

E. A. Wrigley (ed.), *Identifying People in the Past*, The Chaucer Press, 1972.

Interrogation

28 *Caroline Bourlet and Jean-Luc Minel*

A Declarative System for Setting Up a Prosopographical Database

In our collaboration on a Franco-Canadian project to record the Parisian 'rôles de la taille'[1] or Royal Tax Registers, dating from the end of the thirteenth and the beginning of the fourteenth century, and in view of the interest they hold for the medieval historian, we envisage setting up a prosopographical database for the Parisian craftsmen of the time. Based on the registers, this database would be completed by information from other historical sources of the same period.

The volume of information, 70,000 mentions of individuals concerning a population of 15–20,000 craftsmen, justifies recourse to data processing. But the method of building up this database depends on the characteristics of the documents, as well as on the historian's reasoning as he analyses and exploits them.

Analysis of content of the registers

A certain homogeneity exists throughout these registers. They are in the form of a collection of lists, drawn up according to the taxable categories of society: *gros* and *menus*, Lombards, Jews, the dead. For each list, contributions were made by Parish, the bigger parishes being divided into collections (*les quêtes*). Within these divisions the individuals are grouped by street. The order within the street, even if not strict, corresponds to the topography. The individual is therefore relatively well situated topographically by the registers.

Furthermore, the information concerning the individuals is of the same type: firstname, patronym (that is surname), craft, origin, family or craft relationships. An individual is, therefore, always described, either by his particular personal qualities (*Jehan le talemélier*) or by the distinguishing qualities of his next of kin (*le fils Morise le mareschal*).

Nevertheless, it is necessary to note that this wonderful harmony between the registers hides a number of analytical difficulties. Indeed, our lack of knowledge of the principles of description of individuals generates uncertainty about the real value of the content of these registers, and especially of the distinguishing qualities of the individuals. On the one hand, it is not always easy to decide whether we are faced with reference to a craft or a patronym, and on the other hand, when faced with a patronym derived from a craft, whether or not it applies to a craft actually practiced. These uncertainties imply that the indexing system must be open, allowing several interpretations of the distinguishing qualities, and that the reasoning based on these uncertain criteria be tested. Indeed, should the results of such reasoning prove false, it might be proof that the premises were false (i.e. that the analysis of the information was erroneous).

Comparison of the registers

Other difficulties arise when we compare the information from the various registers with a view to finding all the mentions of a same person. It is not rare to find perfect agreement between all registers (cf. Figure 1). Nevertheless, in the majority of cases, a strong disparity in the information on a same individual or all-too great uniformity in the designation of different individuals, makes comparison difficult.

The five major disparities are due (cf. Figure 2):

—to the absence of certain distinguishing qualities: for example we find in 1298 *Guillaume le Chatelain, orfèvre* and in 1299 *Chatelain l'orfèvre*.

—to orthographical variations: the patronym *de cligny* appears sometime as *de cligni*.

—to the use of diminutives of christian names: *Perrot le flamenc* is also named *Pierre le flamenc*.

—to the use of several patronyms to name a same person: *Guiart de Cligny* is occasionally named *Guiart le pesier*.

—and, finally, to the variation of mentions of craft concerning a same person. *Guiart le pesier* has three crafts: *pesier, marchand de poids* and *avenier*.

Inversely, another source of ambiguity is excessive uniformity (cf. Figure 3). Homonyms occurs frequently for Christian names. Twenty-two first names represent about 60% of the occurrences.[2] Therefore, in more than half the cases, we are faced with an individual named Jean, Guillaume, Pierre, Nicolas, Robert, Richart, Thomas and so on. Homonyms occur as frequently for certain types of patronyms; toponym adjectives (*l'allemand, l'anglais, le breton*), craft surnames (*le talemélier, le tailleur*). In such cases, the help of

Figure 1   *Example of perfect agreement between registers*

```
date       distinguishing qualities       street or group of streets

1296 :  Dame Anes d'acre.............  L'Orberie, pl.S.Michel,
                                        La calandre
1297 :  Dame Agnes d'Acre............  pl. S.Michel, la Calandre
1298 :  Dame Agnes d'Acre............  pl. S.Michel, l'Orberie
1299 :  Dame Agnes d'Acre............  pl. S.Michel
1300 :  Dame Agnes d'Acre............  pl. S.Michel
```

Figure 2   *Examples of disparities*

```
a.  Absence of firstname.

Parish of S.Bartélémy:

1298 :  Guillaume le chastelain, orfèvre
1299 :  Chastelain l'orfèvre

b. orthographical variations in patronyms, use of two different
surnames, variations in crafts.

Parish of S.Madeleine:

1296 :  Guiart le pesier
1297 :  Guiart de clyqni, marcheant de pois
1298 :  Guiart de Cligni, pesier
1299 :  Guiart de cligni, avenier
1300 :  Guiart de cligni, avenier

c.  use of diminutives, variations in patronyms and crafts.

Parish of S.Barthélémy

1296 :  Perrot le flamenc, qui fet escuëlles
1297 :  Perrot le piautrier
1298 :  Perrot le flamenc, piautrier
1299 :  Pierre le flamenc
1300 :  Pierre le flamenc
```

Figure 3   *Example of homonyms*

```
Parish of S.Germain le Vieux:

1296 :  Thomas l'englais, épicier      Petit Pont et Marche Palu
1297 :  Thomas l'englois, cousturier   rue aux Fèves
1298 :  Thomas l'englais, couturier    rue aux Fèves
     :  Thomas l'englais, pareeur      l'Orberie
     :  Thomas l'englais, musnier      l'Orberie
1299 :  Thomas l'englais, mercier      Petit Pont et Marche Palu
     :  Thomas l'englais, couturier    rue aux Fèves
     :  Thomas le musnier              l'Orberie
     :  Thomas l'englais, conreeur     l'Orberie
1300 :  la fame Thomas le mercier      Petit Pont
     :  Thomas l'englais couturier     rue aux Fèves
```

Figure 4   *Example of individuals qualified by family relationship*

```
Parish of S.Bartélémy:

In 1296:
     Phelippe de vitri
     Estienne, son fuiz
     Gencien, son gendre

In 1297:
     Phelippe de vitri
     Estienne, son fuiz
     Gencien, fuiz sa femme

In 1298:
     Estienne de vitri

In 1299:
     Estienne de vitri, drapier
     dame Estienne, fame feu Phelippe de vitry

In 1300:
     Estienne de vitri, drapier
```

topographic information is essential to differentiate the individuals.

When an individual is qualified by a family relationship, the information becomes distinctly more complex and permits the reconstruction of the family ties between the individuals (cf. Figure 4).

In brief, then, the historian has homogeneous data at his disposal: first names, patronyms, crafts, origins, family relationships, which he may compare. His reasoning relies on relatively simple logical bases: equality, compatibility, difference and non-difference (that is everything except difference) or absence. But, uncertain of the exact value of the information, and confronted by a multitude of different configurations to qualify a person, and sometimes by implicit information, the historian, on the one hand, calls upon knowledge outside the corpus (crafts the practice of which is compatible, diminutives derived from a same firstname, reduction rules for the phonetic/orthographic differences), and on the other hand, frequently reuses knowledge acquired during a preceding stage of his reasoning: topographical fluctuations, for example, may render void all attemps to find and connect all occurrences of a same person in the framework of the parish or street. It is, then, the immediate neighbourhood of the individual which permits a decision concerning identification. Finally, it is impossible to define *a priori* a reasoning allowing identification of all (or the majority) of the individuals. The historian is able to lay down a sequence of reasoning which may be applied to a series of cases. But, being unable to master the corpus, he knows better than to judge all the consequences by it. The only solution is therefore to consider the reasoning as an hypothesis and to test it in order to improve and validate it.

Data processing

This project to constitute a meta-file of the *taille* payers from the reign of

Philip the Fair presents special characteristics which often occur in historical processing: the methods for identifying individuals found in several registers are not fixed. The historian counts largely on the initial identification to improve his reasoning, to modify it, adding some criteria for decision making, eliminating others.

For this reason a classical Data Base Management System seemed insufficient to us from the outset. Our experience in handling medieval manuscript databases MEDIUM,[3] convinced us that such a system is efficient and effective, when the method of exploitation of the database has been more or less fixed. It is out of the question to consider modifying the underlying relational schema of the database to fit the wishes of a user.

The possibilities offered by the declarative languages, particularly PROLOG, seem to us to be more adaptable. Our choice was directed towards the PROLOG-CRISS language[4] which, while retaining the declarative properties, permits the management of large clause files (several thousand individuals that we can consider as so many 'facts').

Consequently, we have constructed a system whose architecture is the 'classical' architecture of the expert system:

—the facts base (description of the individuals)
—the rules base (the expert knowledge in declarative form)
—the inference engine (PROLOG language)

The strength of the system is in its flexibility. So, from the point of view of the results of the initial identifications, we added rules, without in any way modifying the existing rules. The formalism of PROLOG is close to the expression of reasoning of the historian which is deductive and comparative. Here is an example of this reasoning.

To identify individuals whose craft is indicated either in the patronym (*Guiart le pesier*) or as a craft after their patronym (*Guiart de cligny, pesier*), the historian would announce a rule of the following form:

Two individuals may be identical if:
—they live in the same street and the same parish
—their first names are identical or compatible
—the craft cited in the surname of one is identical to the craft practiced by the other.

Today some thirty rules allow the identification of some 60% of the basic corpus, using a microcomputer (Micromega 32) and the UNIX system.

In conclusion, after these first attempts using a declarative system, it would seem important to stress two points:

The declarative system, allowing step by step progress, is particularly well adapted to the treatment of uncertain and variable data. Not only does it permit treatment at all stages of the reasoning and validation, but also, where doubt exists concerning the interpretation of certain elements, to validate the analysis of the sources. The system, indeed, indicates how it proceeds when identifying individuals.

Finally, because step-by-step progress (to adapt and change the terms of the rules already laid down, adding to the rules basis) necessitates permanent dialogue between the historian and the informatician, their relationship is transformed. The historian no longer presents 'data ready for treatment' which has already been analysed and fixed. The informatician no longer provides a completed interpretable result which he has treated using methods totaly ignored, or almost, by the researcher. On the contrary, constant exchange between them permits movement towards the others field and acts as a stimulant for the creativity of each.

Notes

1. Seven tax rolls; 1292: Paris, Bibliothèque Nationale, manuscript français 622a. 1296-1300: Paris, Archives Nationales, manuscript KK283. 1313: Paris, Bibliothèque Nationale, manuscript français 6736.

2. In his *Études sur les noms de Personne Français* Karl Michaëlsson examined closely the Christian names occurring in the seven registers. Looking at his frequency tables (pp. 60–2) of the 25 most frequent masculine first names, we took only the 22 first names common to the all registers and calculated that they represent from 59% (1292) to 66·6% (1313) of the incidence.

3. See M.-J. Beaud, A. Guillaumont, J.-L. Minel, 'A Medieval Manuscript DataBase', in Robert P. Allen (ed.), *Data Bases in the Humanities and Social Sciences*, 11, 1985, pp. 22–9.

4. Developed by the *Centre de Recherche en Informatique appliquée aux Sciences Sociales*, Grenoble, France.

29   *Jean-Philippe Genet*

The PROSOP System

The PROSOP system[1] has been developed at Paris by a research group sponsored by the C.N.R.S. and Paris I University (Sorbonne).[2] It has already been described in some detail elsewhere,[3] and I shall give here only a brief description of its main features and draw the attention to some points which may be of general interest. The system has been created for a group of people whose chief research field is medieval prosopography and a detailed survey of the different sets of data dealt with is also available elsewhere:[4] it will be enough to say that the set of data which has been used so far is a bio-bibliographical dictionary of authors having produced texts which may be considered in the broadest sense as historical and political in England between 1300 and 1600 (roughly 1600 biographies of people satisfying the specified criteria, with roughly 200 biographies of people not satisfying these criteria, but included with a discussion of the motives for non-qualification). The idea of PROSOP stemmed from the difficulties I have experienced. My first set of data was processed with a system called B.D.P.4,[5] a slowish but on the whole very satisfying package implemented on a Philips P880 with which it vanished, one gloomy day. I had then to turn to SPSS which, despite its well-known qualities, has no proper facilities for dealing with strings of alphabetical characters, which is quite a drawback in prosopography (names, titles, offices and so on). Had I known S.A.S at the time, things could have been different, but I am not sure. Then, I must confess that the results I exhibited in several talks and seminars did not meet with universal applause. Statistics were thought dull but accepted without comments, and the questions were usually concentrated upon some individuals, or the reliability and identification of the sources; I soon realised that when I said that 47% of the writers were members of the secular clergy in the period 1451–75, I had to be able to say at once who precisely they were, and by which process I had reached this figure.

Clearly, all this meant that a prosopographical study, whatever the sophistication of its statistical apparatus, had to be accommodated by a dictionary easy to read, not coded, but in natural language: therefore, a numerically coded database, though a necessary tool for statistical purposes, is not enough. And once the historical result, so to speak, embodied in the statistical figures has been reached, it is tedious to rewrite the biographies to compile a readable dictionary . . . The only reasonable way of handling prosopographical material is, in fact, to start by writing a dictionary in natural language, and then to extract from such a dictionary a numerically coded database to be statistically studied. And this is what PROSOP is all about, with the added advantage that it is independent from existing packages and transferable onto any mainframe (I.B.M. standards).[6] And since the process is wholly computerised, attention has been paid to the dictionary itself, which may be printed from the tape, and which is used to provide automatically all kinds of information. Then, the dictionary is automatically coded and transformed into a numerically coded matrix which may become either a SAS or SPSS (or any other package) data-base.

These are the different stages which we are going to describe briefly now. We shall take as an example the first page of a bio-bibliography, that of Robert Abbot. Here is the image of what has been typed on a microcomputer.[7]

Figure 1

```
1a    2
1b    ABBOT Robert
1d    Eveque de Salisbury
1e    %1560-1617%
1f    %1582-1617%

2a    *Surrey (*Guildford)

3a    Commoner (urbain) : père clothworker.
3b    Frère de $George ABBOT, archeveque de £Canterbury$;
      Frère de $Sir Maurice ABBOT, Lord-Mayor de £London$.
3c    Lord ecclésiastique.
```

```
5a      Grammar=School : *Guildford (Free Grammar School).
5b      *Oxford (Balliol College) .
5c      M.A. (C) %1582% ;
        D.D. (O) %1597% .

6b      Recteur de £Worcester (All Saints);
        Recteur de £Bingham (Nottinghamshire);
        Pretendary de £Southwell (Nottinghamshire);
        Eveque de £Salisbury %1615-1617%.

7b      *Oxford (Balliol College : fellow %1582-15??%) ;
        *Oxford (Balliol College : master %1609-1615%) ;
        *Chelsea (College : fellow %1610-16??%) .
7g      Chapelain royal %1603-161?% .

8c      /Tendance calviniste modérée : prédicateur très renommé ,
        très apprécié de $JACQUES Ier$.

19a     Oeuvre écrite en anglais et en latin.

20d     Théologien, auteur notamment de :
20a1a   &Mirror of Popish Suttleties&
    d   Ed. (T.WOODCOCKE) %1594% : STC 55 .
    e   Dédicacé à $John WHITGIFT, archevêque de £Canterbury$.
20a2a   &The Exaltation of the Kingdom and Priesthood of Christ&
    d   Ed. (G.BISHOP) %160'% : STC 51.
    e   Dédicacé à $Gervase BABINGTON, Eveque de £Worcester$.
20a3a   &Antichristi Demonstratio&
    d   Ed. (R.BARKER) %1603% : STC 43 ;
        Ed. (R.BARKER) %1608% : STC 44 .
    j   Réponse à $Roberto BELLARMIN$.
20a4a   &Defence of the Reformed Catholicke of Mr.$William PERKINS$
        lately deceased , against the bastard Counter-Catholicke of
        $D. BISHOP, Seminary Priest$&
    d   Ed. (G.BISHOP) %1606% : STC 48 ;
        Ed. (G.BISHOP) %1607% : STC 49 (seconde partie seulement) ;
        Ed. (T.ADAMS) %1611% : STC 50 .
        /La première partie (244 p.) est consacrée à la réponse à
        l'épitre dédicatoire de $D. BISHOP$ : on trouve dans cette
        partie beaucoup d'histoire ecclésiastique sans que l'ouvrage
        puisse pour autant etre considéré comme de l'histoire
        ecclésiastique;
        La seconde comporte les topiques théologiques habituels dans
```

The eye is caught by several unusual signs. If we leave apart the & . . . & (the function of which is to produce underlining), we are left with four signs:

=   as in grammar = school, which is a linking sign: it means that grammar = school will be handled as an entity in the course of the indexing process.

*   as in *Oxford, or in *Surrey: it means that the word Oxford will be indexed; if it is followed by a word or a group of words inside a parenthesis, this word or group of words will be printed in the index to qualify the starred word.

$. . .$ as in $George ABBOT, archbishop of £Canterbury$: the entry in the index will be ABBOT George, archbishop of Canterbury.

£   as in archbishop of £Canterbury; here all depends if the sign occurs inside $ . . . $ or elsewhere; in the first case, (as in this example) the entry in the index will be: Canterbury (archbishop of) see ABBOT George; in the second case, as in prebendary de £Southwell, the entry will be: Southwell (Nottinghamshire), prebendary de: ABBOT Robert.

These signs are therefore tools for indexing; but they are a nuisance for an edition and we have to suppress them in order to produce a good print of the data:

Figure 2

```
2
ABBOT Robert
Eveque de Salisbury
1560-1617
1582-1617

Surrey (Guildford)

Commoner (urbain) ; père clothworker.
Frère de George ABBOT, archeveque de Canterbury;
Frère de Sir Maurice ABBOT, Lord-Mayor de London.
Lord ecclésiastique.

Grammar School ; Guildford (Free Grammar School).
Oxford (Balliol College) .
M.A. (O) 1582 ;
D.D. (O) 1597 .

Recteur de Worcester (All Saints);
Recteur de Bingham (Nottinghamshire);
Prebendary de Southwell (Nottinghamshire);
Eveque de Salisbury 1615-1617.

Oxford (Balliol College : fellow 1582-1577) ;
Oxford (Balliol College : master 1609-1615) ;
Chelsea (College : fellow 1610-1617?) .
Chapelain royal 1603-1617 .

/Tendance calviniste modérée : prédicateur très renommé ,
très apprécié de JAMES I(VI) .

Oeuvre écrite en anglais et en latin.

Théologien, auteur notamment de :
Mirror of Popish Subtleties
Ed. (T.WOODCOCKE) 1594 ; STC 55 .
Dédié à John WHITGIFT, archeveque de Canterbury.
The Exaltation of the Kingdom and Priesthood of Christ
Ed. (G.BISHOP) 1601 ; STC 51.
Dédié à Gervase BABINGTON, Eveque de Worcester.
Antichristi Demonstratio
Ed. (R.BARKER) 1603 ; STC 43 ;
Ed. (R.BARKER) 1608 ; STC 44 .
Réponse à Roberto BELLARMIN.
Defence of the Reformed Catholicke of Mr.William PERKINS lately
deceased , against the bastard Counter-Catholicke of D. BISHOP,
Seminary Priest
Ed. (G.BISHOP) 1606 ; STC 48 ;
Ed. (G.BISHOP) 1607 ; STC 49 (seconde partie seulement) ;
Ed. (T.ADAMS) 1611 ; STC 50 .
/La première partie (244 p.) est consacrée à la réponse à l'épitre
dédicatoire de D. BISHOP ; on trouve dans cette partie beaucoup
d'histoire ecclésiastique sans que l'ouvrage puisse pour autant
etre considéré comme de l'histoire ecclésiastique. La seconde
comporte les topiques théologiques habituels dans la littérature
de controverse : Rome est Babylone, le Pape est l'Antéchrist,
discussion sur le libre-arbitre, le péché originel après le
bapteme etc... R.A. montre toute sa sympathie pour le puritanisme
```

Figure 2 has been printed not from the APPLE, but from the mainframe tape on which the content of the diskettes has been transferred, with a high-quality laser printer. In our view, it means that we do not intend to go through the lengthy and costly process of traditional printing of the dictionary, but will be content with the issue of print-out whenever they are needed.

The next example is a sheet from the index (compiled from bio-bibliographies 1 to 216, George ABBOT to Anthony BROWNE). This is the raw index, without suppression of identical entries.

Figure 3

```
Gaunt (John of) , Duc de Lancaster          BEAUFORT Henry
Gelli (Gian-Battista)                       BARKER William
Gentillet (Isaac)                           BRETON Nicholas
George (Saint)                              BARCLAY Alexander
Gerieke (Crispin)                           BAINBRIGG Reginald
Gibbon (John)                               BRIDGEWATER John
Gibson (Thomas)                             BALE John
Gifford (George)                            BARROW Henry
Gigli (Silvestro de) , eveque de Worcester  AMMONIO Andrea
Gilbert (William)                           BARLOWE (III) Willia
Gildas                                      BOLDON Uhtred of
Gilpin (Bernard)                            BROUGHTON Hugh
Glasgow (archeveque de ) cf. Beaton (James) ALDAY John
Gloucester (duc Humphrey de)                BECKINGTON Thomas
Gloucester (Humphrey de)                    ARNOLD Richard
Gloucester (Humphrey, duc de)               BEAUFORT Henry
Gloucester) (Duke Humphrey (of)             BALDWIN William
Glover (Mary)                               BOTT Robert
Glover (Robert)                             BOTT Robert
Godounov (Boris)                            BRERETON Henry
Gulding (Arthur)                            BRENDE John
Goodwin (William)                           BERNARD Richard
Gordon (Sir William)                        BOLTON Edmund
Gorges (Sir Arthur)                         BACON Francis
Gowrie (Earl of ) cf. Ruthven (John)        ABBOT George
```

Gransden (A.)	BEVER John
Gransden (A.)	BROMPTON John of
Gransden (Antonia)	ADYS Miles
Gransden (Antonia)	AMUNDESHAM John
Gransden (Antonia)	BALDOCK Ralph
Gransden (Antonia)	BALE (I) Robert
Gransden (Antonia)	BAVARD Andrew
Gransden (Antonia)	BENET John
Gransden (Antonia)	BEVER John
Gratien	ALYNGTON Robert
Greenwood (John)	BARROW Henry
Gregoire (Maitre)	BREWYN William
Gresham (Thomas)	ACHELEY Thomas
Greville (Fulk)	BACON Francis
Greville (Fulke)	BACON Francis
Greville (Sir Fulke)	BROOKE Ralph
Grey (Catherine)	BEALE Robert
Grey (Henry) , Duc de Norfolk	AYLMER John
Grey (Henry) , Duc de Suffolk	AYLMER John
Grey (Lady Jane)	AYLMER John
Grey (Lord John)	BEALE Robert
Gribaldi (Matteo)	AGLIONBY Edward
Grindal (Edmund)	BRADFORD John
Grindal (William)	ASCHAM Roger
Grineus (Simon)	BENNET Henry
Gringoire (Pierre)	ALCOCK John
Gringoire (Pierre)	BARCLAY Alexander
Grisone (Federico)	BLUNDEVILLE Thomas
Grocyn (William)	AMMONIO Andrea
Grosart (A.B.)	BRETON Nicholas
Gruter (I.)	BACON Francis
Guevara (Antonio)	BOURCHIER John
Guez (Jean-Louis) , De balzac	BAKER Sir Richard
Guicciardini (Francesco)	BARNES Barnabe
Guidericus	BLENERHASSET Thomas

It is at the moment the only documentary facility we have completed; but we have planned many more, which are more fully described in the two above-quoted papers (see note 3).

There are now two features of the PROSOP records which I have not explained so far. First, in figure 1 there is a margin, and in the margin there is a short tag, which identifies a zone. For instance,

- 1a : number attributed to the individual;
- 1b : name of the individual;
- 2a : birthplace;
- 3a : social status of its parents;
- 3c : personal social status;
- 5a : schooling;
- 5b : University . . .

In fact, this amounts to a precoding; but inside the so-defined zone, the historian is free to write whatever he wants, if not free to write in any possible way, because that would make the automatic coding impossible. And here is the second feature: PROSOP admits natural language, but the structure of the sentence has some relevance for further treatments and the PROSOP user has a set of rules at his disposal. Let us take as an example one of the simplest of these rules (the very simplest being a copy of the content of the zone without coding, as for the date of birth or date of death): the first-word rule. For instance, in the 2a zone, the county in which the man has been born is always written first, followed by the birth-place and eventually other comments. It means that I have taken such a decision because I will perform automatic coding on the basis of the county of birth. Other zones are written according to other rules; in 5b (University), the rule is somewhat different, since it is a first-word rule, but with the possibility of having several first words, since a man may have been registered in several universities (Oxford, Cambridge and Louvain or Padua for instance): the first 'first word' will be followed by qualifications and comments, terminated by ';', and then there will be a second first-word beginning the next line. With such a rule, it is possible to generate a table such as that in Figure 4.

Figure 4

```
 4  2a    Berkshire (Kintbury)
 5  2a    Berkshire (Newbury)
 6  2a    Berkshire (Reading)
 7  2a    Bristol
 8  2a    Buckinghamshire (Amersham)
 9  2a    Cheshire
1C  2a    Cornwall (Lanherne)
11  2a    Cumberland (Carlisle)
12  2a    Derbyshire
13  2a    Derbyshire (Foston)
14  2a    Devon
15  2a    Devon (Dartmouth)
16  2a    Devon (Exeter)
17  2a    Devon (Northam)
18  2a    Dorset
19  2a    Dorset (Exeter)
2C  2a    Dorset (Wimborne-StGiles)
21  2a    Durham
22  2a    Durham (Bolden)
23  2a    Ecosse (Dumferline)
24  2a    Essex
25  2a    Essex (Leigh)
2E  2a    Etranger : Ecosse (Edinburgh)
27  2a    Etranger : France (Toulouse)    il serait n< vers 1450
2E  2a    Etranger : Italie (Lucca)
29  2a    Etranger : Italie (Sessclerreto cu Ferugia)
3C  2a    France
31  2a    Gloucestershire
32  2a    Gloucestershire (Gloucester)
33  2a    Gloucestershire (Prestbury)
34  2a    Hampshire
35  2a    Hampshire (Thanet)
36  2a    Hampshire (Winchester)
37  2a    Herefordshire (Hereford)
3E  2a    Hertfordshire (Berkhamstry)
39  2a    Hertfordshire (St-Albans)
4C  2a    Huntingdonshire
41  2a    Huntingdonshire (Great-Stukeley)
42  2a    Kent
43  2a    Kent (pr>s de Sandwich)
44  2a    Kent (Chislehurst)
45  2a    Kent (Gravesend)
46  2a    Lancashire (earlier-Acor   pr>s de Manchester)
47  2a    Lancashire (Farnworth)
4E  2a    Lancashire (Manchester)
49  2a    Lancashire (bossall)
5C  2a    Leicestershire
51  2a    Lincolnshire
52  2a    Lincolnshire (Epworth)
53  2a    Lincolnshire (Stallingborough)
54  2a    Lincolnshire : il est traditionnellement consid<r< comme
55  2a    London
5E  2a    London ( All=Hallows Barking )
57  2a    Monmouthshire (Snlw-las)
5E  2a    N<   l'<tranger : Allemagne (Kesel)
55  2a    Norfolk
```

Such a table is extremely useful for correction. First, everybody can see that Exeter has been located once in Devon, and once in Dorset, which obviously is a mistake. It is easy at that stage to make amendments on the tape by using SPF facilities such as 'find' to go back to the precise location of the mistakes (the same device is also very useful to ensure the good standardization of the sensitive part of each zone). The table given as an example is not a first-word table; it contains the full zone, allocating a number to each different record. If we now restrict the table to the first word, the table will be quite a bit smaller, and a number will be allocated to each county and foreign origin ('N<'). This second stage of the table will enable us to proceed to the automatic coding of the data:

Figure 5

50	ASTON John	M.A.	fl.1385		13851382139200400000000
51	ATKINSON Edmund	Heraut	fl.1550		15501550 000000000000
52	ATKINSON Robert	M.P.	-1607	1607	15601607002700010000
53	ATKINSON Stephen	Metallurgiste	fl.1600		1600159016190024000100000
54	AUDELEY Thomas	Soldat	1492-1554	14921554	15171554000000020000
55	AUSTELL Henry	?Soldat	fl.1586		15861586 000000000000
***	AVALE Lemeke	?	1569	1569	1556 000000000000
***	AVERELL William	?	fl.1585		1585157915900000000000000
56	AVESBURY Robert of	Registrar de Canterbury	-1359	1359	1359 000000000000
57	AWDELEY John	Imprimeur	-1575	1575	15561575002400010000
***	AWSILYN John		fl.1588		15881588 000000000000
58	AYLMER John	Ev. de Londor	1521-1594	15211594	15451594002600020000
59	AYSCU Edward	?Gentleman	fl.1600		1600159016330000002000
60	BACON Ann	Femme de Sir Nicholas BA	1528-1610	15281610	15531610001200020000
***	BACON Anthony	M.P.	1556-1601	15561601	15811601001700020000
61	BACON Francis	Lord Chanc.	1561-1626	15611626	15851626002400020001
62	BACON Sir Nicholas	Ld. Keeper of the Great	1509-1579	15091579	15341579002000020001
63	BACONTHORPE John	O.Carm.	1290-1348	12901348	13121348002600000000
64	BAGNAL Sir Henry	Marshal of Ireland	1556-1598	15561598	15731598000000020001
66	BAINBRIGG Reginald	Headmaster	1548-1606	15481606	15731606003800000000
67	BAKER Geoffrey le	Cl.	fl.1350		13501340135600290000000
***	BAKER Humphrey	?	fl.1562		15621562159800000000000
68	BAKER Sir Richard	M.P.	1568-1645	15681645	15931645002000020001
69	BAKER Robert	Marin	fl.1563		15631562156800000000000
***	BALATINE Allan		fl.1560		15601560 000000000000
70	BALDOCK Ralph	Ev. de Londres, Ld. Chan	-1313	1313	12711313000000000002
71	BALDWIN William	Min.	-1563	1563	15451563000000010000
72	BALE John	Ev. d'Ossory	1495-1563	14951563	15201563003300010000
73	BALE (1) Robert	Scrivener de *London	1410-1470	14101470	14351470002400010000
74	BALE (2) Robert	O.Carm.	-1503	1503	15011503002600000000
75	BALLARD William	March Herald	fl.1470		1470146014850000000020000
76	BANCROFT Richard	Archev. de Canterbury	1544-1610	15441610	15691610002100020002
77	BARCKLEY Sir Richard	M.P.	-1604	1604	15741604001400020001
78	BARCLAY Alexander		1475-1552	14751552	15001550002300000000
***	BARCLAY William	Civiliste Ecossais	1546-1608	15461608	15001550000000000000
79	BARDNEY Richard	O.S.B.	fl.1490		149014851503000000000000
80	BARKER Edmund	Marin	-1595	1595	15911595003300000000
***	BARKER John	?	fl.1569		15691561156900000000000
81	BARKER William	Secr. du Duc de Norfolk	1520-1576	15201576	15451576002600000000
82	BARKHAM John	Chan. de St.Paul	1572-1642	15721642	15951642000800020000
83	BARLOWE Arthur	Marin	fl.1584		15841584 000000000000
84	BARLOWE Roger	Marin	-1554	1554	15261554001200020000
85	BARLOWE (1) William	Ev. de Chichester	-1568	1568	15251568001200020002
86	BARLOW (II) William	Ev. de Lincoln	-1613	1613	15851613002100000002
87	BARLOWE (III) Willia	Arcad. of Salisbury	1545-1625	15451625	15701625003600020000
89	BARNES Barnabe	Soldat	1569-1609	15691609	15931609004100020000
90	BARNES Robert	Théologien protestant	1495-1540	14951540	15201540002600000000
91	BARNFIELD Richard	B.A.	1574-1627	15741627	15901627000000020000
92	BARON Stephen	O.F.M.	-1520	1520	14951520000000000000
93	BARRET Patrick	Ev. de Ferns	-1415	1415	13901415000000000000
94	BARRET Robert	Soldat	fl.1598		15981598 000000000000
95	BARRET (1) William	Marchand	-1584	1584	1584 000000000000
96	BARRET (II) William	M.A.	fl.1595		159515881612000000000000
97	BARROW Henry	Min. puritain	1550-1593	15501593	15751593002600020000
***	BARSTON John	?	fl.1576		15761576 000000000000
98	BARTHLET John	?	fl.1568		15681562156800000000000
99	BARWICK Humphrey	?	fl.1594		15941594 000000000000
100	BASKERVILLE Sir Thom	Capitaine	-1597	1597	15701597001600020001
101	BASSET Peter ou Phil	Soldat	fl.1430		14301420143400000000000
102	BASTON Robert	O.Carm.	fl.1314		13141314133500280000000

Here is an image of the matrix computed from PROSOP using only the zone-copy and the first word rule. There is first the number attributed to the individual (*** for those not qualified as members of the population under study); then the name and a short description of occupation and dates of life in one continuous string of alphanumeric characters, date of birth, date of death, date of supposed beginning of activity, date of supposed ending of activity, and in three columns of four numbers, the place of birth (county), the social status of the father, and the social status of the individuals. And this is a matrix which S.A.S. at least is perfectly able to deal with.

There is still a long way to go before PROSOP may be considered as completed and entirely satisfactory, as will become clear to all those who scrutinize the figures provided. Nevertheless, the first results have given us some confidence in the general principles which have guided the conception and writing of the specific programs of this system so far.

Notes

1. This is a rather free use of the word system. In a sense, 'method' would be a better chosen word; as will become clear, there are few genuine PROSOP programs in the whole process described here, and PROSOP is chiefly used as a bridge between the data and other programs.
2. The U.A. (associated unit) 1004, directed by Professor Bernard Guenée: work on PROSOP has chiefly been the concern of Hélène Millet and myself, associated with Michael Hainsworth, director of the L.I.S.H. (Laboratoires d'Informatique pour les Sciences de l'Homme, C.N.R.S., Paris).
3. See J.-P. Genet and M. Hainsworth , 'Prosop: un système de traitement automatique des données prosopographiques', in H. Millet, *Informatique et Prosopographie*, Paris, 1985, pp. 279–97 and by the same, 'Entre statistique et documentation: un système de programmes pour le traitement des données prosopographiques', in N. Bulst and J.-P. Genet, eds., *Medieval Lives and the Historian: Studies in Medieval Prosopography*, Kalamazoo, 1986, pp. 359–79.
4. See J.-P. Genet, 'Medieval Prosopographical Research at Paris I', *Medieval Prosopography*, I (1), 1981, pp. 1–14.
5. X. Debanne , B.D.P.4, Paris, 1971.
6. Michael Hainsworth intends to write a version which will work on I.B.M. personal computers (XT type).
7. APPLE II, with APPLEWRITER, using a classic typewriter (OLYMPIA ESW K 100) for print-out.

30 *Jon Nichol, Jackie Dean and Jonathan Briggs*

Logic Programming and Historical Research

Introduction

It is ten years since I laid to rest my doctoral thesis, *The British in India 1740–63: A Study in Imperial Expansion into Bengal*. A thick layer of dust now covers this monument to industry if not knowledge. The Ph.D. was indirectly involved with K.N. Chaudhuri's monumental work into the functioning of the East India Company.[1] Although my main interest was centred upon the activities of Clive and his fellow *bandittii*, their behaviour was set against an analysis of the working of a major international corporation, the E.I.C., and the modelling of its functions. The modelling involved computer analysis of raw data dredged from stock books, ledgers and shipping records, and the projection of economic trends based on these statistics. These were the optimistic days which saw the emergence of the bright new dismal science of econometrics.[2] Then the oil ran out. In the early 1970s there was no great demand for experts on Bengal politics of the 1750s. Because of this, by 1976 I had rerouted my academic interests and energies into the educational field. A central thrust of my historical research spilled over into our curriculum development work in history pedagogy. Modelling ideas underlay our pioneering of simulation as a tool for pupil learning. The simulations were serious attempts to analyse the functioning of both social and economic systems within their historical contexts. Simulation is based upon the ability to generalise an historical framework from a series of separate yet similar historical situations.[3] The difference between each simulation is based upon the incorporation of the particular within the functioning of the model upon which it is based.[4] Historical simulation has the premise that their are logical relationships between the decisions and actions of historical agents, and the outcomes of those actions. The rider is that the logic relates to the perspective of the historical agent.

By the mid 1970s a range of historical simulations had been produced. They mirrored historical activity as diverse as the working of an Iron Company, a village undergoing enclosure, the Norman Conquest, the settlement of the American Colonies, The Congress of Vienna, The Scramble for Africa, The Russian Revolution and The Norman Conquest.[5] This was one element in a wider movement, known as The New History, which attempted to engage children more actively in the learning of history. This process led approach to history teaching had as its spearhead the extremely successful Schools Council History Project (1972–75).[6]

At the same time the computer was beginning to make inroads in education. At Chelsea the Schools Council funded a project, Computers in the Curriculum (C.I.C.), which pioneered a range of interesting ideas and approaches. Significantly, in the humanities area, C.I.C. attempted to implement a range of our Longman published and similar simulations.[7] During this period we were aware of computing developments in historical education, but felt that they had little chance of widely affecting practice. Using a mainframe with a telephone link which took two weeks to give a reply to a query did not seem the most sensible way forward.[8]

By the early 1980s the emergence of the micro suggested a change in possibilities for computing in education. In February 1982 we were vividly made aware of a whole new dimension to educational computing through our acquaintance with logic programming, the language adopted for the Japanese Fifth Generation Computing Project.[9] Elsewhere we have discussed at great length our educational work using PROLOG;[10] here I will discuss logic programming's possible relevance to historical research. Richard Ennals examines its more general application to historical research in *Artificial Intelligence — Applications to Logical Reasoning and Historical Research*.[11] The wheel has now turned full circle. From 1971–76 we developed a range of powerful tools for children to learn history. These tools were based upon our historical research methodology. Between 1982–86 we adapted these tools, using logic programming, for pupils to learn history through the computer. Now in 1986 we would like to suggest that similar computing tools can be of use to the historical researcher. Our computing tools, authoring programs, are based upon the nature of PROLOG.

The Nature of PROLOG

PROLOG is a language with which one can program declaratively as well as procedurally. A declarative program tells a computer what it can do to solve a problem, a procedural program how to do it. With a declarative program the computer works out how it will solve the problem or answer the question you have asked it. A declarative or descriptive program consists of two elements, proposition and rules. Propositions are the facts which the rules operate upon. The facts or propositions provide a database which describes to the computer a 'state of the world'.

Any PROLOG proposition has two elements, a predicate or verb, and an object or objects. The object derives its semantic meaning from the way in which the predicate links it to other objects. Thus we can enter into the computer a series of discrete propositions or facts. A small database of facts about feudal England might state

> William status king
> king owns (all the land)
> barons hold-land-from king
> knights hold-land-from baron
> peasants hold-land-from knights.

Thus, hold-land-from is the relation between barons and king. We can ask PROLOG questions about each of these propositions, such as who holds land from whom, and whether William has the status of king.

PROLOG works by pattern matching. Although the number of facts you can enter into the computer is only limited by its memory, the use of PROLOG in this way is essentially trivial. Its power comes from the application of rules to the propositions. For example, we might want to know who owes fealty to William. To do this we write a rule of the kind:

> someone owes fealty to someone else if someone holds land from someone else.

In the form of PROLOG we use the rule appears thus:

> x fealty-to y if x hold-land-from y

To find out who owes fealty to William we need a more complex rule:

> someone owes fealty to William if someone holds land from someone else and someone else holds land from William

When you can ask the question recursively, for example by applying a rule which redefines itself, you have a very powerful tool. For example, if you want to find who are the grandparents or single parent families in a demographic database, you can write rules defining grandparents and single parent families.

Rules can be of the complexity you require, and can be interlocked. They can include negation, which means that you can ask precise questions of elements within your database.

List Processing
PROLOG has another dimension; it enables us to get inside lists of information, and correlate the discrete elements. It is thus an extremely powerful language for handling data which appears in the form of consistently patterned lists, for example Domesday Book entries or place names.

Query The User Facility
The final element in PROLOG is the ability to add to the program answers you give it to questions it asks, and for the computer to explain the logical reasoning in its answer. This means that the program can add information to its database in the form of answers, and gives the machine a genuinely interactive capacity.

PROLOG and Historical Research

The nature of PROLOG has profound implications for the research historian. The facility to add propositions, rules, split lists, to questions the user and build up the program as the user responds to it means that we have a language which can represent some elements of logical thinking involved in historical study. For the academic historian PROLOG has a number of clearly definable uses; the analysis and processing of consistently patterned historical data, the recording and processing of historical sources and the employment of Expert Systems which contain the knowledge of an expert. Below we will discuss a shell DATALOG for processing structured information, the possibilities for using a PROLOG shell LOGBOX to record data in record offices and the field, and the potential use of Expert Systems. Both DATALOG and LOGBOX exist in prototype form for 16 and 32 bit micros.

DATALOG is the shell we are producing for handling patterned data. To use DATALOG we have first to decide upon the pattern of material which we are going to enter into the computer, and then the rules which we will apply to the data. Below we will examine two existing programs, PLACES, for the analysis of place-names, and DOMESDAY, for sorting out Domesday Information.

Both of these will be easy to enter using DATALOG. Our place names data takes two forms, the individual place names and entries in a dictionary of place-name terms. We used the program to analyse place-names within a twenty square mile area around Crediton, Devon. To write the program we split the map up into numbered squares, A1-D4. We then researched all the place-names on the map, and entered them into the computer using two list patterns, one for the place- name elements, the other for the meaning of place

name terms. The bottom line shows the entry for Crediton, PROLOG terms
are entered inside brackets.

predicate	object one	object two
facts	place name	terms of original name, date, square, other information (this may be blank)
((facts	Crediton	((cridie tun) 793 C3 Domesday)))

The entry pattern for the meaning of place-name terms was:

predicate	object one	object two
((means	cridie	(winding river)))
((means	tun	(farm)))

A rule within the PLACES shell correlates the two separate lists, so that
when we ask the computer a question or give it a command, it knows what to
do. Thus, to know about Crediton we type **describe Crediton**, and get the
answer:

    Crediton
    OLD NAME
    Cridie meaning
          (River Creedy (winding))
    tun meaning
        farm

Inside the shell is provision for the user to ask a huge range of questions
about place names. For example, if we want to find all the farms, that is tuns,
we type:

    Which places contain tun?

The program can combine two or more questions. Thus, it can tell us:

    Which places contain tun and before 1200?

PLACES power comes from our ability to add new rules to the program.
Such rules can enable us to test our hypotheses. For example, we might
postulate that the Anglo-Saxons settled extensively near water. If we ask at
present which places are near water, we get no answer. But, using the
program's ability to add a rule we can define the concept of settling near
water in terms of place-names which contain elements indicating such sites.
Such a rule states

> A place is near water if it contains a place-name element which suggests a low
> lying site

As each place name's terms take the form of a list, our prolog rule enables us
to search inside such lists for the terms we want:

> x (the unknown place) is near water if x contains y (the place-name element) and y is a member of a list which contains one of the following place name elements, mill, ford bridge, mere, lake and stream

We add this rule as

> x is near water if x contain y and y mem-of (mill ford brugg brycg mere lacu silver)

Using DATALOG, we can specify an authoring tool for handling Domesday Entries. The section below is completely based upon the dissertation of a student at Imperial College's Department of Computing and Control who examined the application of PROLOG to the production of an IKBS for analysing Domesday Book.[12] Such a tool contains three elements:

a) A structure for putting each proposition in a Domesday Manorial record into the computer and identifying it. (the facts)
b) A network of rules for correlating the information within the propositions.(the rules)
c) A mechanism for explaining the meaning of terms within the individual entries.(a glossary, linked by rules to the program's propositions)

The structure for the manorial entries had to recognise that they were divided between different fiefs, and therefore each manor would need its own separate code. The unique code would be linked to the manor's separate attributes:

unique code	manor attribute 1
	manor attribute 2
	manor attribute n

The attributes were to be entered in a consistent order. The rules enable the user to ask any question according to a prepared list, or any additional ones which occur. The PLACES and DOMESDAY examples give some indication of the possibilities for DATALOG in historical research. Personal names, shipping lists, census and pollbook records would all be amenable to such treatment.

LOGBOX

The structured data handling package, DATALOG, is one which immediately appeals. Another toolkit of great use to the research historian is LOGBOX. We would use it to collect information both in the record office and in the field. LOGBOX is based upon a toolkit called DETECT for 8 bit micros.

What is the specification for LOGBOX? In general terms it must allow data to be recorded, stored and processed in any form the user specifies.

a) The user will be able to state how the source will be indexed. For example, for letters the historian will be able to type into a template the following, or any other, categories: sender, receiver, date, place from,

place to reference.
b)   LOGBOX can then sort the entries into any order in relation to a single or combined number of categories, e.g. date order, alphabetical order, place of receipt, place sent from.
c)   Give numerical totals
d)   Search all the text entries, and pick out individual words, combination of words, and phrases, — an indexing facility
f)   place such lists of words into any order which the user requires
g)   produce a diagrammatic representation of the links between the sources as defined in d)

Such a tool would be stored on a disc and used with a portable micro. The entries for each day could be translated to hard disc and printed off.

Expert Systems

The final area is that of Expert Systems programming — programs which contain the knowledge of an expert in the form of facts and rules. Such programs interact with the user by asking him questions, and recording the answers as additional information. The earliest use of Expert Systems were in the field of medical diagnosis.

Expert Systems are still in their infancy. For the research historian we could think immediately of a large number, dealing with different areas. For example, one on research into the Henrician Reformation might be called:

ELTON

Another to guide the researcher through the British Library manuscripts labyrinth could be called:

MINOTAUR

Conclusion

The application of logic programming to historical research is manifest. With the use of authoring programs to make Intelligent Knowledge Based and Expert Systems available to the researcher, we place history at the cutting edge of the Information Technology revolution. Indeed, in its educational application Fifth Generation Computing is feeding off the expertise derived from history as a domain of knowledge. This comes, of course, as no surprise to the community of academic historians.

Notes

1.   K. N. Chaudhuri, *The Trading World of the English East India Company 1660–1760*, Cambridge University Press, 1978.

2. M. Desai, 'Some Issues in Econometric History', *The Economic History Review*, Second Series, XXI , 1968.

3. B. Barker, 'History Situations', *Teaching History*, 17, The Historical Association, 1977.

4. J. Nichol, *Simulation in History Teaching*, The Historical Association, 1980.

5. B. Barker, J. Birt, R. Bowden and J. Nichol, *Longman History Games*, Longman, 1973.

6. *Schools Council History 13–16 Project*, Holmes McDougall.

7. K. Randell (ed.), *The Use of the Computer in the Study and Teaching of History*, The Historical Association, 1984.

8. D. Daniels,, 'The Local History Classroom Project', in J. Nichol (ed.), *Developments in History Teaching*, School of Education, University of Exeter, 1980.

9. J. R. Ennals, *Beginning micro-PROLOG*, Ellis Horwood, 1982.

10. J. Nichol, J, Dean, J. H. Briggs, 'Powerful Prolog', *The Times Educational Supplement*, 25th October 1985.

11. J. R. Ennals, *Artificial Intelligence Applications to Logical Reasoning and Historical Research*, Ellis Horwood, 1985.

12. S. Townshend, 'Domesday Book and Prolog', Imperial College, London, unpublished dissertation, 1985.

31   *Robert L. Woods, Jr.*

Skills for Historians: Getting Something Done with a Computer

Few things have become more obvious at this conference than the variety of historical uses to which the computer can be put. It can enliven our study by enabling us to ask (and to answer) questions heretofore impossible given the life of one person. It can unburden us from tedious, repetitive tasks. And, under proper supervision, plough seemingly barren data into fertile interpretations. But let us give credit where credit is due. It is not the machine or the data bases which have done so much; it is the scholars who have laboured hard to devise, to formulate, to format, and to finalise the projects and datasets we have just heard about. What we really celebrate here is what historians do for history, and more specifically, how they do it.

This paper, then, emphasises not the computer but us, the historians, who want to use it productively. It begins by assuming that we as historians wish to preserve and to refine the variety of critical intellectual skills developed since the time of Herodotus as we add to them the use of novel mechanical and electronic aids. And it presumes that like any aid to historical analysis, we want — at the least — to be sure of how it worked on our data so that we can identify and account for its shortcomings, presumptions, and prejudices. So, this paper exposes some of the skills we must use to do so, and implicitly makes a plea that historians adopt a common idiom in dealing with computers so that we may exchange our methodologies regardless of our individual specialities and speak clearly to computer science professionals who, only when they fully understand our historical demands, can help us. This paper will also provoke by arguing that we may be losing critical control of history, because too many times we may confuse the successful completion of a computer program with the successful analysis of historical data using a computer program. This paper proposes, then, using skills, not just to get something done on the computer, but to get something important to historical inquiry done.

I hope I have given you reason to pause. After all, you must ask, to whom would historians using computers lose their critical control? Computer centres only do what users ask and the micro responds only to the orders given it through DOS, dBASE or whatever. Certainly, the computer itself could not threaten the integrity of historical work; it is not an independent agent. If you had said so, you would be quite right. The computer *per se* presents no real threat to the integrity of historical inquiry, but the uninformed application of the assumptions surrounding its use does. Remember this famous story? A field anthropologist, intrigued by cultural self-conception went to Alaska to study Eskimos. Earnestly, he asked an Eskimo child to name the elements of the typical Eskimo family. Hardly pausing, the child answered, 'A man, a woman, two children and an anthropologist'. Maybe our answer to a question on the elements producing history would be 'An historian, the evidence, analytic tools of various sorts, and — a software engineer'.

This certainly is not to say that software developers are evil, tyrannical, or even conspiratorial in trying to take over history. Rather, what I am saying is that they are there and are as important an influence to the resultant historical work as Banquo's ghost was to Macbeth's resultant fate. Consider Lotus 1–2–3, the major software spreadsheet for micros and a sophisticated piece of software engineering with built-in analytical routines that calculates, for example, a standard deviation like lightning. Yet which standard deviation? As any elementary statistics text notes, the formula to calculate the standard deviation differs for a sample over a population. Lotus 1–2–3's authors 'helped' the user by calculating it in the one way they saw fit, and allowed no easy substitution, even if intellectually demanded by the situation. Moreover, Lotus so trusted its decision that it buried the formula it used in over 350 pages of documentation and without any index entry (at least in version 1). Why have we not been conscious of the power software engineers implicitly hold over our work?

The present situation in computing is nothing less than extraordinary. With the advent of powerful micro-computers, anyone (serious or frivolous) can have access to processing power which excludes only the largest jobs. IBM micro-computers, for example, now support random access memory to eight megabytes and can access disk storage of over 72 megabytes in one partition. (By way of comparison, the whole Bible takes up only

3 ¼megabytes.) Coincidentally, mainframe developments have opened even more possibilities. For all practical purposes, computer hardware poses no limit to the complexity and size of any analysis. We can gather, retrieve, reform, and question primary material (as well as secondary) in almost any configuration imaginable. The only limit seems to be the instructions to the machine necessary to realise this potential.

For the historian, these developments in computing have been a mixed blessing. On the one hand, we can now afford machine assistance previously monopolised by engineers, mathematicians, and those with large grants. On the other hand, the engineers and scientists also relish the new computer opportunities. Not too surprisingly, they who had the previous experience in machine use, use computer resources selfishly — to solve their own professional problems or to write programs for the market as they and their expertise understand it. With a few, notable, exceptions, the promise of powerful computational resources available in useful applications for historical scholarship has been blunted due to our weak market influence and to the developers' lack of understanding of our individual, professional needs. We are told implicitly to 'make do' with, for example, data base management programs explicitly and overtly written for the needs of business entrepreneurs. What assumptions are built into those programs? Well, they certainly aren't historical.

Now we face a major decision: either we learn the skills to direct the machine in the analyses suggested by our training or we must accept the computer analyses dictated to us by engineers or computer programmers. This decision, however, is made all the more difficult because so many of the available software programs seem to do so much — at least so much when compared with the tedium of doing an analysis by hand. But again, that comparison, though perhaps emotionally exciting, is weak indeed. Since computers are an established reality, a packaged program's output should be compared not to the work of someone not using the machine but to the quality of production by someone using the machine unconstrained by that package. This is not to say that we should not use the packages; they most certainly have their place — and I might say obvious place. But, we must be aware that they are 'ready-made' answers. History, after all, is not answers anyway. Rather, it is a search for a truth of a sort. Not 'The Truth', but the search is what animates the historian and the student of history. That is why we are trained to criticise our documents and interpretations aggressively. To avoid doing so seems to me to betray history; it takes away the intellectual adventure — the challenge — the fun.

What can we expect from the machine, not presently available in package form? Well, first of all respect for the historical method.

Professor G. R. Elton has aptly summarised the process of historical questioning as the immediate give-and-take with evidence.

Right questions mean fruitful questions, questions capable of producing answers. They must therefore be geared to what is contained in the matter to be enquired from: the evidence need not by any means supply answers to all the questions the historian would like to ask. Secondly they must be penetrating; they must really exhaust the possibilities of evidence . . . Of course, questions that at some time seem unanswerable may become answerable in the hands of the historian who realises that the evidence can after all be made to yield relevant replies . . . (*The Practice of History*, 1985)

The historical method is 'interactive' and not rote. We expect, thus, to use the computer to expand our thought on history and its processes.

But is it too much to ask of the machine to help us to think historically — or at least not to force us to think and act a-historically when we use it; too much to accept our idiosyncratic and unique questions of data formed in the way and at the time we think on our evidence? In a way, yes, it is too much: packaged software can only deal with what its authors wrote it for. Yet in a more important way, it is not too much to ask. The machine, after all, will react relentlessly and accurately to any instructions given it. It only demands precise and clear instructions to act on any data. As historians, our existing skills stress precision, logical consistency and clarity of expression, the same skills needed to achieve full control over the computer.

I am not talking of any new skills, just an uncompromising expansion in using the ones which we all had to hone since entering the profession: to apply the highest standards of criticism to our historical data of its genesis, its preservation, its manipulation, and its exposition. To do that suggests that historians can only get something done with the computer if they can order the computer to do what they want. This means that historians must become fluent in a computer language, which will take its place right beside the other languages and tools we need to do our job. Though in principle I do not care what language we might adopt, I would argue that the simplest, most versatile, widely available, non-culturally bound, and most powerful language ought to be used.

In the time that remains, let me make a suggestion for a common computer idiom — APL. Like languages, learning this will require attention to the intellectual concepts which undergird it. But unlike other computer languages, the effort is worth it since it allows a rich individual expression instead of rote uniform notation.

First, APL (an acronym for A Programming Language) deals only in symbols which denote universal concepts and, despite their present unfamiliarity, allow for an economy of expression. Take, for example, the 'grade-up' operator (∇). Used with numbers on its right, it will sort them ascendantly; used with a sort key on the left and data on the right, it will arrange the data in the way defined by the key. Far more powerful than just a sort, 'grade' shows the universal concepts at work in APL. Historians constantly sort and select their data. It is one of the ways we explore our evidence. Certainly, every major package has a sort and a select routine built-in, allowing for ascending or descending ordering. But does a strict alphabetic sort according to the established syntax of the English language exhaust the need for sorts and does it encourage methodological exchange among historians of different cultures and specialties? Certainly we will accept the package sort and use it, but that really is not my question.

A colleague of mine, a year-long exchange scholar from the People's Republic of China, happened to answer my question inadvertently several weeks ago. I explained to him what I was going to do here in London, and he seemed intrigued. I showed him an alphabetic sort, using APL's grade function, and he agreed he too used sorts often. But as a sensitive observer of

our alien culture, he commented on the values implicit in ranking and noted
noted that in China, things would be ranked in an order different to the order
I'd shown him. More importantly, this prompted him to define his sort key
and us to discuss the intellectual results of sorting according to one key or
another. Though not impossible to do with most packages, the assumptions
in their sorts would be hidden from criticism and to sort on a key unique to
the data presented (such as sorting on title from Duke to Baronet in Debrett's
order) would be laborious and involve real familiarity with the package and
its syntax. In fact, given the time, I seriously doubt whether most historians
would even consider pursuing it. At best, they would try to make do in some
other way. At worst, they would avoid asking the question which prompted
the need for an 'irregular' sort in the first place.

APL also encourages the easy solution of unique questions. For example,
in my studies of early modern England, I had to convert lists of subsidy
assessments in pounds, shillings and pence to nominal decimal currency
before applying normal descriptive statistics. As you can see in the
illustration, APL expressions did the task economically and in the order in
which one would explain the process of conversion; BASIC demanded loops
and circuitous machine logic to effect the same transformation, not to
mention careful attention to data format definition. sense dictates the tasks
we need do to convert a table of subsidy assessments to decimal notation.
First, my notes must be transformed from the nominal characters in my data
base to interval numbers capable of being added and divided. Then, that
must be changed from a 240 base number system to a 10 base number system.
Finally the result must be in a form easily accessible to statistical
manipulation.

In APL, the function I wrote called 'lsd2dec' does all the work, and locally
names the data fed to it as 'LSD' within the function. Lines 1 to 3 transform
nominal to interval notation. (I have written expansively here to encourage
discussion.) Since my data were in a table, line 1 first catenates (,) a blank
separator (' ') to the data and then ravels (,) it from a table format to a vector
of numbers and assigns (←) that string vector the name 'LSDvector'. Since I
delimited pounds, shillings and pence in my original data with a dash (-), line
2 searches for all the places where no dash (≠'-'), that is a number, exists and
designates that with a 1, giving a 0 to the places occupied by a dash and then
assigns (←) that result the name 'nodash.' Line 3 does several things. First it
reduces (/) the vector to exclude dashes, according to the pattern of 0's and 1's
in 'nodash ' and then expands (\) it back out again, resulting in blanks
delimiting the assessments as well as the L-s-d amounts. Line 3 continues by
making the character representation of numbers into numbers and assigning
it the name 'LSDnum'. That in turn is reformed (ρ) into the same shape as
the original tabular data, but now it exists as interval data in three columns
called 'LSDnum' and available for arithmetic operations. In the next line the
conversion is made. The ratio 1 20 12, of course represents the relationship of
pence to shillings and shillings to pounds. That decoding (⊥) of 'LSDnum',
however, results in the total number of pence for each assessment. Thus, a
division by 240 calculates the decimal equivalents of each of those old-pence
assessments. Line 5 only tidies things up by rounding the conversions to two
decimal places. Now things are terribly easy: the 'floor' (⌊) and 'ceiling' (⌈)

of the result of this function gives the range of the assessments; the sum, by + /; and the mean, by the sum divided by the shape (.·-) of the result. I do not even want to think about the problems attendant with further analysis using BASIC.

My example, though trivial, illustrates a major point: the solution to problems in APL follow the path of human intellectual discourse and thought unencumbered by machine-dictated 'house-keeping chores'. Packages and other languages are a different story: the conversion would be tedious and long. Lotus 1–2–3 added over twenty steps to APL's five; FORTRAN added even more.

In conclusion let me say that greater familiarity with APL weans one from packages and from the implicit assumptions they force on their users. If I had the time, I would show that APL can calculate the mean, deviation, sum of squares, variance, standard deviations, slope, Pearson's r and r squared, standard error, x and y intercepts, as well as linear regression in only 13 lines of clear notation. If I had the time, too, I would continue to emphasise the interaction APL encourages by showing a one-line function which finds, in a context-sensitive way, specified text in an historical data base.

What skills do we need? None more than what we already have. But we must not be afraid to use them and apply them — not just to the last stages of our projects, but to the whole process of historical analysis. And just as we are not afraid to publish our discoveries in history, this conference teaches us we must not shirk from sharing the methods of how we arrived at those discoveries. This is our responsibility, made all the more urgent by the assumptions hidden in computer use. 'Anybody who thinks the past can't be altered', one wag has noted, 'is rather naive about historians'. Let us keep that monopoly intact.

Figure 1

```
        ∇ lsd2dec LSD
[1]    LSDvector←LSD,' '
[2]    nodash←LSDvector≠'-'
[3]    LSDnum←((1↑ρLSD),3)ρLSDnum←nodash\nodash/LSDvector
[4]    decimalLSD←(1 20 12 1⊗LSDnum)÷240
[5]    0.01×L0.5+100×decimalLSD
        ∇
```

```
10 ON ERROR GOTO 500
20 OPEN "data.dat" AS #1 LEN=55
30 FIELD #1,45 AS ALF$, 10 AS DAT$
40 I%=0
50 I%=I%+1
60 GET #1,I%
70 DASH1%=INSTR(DAT$,"-")
80 DASH2%=INSTR((DASH1%+1),DAT$,"-")
90 LAST%=INSTR(DAT$," ")
100 IF LAST%=0 THEN LAST%=10
110 L%=VAL(LEFT$(DAT$,(DASH1%-1)))
120 S%=VAL(MID$(DAT$,(DASH1%+1),(DASH2%-DASH1%-1)))
130 D%=VAL(MID$(DAT$,(DASH2%+1),(LAST%-DASH2%)))
140 DEC=L%+(S%/20)+(D%/240)
150 DEC=(FIX((DEC+.005)*100))/100
160 PRINT DEC
170 GOTO 50
500 CLOSE #1
510 END
```

Graphics

32 *Renée-Arlette Faugères*

Automatic Cartography in Historical Research

Cartography today is an efficient tool which allows more and more applications in various sciences. Cartography is efficient either for synthetic representation and fast communication of scientific results, or for specific investigations dealing with the relationship between any kind of phenomenon and space this phenomenon occupies. In history, there is a long tradition of the drawing of historical maps. The production of historical atlases has been an important contribution of historians to the enhancement of historical culture in the nineteenth century. In France, the 'Ecole des Annales' has given fresh impulse to cartographic expression, as well as its contribution to the renewed exploration of major historical themes. If we consider the last years' issues of *Les Annales* (1980–85), we note that 17% of the papers do include one or more than one map. The creation of the 'Laboratoire de cartographie historique (E.H.E.S.S)' has strongly reenforced historical studies as a whole, including consideration of space dimension of societies.

Cartography in fact offers a large range of possibilities in data representation. As for history, the data may be political, strategic, ethnographic, as much as demographic, economic, sociological, commercial, administrative, toponymic etc. This data may be organised and made available for fast reading and interpretation, through condensation, codification, symbolic use of graphs, coloured or black-and-white legends. The map emphasises with great effectiveness the relationship between the data and the localities or areas they are related to (*communes, départements,* provinces, *généralités* . . .). In fact, for the researcher, cartography represents a significant commitment. It requires much time, and supposes a specific training for cartographic techniques. These arguments really limit the development of historical maps. Another reason is the fact that each researcher tends to adopt his own system and conventions. There results a marked heterogeneity of representation, and consequently greater difficulty in reading and interpreting maps. During the last year, IHMC has tried out a new approach in cartography, based on automatic process, trying to demonstrate that it is possible to solve some of the problems which have been described above. Automatic cartography for historians, using computers, may easily provide solutions in terms of time, cost, and standardisation.

The Cartographic Process

The cartographic process we describe here is of general application. It should be applicable to all kinds of computer, micro-computers included. The process consists of the following steps:
   —selection of a map contour
   —creation of the map data file
   —creation of the historical data file
   —linkage between map data file, historical data file and diagrams of
      conventions
   —plotting of the map (contour, data, legend).

1·1 Contour selection
Some numeric map contours exist for the more recent years (provided by specialised cartographic institutions or software producers, for example the National Geographic Institute, Paris, the S.A.S. Institute, USA), but for most of their applications, historians have to select themselves their own map contour among the various available sources. This selection must be severely critical: contours have to be as accurate as possible, and the scale compatible with the capacities of the digitising device.

1·2 Map data file
Where no numeric map contour is available, a map data file must be created on the basis of the selected map contours. This map data file is necessary to realise semi-automatic or automatic cartography. There are three ways of creating the map data file. First, the graphic tablet: a magnetic pen is used to follow the contours, which are digitised point by point. The tablet constitutes an input peripheral, and may be connected to any kind of computer. The accuracy of the final drawing will depend on the number of points which are picked up, and, naturally, on the sophistication of the tablet. Second, the 'mouse' which is a facility on some microcomputers, for instance the Macintosh. The mouse is used as a paddle to control the movement of a video-pen on the screen on which the map is directly generated with an accuracy which depends on the screen's graphic resolution. A rather similar technique consists of using a video camera connected to a computer: the map is considered as an image and digitised line by line and point by point. All the contours and any information present on the map are memorised and may be displayed on the screen or saved in memory. The third technique takes much

longer to apply. When no graphic tablet nor mouse or camera is available, it is possible to select a number of characteristic points of the contour, as numerous as possible, in order to avoid too rough a design, the successive points being joined by straight segments. Each point is identified by its co-ordinates: the input of the co-ordinates and of the area identification builds up the map data file.

1·3 Historical data file.
Usually an historical data file contains several variables. For instance, a demographic survey provides information on age, sex, origin and place of birth. Most of them are worth mapping. The data must first be prepared for the cartographic process. For instance, if the data relates to communes, and if the cartographical space unit is the *département*, it is necessary to aggregate the communal data for each *département* and to allocate the result to a departmental indicator such as an INSEE code. The missing data may be replaced by computed values, by extrapolation from the neighbouring data, if a full map is required. In some cases, normalisation may be made when the raw data is not directly significant and preparation is necessary, such as computation of ratio, density or frequency.

1·4 Linkage
A common identifier links the records of the historical data file and the corresponding units of the contour data file. It is often necessary to relate the values to the various elements in a symbol chart. If the values are discrete and not too various, they may be used without re-coding. If the values are continuous it is necessary to divide the data set into classes. When these conditions are fulfilled cartography can be performed automatically.

1·5 Plotting
The drawing is performed on a peripheral colour or black-and-white graphic screen, graphic printer, or drawing table. Various frame formats can be selected according to the output device and, if necessary, scaling, allowing the reconstitution of real ground measurements. In addition, titles, annotations, conventions and footnotes may be plotted to complete the mapping. In most systems there is no real choice in symbolic or key diagrams, forms or colours; there is a restricted set of available patterns. A single pattern is used to fill an area with closed contours.

2. Case Study (SAS cartography)

The case study deals with the geographical origin of French soldiers in 1789. The map figures the number of soldiers for 100,000 inhabitants for each of the 3 *généralités*. The basic map for contour digitisation is a Vidal de Lablache map (*Atlas général*, 1894). The contours have been memorised by manual selection of 3400 points. Each point is stored as ID (identifier), X and Y co-ordinates. The origin of co-ordinates has been taken in the upper left corner. The historical data file contains the common identifier for the *généralités* and the numbers of soldiers by *généralité*:

Part of a Historical Data File
    1 348
    2 449
    3 1164
    ⋮
    ⋮   34 744

Next, six classes have been considered, including a missing data class. The class limits are: 200, 300, 400, 500, 800 and over. The corresponding patterns are selected in the pattern set provided by SAS-GRAPH. The final map clearly emphasised the fact that most of the soldiers came from the eastern part of France, with an exception for the lower Loire valley. The historian should take this evidence into account, together with other evidence from corresponding data for other periods.

From this cartographical data, we have drawn several other cartographic representations: a map of school attendance (1860–1863), an administrative map (1901), and toponymic maps for the investigation of settlement (1982, INSEE database of toponyms).

Figure 1   *Geographical origin of soldiers in 1789*

Number of soldiers by *généralité* per 100,000 inhabitants

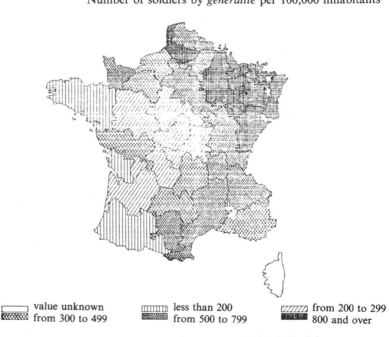

value unknown   less than 200   from 200 to 299
from 300 to 499   from 500 to 799   800 and over

After A. Corvisier, *L'armée française de la fin du XVIIe siècle au ministère de Choiseul*. Cartography by A. Faugères (IHMC).

Conclusion

These first attempts outline the possibility today of realising cartographic representations of historical information at low cost and with little investment of time. Hardware and software are available for any researcher who has a sufficient amount of suitable data which can be related to spatial dimensions. Cartography, a worthwhile endeavour in its own right, can thus be fully integrated in the research process. It is an aid for the visualisation of hypotheses and for interpretation, and a facility for communication. Intensive use of the same cartographic contours may lead — and it is a very important point — to the rapid elaboration of a set of historical maps. A good example is the recent 'Atlas de geographie historique de la Gaule et de la France' produced by S. Sinclair (SEDES-CDU, Paris, 1985).

For some cartographers, this kind of cartography might appear rather approximate and rather far removed from the standards of professional or geographical cartography. However, we must add that at present there exists software (SAS versions) which allows the production of the whole range of traditional and manual cartography (colours, symbols, characters). Some historians might be interested in such sophisticated techniques of automatic cartography. It seems a wise caution to suggest that they cooperate with a specialist. If they do, however, they will necessarily lose some part of the autonomy we have proposed to develop through personal use of the computer.

33 *William Vaughan*

The Automated Connoisseur: Image Analysis and Art History

This paper provides a brief account of 'Morelli'[1], a project being developed in the Department of History of Art, University College London for the automated pictorial analysis and referencing of images. Before going into this, however, I would like to begin with a brief outline of the potential of computer generated imagery for the History of Art.

1. The Digitised Image and Pictorial Analysis

Amongst the many exciting new areas of possibility that the computer has opened up is that of subjecting images to precise investigative procedures. The principal means by which this is done is done is by digitising the image. The process of reducing a picture to a series of precisely addressed reference points, each of which contains measured values of tone and hue, allows us to introduce quantitative methods into the previously enigmatic activity of describing visual display.

In recent years digitised images have been used to aid the restoration of pictures, to reconstruct their original appearance, and to analyse certain aspects of their techniques.[2] But there has been little attempt to use them for referencing or sorting images, or in the areas of formal or stylistic analysis. There are, I think, two main reasons for this, one economic and one methodological.

Let me take the economic problem first. Art Historians quite rightly insist upon 'high quality' reproductions for conducting their debates around pictures. The digitising and manipulation of such images can be very time consuming and costly. Even with present-day technology it can cost literally millions of pounds to store an image with a precision that would rival that of the highest quality reproductions made with conventional photography.

However, it is important to remember that there is a distinction to be made between using digitised images for storage and deriving information from them for reference and analysis. For the latter purposes it is not necessary to insist on images of the highest quality. As is clear from the work done by remote sensing in the interpretation of satellite images, even the poorest of images can yield valuable information if processed in the right way. And while much high level work in this area involved highly expensive equipment, there is a growing awareness of the power that can be achieved even at the micro-computer level in the area of analysis.

The methodological problems facing those engaged in pictorial analysis are of a different order. As has frequently been remarked, verbal and numerical computing have the great advantage over visual computing of having an existing unitary system, that of numbers and letters, on which to base their calculations. Digitisation reduces an image, too, to a set of measurable units. But these units bear no natural relation to traditional means of producing or describing images. Any employment of digitised elements, therefore, involves the researcher in making individual decisions about conventions to be employed which might have no relevance to the problems of other people working in the area. It is perhaps for this reason that computerised visual analysis, where it is applied to the historical consideration of art objects, addresses itself to constrained specific problems. Attention has been paid to areas where schematic simplification is relatively unproblematic and yields immediate advantages. No project, so far as I know, places any confidence in the idea that some general process of image identification based upon formal characteristics is possible.

However the different ventures do underline one general point. This is that the computer is far better suited to the comparison and analysis of form than it is to the interpretation of the subject matter of paintings. Despite all the fascinating advances that have taken place in artificial intelligence we are still a long way from time when a computer will be able to 'read' the subject matter of a picture and decide unproblematically whether the shape that it is scanning is, for example, a Madonna or a sack of potatoes.

This might seem, on the face of it, to be a grave shortcoming. But it could become an advantage. The iconic reading of pictures is essentially a verbal affair, and as such it can happily be left within the context of textual manipulation, for which there are innumerable computerised procedures available. The discussion of form, on the other hand, is a visual matter, for which words have always proved problematic and imprecise. The computer strength in form recognition can here come into its own, generating types of image recognition that need have no dependence upon traditional verbal forms of interpretation. However, this power can only be fully exploited if procedures are developed which will allow that general basis from which comparisons can be made. In other words, some syntax has to be evolved for the manipulation of images. Thanks to the power of digitisation, this syntax does not have to be the derivative of some verbal structure, but can be drawn from the direct consideration of measurable patterns and configurations.

2. The 'Morelli' Project

At this point I wish to introduce a shift of gear, and describe the project mentioned at the beginning of this paper. It is likely that one of the first problems to be faced in the search for a general syntax was that of working out how effective a computer could become in recognising the distinctions between individual works of art. Without the establishment of such discriminatory power, it seemed to me that any system would fall down for lack on some basic unit on which to build.

The means of achieving this was to derive a set of readings from digitised versions of images. These readings recorded various aspects of configuration and tonality. The types of readings were uniform for all images. They were taken using modest resources: a B.B.C. Micro, a digitising unit from Watford Electronics, and a Sony video camera. The total cost of the equipment was under £2,000.

Essentially the system functions by comparison. That is, when offered a new set of readings from an image it has to decide whether these are sufficiently close to any set already in the system to say that the two sets refer to the same picture. For such a system to be operative at a general level it is necessary for it to be capable of containing measurements from a vast blank of images. In my own mind I have thought of it as being capable of taking in all the imagery in a large archival picture library such as the Witt Library, which contains 1·4 million reproductions.

In order to achieve this, the system has to fulfil three central requirements. The first is that it has to work with existing reproductions of work of art, rather than with new highly quality ones of its own devising. However desirable the latter course might be, it is clearly impractical to imagining that the immense resources needed, say, to rephotograph all known examples of Western European art since 1200, is something that could be made available.

Furthermore, even if this stupendous task was performable, it would still not answer the system's full requirement. For there are in existence reproductions of many works of art that have become lost, and it clearly would be absurd to construct a reference system that could not accommodate these. Working from existing reproductions provides a particular challenge of its own. For different reproductions of an image can vary immensely. Any system that sought to identify images simply by their levels of tonality, for example, would come badly unstuck in this case. Obviously one has to turn to another resource, that of pattern configuration and shape. But even here there can be problems. For, as I have frequently found when recording different reproductions of the same picture, most prints cut their source images in different ways. So any system that was dependent primarily upon an absolute matching of shapes would also be likely to fail.

The need to use existing reproductions, therefore, means that the measures have to be taken of a rather limited set of characteristics — and in ways that will allow flexibility of interpretation without loss of precision. There is a further problem about the way they can be taken. Most image recognition systems are built around the desire to identify a certain type of pattern or shape. This system, however, has to be able to cope with an indefinite variety of patterns. It has to be able to be as effective with landscapes as with portraits, with complex narratives as with abstract compositions. I have at present limited it to two dimensional objects, but this can include pictures made with many different media — such as drawings, engravings, oil paintings, patterned tiles, coins and reliefs. It has to be able to compare these without confusing them. The types of measures, therefore, are constructed so as not to be specially used for identifying any one type of image. Rather they function by measuring the different ways in which different types of images perform when exposed to standard criteria.

The third requirement is that the system has to be swift. Any system that is dealing with millions of images is having to make decisions about them very rapidly. This is partly done by use of indexing systems, which cuts down the number of candidates to be surveyed in any case dramatically. But equally important is that the measures of any one image should not be too expensive. When first planning the system I allowed for a maximum of 64 bytes of information per image, that is, the equivalent amount of storage that would be needed to store a single line of text. I am still keeping to that figure, though in the present small version of the system that I have I have found it necessary only to use less than a third of this space per image — to be precise, 20 bytes. As well as having the advantage of rapidity of calculation, such an economic use of measures also enables easy storage. Using the present amount of measures it would be possible to store information essential to make the system workable for 20,000 images in approximately 1 megabyte, or the amount of space needed to store the text of a 300-page book.

When describing the system to colleagues I have encountered two principal responses. One is a frank refusal to believe that it would be possible to reference and compare images using such a tiny amount of information. The other is the question 'Even if it does work, what possible use could it be?' In the remainder of this paper I shall try to deal with these two issues.

3. How Can it Work?

The question of whether the system can work cannot as yet be completely settled. However, I can at least state that there is no theoretical reason why it could not work, and to say that tests made so far give reasons for optimism. The theoretical possibility can be alluded to by a reminder that the space I have allocated for storing the condensed record may be small, but it is still large enough to store a truly astronomical number. The number of separate individuals that could be referenced by a 64 digit number exceeds the largest known archive by several hundreds of billions. Even allowing that in practice there would be liable to be as many permutations of each individual image as there were reproductions and that any reduction will lead to the danger of duplication, I think one can safely estimate that the system would not seriously break down until one had been storing tens of millions of images in it.

I do not, admittedly, have the means of testing this assertion. I have, however, entered data from 1000 digitised images into the system, and have run a test going through the whole of the first 500 of these. Only in one case did the system associate two images incorrectly. In other words there was an error factor of 0·2%. And this was with using no more information about each image than could be stored in 20 bytes. It might be objected that the results of such a small run could be simply a matter of chance. However there are two facts that I think militate against this. The first is that I took care to make a large number of images of a type that was readily confusable with each other. I chose as my base (more than half) the half length portrait. This type of image — which is one of the commonest types in post-Renaissance European art — does not have much formal variation. Since the system was able to individualise between 300 of these while only making one mistake I would be bold enough to claim that it was doing as well as many human observers could.

The second reason why I think that the measures I have are not simply discriminating by chance is that, while the system individualised between different pictures, it was nevertheless able to link together different reproductions of the same image, even when these were taken from widely divergent sources. In one case, that of Raphael's portrait of Castiglione in the Louvre, I used four different reproductions. Two were slides, one dark, one light. The other two were printed reproductions, one a black-and-white from a book the other a colour post card. The system was able to relate all of them together. At the same time it was able to distinguish the reproductions of one picture from other that looked very like it. To test this facility further, I made a series of records of close copies of paintings, to see if it could distinguish the copy from the original. In the case of Raphael Castiglione I used reproductions of a copy by the Flemish artist Rubens (now in the Courtauld Institute Collection, London University). On the evidence of the naked eye we might find it hard to distinguish the one from the other. But the system had no difficulty in separating them.

The ability of the system to relate mechanical reproductions of an image while distinguishing them from manual ones is interesting since it suggests an area where the computerised reading of digitised images might have a practical application. Often it is hard for the human eye to perceive slight changes in form and tonality exactly. But the machine can do this unproblematically. Basically the reason why it can separate manual and mechanical reproductions of an image with such apparent ease is that mechanical reproductions, however bad, tend to bear a regular relationship to their source image while manually made ones do not.

I realise that I am in danger of letting my enthusiasm run ahead of me and claiming too great a success rate for my system. Let me record, therefore, that it was not always as successful as it was with the Castiglione. There were cases where divergent reproductions could not be matched. Of the 500 that I tested there were seven which fell into this category. This was a failure; but it must also be said that the reproductions in such cases were extremely discrepant. As might be expected, dark pictures (for example the Rembrandt Self Portrait at the age of 34 in the National Gallery) prove to be the hardest for it to assess accurately. It may well be that the introduction of additional measures would increase performance in this area; but I would never anticipate that it could achieve total success with such images.

4. What Use is it?

I would now like to conclude with a consideration of some possible uses for the system.

Essentially, these are of two kinds. The first is in the area of image identifying and referencing. The second is in the area of classification and analysis.

Referencing is the most direct and obvious. It has an immediate relevance because we are surrounded on all sides by museums, galleries and archives that are referencing their collections of visual objects by automated means. The multifarious systems in use are based upon verbal descriptions of the objects of their collections. Visual information, where present, is an 'add-on', usually some reference image — perhaps a photograph a microfiche or a video disk. Only rarely is a digitised image employed, and then it is not used in any way that allows direct referencing of its visual characteristics.

A system similar to the one described above would provide a means of directly referencing the objects of a collection according to a code based on their visual characteristics. This could be a valuable addition to current referencing systems, particularly for collections of easily confusable items, where individualisation through verbal description becomes most difficult. It could furthermore become a means of rapidly ascertaining if different collections contain similar items or of finding out if some newly discovered work relates visually to any already recorded in collections and archives.

The second possibility is a more tendentious field and deals with classification and analysis. When designing this system in the first place I was predominantly concerned with finding measures that would identify an individual image with precision. However, the need of being able to relate different types of reproduction of the same image to each other has necessitated the development of comparative procedures which turn out to have a potential beyond their initial purpose. Since the system that establishes the identities of the pictures is a series of measures, it can also be used as a means of expressing degrees of relationship between images. It is possible therefore to discover groups of images that share certain formal features. Amongst the images currently in the system broad flat landscapes with unbroken horizons (such as the frequently painting by Koninck in the seventeenth century and by Caspar David Friedrich in the nineteenth century) have been related.

It seems to me that such associations could provide the basis for a quite different kind of exploration of the system, one that sought to create 'families' of images, or interrelated networks. Such formal analysis as has existed in this area in the past has been on the basis of arbitrary designation. I do not want to fall into the fallacy of believe that the system is in any way 'natural'. Clearly it is based on a highly artificial and arbitrary set of transformations. But it might nevertheless be the basis of understanding the relationships between image types of a sort that could be quantifiable.

These are early days for such claims. Indeed it might be that a totally different way of approaching this problem will in the end prove to be more successful than my avowedly pragmatic one.

One thing is clear: that without experiment in this field there will be no progress. Nor should we art historians leave these problems to those others who work in the fields of imagery — the psychologists, physicists geographers and crystallographers. The techniques that they have evolved are of interest to us and can teach us much. But they each, quite properly, addressing specific problems relevant to their own disciplines, and we cannot expect to take over the techniques that they have evolved unmediated into ours. Issues of style and formal development are special problems for which special techniques are needed. While the 'storage' digital image must remain in the future that of the one for analysis is perfectly feasible now. It is an opportunity that we must grasp.

Notes

1.   Called after the nineteenth-century scholar Giovanni Morelli, who devised a procedure for the identification of pictures through the comparison of pictorial motifs within them. While art historians have, on the whole disparaged his method, it has provided fruitful in the field of archaeology.

2.   See, for example: D. Cappellini, M. Bacci, C. Conese, 'Digital Methods and Techniques for Analysis and Cataloguing of Art Works', in *Automatic Processing of Art History Data and Documents*, Scuola Normale, Pisa, 1984, 2, p. 37. Also K. Freifeld, 'Art Analysis: probing beneath the Image' in *IEEE Spectrum*, June 1986, 0018-9235/86/0600-0066

Computer Methods Used to Analyse and Re-construct the Cadastral Map of the Town of Carpi (1472)

Between 1472 and 1480 the town of Carpi operated a system of land taxes based on the dimensions and number of buildings and building plots owned by individuals. The taxes varied according to the social category of the owners ('castellani' or 'borghesani'), and to the dimensions of the façade of the property. In 1472 the public administration carried out a cadastre in which extremely detailed measurements were recorded. Measurements were given in *braccia* and *once* (1/12 *braccio* = 4·4cm), so that eventual differences due to the fractioning of the *once* were less than 5cm. The survey applied to the front of the house which looked out onto the street or, in the case of corner houses, that which was considered to be the principal façade of the building. The taxes did not therefore take into consideration the depth of houses or the number of floors.

Every entry referring to a property included not only the name of the owner and his social class, but also the 'castello' or 'borgo' in which the property was situated, boundaries, with names of neighbours and topographical elements (streets, moats, walls etc). Each boundary was identifiable according to its geographical orientation in relation to the plan of the property.

The cadastre has always been known to historians, and various studies have been carried out on it using whatever methods were available at the time when the study was done. The most recent study was carried out by one of the present authors in 1978, using however manual instruments and not going into particular detail, and was incomplete because, even though the original document was rich in certain details (orientation of boundaries and names of property owners for example) it was not possible to establish limits of construction (boundaries) due to the fact that the source did not give enough toponomastic information to establish streets already built and places where building was to be carried out. We could see that there were about 850 houses and almost 50 building plots in the town (excluding property belonging to the Church and ruling families who were exempt from paying taxes). We could also see how the town was divided into 'castelli' and 'borghi'. The exact position of the properties however remained uncertain.

It was important to have this vital information in order to answer a perplexing question. Carpi is known as a town which owes its present urban form to works of re-structuring and design carried out in the first decade of the 1500s under the orders of Alberto III Pio, lord of Carpi at that time. However certain zones such as il Borgogioso (Castel Noglioso on the cadastre) were clearly urbanised 1472, but not enough was known about internal articulation or topographical limits to be more precise. Did the town described in the cadastre reach the limits where Alberto III ordered the building of the city walls in 1518, or was there space for the Prince's projects?

In order to answer this question and to answer to the needs of the Town Council who wanted to carry out correct conservation work on the town centre, it was necessary to carry out research on the cadastre using different methods to those previously used. We therefore decided to elaborate the data electronicly. We worked in steps, starting with the formation of a 'data bank' and finishing with a graphic reconstruction of the cadastral map on video (the Computer Aided Design System, known as CAD).

Preparation and codification of data

The register did not contain a particularly large number of entries (there are about a thousand properties registered, each made up of about thirty pieces of information) but it was decided to use a computer filing system in order to be able to rapidly visualise and compare data on different pages of the register. Furthermore, the information could in this way be stored and used later in other fields of research. Firstly, before data was put into the computer, cards were made on matrices corresponding to the memory spaces given to each piece of data on magnetic disks. The information was made as detailed as possible so that if necessary the data could be used for varied types of research. At present the information is available and practicable even for very complex fields of study such as, for example, linguistic research. In all, details referring to 851 houses and 46 building plots were put onto the computer (a simple Commodore Personal).

Elaboration of data

Once the filing system had been established certain specific programmes were carried out in order to elaborate the data. A preliminary print-out was done to check detail, then programmes were elaborated to obtain lists in alphabetical order and lists according to size of façade. In this way we were able to synthetically analyse at a glance the principal characteristics emerging from the document. Finally we set about devising a programme to reconstruct the series of properties. For this we took into consideration the following details:
—the borgo where the property was situated
—orientation of the property in respect to roads
—types of topographical boundaries
—annotation referring to sale of the property
In this way it was possible to automatically reconstruct a grid of buildings in each block. Taking any property as a starting point, it was enough to give the command to the computer to look for the neighbouring property in a particular direction. Once this was done, the computer continued until it came across a topographical point, the sign that the row of houses in that

direction stopped. Then the computer was sent in another direction until all the outlines of the blocks, provided they were surrounded by topographical elements — roads, moats, *androni* (see below) etc. — were established.

Comparison between fifteenth-century blocks and topographical maps

When the work of placing each property in its row and block had been completed, 'grids' were made on transparent pieces of plastic, with the size of each element corresponding to the dimensions of the street front of each property. The scale used was 1:1000, and geographical and topographical boundaries were also included.

This grid was then compared with the oldest surviving and most geometrically precise cadastral map available, that of 1893. One by one the grids were placed on the 1893 map, and the outline of fifteenth-century Carpi slowly began to take shape. If we take as an example of study an important area of the town, the main square with the so-called Long Portico, which is presumed to have been built under the orders of Alberto III Pio at the beginning of the sixteenth century: the houses in those days looked out on the street, and were separated from the castle of the Pio family by a large moat — running through rows of houses on the grid, the correspondence of the outlines is almost perfect. There are only two exceptions: the second boundary (between the properties of Juliano Cochapano and Vinceguerra Rabia) and the sixth (between Damiano and Cristoforo di Ximbroxi). Further to the west (to the left on the image) however the correspondence of outline between the two maps continues. The coincidence between these outlines or boundaries of properties was often more significant internally than on the street fronts: the façades in fact were more often altered in relation to the public road. Another useful piece of information in placing the rows of buildings was the fact that though in general the properties are more grouped together than in the fifteenth century, the formation of the internal courtyards and of the minor buildings gives us an idea of a more complex antique layout: the correspondence between present day and fifteenth century properties may be reduced, but the correspondence between ancient outlines, the corners of buidings, internal courtyards etc. is extremely exact.

Use of aerial relief photographs of the town centre (1983) and research on the wall structure of buildings

Towards the end of 1983 the Town Council of Carpi carried out a series of very detailed aerial relief photographs of the town centre (scale 1:1000). These proved very useful in our research because they gave information which it was not possible to obtain from the cadastral plan. In particular they gave confirmation about the outsides of buildings, the position of doorways and colonnades and the entrances to the courtyards of major buildings. Using these planimetric photographs, in other words, it was possible to outline more precisely the definition between the fifteenth-century boundaries and the morphological characteristics of the buildings. Of particular interest was the position of the numerous passages which gave access to houses and connected the internal courtyards with the streets. These passages are still known today as *androni* and often correspond to the outlines of the fifteenth century.

The only figures given in the cadastre were the lengths of the street fronts of houses. It gives no indication of the depth of plan or the width of roads, nor does it indicate the presence of porticoes. By placing our grids over the actual planimetry however we were able in some cases to find a solution. We were able to match original boundaries, closed passageways (*androni*), and other details which gave us an exact correspondence between the rows of 1472 properties, present day properties and the units on the grid. We took as a starting point a block in Borgo S. Francesco which looked out on the square in those days known as the Piazza Commune (now called Piazza Garibaldi). From here we were able to reproduce all the plans and street façades on a scale of 1:200. It became possible to verify the similarity of fifteenth-century boundries not only with external walls, but also with the complex internal network of the buildings.

The results proved without doubt the exactness of the reconstruction of the fifteenth-century cadastre: from this it was possible to form an idea of structural elements using the matrix and hence to recognise successive phases of building.

Although we worked on a 1:200 scale, it was clear that the measurements of the fifteenth century must have been carried out with great precision. We identified a maximum error of the equivilent of 25cm. per row of houses, that is, 2·5 of a thousand on the overall measurement of the street façade. The positioning of the rows of houses was considered satisfactory when at least 50% of the fifteenth-century outlines of the rows corresponded with similar significant points on the cadastral plan compared to the modern aerial photographs. As an extra guarantee of precision we checked the grid using a method which eliminated any errors made by using the small scale on which it was necessary to operate (1:100).

The CAD System

In the hope of obtaining more precise results and eliminating graphic errors, a new graphic elaborator was used with a graphic plotter and video screen. This system, known as Computer Aided Design (CAD) allowed us to trace the fifteenth-century grids, verifying the dimensions while we drew. The rectangles which were formed in this way produced a mathematical model which could then be elaborated as required (reduced, enlarged, deformed etc.). Using the CAD system we were also able to automatically draw a number of particularly significant thematic maps. It was now sufficient to associate with every graphic element equivalent to part of the cadastre the series of relevant data — the social category, family, profession and place of birth of the owner — in order to obtain an image on the video screen of the relevant property. Colour screens represent the images obtained using this method. We can see blocks marked in different colours representing the various social categories of property owner. In red — the 'nobiles exempti', in diagonal red lines the 'castellani antiqui', in green the 'castellani adiuncti' and in pinkpurple the 'burgenses'. We can immediately visually identify the social organisation of the town, with Castelvecchio and Castel Noglioso clearly recognisable as areas occupied by nobles.

Figure 1   *Reconstruction of the plan of fifteenth-century Carpi (1472)*

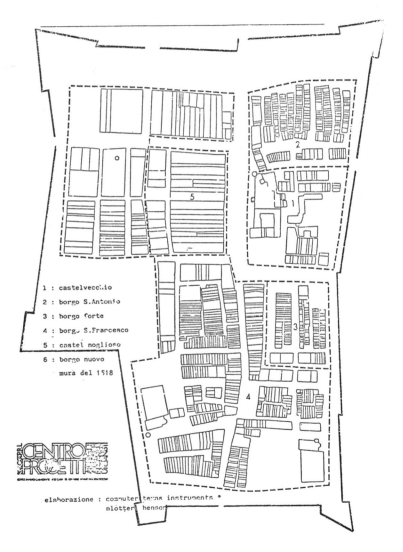

1 : castelvecchio

2 : borgo S.Antonio

3 : borgo forte

4 : borgo S.Francesco

5 : castel noglioso

6 : borgo nuovo

   mura del 1518

elaborazione : computer texas instruments *
              plotter benson

Characteristics of the Electronic Elaborator used for the Carpi study

The equipment used for the electronic elaboration of the data contained in the fifteenth-century register included a Commodore Personal Computer series 4000, with a mass memory, floppy disk of 500 Kbytes capacity. A disk of 5¼ inches contains all archive data and programmes for elaboration.

For the thematic maps a TEXAS INSTRUMENTS electronic elaborator with the following characteristics was used:

—CPU 990/IO
—Central memory:256 Kbytes RAM with ECC (Error Correction Circuit)
—Terminal: video keyboard of 1920 characters
—Mass memory on hard disks of 10 Mbytes

The graphics placement was carried out with:

—GPU (Graphics Processing Unit) with words of 64 bits and 512 Kbytes RAM
—GC3 controller with black and white monitor, colour monitor, digitizer, plotter, with 256 Kbytes RAM interpolate 1·500·000 pilex/sec
—digitizer 11 inches
—20 inch high resolution, long persistency colour monitor
—12 inch monochromatic monitor

The unity of exit was comprised of a Benson plotter with roller.

Text

35 *Lou Burnard*

Primary to Secondary: Using the Computer as a Tool for Textual Analysis in Historical Research

One assumption underlying this paper is that historians are, like the rest of us, primarily interested in reality. As a database designer, it is my task to attempt to define two distinct mappings: firstly that between the reality of the external world and the information which we wish to hold and consider about it; secondly the mapping of that information on to the sort of data structures and functions which a computer can deal with. The most effective way of accomplishing this involves the definition of a conceptual model (to use the jargon), representing real world objects, events and their relationships independent of their representations. The subsequent process of redefining that model in data processing terms — that is, choosing the data structures and processes which will most effectively support the entities and relationships defined to be meaningful within the conceptual model — is one which is well understood (by data processing people, at least!) and on which I will not linger. It is the prior process of defining the conceptual model that is of major importance.

In a very similar way, the historian must distinguish between information and its representation. The historian, perhaps uniquely among researchers, has to maintain a double focus: as well as 'conceptual level' information about events, people and places in the real world, he has to deal with the 'data' which has been used to represent that information in the pre-electronic past. Understanding the past involves both the assessment of 'primary' data, insofar as that can be determined, and the interpretation of the mass of 'secondary' data through which it has percolated to us. If that double focus is not to become blurred vision, it is obviously crucial to distinguish the two, while retaining the ability to integrate them. The task of the historian is thus very like that of the data analyst, above all one of defining a satisfactory abstraction from seemingly ambiguous and unstructured raw materials, many of which are themselves earlier abstractions from the same rich vein. The raw material of the historian is more frequently the representation of information than information itself.

Before the advent of computers, another and simpler word for 'representation of information' was text; an analysis of the nature of text is thus appropriate here. In interpreting text, the trained human brain operates quite successfully on three distinct levels; not surprisingly, three distinct types of computer software have evolved to mimic these capabilities. The case I wish to argue here is for the integration of these three levels.

At the first and most primitive level, we may consider a text as an image on a physical medium. At this level of description, sequences of character strings and other symbols have as much significance as other visible entities such as paragraphs, changes of typeface or layout etc. Most current standardisation effort in data processing is concerned with text at this level, with the establishment of standard generalised mark up languages, document format languages etc. Typically, in describing text at this level, we enter the realm of the word processor and the typesetter.

At the second level of description, we may consider a text as composed of specifically linguistic constructs. Here we are concerned with the identification of lexical items and syntactic structures, irrespective of their physical appearance or the function they perform in a particular context. This is the realm of the simple-minded 'information retrieval' package.

At the third level of description, we are concerned with the intentional aspects of a text: the identification of those real world entities and relationships which constitute the 'meaning' of the text. This is (or should be) the preserve of the database management system.

As a simple example, consider any monumental inscription. At the first level, we might be concerned with the manner in which the inscription was made, the size of its letters and their spacing, and similar concerns, all with the ultimate aim of being able accurately to reproduce the appearance of the inscription and relate it to others of a similar appearance. At the second level, we would be concerned with the words of the inscription, the language in which they are couched, their root forms and variants and similar concerns. We might wish to identify contracted forms of words and identify inscriptions using similar turns of phrase. Finally, at the third level, we are concerned with the intentions of the producers of the inscription. Whom or what does it commemorate? From what historical context does it come? What other evidence do we have for the assertions it appears to make about the past? To answer such questions it is necessary to identify entities and relationships independently of the inscription itself, although this may be the only evidence for their existence.

Of course, in answering such questions, we will frequently wish to use insights implied by second or first level considerations: a particular style of inscription or use of language may well be associated with particular real world events or people. In the same way, aspects of a text which appear to function purely physically (for example, the layout of text on a page or its punctuation) often have an intimate connection with the meaning which we create when reading it. It is only with difficulty that the computer can be persuaded to be equally flexible. Corresponding with the three levels of text description outlined above, present day computer systems offer us word processing systems, what I call rather loosely informaticn retrieval (IR) or word-searching systems and true database management systems (DBMS), each of which tends to be optimised for use at one particular level alone.

Some word processors offer rudimentary information retrieval functions such as the ability to search for specific strings of characters or to consult a simple thesaurus or spelling dictionary, in much the same way as some information retrieval packages often include a simple screen editor. Some database management systems (though very few) grudgingly recognise the existence of text as a rather curious datatype, usually assumed to be a variable length string of bytes. Vanishingly few include ready-made tools for the manipulation of text which even approach the flexibility and power of the tools available for the processing of 'real' data such as numerical values, part numbers or employee codes.

These differences are reinforced by the implementation techniques typically adopted by these three flavours of software. Because word processing systems are primarily interested in the capture and formatting of whole texts, their basic unit of storage is a document, which will typically have an internal structure peculiar to that particular system. The expensive parts of such software are usually concerned with transforming this fairly esoteric internal structure into a variety of external appearances (and vice versa). Because information retrieval systems are primarily interested in searching and displaying syntactically-defined subsections of text, their basic storage mechanism is the inverted file or index. In both cases, the software tends to be of the 'black box' variety, with its own internal structure inaccessible directly to the outside world. By comparison with these, database management systems offer a far wider range of storage techniques and access methods. Moreover, because standards exist for such systems, it is possible to implement a database on one machine with a reasonable expectation of being able to re-implement it on another. Also unlike word processing or information retrieval systems, a database management system will generally offer great flexibility in the types of object that can be manipulated. With a true relational database management system, it is at least theoretically possible to represent almost any arbitrarily complex information structure, not excluding the predicates and rules which characterise 'fifth generation' or expert systems.

For the historian, or anyone else, attempting to process text at all three levels by computer this separation and specialisation can lead to serious problems. If the word processor seems the obvious tool to use for the preparation and display of text, the information retrieval system seems equally essential for the manipulation and exploration of its lexicon. To make any sense of the results, a database management system is necessary for all but the most trivial of applications. If all three are to be used, the user must maintain independently a document store (access to which is available only by the word processor) a lexical store or text base (access to which is restricted to the IR system) and a database. Shunting information between all three components becomes a complex and messy task, involving many ad hoc solutions and much special purpose programming, for which the unlovely term 'data massage' seems appropriate.

What is needed is some way of integrating all three stores into a single integrated information base, accessible by software which is capable of functioning at all three levels. No such system exists as yet, to my knowledge, although there are several postulants. In its absence, the most practical course seems to be to extend the range of applications for which the database management system (surely the most flexible of the tools at our disposal) would be a natural choice to include at least an IR or lexical searching function and also perhaps a document control system.

Integrating database and textbase is not just a matter of finding a database management system which will support variable length records (though this is itself by no means a trivial task); it requires that the sort of distinction which I have presented above as characteristic of the historical method must be directly modelled in the database structure. The conceptual model must include both objects and their representations.

As a simple example, consider the ways in which we might hold information about people in a conventional database. We would start by attempting to define all those attributes which together constitute the entity 'person' and all the meaningful relationships that might exist between this entity and others. Any database management system will allow us to redefine such a model in terms of records and sets or relational tables. However, this simple model will rarely be adequate to deal with the realities of historical data.

One particularly significant attribute of a person might be his name; every person has one, although we might not know what it is. The fact that the same person might have different names, or that the same name might be associated with different people is one which a traditional database management system would prefer to ignore. But the name by which a person is known in a particular context may well be of the utmost importance, as might the problem of determining to which of several candidates a particular name is believed to refer. This indicates that our conceptual model must include the entity 'name' independently of 'person', with some other entity recording the association (in some given context) between a 'person' and a 'name'. Such a conceptual model will thus seek to represent both real world entities and their representations. The great strength of a database management system is that its primitive constructs are sufficiently abstract for this to pose no special problems (see Figure 1).

As a further example, we might wish to include the notion of 'place' within our database. Leaving aside the problems of associating a physical place with a particular name (in itself no different from the problem of people's names already discussed), we will also have to contend with the fact that place names are hierarchically organised. A reference to 'Europe' implies (probably) a reference to 'France' and 'England', just as a request for information about events in 'London' should probably include information about events in 'Wapping'. The conventional database approach might be to normalise all place references, thus requiring of the user an exact mapping of every place name to some neutral set of geographical co-ordinates. This is clearly

Figure 1   *Representing nominal linkage by a relational join*

PERSON		
PNUM	PNAME	BORN
P1	ALFRED THE GREAT	800
P2	ALFRED TENNYSON	1841
P3	ALFRED NOYES	1892

NAME	
NNUM	NFORM
N1	Alfred
N2	Aelfred
N3	Alfie

ASSOCIATION		
PNUM	NNUM	ASSTYPE
P1	N1	PRIMARY
P1	N2	VARIANT
P2	N1	FAMILIAR
P3	N1	FAMILIAR
P3	N3	JOCOSE

Figure 2   *Relational implementation of a simple hierarchy of terms*

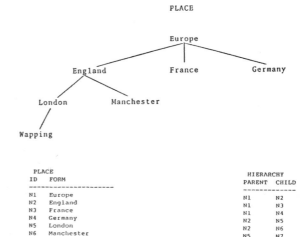

PLACE	
ID	FORM
N1	Europe
N2	England
N3	France
N4	Germany
N5	London
N6	Manchester
N7	Wapping

HIERARCHY	
PARENT	CHILD
N1	N2
N1	N3
N1	N4
N2	N5
N2	N6
N5	N7

impractical for historical data, where often all this is known of a place is that it is 'near' or 'a part of' some other place. The text processing approach is to treat place names in the same way as indexing terms are treated in an associative thesaurus: terms are related to other terms in a number of ways ('broader than', 'narrower than', 'synonym of' etc.); this too can be modelled very simply in a relational database system (see Figure 2).

These two examples indicate, I hope, that it is possible to use ordinary database techniques to implement such apparently purely 'text processing' functions as the handling of polysemy or the construction of thesauri, normally regarded as the province of the IR system. Equally, given suitable tools, there is no reason why a conventional database should not include straightforward running text, as produced by and for a word processing system. Of particular interest here is the availability of specialised hardware such as ICL's 'content addressable filestore' (CAFS),[1] which solves many of the technical difficulties normally associated with the storage and manipulation of large amounts of text. In particular, CAFS makes it possible to maintain in one single integrated system a display form of a text, a searchable form of the same text, accessible in terms of its constituent tokens, and tables of abstract data derived from both.

In both data analysis and historical research, a clear statement of the problem is sometimes as close as we may get to a solution. In this paper, I have tried to examine some underlying causes for the reluctance of current computer systems to process large amounts of text with anything approaching the sophistication of those much under-valued pre-electronic data management tools, the eye, the pen and the brain. I have also indicated the kind of initial adjustments that need to be made if our current electronic systems are to begin to emulate them.

Note

1. I have described in more detail some of the implications of CAFS for free text searching in 'CAFS: a new approach to an old problem', *Literary and Linguistic Computing*, vol. 2 no. 1, 1987.

36 *Ulrike Winkler*

The Austrian Historical Bibliography (AHB)

Introduction

In modern terminology the terms information and documentation are concerned with the conveyance of all kinds of data and facts. In the Arts they are associated with various kinds of bibliography. Of course, although in the field of history this is of prime importance it is by no means the sole function of information and documentation. Attempts to apply them in fields other than reference location have not been unsuccessful. For us, however, reference location involves tracing a title, passing it on to the applicant and, last but not least, the location of the required article or book. The vast amount of material and the impossibility of recording publications have, in the past, presented the individual with a virtually insurmountable task. A solution just had to be found. For several years now electronic data processing has been employed to facilitate access to information. It can be used to perform a nunber of different tasks.

For many years Austria did not possess its own comprehensive historical bibliography although one here should exclude the fields of pre- and ancient history as well as folklore and the history of art which had in fact developed their own records. Whilst a great deal of bibliographic work was done in the realm of regional history, undertaken to a large extent by the individual provinces, a general survey was lacking.

After 1945 Austria experienced a period of independent development, bibliographies of regional history began to show renewed signs of life and became extremely useful sources of information. There was, however, still a need for a national Austrian historical bibliography. When, in 1963, a German journal once again mentioned the fact that Austria was probably one of the only European countries without its own national historical bibliography, this merely drew attention to a state of affairs that was not only well known but even tolerated by a number of prominent historians. This observation was one of the major impulses that finally led to the setting up of the Austrian Historical Bibliography, the first volume, dealing with the year 1965, appearing in 1967.

The Austrian Historical Bibliography (AHB)

The compilers of the first volume of the Austrian Historical Bibliography were able to draw on experiences and material collected by the Institute for Austrian Historical Research in Vienna since 1951. The Institute possessed a comprehensive collection of historical publications which had appeared in Austria from 1945 onwards. This included literature on every branch of history, on its complementary sciences as well as neigbouring and peripheral fields which are often neglected. The selection and allocation of material prepared as the Austrian contribution to the International Bibliography of Historical Science in Paris were based on the same criteria.

In order to avoid confusion, it was decided to include only references to work published in Austria. Thus emerged a bibliography of Austrian historical research undertaken within the borders of the Second Republic. This bibliography contains works on Austrian history as well as the history of other countries published in Austria, and covers not only books dealing with strictly scientific questions and topics as well as essays taken from the limited number of prominent Austrian historical journals, but also more general accounts and surveys plus articles and reports written by amateurs. Whilst, as is only to be expected, major importance is attached to regional and local literature, it also includes current publications whose relevance for historical research and interpretation is not immediately apparent, as is the case with declarations of programmatic contents, political statements and comments on measures and incidents. This literature is similar in many ways to daily news reports as it is also to that of neighbouring fields such as legal science, theology and philology, to mention just the most important. In fact it would be erroneous to talk of a clear dividing line. There exists, at the most, a border zone which allows for liberal interpretation. The criteria of historical relevance decided whether or not anything was included from these disciplines. A very basic system was chosen for the classification of the listed material. Whilst largely following geographical and chronological criteria, it also offers a pragmatic division of history's so-called complementary sciences.

Author and subject indexes provide access to the Austrian Historical Bibliography. From the very beginning the publishers of the Austrian Historical Bibliography have endeavoured to document all the Austrian historical publications since 1945. At the same time they have made every effort to keep up to date by avoiding long delays in publication of the yearly volumes. It was agreed upon that no more than eighteen months should elapse between the period covered by the volume and its actual publication. Up to now this deadline has always been met.

The Science of History Database

1978 the Ministry of Science and Research commissioned the automation of the Austrian Historical Bibliography. It was already obvious that electronic data processors would also be made use of for information and documentation in the field of the Arts. When setting up the database it was decided to adopt the programme system MODOK (modular documentation system), developed and tested by the Institute for Mechanical Documentation(IMD) at the Computer Centre in Graz. This system can be employed to deal with numerous aspects of mechanical documentation. It is modular, that is to say, the parts are interchangeable which guarantees versatility. The next step was, in conjunction with the Institute for Mechanical Documentation, to work out guidelines for the recording of historical bibliographical data. After agreeing on the already existing bibliographical elements in the Austrian Historical Bibliography, these were arranged into categories. Based on these categories, guidelines for data gathering were set up, INSPEC (Information Service in Physics, Electrotechnology, Computers and Control) serving as a model. At the same time it was possible to supplement and expand the required computer programme by employing already existing programmes at the Institute for Mechanical Documentation, thus enabling the publishers to cope with the printing process. The data accumulated by the Austrian Historical Bibliography since 1967 served as a basis for this data. Since 1975 data has been fed directly into the database, subsequently supplemented by material from the years 1945–64. The database therefore contains, as does the Austrian Historical Bibliography, the entire findings of Austrian historical research since 1945, as far as it has been published in Austria. The advantage of the database over the printed version is that it can be added to systematically and at any time, whereas the Austrian Historical Bibliography can only be supplemented in later volumes.

Apart from the storage of authors, titles and the classification of contributions, the database also contains a comprehensive subject index which includes details of contents in key words, categories taken from the title or from the contributions themselves, names of individuals that appear in the title or the article, topographical terms, details of geographical classifications and regional or political units, relevant dates, references to organisations, to complex historical events or defined and established facts. This information is arranged within a framework of collective key words (major key words) (Figure 1).

The database also contains information as to the nature of the document (monograph, journal, periodical, commemorative publication, catalogue, report, thesis, dissertation, post-doctoral thesis, personal and subject bibliography etc). This system permits ready access based on formal criteria and offers the possibility of establishing certain indexes determined by formal criteria as well as the compilation of cumulative subject indexes. It also makes possible the listing of specific thematic bibliographies.

The systematic framework within which the developmental and test work for the organisation of the data input was carried out, can now be regarded as complete. There are hardly any more problems as far as the contents of the programme are concerned. The practical registration work, which also includes necessary modification to details, can now be carried out fully automatically. The complete compilation of readily accessible references is thus ensured, allowing comprehensive searches for any work which has appeared since 1945. The experimentation with this kind of documenting in the Arts can therefore be regarded as a success since the system functions both technically as well as in regard to content.

Figure 1   *Key words*

(some examples from the list)

Absolutismus	– Absolutism	Kartographie	– Cartography
Annalen	– Annals	Kunst	– Art
Bankwesen	– Banking	Liberalismus	– Liberalism
Brauchtum	– Customs	Literatur	– Literature
Bürgerkriege	– Civil wars	Musik	– Music
Chronologie	– Chronology	Münzwesen	– Monetary system
Dritte Welt	– Third World	Politik	– Politics
Einwanderung	– Immigration	Restauration	– Restauration
Erster Weltkrieg	– First World War	Schlachten	– Battles
Faschismus	– Fascism	Sozialdemokratie	– Social democracy
Gesetzgebung	– Legislation	Urkunden	– Documents
Imperium Romanum		Völkerkunde	– Ethnology
Judentum	– Judaism	Wiener Kongreß 1815	– Viennese Congress 1815
		Zweite Republik Österreich	– Second Republic of Austria

Data Gathering

An essential component in the compilation of bibliographic units is a well organised set of categories which establish the contents of the individual bibliographic elements (categories) (see Figure 2). The development of this system was based on already existing systems and uses a three-digit code

Figure 2   *Set of categories*

A selection of available data fields

Code	Contents
001	Control number
010	Type of document (monography, essays, theses etc.)
100	Title
120	Classification code (specified time period)
200	
206	Authors, publishers etc.
.	
250	
130	Special terms, key words
131	Persons
132	Towns
134	Political and/or regional units
135	Dates
150	Journals and periodicals
152	Series
510	Place of publication and publishers
620	Pages, format
810	Year

Example:

001	7503233
010	A
100	George Eliot and Judaism
120	2604
200	Baker, William
130	Literatur Eliot, George; Judentum Eliot, George
131	Eliot, George (d.i. Mary Ann Evans), englische Schriftstellerin (1819–1880)
152	Romantic Reassessment. Salzburg Studies in English Literature
400	45
510	Salzburg: Institut für Englische Sprache und Literatur der Univ. Salzburg
620	III, 321.8+0
810	1975

(characterisation of categories) to characterise single data fields. These characterisations are used to control the print and tracing programmes.

The data units (titles and subject definitions) are given a serial number and a classification code based on the Austrian Historical Bibliography (Figure 3). This is followed by details of the type of document, the author and the title. A different procedure is used for the compilation of specialist titles. The writers of commentaries, prefaces and epilogues, publishers and translators are also listed. Persons or institutions associated with the works, editors and editing institutions as well as the language of the document are also considered. Individual categories are allocated for journals, periodicals, details concerning series or headings of commemorative publications, symposia, catalogues, collections of essays and the like, as well as year and place of publication, publisher, number of pages and details of format. Information concerning whether or not a publication contains sources, bibliographies, illustrations, portraits, appendices, maps, indexes, sketches, charts, tables, diagrams, facsimiles, genealogical tables, summaries, notes or chronologies, round off the formal element of a reference. The data is either extracted from the original document or from the Austrian Bibliography and from the relevant journals, series, symposia, commemorative publications, collections of essays etc. Following the specific classification, indexing and clarification of the formal elements, data input via the terminal is often immediately possible. This cost- and time-saving process can be utilised for approximately fifty per cent of the titles. The rest are either handwritten or copies of titles and indexes or examinations of contributions with additional necessary details and categories. The aim of this technique is to provide the

Figure 3   *Set of classification*

(some examples)		Code
BIBLIOGRAPHIEN - BIBLIOGRAPHIES		1000
NACHSCHLAGEWERKE - REFERENCE WORKS		1200
Kataloge - Catalogues		1210
Berichte - Reports		1220
Archive - Archives		1221
HILFSWISSENSCHAFTEN - AUXILIARY SCIENCES		1600
Paläographie - Paleography		1610
Epigraphik - Epigraphy		1611
Genealogie - Genealogy		1630
Geschichtswissenschaft - Historical Science		1680
ÖSTERREICH - AUSTRIA		
Allgemein - General		1800
Römerzeit, Frühmittelalter	- The Roman Period, The Early Middle Ages	1801
Hoch- und Spätmittelalter	- The Middle Ages (11-15c)	1802
Frühe Neuzeit	- The Early Modern Period (16-18c)	1803
19. Jahrhundert	- 19th Century	1804
20. Jahrhundert	- 20th Century	1805
1945 ff.	- The Post-War Period	1806
WIEN - VIENNA		1810
SALZBURG		1850
KÄRNTEN - CARINTHIA		1870
ALLGEMEINE UND EUROPÄISCHE GESCHICHTE - GENERAL AND EUROPEAN HISTORY		2000
EUROPA: Staaten - EUROPE: Nations		
Albanien - Albanian		2150
Deutschland - Germany		2400
Großbritannien - Great Britain		2600
Italien - Italy		2750
Ungarn - Hungary		3700

Figure 4   *Printed version in the AHB 1975*

164	EUROPA: STAATEN	3233—3251

Großbritannien
Great Britain

3233 Baker, William: George Eliot and Judaism. *Romantic Reassessment. 45. Salzburg Studies in English Literature.* — Salzburg: Institut f. Englische Sprache und Literatur der Univ. Salzburg 1975. III, 321. 8°. Bibl.

3234 Brügel, Johann Wolfgang: Das Echo der Februarereignisse 1934 im britischen Labour-Lager. *Die Zukunft* 1975, 3: 2—5

3235 Debus, Allen G.: Van Helmont and Newton's Third Law. *Paracelsus. Werk und Wirkung. Festgabe J. K. Goldammer:* 45—52. Dok. (s. Nr. 383)

ristengymnasium) 1974/75: 5—14. Bibl.

3243 Schepelmann, Wolfgang: Die englische Utopie im Übergang: Von Bulwer-Lytton bis H. G. Wells. Strukturanalysen an ausgewählten Beispielen der ersten evolutionistischen Periode. *Dissertationen der Univ. Wien. 122.* — Wien: Verband der Wissenschaftlichen Gesellschaften Österreichs 1975. IV, 305. 8°. Bibl.

3244 Weinzierl, Michael: Republikanische Politik und republikanische politische Theorie in England 1658—60. — Phil. Diss. Wien 1975. II, 365, XXII, 4° (Masch.)

3245 Wilder, Frederick Louis: Englischer Sport in alten Drucken. Aus dem

most up-to-date information and ready access to the titles as soon as possible after their publication. However, certain remote titles can remain undocumented for quite some time. In order to organise and coordinate them the compilers have at their disposal a comprehensive journal and series index. After the data has been fed into the terminal, print-outs (data lists) are produced, which facilitate corrections and additions. At the same time, this process prepares the data for printing (Figure 4). The data bank itself is stored on hard discs and can mainly be processed sequentially. Accordingly every bibliographic unit is equivalent to a file of variable length and memory. The ASCII characters which are used by the computer system (UNIVAC 1100) have been extended by the addition of every available special character, accent and the like. Special switching characters are used to encode a special character. In addition, specific typefaces are marked by special characters whereby a complete category (data field) can also be allocated its own typeface. This data bank provides a large range of information output, employing various technological and print-out systems (Figure 5).

Figure 5   *Database output*

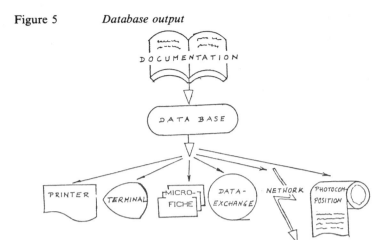

Organisation and Operation of the Centre for the Information and Documentation of History

During the development of the data bank, the documentation which had been carried out by hand became fully mechanised. The following steps were necessary: the choice of the appropriate classification system, the setting up of a memory model, the working out of guidelines governing the inclusion of data, and guidelines concerning indexing as well as the choice of technical equipment and staff. During the test period the system was continually checked to ensure that the user was provided with suitable and accurate information. The following steps were then taken to engage the system: documentation (compilation and indexing), setting up of the data bank, direction and execution as well as supervision of the work process, training of the staff, initiation of the users, carrying out of searches, the periodic setting out of information (yearly volumes of the Austrian Historical Bibliography), improvements and additions to the system.

In practice these systematic steps, necessary in order to set up a system, to a large extent overlap. The needs of the user played a central role in the development and testing of the system. As these needs are in a constant state of flux the information system is continually subject to structural alteration and requires constant surveillance.

History Information Service

The data bank not only provides the aforementioned output, but also allows for the carrying out of reference searches. At present the History Information Service uses the retrieval module MODOK. Based on the combination logic devised by Boole search terms in the retrieval system can be combined at will.

The following combinations are permitted: 'AND' (*), '0R' (+), 'AND NOT' (-), 'NOT" (/). Search term numbers which are assigned individual search commands are thereby combined. Within a search command it is also possible to indicate required data fields as well as search terms of their fragments.

When the request has been entered the problem is analysed so that the appropriate search codes can be determined. The search can commence when the problem has been formulated. During the search, documents are compared with requests and, when in agreement, stored on a hard disc data file. The results of the search can then be prepared for printing and printed out in a nunber of ways. In addition to the relevant references the applicant also receives statistics about the occurence of individual search terms. Figure 6 gives an example of a reference search dealing with the topic 'The Turkish Siege of Vienna 1683'.

Figure 6 *Example of a computer response to an application*

OEHB 84-10 IRD-GRAZ 1984-10-02

CUSTOMER NUMBER
1150 - Kunden Nummer TURKISH SIEGE OF VIENNA 1683
PROFILE – TITLE Profil - Titel : TUERKENBELAGERUNG IN WIEN 1683
ITEMS FOUND Trefferzahl : 20
DOCUMENTS SCRUTINIZED Untersuchte Dokumente: 66347
PRINTING LIMIT Drucklimit : 500

OCCURENCE OF SEARCH TERMS
Haeufigkeit der Suchbegriffe :

NUMBER SEARCH TERMS / LOGICAL PRINT OUT
Zahl: Suchbegriff/logischer Ausdruck:

51 1 135A,0000,135Z=1683N(3)
5 2 131A,0000,131Z=SOBIESKIN(2)
4283 3 132A,0000,132Z=WIENN(4)
20 A=(1+2)*3NN

DETAILS ABOUT THE NATURE OF THE DOCUMENT ARE FOUND UNDER THE HEADING 'TYP' IN THE FIRST LINE OF EACH REFERENCE
In der ersten Zeile eines jeden Zitates finden Sie unter der Bezeichnung 'TYP' Angaben ueber die Art des Dokuments.
LETTER CODE
Der Buchstabe bedeutet:

MONOGRAPH	A Monographie	G Dissertation	THESES DISSERTATIONS
JOURNALS, PERIODICALS	B Zeitschriften, Periodica	H Diplomarbeiten	
COMMEMORATIVE PUBLIC.	C Festschriften	I Habilitationsschriften	POSTDOCTORAL THESES
COLLECTION OF ESSAYS	D Aufsatzsammlungen	J Personalbibliographien	PERSONAL BIBLIOGRAPHIES
CATALOGUES	E Kataloge	K Sachbibliographien	SUBJECT BIBLIOGRAPHIES
PROTOCOLS OF CONGRESSES AND MEETINGS	F Kongreßberichte u. Symposien	M Verschiedenes	MISCELLANEOUS

RELEVANT REFERENCE

(1A) 8200168 / 2733 2003 TYP: (A) (6) (7) (1B)
(2) Barker, Thomas Mack
(3) Doppeladler und Halbmond (Double Eagle and crescent). Entscheidungsjahr 1683
(4) Graz, Wien, Köln: Vlg Styria
S.: 423.8+0
J.: 1982
(5) Deskriptoren:
Kriege Türkenkrieg 1683 (Wien)
Wien Türkenjahr 1683; Europa Türkenjahr 1683
1683

1A: Control number
1B: Number within an ÖHB Volume
2 : Author(s)
3 : Title
4 : Bibliographic entry
5 : Description (Key words)
6 : Special field ("2003" - Europe, modern era, 16-18c)
7 : Type of document ("A" - monography)

In the course of the search 66,347 references were scrutinised. The search term TURKS, VIENNA 1683 produced 3234 titles. The combination of these search terms, as just described, resulted in twenty 'hits'. This shows that in the Arts too this kind of efficient information service can provide an alternative to long-winded manual bibliographies. The database contains approximately 70,000 references dealing with history in its widest sense, published in Austria since 1945, bibliographically documented, subject indexed and immediately retrievable. Through the possibilities mentioned above, it was possible to build up an information service for history which is used regularly in the meantime.

37 *Rainer Metz*

TUSTEP: a Software Package for Source Oriented Data Processing in History

Quantification in history is only one part of computing in history, although both expressions are often used interchangeably. Computing in history, as we understand it, should not be restricted to the mere numerical evaluation of quantitative data, as for example counting tax amounts or calculating the average increase in wheat prices, but should also provide the means for handling textual data in a source-oriented way. As a prerequisite for source-oriented processing it is necessary to make the sources completely machine-readable without changing or modifying the original information in advance by coding or selecting. Later revisions of such modifications, if they proved to be insufficient for processing and analysis, can be undertaken not at all or only with great difficulties. In processing historical sources a number of different basic operations can be distinguished, such as checking data with regard to their logical syntax, selecting and extracting numerical values from textual data, combining information from different sources, sorting and finally preparing indexes of subjects and names. Hence software suitable for processing historical data in a source-oriented way must offer appropriate tools which carry out these basic operations. These functions are usually not covered by numerical software packages.

TUSTEP (*TU*ebingen *S*ystem of *TEx*tprocessing *P*rograms) is a software package which meets the requirements of source-oriented processing to a high degree. TUSTEP has been developed by the data processing center at Tübingen University in the past nineteen years.

The aim in developing TUSTEP was to isolate the fundamental operations necessary for the processing of textual data and to provide for each of these basic functions separate programs, which can be used without any knowledge of conventional programming languages. The single programs can easily be adapted to the specific requirements of the user. He only has to change default parameters or add new ones. To meet the requirements of the different tasks these programs can be combined in any sequence. In contrast to other software packages, the different basic programs are not designed for specific kinds of sources or procedures of analysis. Rather, they can deal with a great variety of source material.

In order to demonstrate the structure and possibilities of the package for historical research, I will first explain a few principles of the program calls. After that, I will discuss the output facilities, because they are of great importance — also from a financial point of view — to people who handle and publish historical sources. Finally, I will try to give a short survey of the different TUSTEP programs. Perhaps this survey will give an impression of how to handle an entire data-base project with these programs.

I. Principles of program calls

The basic structure of the different textprocessing programs is more or less identical and can best be demonstrated by a simple example. Let us assume for this purpose that a file contains all registered transactions of a grain market in a medieval town. From this file only those entries shall be copied which contain the string 'Auswaertige' (non resident) or 'Fremde' (foreigner) and in addition report on transactions which took place on a Wednesday. The program which selects the corresponding entries has the following parameters:

```
#Kopiere,Markt,Ziel,-std-,parameter=*
        Defines the beginning of a new logical unit
aa      /&d/
        Selects units containing the following strings
zf+     /auswaertige/fremde/
        Start reading numerical values after this string
al      /&d/
        Read 3 numeric values
liv     i1 i2 i3
        Calculate day of the week
rr      h0 = id (i3, i2, i1, h1, 1);
        Read next logical unit if the day is not a wednesday
rr      if (h0 .ne. 3) go to 0
*eof
```

The corresponding entries in the data file have the following format:.

```
&d1793.08.24 &s 1 &m 6 &p 19.00 &v auswaertige 01 01 01
&k mechelen 01 01 01 &n schoop
&c Originaleintrag durchgestrichen
&d1793.08.28 &s 2 &m 18   . . .
```

This #KOPIERE program combines several records of the file 'MARKT' to a logical processing unit. Each unit begins with the mark '&d'. The single unit is only selected for further processing if it contains the string 'Auswaertige' or the string 'Fremde'.

In those units which have been selected a date in the form year, month, day is also read and assigned to the integer variables 'I1' (year), 'I2' (month) and 'I3' (day). Starting at the mark '&d' the first three numbers are assigned to the variables 'I1' 'I2' 'I3' consecutively. If the date is a Wednesday — the value of the date function 'ID' being 3 — the unit will be copied into the file 'ZIEL'. All other units will not be copied.

This example illustrates the principles of textprocessing with TUSTEP. In order to be able to process textual data, that means texts which may also contain numbers, in a flexible way, both the logical processing units (cases) and their variables are marked by specific characters. In the following I will use the term text-parts instead of variables. Thus, when editing the source one does not need to keep to a certain sequence of the text-parts, or a certain number of them, which must be defined in advance; nor is one bound to mere textual or numeric information. Therefore, one can edit the data in an unformatted way and in any order the source requires.

All the TUSTEP programs allow the processing of data of such a structure in manifold ways. Procedures which are typical for the processing of textual data can be controlled by the user with the help of so-called parameter cards. The function of these cards is similar to the control cards in SPSS. Such typical procedures are, for example, extracting or rearranging of text-parts, reading numbers out of texts or exchanging characters and character strings. Within the individual TUSTEP programs — for example within the program #KOPIERE — one can use the parameter cards for the following tasks:

1. To specify the conditions on which logical processing units are to be processed. In the example mentioned above this is done by the parameter card 'ZF +'.
2. To define which text-parts (variables) are to be processed in which way, in which function (e.g. as basis for a collation), in which sequence or with which frequency.
3. To determine how the output of the processed text units shall look like.

According to the function of the parameter card, one can specify single characters, character strings, numerical values or within the programm #KOPIERE Fortran-like statements. Hence, a TUSTEP program usually consists of the program call as well as a certain number of parameter cards. The parameter cards normally control very small steps of processing. This provides, on the one hand, an extremely high degree of flexibility for the programs; on the other hand the programs for more complex tasks appear as a kind of metalanguage. Perhaps it may help to imagine the manifold possibilities which are provided by these programs, if I tell you that within the program #KOPIERE alone there are 168 different kinds of parameter cards at the user's disposal to put together a particular program call.

II. Output Facilities

In developing TUSTEP, the production of high quality output has been considered an important task to be performed by the package. The requirements of the humanities arising especially in connection with larger editorial projects have led to the development of a great number of different character fonts. The print programs of TUSTEP support not only the letters of the Latin alphabet, but also those of the Greek and Hebrew alphabets. Furthermore, the user has the possibility to print nearly 200 different characters on standard printers (using photocomposition, there are additional facilities, including the creation of own fonts).

Besides the normal font, small capitals and italics are available as well. Each of these fonts can be printed spaced, bold faced, and underscored either single, double or bold. Super- and subscripts are available, too. In addition to the print programs the TUSTEP composing program #SATZ is of considerable importance, especially in preparing and publishing books and critical source editions. With this composing program textual data can be automatically made up into lines and pages. The composed text is transformed into control codes which drive a composing machine of the type DIGISET or LASERCOMP. So the user himself can produce camera ready pages in an output quality to which one is accustomed from the traditional hot metal typesetting.

This possibility has to be rated very high especially in cases where a lot of time is spent rendering the textual data error-free. By using the traditional composing procedure new errors would come into the material when a compositor is transcribing the text once more. In addition it would entail a considerable expenditure of time and money caused by a renewed proofreading and correcting.

The program allows the user to compose automatically footnotes, marginal notes and up to nine critical apparatuses in different type sizes.

It is impossible to show the wide range of the possibilities which are offered to the user by this program. Therefore, only two examples (Figures 1 and 2) out of the daily work may suffice to demonstrate the advantages of the program. The numbers in Figure 1 are calculated by a #KOPIERE program, which in addition adds the respective control codes for composing. The table is an example out of the research project 'Deutsche Agrarpreisstatistik' at the University of Trier. Within this project also prices for other towns of the Lower Rhine region will be published. Figure 2 shows one page from the complete works of Nicolaus Copernicus.[1]

A further technical feature of this program which distinguishes it from much other composing software is the fact that it produces not only an output file on the tape which will drive the composing hardware, and which is therefore no longer suitable for the rest of the text processing software; in addition, it produces a reprocessable text file which contains the text with the final line and page divisions automatically generated by the composing and paginating procedure, but preserving all control codes used by the composing program. This file may then be used e.g. for automatic generation of tables of contents, lists of figures and tables, for the automatic generation of subject indexes or of indexes of quoted authors. For these purposes one can use this file as input for the respective TUSTEP programs. If one prepares from such a file an index of authors, for example, the reference of the entry refers automatically to its final location in the book. This is only possible because the page and line numbers of the used file correspond to the page and

Figure 1   *Tabular matter produced with the TUSTEP program #SATZ*

```
000004        haefele tab.    21.05.84 16:20
```

◄   DÜREN 1583-1585: Monatstabelle

WEIZEN   ROGGEN

Datum	Anz	DPreis	Min	Max	Anz	DPreis	Min	Max	
1583									
JAN	4	166.50	156.00	174.00	9	135.33	120.00	144.00	5
FEB	7	173.14	156.00	192.00	8	137.25	120.00	154.00	
MAR	11	194.00	174.00	206.00	16	136.31	126.00	150.00	
APR	9	192.33	168.00	204.00	8	150.37	138.00	162.00	
MAI	9	198.00	168.00	216.00	13	160.38	144.00	174.00	
JUN	7	207.43	192.00	222.00	11	162.55	141.00	177.00	10
JUL	15	207.60	186.00	228.00	15	155.73	135.00	168.00	
AUG	4	201.00	186.00	216.00	3	164.00	162.00	168.00	
SEP	8	206.25	186.00	228.00	5	163.20	162.00	165.00	
OKT	2	193.50	192.00	195.00	2	157.50	156.00	159.00	
NOV	1	200.00	200.00	200.00	1	156.00	156.00	156.00	15
DEZ	3	196.00	192.00	204.00	3	152.67	150.00	156.00	
1583	80	196.50	156.00	228.00	94	150.49	120.00	177.00	
ÄQUIV: Weizen 77.421 GS 7.035 GG					Roggen 59.293 GS 5.388 GG				20
1584									
JAN	1	192.00	192.00	192.00	2	151.50	150.00	153.00	
FEB	2	195.00	192.00	198.00	2	153.00	150.00	156.00	
MAR	0	0.00			0	0.00			
APR	3	197.00	189.00	210.00	3	157.33	156.00	159.00	25
MAI	2	215.50	215.00	216.00	2	158.50	158.00	159.00	
JUN	4	196.00	188.00	204.00	4	153.50	151.00	158.00	
JUL	4	191.50	191.00	192.00	7	146.14	136.00	151.00	
AUG	4	188.75	183.00	194.00	8	138.75	132.00	144.00	
SEP	6	185.67	182.00	192.00	3	130.67	129.00	134.00	30
OKT	5	183.60	180.00	189.00	10	132.20	130.00	134.00	
NOV	6	182.50	177.00	186.00	6	131.17	130.00	132.00	
DEZ	3	180.00	180.00	180.00	3	131.67	131.00	132.00	
1584	40	189.40	177.00	216.00	50	140.82	129.00	159.00	35
ÄQUIV: Weizen 74.624 GS 6.781 GG					Roggen 55.483 GS 5.041 GG				
1585									
JAN	1	180.00	180.00	180.00	1	129.00	129.00	129.00	
FEB	3	186.33	180.00	193.00	4	131.50	128.00	134.00	40
MAR	2	195.00	192.00	198.00	2	134.00	134.00	134.00	
APR	2	198.00	198.00	198.00	2	131.00	129.00	133.00	
MAI	4	195.00	186.00	198.00	4	130.50	129.00	132.00	
JUN	1	196.00	196.00	196.00	1	132.00	132.00	132.00	
JUL	5	198.40	192.00	204.00	4	142.50	138.00	144.00	45
AUG	3	192.00	186.00	198.00	6	136.50	126.00	147.00	
SEP	2	185.50	183.00	188.00	3	140.33	130.00	147.00	
OKT	5	219.00	210.00	231.00	8	159.37	144.00	174.00	
NOV	2	229.50	228.00	231.00	3	170.00	168.00	174.00	
DEZ	3	244.00	240.00	249.00	3	198.67	186.00	210.00	50
1585	33	203.82	180.00	249.00	41	147.07	126.00	210.00	
ÄQUIV: Weizen 80.305 GS 7.297 GG					Roggen 57.946 GS 5.265 GG				

line divisions of the printed book.

III. Some TUSTEP Programs

The TUSTEP programs mentioned up to now are only a few out of a great number of different programs which have been developed for handling textual data. The use of the various programs can be best demonstrated in connection with the basic operations which are needed for processing historical sources. Such basic operations are the input and output, checking and correcting, and finally processing and analysing in a broader sense. How

Figure 2   *Block composition with the TUSTEP program #SATZ*

12   NICOLAI COPERNICI REVOLUTIONUM

eo potest intelligi. Quoniam finitores circuli (sic enim ὁρίζοντας⁺ apud Graecos interpretantur) totam caeli sphaeram bifariam secant, quod fieri non posset, si insignis esset terrae magnitudo ad caelum comparata, vel a centro mundi distantia. Circulus enim bifariam secans sphaeram, per centrum est sphaerae, et maximus circumscribilium circulus. Esto nanque horizon circulus ABCD. terra vero a qua⁺ visus noster sit E, et ipsum centrum horizontis in quo⁺ definiuntur apparentia, a non apparentibus. Aspiciatur autem per dioptram sive horoscopium, vel chorobatem in⁺ E collocatam, principium Cancri Orientis in C puncto, et eo momento apparet Capricorni principium⁺ occidere in A. Cum igitur AEC fuerint in linea recta per dioptram, constat ipsam esse dimetientem signiferi, eo quod sex signa⁺ semicirculum terminant, et E centrum idem⁺ est quod horizontis. Rursus commutata revolutione, qua principium Capricorni oriatur in B, videbitur tunc quoque Cancri occasus in D, eritque⁺ BED linea recta et ipsa dimetiens signiferi. Iam vero apparuit etiam AEC dimetientem esse eiusdem⁺ circuli, patet ergo in sectione communi⁺ illud E esse centrum. Sic igitur horizon circulus signiferum qui maximus est sphaerae circulus bifariam semper dispescit. Atqui in sphaera si circulus per medium aliquem maximorum secat, ipse quoque secans maximus est, maximorum ergo unus est horizon, et centrum eius idem quod signiferi prout apparet, cum tamen necesse sit aliam esse lineam quae a superficie terrae, et quae a centro, sed propter immensitatem respectu⁺ terrae fiunt quodammodo similes parallelis, quae prae nimia distantia termini apparent esse linea una, quando mutuum quod continet | spatium ad earum longitudinem efficitur incomparabile sensu, eo modo quo demonstratur in Opticis.⁺

Hoc nimirum argumento satis apparet, immensum esse caelum comparatione terrae, ac infinitae magnitudinis speciem prae se ferre, sed sensus aestimatione terram esse respectu caeli, ut punctum ad corpus, ‖ et⁺ finitum ad infinitum magnitudine, nec aliud demonstrasse videtur. Neque enim sequitur, in medio⁺ mundi terram quiescere oportere. † Quin magis etiam miremur, si tanta mundi vastitas sub 24 horarum spatio revolvatur potius, quam minimum eius quod est terra.

Nam quod aiunt centrum immobile, et proxima centro minus moveri, non arguit terram in medio mundi quiescere: nec aliter quam si dicas, caelum volvi, at polos quiescere,

Fig. 1

5

10

15

20

25

5r

30

4b

───

1 ὁρίζοντας < ὁριζορτας -   *6* a qua < ad quam -   *7* quo 〖definitu〗 〖definiuntur〗¹ -   *9* in e collocatam -   *10-11* principium 〖ori〗 occidere -   *13* signa < signorum   semicirculum < semicirculus apparentia < apparentium -   idem [est] quod -   35   *15* eritque 〖quoque〗 bed -   *16* eiusdem < eius ci -   *17* communi illius esse -   *22* respectu < rec -   *24-25* Opticis 〖Quod eorum quae spectantur vnumquodque longitudinem interualli habet aliquam: qua aduentante non amplius spectatur.〗 Hoc -   *27* et finiti -   *28* medio 〖mundi〗 ᵐ〖mundi〗 terram -

2 posset *E // potest N, B, A, W* -   *9* orientis // exorientis *Ms, M, P* -   *11* AEC // ABC *B* -   *13* terminant // apparentia terminant *Ms, T, M, P* -   idem est quod // idem E quod *M*   *15* tunc quoque // quoque tunc *Ms, T, M, P* -   *16* ergo *deest in Ms, M, P* -   *17* illud E esse // illius esse *Ms, T, M, P* -   *22* quodammodo *deest in Ms, T, M, P* -   *23* continet // continent *Ms, T, M, P* -

24 Euc. Opt. 3 (Heiberg VII, p. 4–7) -

the different TUSTEP programs can be used in relation to these basic steps is demonstrated in Figure 3. The diagram should also stress the fact that, as indicated by the arrows, the different TUSTEP programs can be combined in any sequence and can be repeated as often as needed by the user.

Perhaps it is of some interest to list a few of the characteristics of these programs.

#EDIERE (EDIT); With this program data can be edited and corrected at the display in full screen mode. Compared with other editing programs, the TUSTEP-editor contains very advanced possibilities for the search and exchange of characters and character strings. Another important feature is that the insertion or deletion of one or more lines does not automatically alter the line numbering in the rest of the file.

#VERGLEICHE (COMPARE); The program collates two different text versions, to which I will refer as version A and version B. The identified differences can be listed in a print file in the following form:

```
1.1        Two versions of the same  short text.
  →        ********              + -----
1.1        Two drafts  of the samee      text.
```

whereby an asterisk marks a substitution, a plus marks an insertion and a minus marks an omission

These differences can also be generated in form of correcting instructions and be written in a data file. On the basis of these instructions and the program #KORREKTUR-AUSFUEHRE one can automatically correct

Figure 3   *Basic operations of textdata processing with TUSTEP*

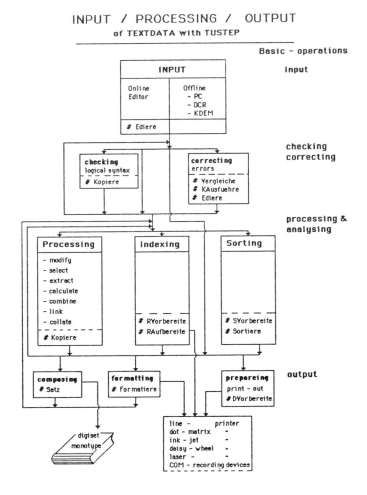

version A. The result would be the text of version B.

Since the program does not rely upon an identical line division in both versions, it can handle automatically also large omissions and insertions, up to the length of one (typewritten) A4-page.

#VAUFBEREITE (COLLATE); In practice there is no limit for the number of text versions to be collated to a basic text. You have only to cumulate the correcting instructions generated by the single #VERGLEICHE runs which collate one version each time with the basic text and use the program #VAUFBEREITE for printing them in a synoptical way. In the print file generated by #VAUFBEREITE the different readings of the versions appear under the respective word(s) of the basic text, for which a deviation was identified. Identities between the basic text and the versions as well as identities between the versions themselves are marked. Figure 4 shows the differences among twenty versions of the beginning of the ninth of the twelve 'Artikel der Bauern' which date from the Peasants' War. Under the line showing the respective text with which the other versions were collated, the variant readings of every other version are printed synoptically.

Because of the modular structure of TUSTEP, the preparation of indexes and concordances requires a combination of three programs, namely #RVORBEREITE, #SORTIERE and #RAUFBEREITE, and not, as one might have expected, one single program. This seems at the first glance to be

Figure 4   *Synoptic print-output of variant readings of a text*

```
1.1        Der Neundt  Artickel .
[v02]      === ======  ======== =
[v03]      === neuude  artickel =
[v05]      === neu%ndt ======== =
[v06]      === neu%ndt ======== =
[v08]      === neu%nd  artickel =
[v09]      === neu%nd  ======== =
[v10]      === neu%nd  ======== =
[v12]      === neundt  ======== =
[v13]      === neundt  ======== =
[v14]      === neund   ======== =
[v15]      === neundt  ======== =
[v16]      === neundt  ======== =
[v17]      === ======  ======== =
[v18]      === ======  ======== =
[v19]      === Neu%ndt ======== =
[v20]      === Neu%ndt artickel =
[v21]      === Neu%ndt artickel =
[v22]      === neu%nd  ======== =
[v24]      === neund   ========
```

```
1.2        Zuom neu%nten  seyen wyr   beschwertt    der      grossen   frefel         / so
[v02]      ==== ========  ===== ===   =========     ===      =======   ======         = ==
[v03]      Zum  neunden   seyn  wir   beschwerd     ===      =======   ======         = ==
[v05]      zum  neu%ndten sein  wir   weschwert     ===      =======   ======         = ==
[v06]      Zum  Neu%nden  ===== wir   beschwert     ===      =======   freuel           ==
[v08]      ==== neu%nden  ===== wir   beschwaert /  ===      =======   fraeffel         ==
[v09]      ==== neu%nden  ===== wir   beschwaert /  ===      =======   fraeffel         ==
[v10]      Zum  neu%ndten sein  wir   beschwert     ===      =======   freuel         = ==
[v12]      Zum  neundten  ===== ===   beschwert     ===      grosen    ======         = ==
[v13]      Zum  neundten  ===== ===   beschwert     ===      grosen    ======         = ==
[v14]      Zum  neunden   ===== wir   beschwert     mit dem  =======   freuel         = ==
[v15]      Zum  Neunten   seien wir   beschwert     ===      =======   ======         : ==
[v16]      Zum  neundten  ===== wir   beschwert     ===      ======    ======         = ==
[v17]      Zum  neunten   ===== ===   beschwert     ===      =======   ======         = ==
[v18]      Zum  newden    ===== ===   beschwert     ===      grossenn  ======         = ==
[v19]      Zum  Neu%ndten seindt wir  beschwert     ===      =======   freuel         = ==
[v20]      Zum  Neu%ndten / Seind wir beschwert     ===      =======   freuel halben  = ==
[v21]      Zum  Neu%ndten / Seind wir beschwert     ===      =======   freuel halben  = ==
[v22]      ==== neu%nden  seyn  wir   beschwert     ===      =======   freuel ====== = = ==
[v24]      Zum  neu%ndten ===== wir   beschwert     ===      =======   ======         . ==
```

complicated but allows an unrivalled flexibility of the system. Especially when one considers that the user may also process the intermediate results provided by these programs with the help of other TUSTEP programs, or even with own programs.

#RVORBEREITE (PREPARE INDEX) decomposes a text into its elements (index entries) and/or selects marked text parts as entries from a text. What constitutes a text element depends on the information given by the user on the respective parameter cards. From these entries up to three sort keys can be set up. The sort keys are only used for sorting and are automatically eliminated after the sorting. In the sort keys the user can freely delete, exchange and add special character strings in order to achieve the desired sequence on the following sorting. The entries may be completed by a reference which indicates their location in the underlying text. This reference can be taken from the page- and line-number of the input file as well as from especially marked text parts. The reference may also be combined of several parts.

#RAUFBEREITE (GENERATE INDEX) combines sorted entries or text units and edits them to indexes. The index can be printed in any format, with running titles and sub-titles. In order to be able to differentiate typographically between different types of entries, they can be marked by special characters. The program can also calculate absolute and relative frequencies for the entries.

For the sorting of text units like bibliography entries you need the programs #SVORBEREITE and #SORTIERE.

#SVORBEREITE (PREPARE SORT) prepares sort units which can consist of several input records. It is possible to specify with parameter cards which text parts are to be considered for sorting and in which sequence. These text parts may appear in any sequence at any location and in any length in the respective text unit. Out of the selected text parts one can set up as many as three sort keys in the same manner as in the program #RVORBEREITE. The sort units which are prepared in such a way are sorted by the program #SORTIERE.

With the programs #DVORBEREITE (GENERATE PRINTING) and #FORMATIERE (FORMAT) textual data can be prepared for printing on a line printer, wheel printer, matrix printer and laser printer.

#DVORBEREITE (GENERATE PRINTING) edits the data in that form in which they are stored in the file. Control characters which are included in the text are printed, but not interpreted. Such control characters are needed, for example for the program #FORMATIERE.

#FORMATIERE (FORMAT) formats textual data according to any format given by the user on parameter cards and according to the format instructions which are included in the text. This program includes automatical hyphenation and automatical line and page make-up, with line justification and an automatic handling of footnotes.

For the output in professional typographic quality TUSTEP contains the program #SATZ which I have already mentioned at the beginning of this paper.

This overview shows that the basic programs are not designed for special applications only, but serve for a multitude of different tasks. The single programs are relatively independent from each other,on the other hand they can be combined almost arbitrarily, since the output of any of the programs, including the composing program, may serve as input for any other program. This basic 'philosophy' of TUSTEP — namely to split up the different basic operations of textprocessing to a high degree — is the reason for the fact that for generating an index for example one needs three different programs, namely #RVORBEREITE, #SORTIERE and #RAUFBEREITE, whereas with other packages this is normally done with only one program call.

Although some of the functions of these basic programs are also available in other packages or on word processors, it is essential, especially for larger projects in the field of historical research, that the required functions are available not in isolation, but incorporated into a system of compatible programs which cover a great variety of problems and which are powerful enough also to handle large amounts of data.

In addition to the programs for handling textual data, TUSTEP contains programs of a more organizational nature, like file allocation, magnetic tape handling or defining own command macros. This has the effect that TUSTEP appears to the user to be independent of different hardware and different operating systems. Therefore, logging-in, logging-out and initializing TUSTEP are typically the only system-dependent JCL commands needed by the TUSTEP user; all the other commands needed by the user are TUSTEP commands which are identical on any system. So far TUSTEP has been installed under the operating systems OS/1100 (SPERRY UNIVAC), MVS (IBM) and VM (IBM) including VM/PC on the IBM-PC AT/370. An installation under the operating system VMS (MICROVAX) is presently being developed and will be available for the user probably in 1987. An implementation on Personal Computers beyond the AT/370 is planned.

Note

1.   Nicolaus Copernicus, *De revolutionibus libri sex*, ed. H. B. Nobis and B. Sticker (Nicolaus Copernicus Gesamtausgabe, vol. II), Hildesheim, 1984.

Computer-Assisted Editions of Medieval Historical Texts

The Monumenta Germaniae Historica, where I work, was founded in the early nineteenth century to edit the sources for medieval German history (interpreted very widely). Until fairly recently we have prepared all our editions traditionally, but both in the main institute and among our associates, computers are in use for a number of purposes, ranging from simple word-processing through typesetting from diskettes to the preparation of complete editions from cradle to grave using computers, as I am doing now. Now it is obvious that you can use a word processor for preparing the typescript of an edition. What I want to discuss is how to go beyond word processing in such a context; what do you need besides a good text editor to make life easier? The answers are not just for medievalists; they are relevant to anyone concerned with the edition of historical sources, though if you want to do a lot of statistical analysis of your material then you probably need to go about things differently.

The edition of historical texts presents the same sort of problems as those encountered in the writing of monographs and articles, but they are sufficiently different to require special treatment. Editions are often very large and typographically complex, with several layers of apparatus. Printing them is expensive. There are therefore good reasons for doing your own typesetting, that is, supplying the firm doing the printing with data for the phototypesetter in the form of ready-laid-out pages. The more complex an edition typographically, the greater the cost of production, and the greater the risk of expensive author's corrections. Cost here means one's own time as well as printing costs; it is not unknown for a large and complex edition — say 500 or more pages of quarto — to take three years to be printed. There is a further good reason for doing your own typesetting. The core of a good edition is proper indexing; only then has the user full access to the text. Whether such an index is selective, as ours are, or made in the form of a lemmatized concordance is a matter of taste. In either case it is often necessary to have page- and line-information, and though this is available in principle in the output from the phototypesetter it is not there in a decodable form. You can of course — if you have used a word processor to prepare a traditional typescript — go though your files inserting page-numbers and line-endings after you have received the mounted page-proofs and then make a KWIC index, but this is neither fun nor reliable.

From these considerations we have the first requirement of a software package for assisting editors; it should contain the means of transforming an electronic typescript into data which can be used by a phototypesetter.

Editions are complex typographically because they are complex structurally. Keeping track of everything is difficult, so one wants help in preventing errors creeping in. This is particularly necessary because even less than articles and monographs can editions be begun at the beginning and ended at the end. You are constantly revising editorial decisions — not just those of establishing the text, but those of presentation as well. The apparatuses tend to grow haphazardly, which means for example that footnotes and cross-references need constant re-numbering. Moreover, editions are very often prepared for inclusion in a series with its own particular rules. Not only are such rules subject to change; you may also find that you want to publish your edition in a different series with different rules. Consistency here is very important. And contrary to what is often claimed, computers are not in themselves the answer to problems of standardization and consistency in editions. If you have consistently used abbreviation and formulation 'A' then you can replace it by 'B' with little trouble; but if you have not been consistent in the first place then you will have to search through for all the occurrences by hand. No word-processing package will enforce consistency of usage.

From these considerations come the next set of requirements for any software for edition; it must make the problems of unplanned growth and of consistency easier to deal with.

A third point concerns the users of any such package. These will evidently be prepared to use a computer for word-processing purposes, but they will not necessarily be or want to become experts in data processing. This means that the workings of the programs they use must be transparent, and it should be easy to rescue the situation if anything goes wrong. Nor should users have to change their working habits more than is absolutely necessary. The changes enforced by aiming at direct transfer to print are sufficient; you have to learn to do your copy-editing 'as you go' rather than at the end of the process.

A fourth point is that of data security. This means a lot more than simply the protection of the physical (and logical) existence of the data, though that is of course very important. It also means that you need to protect your material against unintentional change — text editors are dangerous things. Moreover, the time over which an edition is prepared must be borne in mind — you do not want to find yourself sitting on files for a machine which can no longer be repaired which are written in a format which no-one else can read. For this reason it is highly desirable to have access — data-transfer access — to a mainframe, even if you are using a micro to do most of your work.

This still does not say anything about how to go about organizing a computer-assisted text edition. One obvious approach is to put the edition into a databank form. I have not gone along these lines for a number of reasons. First, there is the question of size. The text I am currently editing, the letters of Wibald of Stablo, contains some 120,000 words (lexical, not machine) without any additional editorial material. This is by no means untypical as regards size; in my view it rules out the database approach. I cannot see how the main record-item in a hypothetical editorial database could be anything but the individual word in the text; but that means you are talking about data files of 10MB and more, and retrieval tables which would probably not fit into the memory of most micros. A mainframe of course could cope, but in my experience such programs are highly machine- and operating-system dependent: there is no guarantee that anything I could write for the purpose using our mainframe, for example, would be easily portable except to other CDC machines; and in any case, not all users have unlimited access to a mainframe. Second, there is the question of repairability and transparency I mentioned earlier: if your system crashes during access or the database becomes inconsistent for some reason it can be hard to make repairs unless you know something about how such structures are organized. Moreover, you have access to the raw data only via their transformations (through 'print-out' programs, for example): there is no transparency.

The alternative approach is to use sequential text-files. In the early stages these can be created with a normal word-processing package, but beyond a certain point I do not recommend editing your files with a word-processor: it is too risky. The danger is not so much that of losing all your files — that can be guarded against by making security copies — but of making small changes unintentionally. For this reason the technique I use for making changes is a batch one. The edition exists in one or more 'basic' files. You prepare in advance the changes, deletions or additions you wish to make, feed these together with a copy of the 'basic file' into the program, and get a new file with the changes incorporated plus a log of what you have done. If you are satisfied, you can then make the file with the changes the new 'basic file', print it out, and destroy the old one (or better, save it on disk or tape). This is not at all elegant, but it is safe and controllable. It also means that you do not have to work online if it does not suit your working habits. You can also use an editor to make global changes to the basic files directly, but here great care is needed.

There are two possible ways of organising the raw files. One is to keep everything, apart perhaps from the introduction and bibliography, in one file: the information for the various apparatuses is simply inserted into the main text at the appropriate point and separated off by coding. Anyone who has a word-processing program with a footnote facility will be familiar with this technique. The other way of doing it is to keep the apparatuses in separate files, and put markers into the main text. This has the advantage of increasing speed and giving you several smaller files instead of one large one, but it requires a little more organisation. The package allows you to do either, because you can separate and combine files at will: in the final typesetting stage it is desirable for programming reasons to have all the information in one file, but you are not forced to work like this throughout.

The raw files are readable and editable, but not instantly recognisable as their final content for three reasons. First, it is only when processed that all the footnote numbers and cross-references are inserted into the text. What I use as my working text is a hard copy of the raw files as they stand (so I can check the source of any possible errors) plus a formatted printout. Second, the use of abbreviations is, though not compulsory, a good idea: it reduces the size of the raw files and is the safest way to guarantee consistency of editorial approach. By 'the use of abbreviations' I do not mean that one consistently writes 'MGH' for 'Monumenta Germaniae Historica', but that one uses a standard coding sequence plus an alphanumeric code to which one assigns a meaning. This is the most significant change from 'traditional' working methods — but it is an optional extra. It does, however, cope well with a number of trivial but potentially time-consuming problems. Thirdly, the files have coding information of various kinds scattered through them — codes to govern printing, characters not normally found on keyboards, and so on. Again, this is a technique familiar to anyone who has used a word-processing program: the difference is only that the coding system is much more comprehensive and only uses printable characters, both because these are more easily entered and edited and also because it ensures that there are no problems with data transfer. This approach has been retained even for the more complex typesetting programs — all files produced by all programs are ASCII-files, thus making it possible to edit the files at any stage (in order to do things which the programs cannot or cannot yet do, for instance).

The package I have repeatedly mentioned falls into two parts. First, there is a series of utilities for doing such things as: separating and reuniting the different parts of editions; providing formatted printouts at any stage; simultaneous multiple string replacement (for conversion to and from word-processing formats and other uses); managements of bibliographical information; checking for consistent and sensible use of the standard coding, and so forth. The second part consists of or will consist of the typesetting programs together with indexing facilities. I cannot offer a fuller description, partly for reasons of space, but mainly because although the coding and most of the programs in the package as I now conceive of it exist, they have evolved gradually out of *ad hoc* responses to problems I have met which I could not solve with available software. This means that the various bits were originally written in a number of different languages, that the coding which is essential for this kind of data processing has been very *ad hoc*, and that in my early enthusiasm for programming I tried to produce programs which were egg-laying, wool-bearing, milk-giving pigs rather than simple and straightforward tools. I am now in the process of rewriting all the programs in a much more generalised form and in one language, standardising the coding, separating separate tasks into different programs, and looking around for solutions which already exist. The intention is that the separate programs should be useful on their own as well as forming part of a package. The emphasis is on simplicity rather than elegance: no windows, no mice, no pull-down menus. Not only do these have a nasty tendency to be hardware dependent, they are not necessarily perceived by the inexperienced as user-friendly, to judge by the reactions of less computer-minded colleagues. Except for the necessarily more complex typesetting programs, which exist at the moment only as fairly simple skeletons, all programs will need not more than a sheet of A4 to describe their operations (at least, that is my aim); and most will operate on their own after being fed with a command line or command file.

Once the programs have been generalised and thoroughly tested it is our intention to make them available to our associates and probably on a more general basis as well. The only restrictions as far as micros are concerned will be that the operating system must be either CPM or MS-DOS, and on mainframes will need a C compiler (most of the programs were written in PASCAL but in the interest of portability as well as of speed and flexibility I am in the course of rewriting them in C, though in the micro version I have written some of the most frequently used routines in assembler for reasons of speed and space). If you are going to use the programs to do typesetting you will need to make sure that you can get the data from your computer to the typesetter, and you also need information about fonts and control sequences used by any printing-devices you want to use, both for final typesetting and for the production of proofs; otherwise all you need is access to a computer and a text-editor. From the start I have not thought it necessary to write a text-editor, since there is no shortage of good ones. I hope also to avoid having to write a complete typesetting program, but at the moment I know of none which is available to us which will do the things we want.

I should like to close by talking briefly about other uses of data-processing in the course of preparing editions. One editorial assistance I have not mentioned is the old-fashioned and much-maligned KWIC index. In my view it is worth putting the text of an edition you are doing into machine-readable form and having a KWIC printed out for it — at an early stage in the edition — even if for one reason or another you do not otherwise intend to use computers in the course of your edition. You can use a KWIC for all sorts of things — checking consistency of punctuation, identifying self-quotations within an author's work, and so forth. We also make use of them for identifying dependencies of one work or another — a program compares two KWICs and prints out all the possibly identical passages. The output contains a lot of pseudo-dependencies, where there is in fact no connection between the two texts compared, but it is nevertheless very helpful where there is a substantial use of one text by another — one classic example is the identifying of quotations from the Vulgate in medieval Latin texts. These advantages are there even if you are not planning a computer-based edition; but if you are it is even more helpful. The standard coding mentioned earlier allows for this: you can fill the text of your raw files with as many 'references' of the kind used by packages like OCP or COCOA as you like. You can therefore in the course of your edition make KWICs of whatever parts of it you want — which goes some way towards the loss of database facilities entailed by the approach — and the 'typesetter' can also use these to create a file suitable for such processing with page and line references. This is helpful should your indexing demands be more complex than can be met by using the indexing facilities of the package: you can create the raw material for a selective word and phrase index, for example.

There are other possible applications which we have not so far explored. I have so far not tried computer-assisted collation either as a mechanical process or with additional statistical computations to produce a textual apparatus. Another area to be considered is that of the electronic edition. This could be particularly interesting with texts where there is a large manuscript tradition and where the user of editions wants to be informed both about the author's original intentions and about what his subsequent users read. The 'flat' nature of printed editions as a representation of the text edited is here a serious drawback. In principle it ought to be possible to devise a 'requestable' edition, which coupled with a computer and a printing device provides the edition in the format the user wants, though the practical difficulties, particularly as regards portability, are very evident.

History and Computing: Implications for Publishing

Ten years ago a conference on history and computing would have attracted a very different audience. It would have been smaller and more concerned with the details of computing hardware. If we imagine another such conference in ten years time, how will things have changed?

It is arguable that there will no longer be a need for a conference on history and computing. By then the uses of computers in historical research will be so well understood and so much a part of the fabric of scholarship that it would be as unnecessary as having a conference on libraries and history. I predict that there will be a history and computing conference in 1996, but I have some sympathy for the view that there is nothing of importance, apart from the historical content, that is unique about historical research and computing. There can be very few computing techniques which are solely of interest to historians. Many of the papers read at this conference should be of methodological interest to scholars in other disciplines in the humanities.

If history, like other disciplines, is finding increasing scope for computing techniques this is a simple consequence of the fact that computing is an extraordinarily pervasive technology in our culture. Or, more precisely, computing is an aspect of a broad coalition of information technologies — microelectronics, telecommunications, optical storage, video etc. — which feed upon each other to grow with ever-increasing vigour to offer new and unexpected channels and modalities for communication. These technologies are having and will continue to have a deep effect on the teaching of history and on scholarship because they will alter many of the practices of all those who work with knowledge. Their initial impact will be on bulky and repetitive information processing tasks and in those sectors of the economy where there are mass markets or where information has an immediate high cash value, but as computers become more interesting and more subtle we may expect historians and other scholars to start taking advantage of the possibilities the medium offers for recording, distributing and publishing the results of research. This should lead to publications which are quite unlike books or journals printed on paper. They will exploit the computer's ability to present images, moving graphics and text, of the ability to search large bodies of information swiftly and accurately, of the capacity of computer software to be highly interactive and responsive to the interest of a particular user, and with the development of artificial intelligence techniques of methods of knowledge processing.

The growth of new methods and media for research publication is quite consistent with the survival and continued success of traditional methods. The death of the book has been been frequently but mistakenly foretold: as though computers were, like a fierce breed of colonists, displacing books from the continent of knowledge. I suspect that most publishers are quite optimistic about the continuing future for the book. My own optimism is based on a simple truism: what the book does best will continue to be done best by the book. This truism lacks predictive power since it does not tell us 'what it is that books do best', or 'what computers might do better', but the important point is that they can be expected to be broadly complementary modes of publication. In this paper I shall say nothing about the technical problems which beset authors and publishers who are increasingly using word processing files to drive typesetting machines. This is a less trivial challenge than is generally appreciated but it seems to me that the really profound implications of computing for historical publications are to do with the possibility that the technology will not only offer historians new techniques for historical research, but that the use of these techniques will encourage computerised modes of publication.

The words 'technique' and 'technology' connote means rather than ends, method rather than purpose. When we think of the potter's technology we think of his tools rather than his clay or his vases. Viewing computing as a technology which can assist the historian in his research, we may ask ourselves with which traditional tools is the computer to be compared. Ten years ago we might have selected a different model from today. The earliest uses of computers in historical research were for large-scale data processing, particularly of statistics. The computer was used as if it were a very powerful, multidimensional but awkward, card index system. The computer now appears most prominently to the historian or scholar as a technology for generating texts. If the first generation of historical computing saw the computer being used on the model of the card index, and the second generation sees the microcomputer displacing the mechanical typewriter from the author's desk, what historical tools remain to be displaced or supplemented? There is of course a very important difference between technologies which replace and those which supplement existing methods. It seems very likely that card indexes and typewriters will soon be as obsolete for serious historians as slide rules and log tables are for mathematicians. But books are so central to, and so constitutive of current methods of historical understanding that it may seem absurd to characterise the third generation of history and computing as the one in which computers are used for communicating historical knowledge in ways somewhat similar to the conventional book publishing process.

It is only absurd if we see the use of the computer to disseminate information or knowledge as *displacing* the book. Of course there are respects in which the the book and the computer may be in direct competition. The subscription to an on-line database may come from the same budget as the book acquisitions, the Professor who is using a terminal screen is not at that moment reading a book. But computerised information systems may compete with print on paper technologies while at the same time coexisting with the book and the journal; in much the same way as automobiles and airplanes compete with rail and sea transport as well as complementing them. Many reasons could be adduced for believing that books are not going to disappear in the foreseeable future. One could go further: there are convincing reasons why the writing of books will always be important within universities. The usefulness of computer-based information systems *vis a vis* books will be comparable to the happy coexistence between the spoken lecture and the printed treatise. Books will retain their centrality for many years to come because there are too many things which the book does so well that they could not be done better by some other technology or medium. But there are types of information service that computing technology can supply much better than any print on paper technology. It is in these areas that we can expect computer based publishing to flourish. So, I predict that in ten years time a conference on history and computing will be concerned with questions about the electronic or computer-based publication of research. Computer software and databases will be important not simply as tools for research but as the product, outcome, or record of research.

Computer-based or electronic publishing will be quite different from book publishing in important respects. The differences are more to do with function than content. There can be no point in writing, publishing, or reading electronic publications unless they meet a different need from the book — it is not as though books are impossibly expensive to produce. Let us consider some hypothetical examples which show why a historian might think it useful to publish a work in an electronic mode. Suppose that someone has completed an exhaustive study of the dispositions of British forces during the Boer war. This information is available in the form of large files which give all the information collated during the research. These files could be used by the scholar to establish the points of military history which he chooses to make. But the data may be of use to other students of the period and could conceivably be published in such a way that readers could examine and interrogate the data collected. It is also likely that once a scholar begins to think about publishing his research materials in this way, the very act of readying the material for publication will suggest further conclusions and hypotheses. Data which is prepared for interactive publication is open to reinterpretation. There is a possible analogy with the way in which the use of spreadsheeting software has led accountants and financial managers into a new activity: the so called 'what iffing' in which many hypothetical alternatives can be rapidly considered. There is a tendency to suppose that databases are simply collections of data, from which it seems to follow that they must ignore the really difficult questions which are to do with argument, assessment, and the interpretation of facts. This line of argument overlooks what may be the most important aspect of database software. Namely, that it gives us new models for the arrangement of information and thus for the generation and expression of knowledge.

The potential, and in some sense the necessity, for computerised books is strongest in the case of those very large reference books or tools of scholarship which threaten to become unwieldy in book form. These books are in many cases only accidentally printed as linear texts. The need to computerise major library catalogues, such as the British Library's Eighteenth Century Short Title Catalogue, is a consequence of the fact that it will only be possible to maintain an adequate control of bibliographic information through computerised systems. The stock of published material is growing at a rate which defeats traditional cataloguing methods. In an analogous predicament, Oxford University Press realised that it would not be possible to produce a printed supplement to a supplement, and the only way in which it would be practical to continue the lexicography of the *Oxford English Dictionary* and its *Supplements* would be by integrating the two works. The only feasible way to do this was by computerising the whole corpus. The production of the Eighteenth Century Short Title Catalogue and the *New Oxford English Dictionary* was not undertaken primarily for reasons of historical research, but there can be little doubt that major by-products of these computerisation projects will be databases of great value for historical research.

The computerisation of these corpuses is not significant in its addition to the stock of human knowledge, but in the way it makes this knowledge accessible. It is not as though we had discovered a trunk of Napoleon's archives and thereby acquired new knowledge. It is rather that what is already known is more accessible, because information held in computer memory is more usable than information held in book form. The data which these databases contain is very similar to that which appears in the printed or typed records from which they are descended. The computerisation of these large books will be significant to historians primarily because it will make it possible to get immediate answers to such questions as: according to the OED, which words with a medical definition entered the English language from Dutch in the seventeenth century, or, how many pamphlets on medical matters were printed in the English language by Dutch printers in the seventeenth century? The answers to these questions are simple statistics, but a listing of these words, or of these works, might be extremely suggestive and useful to certain sorts of historical inquiry. So much information is implicit in our printed records but in practice much of it is quite inaccessible.

A major database, such as a large catalogue or a multi-volume dictionary or encyclopaedia may seem to be rather remote from the concerns of many historians. The very scale of these large publications may seem inappropriate for the work of many scholars. Can one envisage smaller scale computer publications which might fall within the ambition of one, two, or a small group of scholars? How might such publications work? Since I am not a historian I shall not try to suggest what projects might be justified on grounds of scholarship. It would seem to me that several of the research projects discussed at this conference are strong candidates for software or database publication. The important thing is that this should be recognised and that scholars will in the future consider whether distributing some electronic or software publication may not be more appropriate than the publication of papers or monographs. If this is so, then we may expect some of the criteria which have application in paper publishing to cut in a rather different sense on the grain of a new method and a new medium. It may be useful if I sketch some of the criteria which might be invoked in assessing computer-based projects in history.

When considering an unfamiliar computer-based publishing project, I always try to get clear in my mind whether the author has a product which is primarily a technique, a program or method which other historians may wish to employ, or whether it is primarily a set of data which may be of use to the peer community, or to students. In most subjects, useful tools are rarer than interesting packets of data. The good craftsman needs to be familiar with a limited set of tools, but scholars have a nearly unquenchable thirst for extensions to the library. We do not like changing our working methods too quickly but are often curious about new information. The distinction between programs and data is not rigid, but it is probable that relatively few programs or software tools are specific to history. We may expect historians to use tools developed for, and used by other disciplines, for example: databases, time series packages, concordance programs, statistical packages, and word processors.

But history is characteristically very rich in data and we may expect historical research projects to involve large and heterogenous sets of data. In which case a publisher may be particularly concerned to reassure himself that the data is good, the capture reliable, and the way in which the data has been classified is appropriate to the research interests. It may also be necessary to think very early in the project about the expense of capturing the requisite data.

It is arguable that the database may become the paradigm of a new kind of historical publication which will serve a different function from the monograph or article. But one should be careful not to conclude that historical databases will be concerned with *mere* data. One often finds a defensive reflex among those who are anxious about information technology. With satisfaction, and presumed finality, it is pointed out that computers can handle mere facts, data or information: 'But computers cannot deal with argument, value, insight, or knowledge.' The trouble with this line of argument is that computer software is on all fours with books when it comes to handling or representing knowledge and argument. We do not yet know how informative, or deep, databases or knowledge bases will become, but we can be sure in advance that whether or not they are any good or will depend on the ability and judgement of their authors.

A publisher who is considering whether to commit his firm to a publication in historical computing will need to consider many other factors which have their analogies in book publishing: is the subject of wide enough interest? Can a large publication be approached in stages? Is it likely to bring an adequate return? These questions do not seem to have any unusual bearing on computer-based publishing projects. But there are some issues which are peculiar to computer-based publishing.

We all think that we know what is required to write a book. We assume that a good scholar can write a book. The question of the technical competence of the author does not, in general, arise. The position with computer-based publishing is rather different. A historian who plans a major research project involving the use of computers will either need to be technically competent with software, or need to know how to secure good technical advice. The technical assessment may go to the heart of the project in a manner which is unfamiliar to the authors of books. We may discover that there is a premium on good team work, as there is in some fields of scientific research.

Given the extreme novelty of low-cost, personal, computing it is not surprising that we do not yet know how best to exploit the technology for publishing purposes. But it is not simply the novelty of the technology which is the cause of uncertainty. Computer hardware and software is still evolving at such a rate that the consequent lack of uniform standards is itself an obstacle to effective publishing ventures. For this reason the most important feature of the IBM PC standard is that it has created a nearly universal basis for computer software of the kind which can be afforded by individual scholars. The lingua franca of MS/DOS will become the substrate for serious attempts to use computer media to publish works of historical research in the next five years. Historians who wish to use computers in their research or teaching should concentrate on the possibilities offered by standard spread sheeting, database, word processing and statistical packages.

In this paper I have predicted that historians, like other scholars, will increasingly be able to use computers as a publishing medium which is complementary to the printed book. I have also speculated on the form these publications might take. But leaving on one side the question of whether or not historians will be able to use computers in this way, it is open to us to consider whether or not historians should be encouraged to think about new methods of publishing historical research. This is difficult terrain for the amateur, but there may be quasi-ethical reasons for publishing historical data in a computerised form in which it can be easily examined by other historians — it is the scholar's duty not only to make conjectures and fashion theories, but also to publish the evidence. These quasi-ethical considerations will count for more if the cost of publication is low, and as we know the simple manufacturing cost of electronic media is very low. Information about birth and dèath rates in urban and rural parishes in nineteenth century England might make for extremely tedious reading if published in book form, but could generate highly testable hypotheses if the information was held in a computer database. It may appear very bold and innovative today to publish a book with an accompanying database, but perhaps in ten years time the carping critic may object that an otherwise excellent book on urbanisation and industrialisation in nineteenth century England is not accompanied by a database which covers the relevant research, as we might today complain of the absence of a good index. It should be unthinkable for anyone now planning a definitive edition of some great author to overlook the need to produce an electronic and archival edition of the text, even though the immediate market for an electronic text is slight. For several years, published historical databases may be rare and exceptional, but we should be willing to accept and use them as useful extensions to the form of the historical monograph. They should perhaps be seen as illustrations of historical monographs, analogous to the bibliographies, tables, appendices, or critical apparatus — perhaps even to the extent of being tucked in the binding of a book like a microfiche facsimile in a critical edition. Historians will decide which software and database approaches are particularly appropriate or helpful in history, but when the appropriate methods have been proven then the researcher's peers will need also to have access to the results and techniques of the computer-based research.

Demonstrations

40 *Lorna Weatherill*

Using 'Datatrieve' to Analyse Data from a Sample of Probate Inventories

The purpose of the demonstration was to show, on line to the St. Andrews mainframe computer, how I had used a data-base-management system to explore and tabulate data about ownership of household goods from probate inventories. This summary gives a brief outline of the demonstration: the note at the end refers to the origins of the research and publications arising from it.

Datatrieve is an interactive programme designed by DEC for use with VAX data files. The particular data used here was obtained from a sample of 2092 probate inventories from eight parts of England. Data from each inventory occupied one line in the data file, with fields giving coded information about the inventory and whether or not 21 household goods were recorded in it. Example 1 shows the lay-out of the file, and this was discussed at the demonstration.

This is obviously a simplification of the information from the documents. My demonstration showed how relationships could be explored in this very large body of information. Example 2 shows a brief extract from a Datatrieve session, in which the ownership of one of the goods (china) is explored. Frequency tables can be constructed from these sessions and Example 3 shows a completed one of these.

In the demonstration I showed how it was possible to examine quite complex relationships between the variables contained in the inventories and the ownership of the household goods. There was a lot of discussion and it was felt that a database management system is an effective way of exploring data with regular patterns. Datatrieve itself can be used in other ways and data need not be coded. Its main drawback is that you need to be able to use it before you can understand the manual!

Note

The research reported here was undertaken as part of an ESRC project entitled 'Consumer Behaviour and Material Culture, 1660–1760', which has led to two articles and a book (forthcoming) with the same title as the project. See Lorna Weatherill, 'A possession of one's own; women and consumer behaviour in England, 1660–1740', *Journal of British Studies*, 25, 1986, pp. 131–56; 'Consumer behaviour and social status in England, 1660–1750', *Continuity and Change*, 2, 1986. I am grateful to Angela Lamb and John Henderson for their help.

Example 1   *The layout of the Datatrieve file used in the demonstration: the first 16 entries*

REC NO	YEAR	DIOCESE	LOCATION	OCSTAT	ECON MAIN	ECON SUB	SEX	GEN CLASS	SOCIAL STATUS	TOTAL VALUE	HOUSE VALUE	G1	G2	G3	G4	G5	G6	G7
0001	1675	01	3	108	04	e	1	04	05	0073	004	0	0	0	1	1	0	0
0002	1675	01	1	013	08		1	08	10	0472	004	0	0	0	0	1	1	0
0003	1675	01	1	008	01		1	03	06	0013	004	0	0	0	1	1	0	0
0004	1675	01	3	046	04	f	1	04	05	0012	009	0	0	0	1	1	1	0
0005	1675	01	1	001	08		1	01	01	0181	028	1	0	0	0	1	1	1
0006	1675	01	1	003	08		2	07	08	0025	016	0	0	0	1	1	1	0
0007	1675	01	2	054	06	d	1	05	02	0043	012	0	0	0	1	1	1	0
0008	1675	01	2	055	04	g	1	04	05	0008	006	0	0	0	1	1	1	0
0009	1675	01	2	003	08		2	07	08	0016	009	0	0	0	0	1	1	0
0010	1675	01	2	011	08		1	08	10	0009	007	1	0	0	1	1	1	0
0011	1675	01	3	001	08		1	01	01	0673	048	1	0	0	1	1	0	1
0012	1675	01	1	005	01		1	02	04	0060	003	0	0	0	0	1	1	0
0013	1675	01	2	055	04	g	1	04	05	0621	081	0	0	0	1	1	1	1
0014	1675	01	2	065	05		1	05	05	0031	025	0	0	0	1	1	1	0
0015	1675	01	1	005	01		1	02	04	0028	022	0	0	0	1	1	1	0
0016	1675	01	1	001	08		1	01	01	2572	180	1	1	0	1	1	0	0

Notes

Each inventory was given a record number (REC-NO).
The sample was taken every tenth year, beginning in 1675 (YEAR), from eight dioceses (DIOCESE).
The LOCATION is coded as to whether the inventory came from a rural area (1), major town (3), other town (2) or London (5). Occupation and/or status (OCSTAT) was coded from the entries in the documents.
This was subdivided in three ways, economic sector (ECON-MAIN and ECON-SUB), a general classification (GEN-CLASS) and social status (SOCIAL-STATUS).
Gender was coded as 1 for men and 2 for women.
Inventory value (TOTAL-VALUE) and the value of household goods (HOUSE-VALUE) were entered to the nearest £1.
The possesison (1) or not (0) of 21 household goods is also recorded (G1-G2); only G1-G7 are shown here as examples.

Use of Datatrieve involves using commands in a version of English, as example 2 shows.

Example 2   *A Datatrieve session and some commentary*


```
DTR>
DTR>
DTR>
DTR> print count of lw-survey
```
my instruction to count the number of records with particular characteristics. LW-SURVEY is the name for all the records.

```
COUNT

  2902
```
These are printed at the terminal by Datatrieve.

```
DTR> print count of lw-survey with g16=1

COUNT

   109
```
It counts all the records with china

```
DTR> print count of lw-survey with g17=1

COUNT

   115
```
it counts all the records with knives and/or forks

```
DTR> print count of lw-survey with location=5 and gen-class=4,5

COUNT

   199
```
it can also count records with complex characteristics. Location 5 is London; gen-class 4 and 5 are craft and dealing trades.

```
DTR> print count of lw-survey with location=5
                                      (London)
COUNT

   319
```

```
DTR> print count of lw-survey with location=1 and gen-class=4
                                      (rural)        (craftsmen)
COUNT

   278
```

```
DTR> print average total-value of lw-survey

AVERAGE
 TOTAL
 VALUE
                          i.e. £128
 0128
```

```
DTR> print average house-value of lw-survey

AVERAGE
 HOUSE
 VALUE
                          i.e. £24
  024
```

```
DTR> print average house-value of lw-survey with location=5 and gen-class=4,5
```

AVERAGE
HOUSE
VALUE

032

It is also useful to be able to search smaller sections: this can be done by making a 'collection' of records with certain characteristics. Here china is selected as the current collection.

```
DTR> find lw-survey with g16=1
[109 records found]
DTR> print count of current with location=1
```
COUNT   (rural)

   28

```
DTR> print count of current with sex=2
```
COUNT   (women)

   16

So the same proportions of women owned china as in the whole survey (3·7%). This usually has to be calculated separately.

```
DTR> print count of lw-survey with sex=2
```
COUNT

   430

```
DTR> print count of current with gen-class=4,5
```
COUNT

   63

```
DTR> print count of current with location=5 and gen-class=4,5
```
COUNT

   27

```
DTR> print count of current with location=2,3 and gen-class=4,5
```
COUNT   (urban)

   24

```
DTR> print count of current with location=1 and gen-class=4,5
```
COUNT

   12

Note
Many of the commands can be pre-set, which makes sessions faster.

Example 3   *A three-way frequency table constructed using Datatrieve: ownership of four selected goods in different places in each decade from 1675 to 1725.*

Percentage of inventories with **clocks**

%	1675	1685	1695	1705	1715	1725
London	11	15	19	24	52	51
Major town	7	3	8	28	33	26
Other town	17	16	19	15	31	43
Rural	8	8	13	19	29	31

Percentage of inventories with **pictures**

%	1675	1685	1695	1705	1715	1725
London	9	26	21	57	60	60
Major town	30	30	32	49	60	48
Other town	21	24	21	6	43	47
Rural	2	3	3	5	9	10

Percentage of inventories with **window curtains**

%	1675	1685	1695	1705	1715	1725
London	23	30	43	39	60	62
Major town	20	20	13	31	33	52
Other town	6	13	17	11	29	26
Rural	4	5	5	6	7	10

Percentage of inventories with **china**

%	1675	1685	1695	1705	1715	1725
London	0	0	0	7	33	35
Major town	0	0	11	13	13	9
Other town	0	7	8	8	17	11
Rural	0	1	1	2	2	4

41   *Peter Adman*

Micro-MIST

This paper outlines the project 'Micro-MIST' which is a derivative of the mainframe computer package MIST. In particular, one of the commands,

CLUSTER, is described in detail with numerous examples.

Most readers will be familiar with databases: files that are designed for getting quick answers to queries and producing results. Their essential feature is that they are all structured in some way. They are organised into records and fields and then indexed in order to enable fast retrieval of required information.

Micro-MIST is a set of software tools rather than a database system. For a start there is no indexing to be done. The text is kept and retrieved by the user exactly as it was originally typed. The user is provided with various facilities to compress or encode the data e.g. SOUNDEX, SPELLX. There are other options also for fuzzy matching which allows linking of nearly equal fields and a 'short-match' capability.

MIST stands for *M*anipulative *Interactive Software Tools*, and is a result of a joint venture between the departments of History and the Computer Centre of Hull University. The original package was written in FORTRAN 77, Micro-MIST is written in BASIC and is available for the BBC computer.

Micro-MIST is designed with the following characteristics; l) it is general, and will work with any nominal data: 2) it is interactive: 3) it is menu driven: 4) it has embedded help: 5) it is transportable — written in BASIC: 6) it is modular, and includes graphics & statistical modules: 7) it is layered, having various levels of access through generic commands.

The current state of Micro-MIST development can be best shown by comparing it with the facilities in MIST. The mini/mainframe version featues listing, sorting, cross-tabulating, selecting, checking, matching, merging, recoding, input/editing and clustering. Micro-MIST at present features listing, clustering and simple histograms; full plotting facilities, 3-D histograms, frequencing, pie charts, a pop-up calculator, a full screen editor and spread-sheet have been written but not yet incorporated. Windowing, icons and mouse control are to follow.

The data consist of nominal records made up of fields separated by commas (or any other defined separator). The information in each field may be alphabetic, numeric, coded, uncoded, and variable or fixed length. For example:

NICHOLAS,l,BECKSIDE,JONATHAN,MUSGRAVE,HEAD,M,MALE,43,
JOINER,YORKSHIRE BEVERLEY

Fields may be referenced either via their positions, or via their header keywords which are defined by the user and are often different for different set of data.

From this point on I shall concentrate on describing the CLUSTER command which enables the analysis of grouped data such as families, households etc. A typical call to CLUSTER may be thus:

RELATION-TO-HEAD = SON,DAUGHTER
AGE > 18
BIRTH-PLACE = YORKSHIRE BEVERLEY,HULL
MARITAL-STATUS#UNMARRIED

to give frequencies per household, of all SONs or DAUGHTERs under the AGE l8, who were born in YORKSHIRE BEVERLEY or HULL but were not **UNMARRIED**. Alternatively the user may simply type

> FIELD 6 = SON,DAUGHTER
> FIELD 9 > 18
> etc.

When CLUSTER issued a program is called in and executed producing a running frequency chart such as shown:

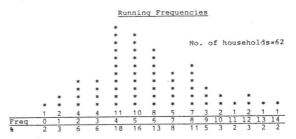

It also displays cumulative values and their percentages.

The general format of the CLUSTER command is as follows:

> CLUSTER filename
> Head of household definitions
> Terminator for above
> Details of individuals to be selected
> Terminator

The head of household definitions and the details of individuals to be selected have two possible forms; (a) 'field header = text1,text2,. . .': (b) macro definitions. These are similar to 'words' used in the computer language 'FORTH'. Each 'word' is defined in terms of words which are already defined in the Micro-MIST dictionary and is implemented as a threaded-list.

In the rest of the paper I illustrate the possible usage of CLUSTER through sample questions. I used the data from 1861 Census for the parish of St. Nicholas in Beverley with the following field header-keywords:

FIELD 1 = PARISH	(e.g. St Nicholas . . . St Martin)
FIELD 2 = SCHEDULE	(house number)
FIELD 3 = ADDRESS	(e.g. BECKSIDE . . . WEDNESDAY MARKET)
FIELD 4 = FIRST NAME	(e.g. EMMA . . . THOMAS)
FIELD 5 = SURNAME	(e.g. WATSON . . . BROWN etc.)
FIELD 6 = RELATION-8-HEAD	(e.g. Son . . . Daughter . . . Sister)
FIELD 7 = MARITAL-STATUS	(Married . . . Unmarried . . .Widow)
FIELD 8 = SEX	(Male . . . Female)
FIELD 9 = AGE	(age in years)
FIELD 10 = OCCUPATION	(e.g. Scholar . . . Cabinet Maker)
FIELD 11 = BIRTH-PLACE	(e.g. Yorkshire Beverley)

The first line of the data is as follows:

N,1,NRWD VLNT SLDR,PHINEAS,MUSGRAVE,HD,M,M,52,VCTLR,Y B

Note that some of the fields in this data happen to have been compacted. In all the tables obtained, column 1 represents the number of people per household, 2 represents frequencies, 3 represents the percentage of frequencies, 4 represents cumulative frequencies, 5 represents the percentage of cumulative frequencies.

Question 1. Size of Households

Type: PARISH = N

Number in a family	Freq.	%	Cum.	C. as %
0	0	0	0	0
1	17	5	17	5
2	66	20	83	25
3	59	18	142	43
4	58	18	200	61
5	42	13	242	74
6	29	9	271	83
7	28	9	299	91
8	14	4	313	96
9	6	2	319	98
10	2	1	321	98
11	1	0	322	98
12	2	1	324	99
13	1	0	325	99
14	1	0	326	100
15	0	0	326	100
16	0	0	326	100
17	1	0	327	100

Total number of families = 327

Question 2. Children aged under 15

Type: AGE < 15

Number in a family	Freq.	%	Cum.	C. as %
0	129	39	129	39
1	62	13	191	58
2	38	11	229	70
3	42	12	271	82
4	30	9	301	92
5	16	4	317	96
6	3	0	320	97
7	4	1	324	99
8	2	0	326	99
9	1	0	327	100

e.g. 39% of the households had no children.

Question 3. Children aged under 15 still at school

Type: AGE < 15
Type: OCCUPATION = SCH

Number in a family	Freq.	%	Cum.	C. as %
0	204	62	204	62
1	41	13	245	75
2	35	11	280	86
3	28	9	308	94
4	11	3	319	98
5	5	2	324	99
6	3	1	327	100

Two-thirds (62%) of the households had no children (aged under 15) still at school.

Question 4. Servants

Type: RELATION-TO-HEAD = SRV

Number in a family	Freq.	%	Cum.	C. as %
0	305	93	305	93
1	18	6	323	99
2	1	0	324	99
3	2	1	326	100
4	0	0	326	100
5	0	0	326	100
6	0	0	326	100
7	1	0	327	100

Except for one household with seven servants, there were only 26 servants, mostly one per household.

Question 5. Servants born in Beverley

Type: RELATION-TO-HEAD = SRV
Type: BIRTH-PLACE = Y B

Number in a family	Freq.	%	Cum.	C. as %
0	318	97	318	97
1	7	2	325	99
2	1	0	326	100
3	0	0	326	100
4	1	0	327	100

Very rarely were the servants born in Beverley Yorkshire (i.e. Y B). Remember, however, that St. Nicholas did not have many servants anyway.

Question 6. Widowed heads

Type: RELATION-TO-HEAD = HD
Type: MARITAL-STATUS = W

Number in a family	Freq.	%	Cum.	C. as %
0	284	87	284	87
1	43	13	327	100

Question 7: Children aged under 15 where the head of family is aged under 60

Type: RELATION-TO-HEAD = HD
Type: AGE < 60
Type: +
Type: AGE < 15
Type: .

Number in a family	Freq.	%	Cum.	C. as %
0	148	45	148	45
1	49	15	197	60
2	36	11	233	71
3	38	12	271	83
4	30	9	301	92
5	16	5	317	97
6	3	1	320	98
7	4	1	324	99
8	2	1	326	100
9	1	0	327	100

There were 16 households (column 2) consisting of 5 people (column 1), i.e. 5%.
317 households consisting of up to 5 people, i.e. 97%
301 households consisting of no more than 4 people.

Bibliography

P. Adman, 'MIST: Manipulative Interactive Software Tools', *ESRC Software Bulletin*, May 1984, pp. 22–3.

P. Adman, 'A General Method and Notation for Matching Text Contained in Fields', *University Computing*, 7, 1985, pp. 85–8.

P. Adman, *MIST Userguide*, University of Hull, 1986.

P. Adman, 'Applications of computers to Historical Data', *Computer Education*, 54, November 1986.

42 *Brenda Collins and John Power*

Families, Individuals and Fertility in Ireland: the FIFI Project

This brief presentation is designed to indicate the capabilities of SIR as a data management system in the collation and analysis of census enumeration data. The research is part of an E.S.R.C. financed project (G 00 23 2224) 'Fertility, Religion and Social Class in Early Twentieth Century Ireland'. The data base used is that of a stratified sample from the household census enumeration schedules of Londonderry in 1911.[1]

The aims of the project are two-fold: first, to test the applicability of SIR as an easily available package for the analysis of such data, and to develop a standardised set of procedures with which the investigation can be extended geographically; and secondly, to examine the connections between the demographic strategies of marital fertility, celibacy, emigration and the labour market.

One of the major aims of computer analysis of census enumeration data is to achieve a data set structured in such a way that analysis can take place, flexibly, across several levels — community, household, family and individual — without 'flattening' or 'rectangularising' the data. The units of analysis are thus at each of these levels with each household being assigned a unique identity number which is tagged onto the family and individual records. Because SIR is a hierarchical data base system in its physical form, each record is stored following the record to which it relates. Thus each HSEFULL (identity number of household) which is a CASE in SIR, points to three RECORD TYPES, where SCHEMA 1 equals HOUSE level, SCHEMA 2 equals FAMILY level and SCHEMA 3 equals INDIVIDUAL level. Each of these SCHEMAS contains several fields or VARIABLES structured from the original data. In addition, because dummy variables have been created in each SCHEMA, RETRIEVAL UPDATES provide the means of adding computed variables into the database, for example getting the computer to calculate the number of resident offspring in each household.

It is also desirable that the collection file should mirror as nearly as possible the raw manuscript and remain unaltered while providing a base for manipulation and analysis. Thus these data have been entered on coding sheets in a controlled transcript form where the most detailed unit of household residence, the rural townland or urban street, and the first names, surnames and occupations of the individuals are retained in alphabetic form as in the original schedule. The data was then typed up by the Data Preparation department of the University Computer Centre and submitted to an ICL Estriel computer.

Figure 1   *Example of raw data file from Derry sample, 1911 census*

```
            NB  Addresses and names are fictitious

Record Schema 1  HOUSE
01   445   48   1    45   DERRY   BAKER   ST   61
Record Schema 2  FAMILY
02   445   1
Record Schema 3  INDIVIDUAL
03   445   1    1    1   JANE   WILSON   212   34
     3    1                    GROCER
```

Some of these codes are actual transcripts of numeric data, for example age of 34 years, while others are codes, for example relationship to household head and relationship to family head. The flexibility of being able to retain the information that a family head is a son-in-law of a household head should be apparent to anyone who has struggled with SPSS.

RETRIEVAL UPDATES have also been used to handle occupational coding. Initially each unique occupation was sorted alphabetically and assigned a sequential number. Each occupational title was then coded on three levels. Firstly, a basic 4 digit code was assigned following the categories of the published Irish census tables of 1911. This is the same classification scheme as that employed by the census authorities in England and Wales from 1851–1901. It thus facilitates comparability both with other synchronic Irish material and with ongoing research on English and Scottish census enumeration material. It was felt that the virtue of compatibility overrode the well-known anomalies of the published classifications. Moreover, greater precision was achieved by coding on an additional two levels, ECONOMIC

ACTIVITY and HIERARCHY. The computer was used to perform the recodes which were then entered into dummy variables as RETRIEVAL UPDATES to remain as additional variables in the data base.

The data base consists of 751 households, of 3526 individuals. Of these 705 households are of a single family unit, 45 are of two, and 1 of three families. Definitions of family units follow those of the Cambridge Group. As an example of the complex analysis which is possible, Figure 2 gives a sample run illustrating the number of children born alive to Roman Catholic wives married ten years or less and living in Derry city in 1911.

Figure 2   *Number of children born alive to Roman Catholic wives married ten years or less and living in Derry city in 1911*

```
10  RETRIEVAL
20  PROCESS CASES
25  IFNOT (HOUSE04 EQ 45 OR EQ 17)NEXT CASE
30  PROCESS REC 3
35  RECODE MARDUR=IND11(99,1 THRU 10=1) (11  THRU 25=2)(26 THRU 40=3)(ELSE=4)
40  MOVE VARS IND12 IND13
50  IFNOT (IND01 EQ 2)NEXT REC
52  IFNOT (MARDUR EQ 4)NEXT REC
55  IFNOT (IND06 EQ 1)NEXT REC
60  PERFORM PROCS
70  AUTOSET
80  END PROCESS REC
90  END PROCESS CASES
100 FREQUENCIES GENERAL=IND12(100) IND13(100)/HISTOGRAM/STATISTICS=ALL
110 END RETRIEVAL
52 IFNOT (MARDUR EQ 1)NEXT REC
RUN

IND12    CHILDREN BORN ALIVE
```

VALUE LABEL	VALUE	ABSOLUTE FREQUENCY	RELATIVE FREQUENCY (PERCENT)	CUMULATIVE REL FREQ (PERCENT)
	1.00	12.00	34.29	34.29
	2.00	7.00	20.00	54.29
	3.00	6.00	17.14	71.43
	4.00	5.00	14.29	85.71
	5.00	1.00	2.86	88.57
	6.00	2.00	5.71	94.29
	7.00	1.00	2.86	97.14
	8.00	1.00	2.86	100.00
	TOTAL	35.00	100.00	100.00

This research is ongoing and copyright. Further details will be published by the authors as the work progresses. It is intended that the networking procedures which are contained in SIR will be extended to cover other contemporaneous Irish census data and linkages with property valuation registers.

Note

1. These original data are available for inspection at the Public Record Office, Dublin.

Appendix   *Initial Schema Definition*

```
CASE  ID  HSEFULL
COMMON  VARS  HSEFULL  HOUSE01  TO  HOUSE05
RECORD SCHEMA 1, HOUSE
VAR LABELS  HSEFULL  IDENTITY NO. OF HOUSE/ HOUSE 01
LOCATION ID 1/ HOUSE02  LOCATION ID 2/ HOUSE04  PARISH/
HOUSE05 TOWNLAND/
RECORD SCHEMA 2, FAMILY
SORT IDS FAMID
VAR LABELS FAMID/ FAMILY IDENTIFIER
RECORD SCHEMA 3, INDIVIDUAL
SORT IDS FAMID, INDID
VAR LABELS  IND01 STATUS IN HHD/ IND02  INFERRED STATUS/
IND03 FAMILY STATUS/ IND04 FIRST NAMES/ IND05 SURNAME/
IND06 RELIGION/ IND07 LITERACY LEVEL/ IND08 SEX/ IND09 AGE/
IND10 MARITAL STATUS/ IND11 YEARS OF MARRIAGE/
IND12 CHILDREN BORN ALIVE/ IND13 CHILDREN STILL ALIVE/
IND14 PLACE OF BIRTH/ IND15 IRISH LANGUAGE/ IND16 DISABILITIES 1/
IND17 DISABILITIES 2/ IND18 OCCUPATION
```

43   *Eric C. Griffiths*

A Poll Book Analysis Package for Eighteenth-Century Elections

1. Introduction

The data analysed by the program was part of the Middlesex poll book covering the elections of March and December 1768, and April 1769. This was a rich source of information giving great scope for quantitative analysis.[1] The county itself was divided into geographical areas called hundreds. Each hundred was further split into parishes. In addition to the way each freeholder in the poll book voted at the elections, he might also have a description of the type of freehold he held (e.g. business premises) and his social status (e.g. being a doctor or member of the clergy).

A traditional computer method for analysing the information in poll books of this type is to match a logical expression against each record of the poll book and count the matches. This was the method used by W. A. Speck and others in the 1970's.[2] By varying the logical expression, and scanning the whole file of records each time, different quantitative aspects of the data can be inspected.

This method of querying the data was unsuitable for the potentially inexperienced users expected to use this system, as it required them to understand the logical complexity of the queries and the intricacies of Boolean algebra. To make query formulation easier, a different approach using screenfuls of information/instruction was adopted (see Section 4, below). This method assisted the users to formulate accurate logical expressions without requiring them to understand Boolean algebra at more than a superficial level.

However, an experienced user could still use the old 'logical expression' method (Section 5) even though the system was capable of building up a logical expression from the 'menu mode' and displaying this to the user (Section 6). As the computational aspects of the system were hidden from the users, it was necessary to indicate to them that the system was still active when processing a logical expression against the data. This was achieved by the dynamic display described in Section 7.

2. Hiding logic from the user

One of the main principles aimed for in designing this system was that of hiding the formal logic of query formulation from the user. The interface achieved this by allowing a user to take a 'natural' course of action at the terminal, entering meaningful information and not formal logic, while the program took care of constructing the required formal query. This would benefit a user by making it as easy as possible for him to enter into the computer information that was close to his view of the query he was trying to formulate.

3. Menu mode

It was decided that the objectives of the system would be best achieved by a program with a menu-driven interface. The main menu (see Figure 1) displayed on initiation of the program (signalling that it had started to run) gave options to descend to lower levels. A lower level would be dedicated to the selection, by the user, of one particular aspect of the data available such as candidates, parishes or types of freehold. E.g. selecting option 1 from the main menu would cause a descent to the candidate menu (Figure 2) giving a display of all candidates and allowing the user to select those he wished to investigate further. (The figures show screens displayed to the user, '_' indicating the cursor's position.)

4. Screen display

The display presented to the user was screen-oriented. While using the

Figure 1   *Main menu*

```
**************************************************************************
* * * choose from below:  _ * * * * * * *
*------------------------------------------------------------------------*
* choice action letter * * * * 1 choose candidates * * 2 choose hundreds
n * * 3 choose divisions d * * 4 choose parishes p * * 5 choose types of
freehold t * * 6 choose social statuses s * * c change operating mode *
* p process request * * q quit program * * *
*------------------------------------------------------------------------*
* query:  * * * * *
**************************************************************************
```

Figure 2   *Candidate menu*

```
**************************************************************************
* * * * c)hoose number(s) m)ain menu * * * * choose a letter:  _ * * *
*------------------------------------------------------------------------*
* no.  month year candidate * * * * 1 mar.  1768 sir william beauchamp
proctor * * 2 mar.  1768 george cooke * * 3 mar.  1768 john wilkes * * 4
dec.  1768 sir william beauchamp proctor * * 5 dec.  1768 john glynn * *
6 apr.  1769 henry lawes luttrell * * 7 apr.  1769 john wilkes * * 8
apr.  1769 whitaker * * * *
*------------------------------------------------------------------------*
* query:  * * * * *
**************************************************************************
```

Figure 3   *Altering Aldgate to Bethnall Green — just before correction*

```
**************************************************************************
* * * c)hoose number(s) h)elp m)ain menu * * * * choose a letter:  _ * *
*
*------------------------------------------------------------------------*
* no.  parish * * * * 1 acton * * 2 aldgate * * 3 ascott * * 4 bethnal g
* * 5 blackwall * * 6 bow and b * * 7 brentford * * 8 brompton * * 9
chancery * * 10 charlton *
*------------------------------------------------------------------------*
* query:  * * (p?) * * *
**************************************************************************
```

Figure 4   *Altering Aldgate to Bethnall Green — selection of latter*

```
**************************************************************************
* * * c)hoose number(s):  4 * * * * * * *
*------------------------------------------------------------------------*
* no.  parish * * * * 1 acton * * 2 aldgate * * 3 ascott * * 4 bethnal g
* * 5 blackwall * * 6 bow and b * * 7 brentford * * 8 brompton * * 9
chancery * * 10 charlton *
*------------------------------------------------------------------------*
* query:  * * * * *
**************************************************************************
```

Figure 5   *Counting 1768 voters for Sir William Proctor and George
                Cooke*

```
**************************************************************************
* * * * * * * * *
*------------------------------------------------------------------------*
* * * * * * counting ...   * * * *
!******************************....................................! * * * * * * * * * *
* * *
*------------------------------------------------------------------------*
* query:  * * ((1&2)) * * *
**************************************************************************
```

Figure 6   *Freeholders voting for Sir William Proctor and George
                Cooke in 1768*

```
**************************************************************************
* * * n for main menu _ * * * * * * *
*------------------------------------------------------------------------*
* * * * * * * counting ...   * * * *
!********************************************! * * * * no.  of
matches = 637 / 3546 = 18% * * * * * * * * *
*------------------------------------------------------------------------*
* query:  * * ((1&2)) * * *
**************************************************************************
```

menu-driven interface, the screen was split into three distinct sections (Figure 1). The top section of a few lines (about a quarter of the screen's area) typically contained brief instructions on the input allowed at that point in the program. The middle section (about half of the screen area) contained information pertaining to the selections in the top section, displayed in the form of a menu. The bottom section gave a summary, as a logical expression, of the query being entered. This was equivalent to the query the user could have typed had he entered the query as a logical expression. The summary line was updated during query entry as the whole query was gradually built up by navigating systematically through the menus.

With this approach, when selecting the desired data (candidates, parishes, social statuses etc.) using the menus, certain constraints were placed on the user with respect to the logical expression that was developed. These helped the user as the system made an appropriate choice of logical operator for the query. For example, each elector in the poll book was registered in one parish only. Consequently, if more than one parish was specified in the query, it would make sense to assume that the logical operator required was 'or' so that voters in either parish would be counted. If logical 'and' were used instead, there would be no matches because no voter was registered in more than one parish.

5. Change of operating mode

Despite this constraint, it was possible to enter queries using logical expressions by changing the mode of use of the program. However, this method of query entry was not intended for novice users.

6. Query summary

The summary of the query input using the menus appeared in the dedicated bottom section of the screen. This grew as the selections from the various menus (candidate, parish etc.) were made. The selections from each menu were parenthesised to aid readability. The query could be edited by re-selecting the appropriate menu. For example, to change 'Aldgate' to 'Bethnal Green' in Figure 3, the parish menu would be re-selected and the new parish number (4) entered having selected 'c' ('choose numbers' in the top section of the screen) giving the corrected version shown in Figure 4. Similarly, the inclusion of one or more parishes could be deleted by selecting no parish numbers when prompted. Any changes made in these ways would be reflected by the summary in the bottom section of the screen. The logical operands used here were the same as those which would be used if entering the query using a logical expression; i.e. the summary could contain

1) operators: 'and', 'or' and 'not';
2) brackets: '(' and ')';
3) operands: candidates, types of freehold, social statuses and the geographical regions described above (parishes etc.).

7. Display during match-counting

Having entered the query, the user instructed the computer to count the number of matches by the appropriate main menu command: 'p' for 'process request' (see Figure 1). As the amount of data was large, there could be considerable delay between the invocation of this command and the display of the result while the computer processed the poll book data sequentially. This delay could be typically anything up to a minute but possibly even longer, depending on

1) the complexity of the query;
2) the different data types in the query (candidates, parishes etc.);
3) the number of users currently using the machine (not just those using the poll book program).

This meant that it was necessary to

1) maintain the user's interest;
2) show him that something was really going on (i.e. counting).

To achieve this, while processing the query, the program would display a lengthening line of asterisks on the screen. These would indicate how far counting had progressed through the data. Thus the user was aware that the program was active during the counting phase. If desired, he could estimate roughly how long his wait would be by observing the rate at which the line of asterisks was growing, rather than looking at a static screen for what might seem a prohibitively long period of time (Figures 5 and 6). The dots indicated the amount of processing still to be done.[3]

Notes

1. G. Rudé, *Wilkes and Liberty*, Oxford University Press, 1962
2. W. A. Speck and W. A. Gray, 'Computer Analysis of Poll Books: an Initial Report', *Bulletin of the Institute of Historical Research*, Volume XLIII, 1970, pp. 105–12: W. A. Speck, W. A. Gray and R. Hopkinson, 'Computer Analysis of Poll Books: A Further Report' *Bulletin of the Institute of Historical Research*, Volume XLVIII, 1975, pp. 64–90.
3. For further information, see E.C. Griffiths, 'The construction of simple user-interfaces for historical databases' (to be submitted). I wish to thank W. A. Gray and Dr. N. J. Fiddian for their help in writing this article.

Post-authoring a Videodisc

The demonstration, which was of particular interest to art historians, was divided into two parts:

(i)   a formal introduction to videodisc technology and post-authoring;

(ii)   a CAL tutorial on post-authoring which delegates could follow individually.

(i) The formal sessions started with a general outline of videodisc technology, focusing on the different kinds of disc available and the configuration in use: player, BBC micro, Microtext on ROM, with the Microtext extension commands and the authored program on floppy disc. Delegates were then shown various menu-driven programs which allow rapid access to still images and moving sequences held on videodisc. The menu options illustrated a number of possibilities offered by the medium, including subtitling and alternative German and English audio tracks. Following the initial demonstration of the system's capabilities, attention turned to the process of creating and editing programs using Microtext. The two main types of command were illustrated: those used to control the player (the extension commands), and those concerned with the presentation of material on screen. The latter are also of two kinds: commands visible in edit mode only which ensure that textual material appears correctly formatted on screen at run time; and commands which create embedded (and normally hidden) codes for graphics and colour. Finally, a program written for computer-assisted language learning (CALL) was used to demonstrate further aspects of the system relevant to both teaching and storage/retrieval. The CALL program illustrated the option of branching rapidly between the two audio tracks on a videodisc within an interactive tutorial — allowing access to alternative languages or alternative commentaries in one language. Also shown by the CALL program were the flexible response-handling capabilities of Microtext. Designed originally for tutorial purposes, these provide a way of checking user responses which is both flexible and relatively quick to author. These facilities also offer the possibility of accessing individual frames or moving sequences held on videodisc by typing in one term or a combination of terms which define the search criteria. Thus Microtext provides scope for retrieval beyond the level of simple multiple-choice menu options.

(ii) Between the formal sessions a computer-based tutorial on post-authoring was left running on the system. This outlined (using graphics) the hardware/software configuration on display, and illustrated the basic commands employed in controlling the videodisc player. An integral part of the tutorial was the opportunity for delegates themselves to practise using the commands to control the player in real time.

Hardware: Philips VP831 Videodisc Player, BBC Micro

Software: the Authoring Language Microtext

45 *Rob Dixon*

System for Tabulating and Indexing People, Possessions, Limnings and Ephemera

STIPPLE is a unique multi-user computer system for recording and linking the history of the fine and applied arts and social, economic, political and military history. STIPPLE allows the creation of a 'knowledge base' of historical data containing millions of records and is available as an on-line real-time service from STIPPLE Database Services Ltd., who have created a unique facility, a world computer centre for historical data. STIPPLE is equally suitable for large and small users in any part of the world, including institutions such as museums, galleries or libraries, and individuals such as archivists, curators, keepers, historians, administrators, book and art dealers, and private collectors and researchers. All can contribute to and draw from the continually growing database of shared information, which includes union catalogues, the *STIPPLE biographical dictionary*, the *STIPPLE historical events directory*, etc. Complex catalogue entries, chronologies and bibliographies can be created, all fully integrated and cross-referenced to each other; to people, places and events; to words, phrases, ideas, iconographical indexes, etc., in the powerful thesaurus: and to the source of information. Operators can browse through all data to which they are authorised in the totally integrated database, bypassing menus if they wish.

STIPPLE has a very flexible method of storing data that allows records to be extended as new data is discovered and the structure of records to be changed as users' requirements evolve. Records can contain unlimited amounts of text or any other data, but only occupy as much space as the information currently contained in them requires.

Any record can contain data that is publicly available to operators (of any user) with adequate authority, and further private data that is only available to authorised operators of the particular user that owns that data. Each user or institution can have their own version of this extra data so that operators of different users who request the same records will nevertheless see different data. This unique record structure, only available in STIPPLE and other applications developed (without any programming) from ERROS (*E*xpert *R*eal-time *R*elational *O*pen *S*ystem), is called a virtual record. The virtual record facility of ERROS allows users to share commonly available information, yet still record their own researches and other data separately where they wish these to be kept private (perhaps pending publication).

Different views of records are also possible, so that operators only see those parts of a record appropriate to the job they are doing, and to which they are authorised. STIPPLE has a complete audit trail of all changes. It is a most secure system with considerable flexibility provided by its easy-to-use security features. Changes to the record structures, the facilities available, to the 'views' of data, to indexes and other access paths, to relationships between records and to security can all be made whilst STIPPLE is being used.

All user administrative requirements, such as collections management, conservation history, office automation (including 'mail boxes' for text and message transmission), etc., can be handled very efficiently by STIPPLE. User data is only available to authorised operators of the user who owns the data. Any information can be extracted, indexed, typeset and printed on a laser or other printer.

STIPPLE can be accessed by using privately leased lines, dialled calls on the public telephone network, or packet switching. Users can have several terminals and printers which may be at more than one location. The advanced computer used, an IBM System /38, can store over 14,000,000,000 characters of information and can be used by over 300 operators at the same time. The software may be rented for use on user's own similar computers.

STIPPLE has been used daily for the last three and a half years to record information on British prints produced before 1900. A large database of related information is being established and subscribers who use the STIPPLE service available from ERROS Computing Services Ltd. may wish to access this.

PART III

Teaching

CAL

46 *Frances Blow*

'A fertile error is more productive than a barren truth': Computer Assisted Learning in History

In 1980 the Schools Council History 13–16 Project and the Computers in the Curriculum Project entered into a combined project for the production of software for use in teaching History in Secondary Schools. This year sees the publication of results of that venture: eight units in Computer Assisted Learning published by Longman. The CAL packages, each of which consists of a teachers' guide containing suggestions for use of the unit in the classroom and possible learning outcomes, and students' leaflets, as well as a disk for a micro-computer, were put together by a development team of teachers and professional programmers. The starting point for each program was a learning problem encountered by pupils in the History classroom and which was known to be widespread and not a product of a particular teaching style. Each package was tested in up to twenty schools across the U.K. and the feedback from these trials has been of great value — not only in testing the technical efficiency of the materials but in providing useful data on the learning processes of pupils working with CAL. Experience as a co-ordinator of this project and the trials' evaluations of CAL units suggest that computer simulations can be effective in teaching historical concepts.

The development team of this project shared a particular philosophy of History education and designed software that rested on certain pedagogical principles. The Schools Council History 13–16 Project is based on a belief that History should be taught as a form of knowledge with a distinctive methodology and conceptual structure, rather than as a body of knowledge. It aims to teach pupils to think historically; to evaluate and interpret evidence; to assess the validity of historical accounts; to understand world views and value systems of individuals and groups in the past that were different from their own; to construct historical explanations demonstrating an understanding of such concepts as change and cause. In this way pupils, it is argued, will not simply learn about the past, but about the nature of History, and in such a way that is useful to them — if only to help them make sense of the present.

The pedagogical principles that underpinned the CAL materials related to this philosophy of History education, were those associated with active learning. This pedagogy rests on a belief that the way in which pupils learn is as important as what they learn. The way in which something is learnt can significantly affect pupils' perception of the relevance and use of the new information or ideas they have just encountered or acquired. Active learning often involves pupils in problem solving. Problems posed within a CAL package can encourage pupils to reflect on and analyse their own assumptions and misconceptions, and the implications of their historical understanding.

These points can be illustrated by reference to a particular program, a simulation related to the Arab-Israeli conflict and called *Palestine 1947*. Historical simulations using a computer are often seen as opportunities to re-enact or dramatise the past, to relive the story as it was. In consequence, adherence to a generally accepted narrative is seen to be of major importance. However an alternative approach is to use a simulation based on a model of the structure of the past. Causal models are often employed in the physical and social sciences and provide a means of visualizing what cannot be directly observed, and for making predictions about the performance of physical and social systems under extreme conditions. Such models might not appear appropriate in History which is not subject to covering laws in the same way as is physics for example. But it is a useful aid in revealing to pupils the underlying structure of events in an information rich subject. The difference between the re-enactment and the model might be compared to the difference between the Ordnance Survey map and the London Underground map — both provide different representations of reality. It is often said that because of the restrictions on the memory size of a computer, computer simulations over simplify the past, and therefore are not helpful for explaining the complexity of the past. Unfortunately in order to convey that complexity it is often felt necessary to provide a huge quantity of detailed information which can obscure rather than illuminate. Understanding the underlying logical connections, and the relationships between the component parts of an historical event is a necessary precondition for perceiving complexity. It provides a framework that can facilitate the assimilation of detail. By using a series of algorithms, the logical patterns of cause and effect in history can be emphasised and the past which can appear to children as simply a catalogue of random occurrences, can be presented as coherent and explicable.

Palestine 1947 is a program designed to help pupils understand why the United Nations' plan for the partition of Palestine in 1947 failed to solve the Arab-Israeli conflict. The 'inspiration' for the unit was the belief by many pupils that people in the past must have been of inferior intelligence not to have resolved this conflict by an obvious, rational and simple solution, that of dividing Palestine between the Arabs and the Jews. When discussing this limited understanding of pupils, the development team diagnosed an underlying failure to grasp certain basic aspects of causation in history. These basic principles are that there is usually more than a single cause of an event in the past; that causal factors interact with each other and that 'cause' is not simply one factor over-riding all the others; that the relationship between motive, actions, and outcomes is complex, and that outcomes are not always predictable, and are not always the ones desired by the participants. Out of this analysis grew the computer program *Palestine 1947* which rested on a counterfactual model. The counterfactual is defined as a logical conditional whose antecedent is or is presumed to be contrary to fact. In this CAL unit it enabled pupils to make a decision and be given a consequence regardless of whether their decision corresponded with that taken in the past. This provided teachers with a means of presenting both actual and alternative pasts to pupils, and encouraging them to consider how a range of possible options existed for decision-makers in the past, and that what did happen was not inevitable. Children can too easily acquire a determinist view of history and the explanation of what did not happen can deepen pupils' understanding of why events turned out as they did. The program invites pupils to alter the policies of five powers within a limited number of moves in order to implement the United Nations' plan for the partition of Palestine. A set of alternative policies is provided in the program for each of the powers and there are over 700 possible combinations of policies. The game begins and ends in 1947 and all the possibilities in the program are restricted to what is thought to be historically plausible in 1947. There are four possible outcomes to the game: stalemate or failure to implement the plan (this is the most common and most likely); implementation of the plan; a joint Arab-Israeli state; the third world war. The players are not obliged to take on a particular role but are encouraged to consider the point of view of each of the participants in turn. This program constitutes the base model. Two variations of this structure could enable pupils to advance to an exploration of other aspects of causation. In the second version of the counterfactual pupils might consider the function of motive as cause. Pupils would be required to take on the role of one power and devise a strategy for a given purpose. In the realisation of this strategy, the pupils would play against the computer whose moves would be reactive and logical but not controlled by the pupils. The computer in this version would play the other four powers. Such a program could help develop a more complex understanding in those pupils to whom the intentions of a participant constitute an essential cause of and not merely a possible influence on events. It might assist children to realise that it is possible for there to be common objectives amongst a group of people but that the interactions between a combination of actions can precipitate undesired results. Version three of the counterfactual would allow pupils to construct their own models of causation. Players would need to select from a range of causal factors, assign values to each of them and then play the game. An analysis of the differences between the outcomes of the game and events in the past, could highlight the relative importance of individual factors. It might also lead to a discussion of how historians can construct differing interpretations of the past depending on their selection of and the value attributed to causal factors.

Version one, *Palestine 1947*, has been developed and published; versions two and three await development. However evaluation of version one by trials in schools has confirmed that a simulation with a limited amount of detail does not automatically result in a low level of intellectual response to the issues in it. Instead it can provoke some complex responses.

Feedback from teachers' and pupils' replies to questionnaires, and from the analysis of pupils' discussion recorded on tape, have indicated a range of responses. History can appear very remote and abstract to pupils but by becoming involved in a decision-making game, pupils began to perceive that the past is about real not invented people. They began to realise that people might have had to make the sorts of decisions and weigh up various factors as had they themselves. They felt the responsibility and dangers of decision-making.

Pupils were also encouraged to reflect on their own ideas and to consider how far their own approach was constrained by the culture and context of the 1980s. One group when asked what they were trying to find out by playing the game, replied 'to see if we thought the same as the statesmen then'. This group clearly had realised the importance of period context and its influence on decision-making and historical interpretation. Other pupils commented that they had realised the importance of inter-relating decisions, of drawing-up a strategy, and not simply responding to circumstances, and of not choosing randomly from the options presented. They began to focus on significant terms and to debate their meaning. They saw that entering into negotiation over a plan was not the same as accepting a plan. In their own words they recorded that 'positive decisions have to be followed by positive action'. They saw that a decision might extend no further than an expression of intention; that intention does not guarantee action; that action can not determine outcome. Pupils frequently discussed individual predictions about the results of collective decisions. For instance, they discussed how far the super powers might unduly influence events; to what extent they could encourage aggressive attitudes in both of the major participants without precipitating conflict; once they had manoeuvred themselves into a situation they did not like, what were the possibilities of manoeuvring into a more advantageous position within the limited number of moves still available to them. In so doing pupils were involved in considering the nature of cause and effect. They saw that stalemate was a direct consequence of a series of decisions and not simply predetermined from the outset.

Throughout their explorations at the keyboard (and pupils usually wanted to play the game frequently) they began to realise that working out in advance and automatically implementing a strategy could not guarantee success. Some teachers gave pupils lists of all the policy variations available for each of the five powers before they came to the micro. Working in groups, pupils then planned sequences of policy changes. As they played the game they came to realise that the means to achieve a particular goal might have to alter because they did not have total control of a situation. As causal factors interacted and as circumstances changed so their strategy also had to change even though fundamental aims remained constant. This experience gave pupils useful insights into the relationships subsisting between intentions, policies and strategies, and into an aspect of assessing change in history.

Finally some pupils, reflecting on the game, said afterwards: 'Basic attitudes of the Jews and Arabs must change to get the plan to work. Pressure might force them to change their attitudes but it's not very likely is it?' In the game there is the option for both the Arabs and Jews to accept the plan, an option which was theoretically possible. The pupils' comment indicates how the pupils were making distinctions between what was necessary but unlikely in the circumstances. They were distinguishing between logical possibilities — those which were theoretically possible but unlikely given the particular historical constraints of time and place — and causal possibilities. Causal possibilities would be those that take into account period factors. Student leaflets accompanying the program were designed to prompt pupils' memories about such period factors. They include for example references to the large and influential Jewish population in the USA, and to the fact that Palestine was the traditional homeland of the Jews but also the homeland of many Arabs.

From the evaluation studies to date it is apparent that this CAL unit has potential for use in a variety of syllabus contexts in secondary schools. It could provide a model for the type of program that could be used in undergraduate teaching. For example, such programs might be included in courses on the discipline of History and concerned with teaching historical concepts, as well as within period studies.

This paper borrowed its title from Hugh Trevor Roper : 'a fertile error is more productive than a barren truth.' A Computer Assisted Learning unit can provide a means of exposing errors in pupils' understandings but in such a way as to enable them to explore their own reasoning, not simply be 'put right' by corrective feedback either from the computer or a teacher.

47   *Martyn Wild*

Information Handling, History and Learning. The Role of the Computer in the Historical Process.

This paper is concerned with the role of the computer as a 'learning tool' and as an agent of change in the teaching and learning of history. Undoubtedly the computer is seen by most historians as a machine which aids the more mundane aspects of research, a notion reinforced by the popular characterisation of the computer as a 'number-cruncher'. Indeed, the computer is often held to be a glorified memory-machine, being possessed of mathematical qualities and little else.

However, equally important to the historian, particularly s/he who has an interest in the teaching and learning of the subject, is the potential the computer represents for putting the historical process within the hands of the student. That is, to recognise the computer as a tool which is able to mirror the processes involved in 'doing history' and thereby enhance the learning process for history students.

Initial observations and research[1] has shown that certain software tools, namely those of an information handling variety, can be used to create learning environments of a type which involve the student in important cognitive processes especially relevant to history. For example, the nature of making and testing hypotheses to form deductions, that is a hypothetico-deductive process, becomes essential practice to students who use a powerful data handling system in their work. Moreover, using the computer in this way may serve to heighten a student's conceptual understanding of historical methodology.

The Context

History teaching is changing. The introduction of the sources of history into the classroom has been the vanguard of a movement to get students to think in history and to think historically. At the same time there is no clearly defined notion of what students should be thinking or indeed how they are to go about it. One influential viewpoint here is characterised by Piaget's work, where identification of specific stages of cognitive development related to physiological change has served to limit teachers' expectations of students in history.[2] However, it is fair to reflect on the more pragmatic approaches of some teachers who insist that students can do worthwhile things in history. This reflection must stand alongside an acknowledgement of the view that history is fundamentally too difficult a subject to study in any serious way until later in life.[3] Perhaps in this context it is going too far to suggest that the historical process, that is the whole process embodied in studying history, is one which is within reach of the student. However, it is this notion that I seek to promote here.

The Nature of History

At the heart of the subject lies the prospect of handling information, whether it is of a primary or secondary nature. The historian uses that information in the process of making and testing hypotheses, doing so against a background of knowledge structures. These structures grow with the assimilation of process (the process of doing) and objective (the result of doing) knowledge gained by testing such hypotheses. The result of this historical process is historical understanding. Moreover, the historical process is a perpetual one in which hypotheses may only be proved false, never true.[4] So, one hypothesis gives place to another, each increasingly more refined.

The complex nature of historical information as sources, however, can cause difficulty. To use source materials in historical explanation for example, needs an appreciation of:

—the structure of the information;
—the scope of information to be handled for the explanation to be plausible;
—the concepts and ideas which must form part of that explanation.

Before now source materials have not generally been made accessible or relevant to the student. Moreover, when sources have been presented it is not in a form or alongside the tools that allow them to be effectively handled. This hinders historical understanding. That is to say, the forming and testing of hypotheses must be a realistic process in which hypotheses can be falsified — this will only be so when a range of information is made accessible for testing conjecture. By the same token, any amount of information available which cannot be handled effectively remains of little use.

Information Handling and the Computer

Using information handling programs on the computer can help unlock the historical process in a number of ways:

The characteristic memory powers of the computer allows rapid handling of vast amounts of data, providing the freedom for students to actually use and think about the information effectively — as a historian might.

Information handling programs also provide both flexibility, (allowing the student a degree of control over his/her own learning), and control, the student being able to manipulate the information to any requisite.

Used in a social context they encourage the exchange of ideas and information between peers and between teacher and student.

Finally, the information handling program demands that students consider the structure of the information they are using.

QUEST is an example of an information handling program used widely in education, at both tertiary and school levels. It allows you to put your own information of a written kind into the computer or to interrogate such information made available by someone else.[5]

How it Works

QUEST handles information in files, each of which is made of records and fields. It operates to a command standard where the user has the full range of possible commands available to address the computer at all times. That is, the user is constantly in control, not the computer. This is an essential feature of powerful information handling programs. Other information handling

292

programs which are not command-driven in this way are often said to achieve a greater degree of 'user-friendliness' but at the expense of severely limiting what can be done with the information.

The Historical Process in Action

Consider the historical process as it is represented in the following example, where the computer plays an important role.[6]

Plague was being considered as a possible factor in the pattern of local community development in the seventeenth century. Some initial observations about the nature of source materials of this period suggested considerable potential in the study of burial registers. Considerations about the nature of burial registers ('What is a burial register?'; 'What sort of information might it convey?') prompted the construction of a fictitious burial register, originating with imaginative responses from the students. In the construction of such a 'historical source' certain issues arose:

'What happens to those who were not part of the official church?'

'Should there be a record of where we died?'

'Do we record the cause of death?'

From this non-historical context the nature of burial registers, as a document contemporary to the students and then as a historical source could be considered. The historical context was then provided by the introduction of

Figure 1   *A page of the parish register of St Mary's, Ware. Hertfordshire Record Office (D/P116 1/3).*

the original statute initiated by Cromwell in 1538 that called for the keeping of 'records' by all parishes. To re-consider the construction of the students' burial register in light of this document provided not only the historical context but the incentive to consider the reasons for the inception of the document (since this would determine, in part, how it was to be responded to):

Was it issued to keep account of the poor moving from parish to parish when looking for work?

Was it to be used as an aid for the authorities to monitor the spread of plague?

The situation of the local ecclesiastic being suddenly confronted with Cromwell's order also prompted discussion: how would he be likely to respond?

From this point the students' own fictitious burial register could be completed, both in form and content. The introduction of original burial registers to compare with the students' own led to a full discussion about the extraneous factors which had influenced the content of seventeenth-century burial registers. The reasons given for such a variation in content ranged from inefficient responses of individual local incumbents, to a situation of dichotomous local and national interests, where local interests withstood the pressures from central government (this, it was ventured, might be expected of parishes that were geographically more distant from the centralised control of the government in London).

Throughout this exercise so far the students had been forming hypotheses about burial registers which needed testing. The possibility of this could be provided with the introduction of burial registers in the form of a datafile containing some 1100 records, (this datafile forms part of a History Investigation pack called PLAGUE — see References, below). With the aid of a contemporary map of the parishes under investigation, (which were Hertfordshire parishes in the period 1664–66), the students could begin to explore hypothetical notions about plague and the communities embodied in these parishes against an appreciation of the nature of the sources with which they were dealing.

Particular questioning strategies that were developed in this instance concentrated on:

the role of women (as seen from their occupations);

the incidence and spread of plague (ascertained by tracing the numbers of deaths from the disease in each parish);

how plague was introduced into the parish (that is, suddenly or gradually and by whom);

the effects of plague on the family constitution (studied from the number of deaths that occured in a range of families that contracted the disease).

Following through such questioning strategies the students necessarily experienced a research process that consisted of:

Figure 2   PLAGUE

The following is a description of the information contained in the datafile. The different categories of information are called FIELDS - thus, DAY is one fieldname; PARISH is another fieldname and so on.

DAY   : The day of burial

MON   : The month of burial

YEAR   : The year of burial

DATE   : The date of burial in numeric form, i.e. YYYYMMDD (e.g. 16640620). This allows the datafile to be sorted chronologically.

FORENAME : Forename

SURNAME   : Surname

EDSUR   : This contains a standard way of spelling the person's surname

ADDRESS   : The person's address or the name of the parish where s/he lived

PARISH   : The name of the parish where the burial took place

CAUSE   : The cause of death. 'P' or 'Plag' is often used in the registers to indicate death as a result of plague

OCCUP   : The occupation or status of the buried person

REL   : This shows the relationship of the buried person to the rest of the household in which s/he lived. For example, daughter, son, child *

FNAME   : The name of the father, husband or husband of nurse

MNAME   : The name of the mother or nurse

REMARKS   : Any extra information contained in the burial registers

* REL   The following abbreviations are used in this field:

B = bastard	NC = nurse child
CH = child	S = son
D = daughter	SER = servant
G = grandchild	W = wife
I = infant	WID = widow

Examples of the information contained in PLAGUE

ADDRESS : Chesterton
PARISH   : Royston
CAUSE   : Killed with a Cart
OCCUP   : a poor man
REL   :
FNAME   :
MNAME   :
REMARKS :

DAY   : 24
MON   : Sep
YEAR   : 1665
DATE   : 16650924
FORENAME : Hugh
SURNAME : Ward
EDSUR   : Ward
ADDRESS : Royston
PARISH   :
CAUSE   : of the plague
OCCUP   :
REL   :
FNAME   :
MNAME   :
REMARKS : the first that dyed of the plague

DAY   : Jun
MON   : 1664
YEAR   : 16640600
DATE   :
FORENAME : Susanna
SURNAME : Croft
EDSUR   : Croft
ADDRESS :
PARISH   :
CAUSE   : Reed
OCCUP   : Of a consumption
REL   : D
FNAME   : Edward
MNAME   :
REMARKS : [ex Commd & had not X'an buryall - buried in her fathers garden]

—the forming and testing of hypotheses;
—making deductions;
—reconstructing elements of the past;
—explanation;
—communication.

In communicating their findings the students were able to reach a number of tentative but important conclusions. For example:

(i)   There was evidence to suggest that main routeways were instrumental in spreading plague, but not rapidly;

(ii)   Nurse-children were primary factors in the introduction of plague into parishes within a 50 mile radius of London.

More importantly, both the limitations and potential of burial registers as evidence of social life in the seventeenth century were now better appreciated. The need to turn to other source material, to test further and more refined hypotheses also became apparent.

Comments

Throughout the example cited above, the students were effectively party to the historical process, directing their own learning, thinking historically and using sources creatively. It may be argued that the computer is not a necessary tool to develop the skills and conceptual understanding involved in learning to handle historical information, or indeed, to immerse the student in the historical process. On the other hand, it may be true that using the computer in the way described provides a focus for learning which could not be achieved by any other means.

Certainly there are pointers towards the latter direction of thought. It may be possible to test this notion further by simply monitoring the interaction between teacher, students and computer. Certain phases in the development of historical understanding can be identified by simply watching and listening, in noting students' use of language, knowledge and concepts and their approach to historical information. An assessment of these factors will provide a better understanding of the effects the computer has on students' experiences in history in the classroom.

I have drawn attention to historical information largely of one type. More powerful and extensive information handling tools, such as those facilitated by Interactive Video Disc technology and Intelligent Knowledge Based Systems, will enable the student to access historical information of a visual, documentary and facsimile kind and in almost any quantities.[7]

At this stage attention might be drawn to the lack of reference made to the age of the students referred to in this paper. This has been deliberate. It is my experience that what has been discussed here in relation to the potential role of the computer in this educational context is applicable to teaching and learning in history whatever the age range of the students. For the record my initial research has been in the 11–19 age range, in schools and colleges.[8]

Conclusion

The computer is quite obviously a powerful research tool in the hands of the historian. It is an equally powerful tool and perhaps a more important one, when it is used for putting the historical process within the grasp of the student.

Notes

1. The research that this paper is based upon is described in the *First Interim Report of the Computers in History Project* (unpublished). Contact Martyn Wild (AUCBE) for details.

2. A good introduction to the work of Piaget is M. Bodin, *Piaget* (1979). Also see J. Piaget and B. Inhelder, *The Growth of Logical Thinking*, 1958. For the application of Piaget's ideas to history, see R. N. Hallam, 'Piaget and Thinking in History', in M. Ballard (ed.), *New Movements in the Study and Teaching of History*, 1972.

3. G. R. Elton strongly represents this view particularly with regard to the nature of historical study that is suitable for school and undergraduate students. See G. R. Elton, *The Practice of History*, 1967.

4. For a full discussion of the nature of hypothetico-deductive reasoning, see K. Popper, *The Logic of Scientific Discovery* (1959). For a critical view of the nature of the relationship between computer, knowledge and learning, see T. O'Shea and J. Self, *Learning and Teaching with Computers: Artificial Intelligence in Education*, 1983.

5. QUEST is available for various microcomputers and in a number of different forms. See references, below.

6. For a full discussion of the role of information handling software, such as QUEST, in the teaching and learning of history, see M. Wild, *QUEST in History* (1986). Also see M. Wild, 'What's This got to do with History, Sir?', *Times Educational Supplement*, 13th June 1986.

7. For a full discussion of the future applications of technology to teaching and learning in history, see M. Wild, *History: a Soft Option?*, 1986, and, F. Blow and A. Dickinson (Eds), *New History and New Technology: Present into Future*, 1986.

8. The Computers in History Project is concerned with, amongst other issues, the effect the computer has on student's thinking in history. A booklet, *Children, History and the Computer*, which describes and discusses the project in detail is available from AUCBE (see references, below).

References

QUEST is available for a variety of microcomputers. The illustrations and curriculum materials described within this paper form part of PLAGUE, a History Investigation pack, based upon the use of seventeenth century burial registers as datafiles. The pack includes full student and teacher support materials. PLAGUE is one of a series of History Investigation packs based upon a wide selection of historical datafiles.

QUEST IN HISTORY is a software package that discusses and describes the processes involved in applying information handling software (*QUEST* in particular) to teaching and learning in history.

VIEWDATA IN HISTORY explores the potential — and applications of viewdata in history teaching.

CHILDREN, HISTORY AND THE COMPUTER outlines the Computers in History Project, which is researching the impact of the computer on the cognitive development of history students.

All materials listed above may be obtained from: Advisory Unit for Computer Based Education (AUCBE), Endymion Road, Hatfield, AL10 8AU, England (Tel. 07072 65443)

48 *Richard H. Trainor*

An Experiment in Computer-based Teaching and Research: the DISH Project at Glasgow

This essay examines the goals and initial implementation of the DISH Project.[1] It includes a preliminary assessment of the advantages and problems arising from the approach to computer-based teaching and research in history adopted at Glasgow. The accompanying essay by Nicholas Morgan examines the ways in which machine readable sources and traditional materials have been combined in the DISH Project's research and teaching. It is hoped that these two papers will identify some key issues to be faced in computer-based history teaching — especially, though not exclusively, in higher education — while making the case for linking that teaching to research.[2]

DISH stands for the Design and Implementation of Software in History. The Project, which forms part of the Computers in Teaching Initiative sponsored by the Computer Board and the University Grants Committee, was awarded its two-year grant in April 1985 and began spending it at the start of the academic year 1985–86.

While drawing considerable assistance from Glasgow's Computing Service and its Computing Science Department (both of which are represented in the Project Team), DISH is primarily the work of four history departments: Economic History, Modern History, Scottish History and the University Archives. The participation of the Archives emphasizes one of the Project's central assumptions: the need to base computer-related teaching on research, using databases generated at Glasgow University where possible, so that instruction and scholarship can enrich each other.[3] The involvement of four history departments indicates a broad approach to the discipline, encompassing 'arts' as well as 'social science' history and dealing with distant as well as local settings. Both these aspects of the Project are embodied in DISH's close ties to Glasgow's interdepartmental research group, *Enterprise, Public Policy and Society*, which is studying the relationship between business enterprise, government action and social conditions in Britain and the United States since the beginning of the nineteenth century.

DISH seeks to develop the software and teaching methods required to give history students access in the classroom to highly structured data without requiring them to master difficult operating systems. The basic objective is to render complex sources such as the nineteenth-century census — sources with many fields, some numerical, some alphabetic, many requiring sophisticated analysis — as accessible as the printed word. We are trying to enhance the historical understanding of undergraduates while also providing them with valuable transferable skills in basic information technology.

In recent years the history departments at Glasgow have won substantial outside funding for the creation of large databases. However, while these data were being extensively exploited for research, previous to DISH they remained largely untapped in teaching.

Yet computer-based teaching is especially well suited to history. For instance, using the computer in the classroom allows students to take an active role in evaluating the important body of historical literature based on machine-processed data — a literature which, until now, they have usually had to accept at face value. More generally, computer-based instruction fosters two of history's principal objectives: the critical assessment of evidence and its systematic handling. Having examined facsimiles of an original source, students can manipulate a machine readable version of the documentary record with great speed and accuracy. Since students must bring to bear considerable imagination and precision in order to devise strategies for interrogating these databases, such computer investigations are intellectual challenges rather than mere mechanical exercises. Similarly, the interpretation of the subsequent 'output' in the context of the general historical issues involved is an academically demanding process.

Likewise, for a word-intensive discipline such as history, the computer's text processing facilities offer considerable educational advantages during the subsequent 'writing-up' of conclusions, allowing students to enhance the coherence and the clarity as well as the elegance of their prose.[4]

This approach to computer-based history teaching requires suitably tailored hardware and software. Networked microcomputers, especially if they incorporate access to mainframe machines, offer easier and more flexible student access to complex data than does the sole reliance on mainframe computing which has previously dominated such teaching in higher education. DISH's hardware consists of Research Machines' Nimbus micros — sixteen in our History Computing Laboratory, supplemented by eight in the participating departments. The Nimbus was chosen for its networking capability, graphics, speed, price and widespread use in education. The micros in the lab are linked, through a network fileserver, to a single hard disk and, via a communications PAD, to the University's ICL 2988 mainframe. Thus databases can either be downloaded onto DISH's local area network or accessed directly from the mainframe.

Concerning software, existing packages fall short of DISH's needs in two basic ways. Complex mainframe packages such as SPSS, while powerful, have led to university instruction which often focuses on computers and statistics rather than on history itself. Also, such packages sometimes encourage historical teaching and research which is restricted to statistical analysis of easily coded databases.[5] At the other extreme, simple microcomputer programs such as QUEST, which successfully expose school pupils directly to sources, are less well equipped with the analytical facilities (such as cross tabulations) necessary for the generation of meaningful results in higher education.

The project's approach to software development, then, stems from its desire to achieve the easy yet systematic classroom availability of complex alphanumeric databases such as company records, marriage registers, pollbooks and rating ledgers. In order to turn the bulk and complexity of these sources into educational advantages, DISH is developing software (with special attention to data entry and analysis systems) which will enable students to access and scan such files with ease and to submit complicated search, correlative and quantitative requests. This is being done by developing an interface which will employ user-friendly approaches such as windows, icons and mice. Yet DISH is not avoiding use of keyboards where they are appropriate either for classroom convenience or for the development of computer skills. With other 'arts-based' subjects as well as other history departments (in secondary as well as tertiary education) in mind, transferability and portability are important considerations.

The Project Team believes that effective software as well as novel teaching methods can best be developed alongside the active classroom use of the computer. In this way the new programs which are emerging will be firmly rooted in experience gained in computer-based teaching. Accordingly, students began using our new History Computing Laboratory in November 1985. So DISH has necessarily imported and enhanced programs (and, to a lesser extent, data) in these early stages. Meanwhile, in consultation with the participating historians, our programmer has been able to plan DISH's own software taking into account the shortcomings of existing programs in relation to DISH's needs.

The Project teaching has been integrated both into selected existing honours courses — which emphasise subject matter while also developing basic computer skills — and into a special introductory course on historical computing for all honours students in their penultimate year. This introductory course concentrates on skills. In part these are computer skills such as the ability to create and manipulate files. These aspects of information technology in turn are linked to historical skills like the capacity to relate different texts to each other and the ability to decide how (and whether!) to apply basic statistical operations to various types of historical data. In both types of course, machine-readable sources and computer manipulation are being combined with traditional evidence and methods. Thus DISH should be able to enhance the students' general comprehension of history while providing them with basic computer literacy.

There are four stages in DISH's teaching: (1) simple classroom illustrations and exercises (these become increasingly open-ended as the courses proceed, allowing students to formulate and test their own hypotheses); (2) supplementary assignments carried out on the computer independently of the instructor; (3) integration of output with text in the writing of essays; and (4) more extended applications in dissertation work for those who have profited most from the first three stages. The latter two stages involve small, self-generated databases, so the project includes training in data preparation and management as well as in information retrieval and analysis. Students are taught word processing in conjunction with data analysis. This approach reflects the Project Team's view that the computer is an educational and research tool rather than simply an enchanted typewriter. Also, in practical terms a more prominent place for word processing might overwhelm our already heavily used lab.

Likewise, although other computing skills are taught directly, they are presented in the context of the historical issues and exercises to which they relate. This approach is reflected in the format of the teaching sessions. After a recapitulation of the previous exercise the first ten minutes or so consist of a briefing (which builds on handouts distributed in advance) on the historical problems and sources concerned. The second segment is an explanation by the lab manager of new computing skills relevant to the week's exercise. Then, after comments by the instructor on the specific database and exercise concerned, students work through the exercise itself, calling for assistance (or, increasingly, providing it for each other) as necessary.[6] In this fashion students build up their computing abilities gradually and in a fashion that seems directly useful for their historical comprehension and skills. Inevitably some computing virtuosity is missed in this way, but for the successful student basic computer literacy will emerge. It is such general competence in computing, rather than specific wizardry, that DISH is trying to encourage.

An assessment of the utility of DISH's approach to computer-based teaching is difficult after only six months of the Project.[7] Student response is generally encouraging. For example, many attend the supplementary work sessions made available each week (though such use tends to decline late in the terms when essays for other courses are due). Also, there are more than a few volunteers for optional computer-based essays and, even more encouragingly, for source-based dissertations. On the other hand, some students — especially those who have never previously faced a keyboard, let alone a computer — have significant initial problems. Yet, if the computing tasks required are kept relatively simple in the early stages, it seems that nearly all students can develop a modicum of skills within a few weeks of their first exposure. (Oddly enough, student absence from the lab over Christmas evidently allowed their skills to 'settle in': after a brief 'refresher' session in January, they proved significantly more adept than when we had last seen them !) Motivation is little problem, in part because students realise that they will eventually need to come to terms with computers, if only to complete successfully with younger siblings! Also, they seem very pleased to be able to manipulate as well as examine sources.

Nevertheless, DISH's early experience indicates that exercises and techniques need to be constantly refined in order to incorporate the lessons which continually emerge from such teaching. The necessarily experimental 'handouts' for the exercises — even when pre-tested by the instructors on themselves — need even more revision than lecture or tutorial notes before they can be used again. More general changes must also be implemented. For example, our external assessor has suggested that the Project's students require more time to think about their exercises before touching the computers. Advance distribution of exercises will help to reduce this difficulty, but the time allocated to various activities within the already crowded two-hour sessions may also need to be reconsidered. Similarly, increasing penetration of history teaching at Glasgow and elsewhere will mean difficult trade-offs with other teaching formats such as conventional group discussions. In addition, computer-based history teaching must deal with problems such as the need for continuous and final student assessment and the desirability of countering students' too easy acceptance of computer-generated 'results'.

Staff response to DISH, though uneven, has also been generally promising. Three colleagues have already enlarged the initial 'inner circle'. With externally provided staff training sessions in prospect, the outlook is good for the extension of the Project into at least two second year courses as well as additional third and fourth year courses. Admittedly such expansion brings its own problems. The 'pioneers' find themselves enmeshed in an ever more complex web of commitments — the generation of teaching exercises, additional contact hours, the initial proselytising and instruction of their colleagues, and the burgeoning administrative needs of their mini-empire. If a 'fad' is to become an established part of history teaching, arrangements for significant reductions in other duties will have to be devised. Finance is a further worry. At the moment DISH is 'priming the pump' furiously but has to face the possibility that, given the current dismal prospects for university budgets, the well may run dry after two years. This resource problem — even more acute in the absence of grants like ours — requires attention centrally as well as within particular institutions.[8]

Yet it would be misleading to conclude on a negative note. Administrative and financial worries have not diminished either our enthusiasm for research-related computer teaching in history at Glasgow or our desire to help make such computer-based instruction more widespread elsewhere.

Notes

1. An earlier version of this paper was presented at a seminar on computer-based history teaching at the Woodland Teachers' Centre, Glasgow on 4 March 1986. It can be found in J. M. McArthur (ed.), *Databases in History Teaching*, Glasgow, Strathclyde Regional Council, 1986.

2. Among the most useful previous discussions of computer-based teaching in history (mainly in schools) are: F. Blow & A. Dickinson (eds.), *New History and New Technology; Present into Future*, London, Historical Association, 1986; J. Francis, *Microcomputers and Teaching History*, London, Longman, 1983; J. Nichol, 'CAL in History', in M. Yazdani (ed.), *New Horizons in Educational Computing*, London, Ellis Horwood, 1983; K. Randell (ed.), *The Use of the Computer in the Study and Teaching of History*, London, Historical Association, 1984; J. Wilkes (ed.), *Exploring History with Microcomputers*, London, Council for Educational Technology, 1985.

3. Adapting research datasets for teaching can do much to help historians discover

the strengths and limitations of their data. For discussion of the value of the computer in historical research, see among others: B. Collins, 'The Computer as a Research Tool', *Journal of the Society of Archivists*, 7, 1982; R. Jensen, 'The Microcomputer Revolution for Historians', *Journal of Interdisciplinary History*, 14, 1983; R. J. Morris, 'Does nineteenth-century nominal record linkage have lessons for the machine-readable century?', *Journal of the Society of Archivists*, 7, 1985; K. Schurer, 'Historical Databases and the Researcher', *Computers in Genealogy*, 3, 1984; E. Shorter, *The Historian and the Computer*, New York, Norton, 1975.

4.   For a discussion of the intellectual advantages of computer-based teaching in 'arts-based' disciplines generally, see my chapter in S. Rahtz (ed.), *Computers and teaching in the Humanities*, forthcoming, Ellis Horwood, 1987.

5.   It should be noted, however, that recent versions of SPSS (notably SPSS-X) while still highly complex and statistical, no longer require initial numerical coding. These remarks also apply to analogous packages such as SAS.

6.   For specific examples see the accompanying essay by Nicholas Morgan.

7.   Since this paper was delivered, DISH has submitted (August 1986) to the Computer Board a report on its first academic year of operation. The report contains additional information on topics such as software development, evaluation and external collaboration.

8.   In late 1986 a few projects in the Computers in Teaching Initiative received assurances of a third year of support either from their own institutions (as in the case of DISH) or from the Computer Board. Yet the longer-term and more general problems of funding in the field remain.

49   *Nicholas J. Morgan*

Sources and Resources: the DISH Project at Glasgow[1]

The DISH project owes its origins to a joint initiative, by the University Archives and the Department of Scottish History at the University of Glasgow, intended to raise funds for the development of software that would enhance the possibility of substantial mainframe databases (either already completed or under construction) being accessed, either in total or in part, by students in the classroom. This reflected a desire both to link the research process to teaching, and to place more emphasis in the classroom on the skills involved in manipulating and analysing primary source material. In addition it mirrored a growing awareness of the fact that the time and expense involved in constructing large historical databases was increasingly difficult to justify during a period of contracting research resources. Frequently, despite the best possible intentions, limited time and funding has restricted databases to being research-specific. The products of such work generally gather dust in a mainframe filestore or sometimes in a data archive, condemned to inactivity due to their problem-orientated structure. It is our belief that the investment of time and money involved in database construction can only be justified by ensuring that large generalised databases (preferably reflecting the structure and entire content of a specific source) are available to the largest possible constituency (of researchers, students, schools and members of the public). Part of the process of ensuring such availability lies in the development of sophisticated but friendly data handling software.

History teaching at universities frequently confines the use of source materials to highly specialised final-year special subjects. In these classes emphasis has tended to be placed on studying the provenance and specific content of selected gobbets or extracts drawn from textual (and often impressionistic) sources rather than on the skills involved in organising and analysing raw data at first hand. The traditional approach provides necessary, but not sufficient, skills for historians to work with. It is our belief that it is essential for history undergraduates to understand the techniques and possess the skills to handle critically large amounts of information, with or without the use of the computer. In the context of the DISH project the machine is secondary to the skill it is helping to impart.

Nineteenth-century historians generally, and those historians of Scotland particularly, are lucky to have access to large numbers of sources which contain information recorded at the level of individuals. Prodigious in their size and complexity, such sources (with perhaps the exception of the census) have until recently only rarely been used by historians in any systematic manner. The ability to access these otherwise inaccessible sources in the classroom through the use of the computer therefore not only teaches the student valuable skills in information handling, but also offers them the opportunity to appraise critically the value of general secondary historical writing. Conclusions based on the use of impressionistic evidence from sources such as parliamentary papers, newspapers and journals, or aggregate data from statistical enquiries or the reports of government boards or departments can be tested against disaggregate data drawn from central government records, local authority archives and business records. In the same way access to datasets allows students to test the validity of conclusions drawn from them by their authors and teachers.

In the process of asking our students to 'do history' (albeit in a limited context), there is no attempt to shield them from the many problems of using raw data. They are placed in the position of discovering for themselves whether a particular computerised source will yield an answer to the problem or issue under consideration — rather than being presented with a dataset of aggregated data contrived to yield certain answers in an allotted teaching period. In some respects the 'right answer' is secondary to the 'right method'. It follows from this that emphasis is also placed on familiarising students with the process of constructing databases from primary sources — they are not allowed to take for granted the many influences which might have corrupted the data they see on the screen in the process of its transition from original document or volume. Before being introduced to a dataset on the computer in the classroom they are made familiar with its original physical form and content, with its administrative or organisational origins, and its archival history. At some point they are themselves placed in the position of selecting, classifying and where necessary coding data, and structuring databases for use — in the process becoming familiar not only with the constraints that the computer can place on conveying the impact of raw data, but also with the tedium (and consequent dangers) of data entry. At Glasgow, we have now conducted this exercise using as data sources both nineteenth century admissions records for the city's Royal Infirmary, and Glasgow University records of matriculations.

The range of sources used for teaching in the DISH project naturally reflect the research interests of those involved in the project. As the database approach to history becomes increasingly integrated with traditional research at Glasgow, so the opportunities for extending the scope of our teaching increase. The link between teaching and research has many well-known and acknowledged advantages — in the field of computer-based study it has particular benefits but also some drawbacks. Even limited experience shows that the time needed to prepare teaching datasets and the necessary documentation to support them is massive — both the technology and the students demand a higher standard of preparation for a computer workshop than one might be able to get away with for a lecture or tutorial. Working on research-generated data and other research materials for classroom preparation has a feedback into research proper and optimises the use of what otherwise might be wasted (or at least unappreciated) hours. Even so the process is generally time-consuming, particularly when the lack of sufficient infrastructure (communications to the Glasgow University ICL 2988) condemns those involved in preparing and downloading even small sets of data from large mainframe databases to frequent interruptions on a busy (and overcrowded) system with almost inevitable recourse to working anti-social hours in order to achieve what are often very simple objectives. Similarly the preparation of supporting documentation — copies of original source materials, explanations of data and field structures and relevant contextual information — all place demands on time which are almost prohibitive.[2] A further disadvantage of working on research-generated data is that whilst colleagues are willing to allow such material to be used within their own institutions they are less willing to allow such materials out of their sight when they are still the subject of primary research. Data exchange is necessary and desirable but there are many constraints acting against the immediate attainment of the ideal.

The two largest datasets in use currently by the project are the Sequestrations database and the Valuation Rolls database. The former, compiled in the University Archives by Arnot Wilson and Michael Moss, contains some 13,000 records on personal bankruptcies in Scotland between 1839 and 1913. The database — its size is 8Mb — can be searched online on Glasgow's mainframe using the PARCH suite of programs developed in the Archives.[3] Although some controversy surrounds the use of such statistics relating to business failure as a measure of economic performance (itself a good starting point for a class) subsets of data for particular counties or towns provide an admirable barometer for observing the influence of national economic events on local economies.[4]

In this context it should be observed that anything 'local' is generally more interesting to our students than things national, regardless of the fact that the locality being studied may not be their own. Sequestrations for particular occupation groups (for example the building industries in Glasgow) have been downloaded in order to discuss sectoral vulnerability and resistance within the Scottish economy to financial catastrophe and cyclical downturns in trade. The Valuation Rolls database (currently under construction by Nicholas Morgan with the help of generous funding from the ESRC) will contain data on the value and ownership of all residential property in Glasgow at the years 1861, 1881 and 1911.[5] It will comprise some 70,000 records, size approximately 15MB. At present data for 1861 and 1881 (some 37,000 records) can be searched on the mainframe at Glasgow using ICL CAFS hardware and software, with simple interfaces developed by the University's Computing Service. However, despite the fact that CAFS provides high speed searching (35,000 records in 20 seconds) of an infinitely flexible nature, term-time congestion of mainframe facilities during peak teaching hours has led us to download sets of data (using CAFS to define the characteristics of the dataset required) to the DISH network for teaching.

Students have been presented with chunks of data for various years and areas in the city and asked to use rental and tenural data to assess the status of different residential districts, and the spatial segregation of status groups within those districts. They are asked to compare this 'measured' status for certain well known (and notorious) areas in the city with inferences of urban decay and degeneration contained in traditional accounts of Glasgow for the period. In addition they have been asked to identify certain characteristics of property owners in the city over time and compare these with what are generally misleading accounts and descriptions of landlords and the structure of the housing market contained in impressionistic sources such as the parliamentary papers.

As with all similar exercises the computer does not provide the answer to the problem. Just as students ask questions of the datasets, so they are encouraged to go away and ask questions of the results they obtain, thereby developing their skills of critical interpretation.

The Confirmations database, developed in the Scottish History Department by Nicholas Morgan contains details of the 1200 or so individuals who died in Glasgow in 1901 and whose estates were confirmed in the city's Sheriff Court, ranging from a grocer's assistant who left personal estate worth £2·00 to the ironmaster Sir William Laird who left some £313,648.[6] It is currently being upgraded to include age data and information concerning the location (registration districts) of individual confirmees in the city in order to allow closer correlation with other social and medical data. Research into the dynamics of Victorian wealth is a subject that links many of the individuals involved in the DISH project and the Confirmations database has been a successful pilot for what will be a far more ambitious undertaking. In teaching the material is used in the context of the debate over wealthholding generated by the work of W. D. Rubinstein; students are asked to identify in what sectors wealth was generated in one Victorian city and to study the distribution of that wealth and the clustering of wealth levels.[7] Given the concentration of the majority of the wealth- generating classes in the middle ranges of wealthholding they are asked to consider how relevant it is to study exceptional wealthholders (millionaires) as opposed to the more typical in order to meaningfully assess the process of wealth generation in nineteenth-century society. In addition to this general study of wealth-holding the University Archives have developed a dataset relating to the financial transactions of a prominent Clydeside businessman and shipbuilder, Peter Denny.[8]

Our concern is also with the businesses which created wealth. Students have performed simple statistical exercises (incorporating graphics) on a set of data developed by Michael Moss concerning shipments of wines and spirits into the Clyde ports by a prominent firm of wine and whisky merchants. As with Sequestrations, so with this, they are asked to explain the specific against the general; the impact on imports of the crash of the City of Glasgow bank in 1878, or the way wine merchants responded to agricultural crises, for example epidemics of phylloxera at about the same time in France and later Spain. Of the databases currently under construction several are connected with business history. The most extensive is the prosopographical database arising from the Scottish Business Biography Project under the direction of Professor Tony Slaven.[9] This will contain records on the lives, families and careers of 1000 prominent Scottish businessmen active during the period 1860–1960. The other large database not yet in use for teaching has been developed by Rick Trainor and relates to marriages in the West Midlands *c.*1850–1900. This will be used to trace changing patterns of social mobility and of interaction among social groups in a region where class formation was especially complex and influential.[10]

We have, of course, needed to borrow data in order to plug gaps in our own resources. We have been grateful to the Glasgow Division of the Strathclyde Regional Educational Department (and indirectly to Michael Anderson's 1851 census project) for allowing us access to census clusters for Glasgow and the West of Scotland, and also to a small dataset (*c.*700 records) drawn from Poor Law Applications made to the Inspector of the Poor in the City in 1867.[11] In addition we have participated in discussions concerning their plans to launch a large scale programme of computer based history teaching into secondary and primary schools in the region in the very near future.

However the need for cooperation that is essential to the success of such a project extends beyond this relationship. The involvement of the Glasgow University Archives (and by association the Greater Glasgow Health Board Archives) in the DISH project from its inception has guaranteed not only flexible access to a vast amount of raw materials but also to a large number of machine readable databases.[12] In addition it has provided a degree of archival supervision (not always so readily available to historians) of the methods of database construction that we are employing. We have excellent relationships with the Strathclyde Regional Archives, who have allowed us to use databases held there concerning the Clyde sailing fleet of the nineteenth century, and planning and building applications made to the City's Dean of Guild Court during the Victorian and Edwardian era.[13] Our colleagues in other institutions of higher education, notably Edinburgh University and

Jordanhill College of Further Education, are not only active in the sharing of data but also in the exchange of ideas and approaches to using the computer in history teaching. In addition the enthusiasm of our students, particularly those who undertake dissertations, is leading to the compilation of a variety of datasets that will (with little adaption) be suitable for teaching in future years.

The computer can be used to give students access to sources in the classroom which they would not otherwise come into contact with. They can be shown how large amounts of data can be organised and analysed in order either to challenge findings based on impressions alone or to test the conclusions and methodology of those who have worked with the same data. We are hopeful that we are on right path to develop databases, software, and an approach to teaching that will maximise these objectives whilst keeping to a minimum the amount of traditional computing that we need to teach our students. In particular we seek to achieve this aim by exploiting a variety of non-linguistic forms of communication between user and machine. However we are aware that our students must be taught traditional skills alongside (and possibly enhanced by) the new. It remains imperative that they should know that impression and empathy (not easily quantifiable, even by the most friendly computer!) are as essential a part of the historian's tool-kit as quantity and the computer.

Notes

1. An earlier version of this paper was presented at a seminar on computer based history teaching at the Woodlands Teachers' Centre, Glasgow, on 4 March 1986. It can be found in J. M. McArthur (ed.), *Databases in history teaching*, Glasgow, 1986.

2. It is difficult to overstress the importance of quality documentation to support teaching datasets. For two excellent examples see T. C. Lewis & G. S. Nunn, *Quarry Bank 1851*, London, 1983; Alison Gray, *Sandyford Census Database*, Glasgow, 1986.

3. These programs are explained in a A. T. Wilson, *PARCH Prospectus*, Glasgow, 1983.

4. See M. S. Moss & J. R. Hume, 'Business failure in Scotland 1839–1913: a research note', *Business History* 25 (1983); R. G. Rodger, 'Business failure in Scotland 1839–1913', *Business History*, 27, 1985.

5. For the details of this project (ESRC D00232126) can be found in N. J. Morgan, *Property ownership in Victorian and Edwardian Glasgow — a progress report*, Glasgow, Centre for Housing Research Discussion Paper, forthcoming, 1986. See also N. J. Morgan & M. J. Daunton, 'Landlords in Glasgow: a study of 1900', *Business History*, 25 , 1983.

6. For a discussion of this source see N. J. Morgan & M. S. Moss, 'Listing the wealthy in Scotland', *Bulletin of the Institute of Historical Research*, hereinafter cited as *BIHR*), 59, 1986.

7. See W. D. Rubinstein, 'British millionaries, 1809–1949', *BIHR*, 47, 1974; *Men of property: the very wealthy in Britain since the Industrial Revolution*, London, 1981; R. Britton, 'Wealthy Scots', *BIHR*, 58, 1985.

8. For Denny see M. S. Moss, 'Forgotten ledgers, law and the business historian: gleanings from the Adam Smith business records collection', *Archives*, 16, 1984. A detailed example of the study of an individual fortune is contained in M. S. Moss, 'William Todd Lithgow — founder of a fortune', *The Scottish Historical Review*, 62,

1983; Morgan & Moss, 'Listing the wealthy in Scotland'.

9.   See A. Slaven & S. G. Checkland (eds.), *The Dictionary of Scottish Business Biography*, Aberdeen, 1986.

10.   The general social and political background to this database can be found in R. H. Trainor, 'Peers on an industrial frontier: the Earls of Dartmouth & Dudley in the Black Country *c.*1810–1914', in D. Cannadine (ed.), *Patricians, power and politics in nineteenth century towns*, Leicester, 1982.

11.   Details of these databases can be found in McArthur (ed.), *Databases in history teaching*, Appendix 2.

12.   Some of the business records in the archive are discussed in P. L. Payne (ed.), *Studies in Scottish business history*, London, 1967; M. S. Moss, 'Forgotten Ledgers'. For medical archives see D. Dow, 'The archives of the Greater Glasgow Health Board', in O. Checkland & M. Lamb, *Health care as social history: the Glasgow case*, Aberdeen, 1982.

13.   For the history of this institution see A. M. Jackson, *Glasgow Dean of Guild Court: a history*, Glasgow, 1983. The uses of building plans are explored in P. J. Aspinall, *Building applications and the building industry in 19th century towns*, Birmingham, Centre for Urban and Regional Studies Research Memorandum 68, 1978.

Information Handling

50 *R. J. Morris and Charles Anderson*

The Edinburgh Computers in Education Project (Economic and Social History Department). Fears and Enthusiasms

The Economic and Social History Department of Edinburgh University is co-operating with CAST (Centre for Applications Software and Technology) and the Education Department in the University in a project jointly financed by the Computer Board and CAST. Our part of the project has two aims:

i)   the production of user friendly software for the exploration and analysis of tabular and nominal data sets in the context of undergraduate teaching in history and related subjects.

ii) the evaluation and development of teaching strategies appropriate to the use of such software.

History of the project

Since the late 1960s, research in economic and social history has made increasing use of mainframe computers. This has made possible the handling of large blocks of data both numerical and nominal. It has made possible the examination of different research methodologies at a tactical level. The analysis of manuscript census records, rate books, trade directories, marriage records rate books and commercial records are a few of the sources so used.

This has created a problem in undergraduate teaching. It is difficult, when examining the results of such work to give students critical access to the intellectual links between sources and conclusions. A student may read Norman McCord on *The Anti Corn Law League* and then go and look at the parliamentary debates in *Hansard* as part of a week's assignment of work. It is not possible to do the same for Robbie Gray on *The Labour Aristocracy in Victorian Edinburgh* and the marriage data on which some of his conclusions depend. In 1978, the department mounted a course for third year students to teach quantitative methods for historians. The course was very successful for research students (gaining recognition from the SSRC/ESRC). It was less successful for first degree students. We used the ERCC (Edinburgh Regional Computing Centre) mainframe computers. Students spent too long learning the system and too little time 'doing history'. Students had first to learn the operating system, then learn to use the editor, then the package (SPSS), then gain an appreciation of the statistics and the data sets involved. Too much energy was spent computing rather than discussing the very interesting problems of methodology and interpretation involved. The slow response time of the mainframe, especially in batch processing mode meant that students lost momentum as quite small mistakes in key punching caused substantial delays. The availability of the new generation of microcomputers, their increasing capacity and increasingly user friendly software provides an opportunity for solving some of these problems.[1]

In many ways the secondary schools and even primary schools are ahead of the universities in taking advantage of this opportunity. In part this is because secondary school teaching demands a more direct approach to the basic outline and principles of a subject. This suits the compact nature of the microcomputer and its limited capacity for data. Hopefully universities give their students a more critical awareness of the complexity of their subjects and the intellectual processes involved. This requires larger data sets and more complex ways of manipulating those data sets. The very successful Macro-economic data base produced by the Esmee Fairbairn Research Centre of Heriot Watt University's Economics department[2] is accessible, easy to use and has a rapid response rate. In order to achieve this success many simplifying decisions were taken. There is only one series for Money Supply. It is M1, notes, coins and sterling current accounts held by private sector residents. Now, much recent debate in economics depends on the different movements of about five different measures of money supply. The decision to keep the data set compact and straightforward was a good one, but it excludes a variety of learning strategies in a higher education context. Nevertheless, an increasing number of students are coming and will come from schools with some experience of using computers in their work and will be disappointed by the lack of computing in their university work.[3] There is a danger that teachers in universities will become like hunter gatherers teaching neolithic man to improve food production.

We also face another danger and challenge which arises from the increasingly insecure position which the practice of history has come to occupy in a society where the argument from numbers is becoming a key part of the everyday negotiation of power. Much historical literature is still being written, quite properly without reference to even the most elementary forms of numerical analysis — like a table or a percentage. This means that we tend to attract students who believe themselves innumerate but in fact are anumerate. There is a danger that the 'last did maths at O level' brigade will be afraid to tackle courses which involve even the simplest use of numbers and computing. Yet we know that they will enter a world in which the argument from numbers is part of the stock in trade of power broking. For example we have just seen the end of an important industrial dispute in the British mining industry. A crucial part of the political debate surrounding this dispute turned on the concept of a 'loss making pit'. This is in fact a highly numerical argument. A document produced for the Scottish NUM by an historian and an economist challenged the notion that large numbers of British pits were loss making.[4] It did so by looking at tables of figures and asking questions which are basic to an historian's skills:

—Where did the information come from?
—How was it produced?
—How was the concept of cost per unit calculated for individual pits?
—What were the circumstances in which coal prices were negotiated?

The historian involved showed that quite simple methods of numerate historical criticism could be very effective. There was not a correlation coefficient in sight still less a regression. The subsequent history of that document showed the complete inability of the trades union and labour movement to profit form the work done and to deal effectively with NCB arguments once the ground had moved from, political rhetoric to 'the figures'. This is one of countless examples of an inability to argue from numbers weakening one side in just the sort of debate for which the traditional skills of historians make them most suited. Our students need to be tempted and cajoled into shrugging off the fear of numbers. The potential accessibility and user-friendly nature of the new generation of micros is a means to doing this. History as always needs to respond to the culture within which it is being created. We live in a culture in which the argument from numbers is vital. We inherit a large number of students and also colleagues for whom fear of numbers is a defining characteristic. Propaganda and reassurance is needed to draw them in. Without this the doing of history will lose contact with powerful aspects of late twentieth century culture and thus assist its own threatened marginalisation as an up-market entertainment industry.

Software — aims and principles

With this background, we came to discuss the principles and aims of our software. A full specification for this has now been written.[5] I want to discuss the principles behind the specification rather than the details of its functionality or technicalities of implementing it.

i)   Extreme user friendliness. To this end we have chosen a mouse and windows approach, with pull down menus. This will make the system fun to use and tend to reduce the inequality of computer expertise amongst students. The learning curve tends to be shorter for mouse-windows systems than for keyboard command driven systems.

ii)   A rapid response time. These first two features will enable students to get meaningful results — say a simple tabulation — within an hour.

iii)   We need to handle two sorts of data in terms of size; relatively small tabulations, such as those extracted from 19th century Parliamentary Papers, and the larger data sets, like the poll books and directories which dominate much research. We have specified up to 8000 cases with 12 variables and the capacity to create up to 20 new variables. History like most of the social sciences tends to require large data sets. There will be some tension between this requirement and the need for rapid response times, which can only be resolved by practice.

iv)   With teaching requirements in mind, we shall include both a log, which will record the major interactions of user and machine, and a notebook facility where the user can record the logic of decisions taken.

v)   The system will work at two levels; those of builder and enquirer. At builder level, the user will be able to create and modify data sets. At enquirer level, the user will be able to create new variables, and to explore and analyse the data, but not be able to alter the initial data set. We anticipate that the user's initial experience will be as enquirer.

vi)   The system will handle a two-dimensional data block. The user will conceive these dimensions as cases and variables.

vii)   There will be a range of modifications to enable the user to create new variables, such as the basic four functions, logs, a facility to lag variables etc.

viii) The enquirer will be able to select sub sets of cases for exploration and analysis.

ix)   The user will be able to add, subtract etc. the cases. This facility will enable the user to mimic some of the effect of hierarchy.

x)   There will be groups of simple statistical functions.

xi)   It will be possible to present results through a variety of graphical means, graphs, bar charts etc.

xii)   Essentially this will be a teaching tool and not a tutor. Much of the action will take place away from the screen in lecture, library and blackboard work.

The chosen development and the target machine will be the Macintosh Plus, although the need for eventual portability will be kept in mind during the project. This machine was chosen because of its attractive and user friendly interface, and because it had a well tried and tested software technology.

The presentation will include the availability of a browser for the data set. This will always be available. The data will have a central place in the presentation and documentation of this system. This is a practical aspect of our philosophy that history, in this case the data, comes before the system, especially in terms of presentation to the user.

Teaching Strategies

We need to think very directly about the kind of teaching strategies which will use this software to best advantage. It is vital that we develop strategies which ensure that 'doing history' remains the central focus of our teaching, and that using the machine remains solely as a means to an end. The machine can extend possibilities, but must not dictate them. The danger is great because the machine is exciting to use and greedy for attention. There is a danger that course design and student work will become 'possibility driven'. The user is tempted to ask, what can I do next? Which of my skills can be displayed in this session? We shall need to be very explicit about the need for strategic thinking. Students must be encouraged to plan work sessions away from the machine, to frame the historical questions they want to ask, and then seek to make those questions operational.

At the same time we must acknowledge that learning takes two forms:

a) proficiency gaining activity. In this case exercises will be illustrative, designed to acquire skills. This necessary stage has the danger of encouraging 'possibility driven' activity.

b) historical enquiry. Here questions must be framed with reference to the broader task of improving historical understanding. Of course we do both in chalk and talk teaching, but the machine requires that we be more explicit about the distinction.

The log and notebook facility will enable student and tutor to retrace steps taken in a work session. For example, by looking at the major interactions, they will be able to decide if an unusual result was due to a mistake in using the system, a fault in the data, or a new and unexpected discovery. The notebook will continually prompt the user with demands to record the logic and purpose of each step taken and modification made.

We need to go further than this and ask what the machine will do to the teaching of history. Will it distort and bias history as taught towards certain styles of enquiry, towards certain types of answer and subject material? I have sympathy with my colleague who asked at a presentation of this project, if we would still buy books for the library. We live in a generation which has taken aboard the ideology of 'information technology'. The very phrase is a significant piece of ideology, leading us to forget that many important and legitimate forms of information have little to do with this micro-electronic technology. Now, machines ask for information in particular shapes and designs. They prefer information in repeatable, standardisable forms. They are most effective with questions that involve the endless repetition of quite simple enquiries. Will this be at conflict with the particular nature of history with its focus on specific events in time and place?

The research experience of the past fifteen years has made us aware of some of the problems. Historians have long recognised the dangers of pre-coding. Historians and historical geographers have developed techniques for dealing with data which is structured in a loose and irregular fashion, like probate inventories and wills.[6] The value of linking nominal records has been widely acknowledged and some discussion has taken place concerning the influence of methodology of results.[7] In most cases these advances in methodology enable us to delay the point at which classification and standardising decisions are made. These advances increase the historian's control over the process of generalisation. There still remains and always will remain a tension between the enormous power of these techniques to generalise, abstract and theorise about huge quantities of information, and the concern of the historian with the individuality of particular people, places and events. Historians must face the problems of philosophy and practice which this tension poses if the practice of history is not to fragment. Even if we ignore the wider problems for a moment, these advances in methodology pose problems within the teaching environment. If we advance beyond the simple two dimensional, cases and variables, pre-coded data set, then the work becomes time consuming both for the machine and the student. For example if the pre-coding of nominal data is rejected (as it should be), then we need to construct and have available within the machine a directory. One of the valuable experiences of teaching with a micro with the right software will be the ability for students and tutors to experiment with different methods of coding and compare results. Preparation within these methodologies is always more time-consuming. The need to flag data fields and data types in loose and irregular data structures is fully justified in a three-year research project but within a week's assignment in a first degree course could distract all attention from the central purpose of such a course which is to understand and analyse history. The time has long gone thank goodness when such students were excluded from getting any glimpse of the research behind the secondary literature, but they can feel cheated if we go to the opposite extreme and focus so much attention on technique that they learn very little history.

Clearly the answer to all these questions depends on the way in which the machine is used in teaching, but we need to ask the questions and not let the machine take charge. Indeed, the question, what does IT do to a subject is one which should be brought to the front in teaching. If the universities and other agencies of higher education are to teach the methods of critical intellectual enquiry and not be restricted to limited utilitarian activity, then an appreciation of what information technology does to information should be a crucial part of the experience which students take away with them.

The enthusiasm which we all feel for the opportunities we now have for the use of microcomputers in teaching must not blind us to the need to face questions about many aspects of practice which the opportunity will present. If we fail to face, discuss and answer these questions we shall lose the support of many colleagues and potential students. Their caution is not just based upon fear of the machine, it is based upon deeply held fears over the impact of information technology on the quality of the history we shall write in the next few decades. If we fail to argue and convince then the practice of history will continue to fragment. History as an academic subject will continue to weaken and historians will fail to make their contribution to that late twentieth century culture in which the argument from number has become so important. That particular ability of historians, especially those who locate their methodologies at the conjuncture of the arts and social science traditions, to appreciate the qualities of the general and of the particular will be especially valuable in such a culture.

Notes

1. Richard Jensen, 'The Microcomputer Revolution for Historians', *Journal on Interdisciplinary History*, 14 (1), pp. 91–112.

2. Keith Lumsden and Alex Scott, *Macro-economic Database*, Longman Microsoftware, 1984.

3. R. J. Morris, 'The Historian in the machine', *Social History*, 9, 1984, pp. 414–16.

4. George Kerevan and Richard Saville, *The Case for Scottish Coal*, 1985.

5. This paper represents the state of the project and our thinking as it stands at the end of February 1986.

6. K. Shurer,' Historical Research in the Age of the Computer; an assessment of the present situation', *Historical Social Research*, 36, 1985, pp. 43–54; Mark Overton,'Computer analysis of an inconsistent data source: the case of probate inventories', *Journal of Historical Geography* 3, 1977, pp. 317–26; R. S. Schofield, 'Computing, statistics and history', *Historical Journal*, 15, 1972, pp. 325–30.

7. R.J. Morris, 'Does 19th century nominal record linkage have lessons for the machine readable century,' *Journal of the Society of Archivists*, 7, October 1985, pp. 503–12; John A. Phillips,' Achieving a critical mass while avoiding an explosion: letter cluster sampling and nominal record linkage', *Journal on Interdisciplinary History*, 9, 1979, pp. 493–508.

8. Strathclyde Regional Council, Department of Education, Glasgow Division has produced two teaching data sets with documentation from Michael Anderson's 1851 census data set. *Bonhill* and *Sandyford* were produced under the guidance of Alison Gray with the help of MSC labour. They are designed for secondary school teaching but are a warning of the substantial amounts of labour required to provide backing for quite a modest data set. Each set contains some 400 to 500 cases.

The Teaching of Computing for Historians in Austria

The teaching of computing for historians in Austrian universities now has a tradition of some years' standing. It has its beginnings in the formation of a group of historians for the promotion of quantitative methods in Austrian history. Among other goals this group was trying to foster the spread of knowledge in social scientific methods, statistical techniques and electronic data processing skills. Since 1978 an annual introductory course and workshop on quantification in history has been organized.[1]

During the first years these meetings were mainly devoted to discussing problems of quantitative research on a theoretical level and to exchanging information on current research projects. In 1981 there was a major shift in the content of this annual meeting. Located now at the University of Salzburg, the 'Quant-Kurs' — as it is called — became a training course for basic and advanced skills in quantitative history.[2]

Since that time the concept of the course has been to combine theoretical learning with the practical use of computers. This combination is possible because the computer centre of Salzburg University generously offers for the full length of the course — about ten days — a good deal of its capacity. That means that all participants can work at a microcomputer or at a terminal during the whole course, thus covering each step in practice as well as in theory. For some years the 'Quant-Kurs' has been split up into one branch for beginners and another for advanced and already experienced participants. Beginners learn basic skills in statistics and the usage of statistical program-packages such as minitab or SPSS. Advanced participants partly deal with the use of computers for special historical reasearch problems such as medieval every-day life or the making of the nineteenth-century working class, and partly discuss methodological questions such as advanced statistics or non-numeric data processing.

This concept has proved to be rather successful. A good proportion of all Austrian historians who are actually using computers in their research have joined in the 'Quant-Kurs' during the last years, lecturers as well as research students. As a result some former participants are now giving their own lessons and the teaching of computing for historians has spread from Salzburg to other universities, mainly to Graz and Vienna. Within this process of decentralisation I myself started lessons in computing for historians at Vienna University in 1984.

As Vienna is a very large university with more than 3,000 history students and teaching and research activities in almost all fields of history, I tried to find a concept for an introductory course which might satisfy the needs of a large variety of historical research. By talking with those students and researchers who were already using computers in their work, within the variety of their actual research three common elements became visible: first, most of them use the computer for quantitative historical research, mainly for descriptive statistical analysis. Second, most historians do not work with existing machine-readable data files or databases but create their own data files by processing special historical sources. Usually these are sources with a complex structure such as inventories, census lists, church books and so on. Third, when historians trained themselves to use the computer they faced a common experience. It was not so much a problem to get training in statistics, because social scientists such as sociologists or psychologists are continually offering courses on that field. It was also not a problem to get some advice in programing and the use of statistical packages, because such courses are offered by the university's computer centre. Obviously the main grievance was a complete lack of training possibilities on the application of the computer and of popular software for the specific problems of processing historical sources of the type mentioned above. I had had the same experience in my own research dealing with family history based on census lists.[3]

It seemed to me therefore that this basic need — how to compute complex historical sources — should be covered by an introductory course on computing for historians. In my opinion this can be done best by organizing the lesson as a real little research project in the course of which all major problems of computer-aided historical research will emerge. As such a project should actually be of interest for all participants, I decided to carry out an analysis of all the history teaching offered to the students in the current university term, and as the basic source I am using the actual university prospectus.

The prospectus fits very well as an historical source. It is a listing-type source which should give constant information but in fact is full of gaps and ambiguities. There is numeric as well as alphanumeric information at different levels of complexity: some is quite simple and easy to handle like the type of the lesson or the rank of the lecturer. Other information, for example concerning methodological approaches, is rather complex, and some, such as the time-span or region covered by a lesson, comes in between. This variety of information allows intensive discussions of input formats, coding systems and so on. The number of about 200 history lessons each term is large enough for statistical analysis and small enough to master the project in a limited course.

In analysing the prospectus all steps of a computer aided research project are carried out:
—articulating problems and formulating hypotheses;
—conceptualizing;
—defining an input format;
—entering the data into the computer;
—transforming the raw data input into an analytical file;
—analyzing the data by means of a statistical package which in this case is SPSS.

In the course of the project it should become clear that it consists of a series of points where decisions have to be made. The students should learn that it is their task to find appropriate solutions and they should become aware of the factors they have to keep in mind in decision making: — the questions that should be answered; — the character of the source; — the locally available hard- and software; — and last not least economy of time. They also should learn that the result itself will largely be influenced by the actual form of data processing.

In my view it is very important to encourage discussions at each step and to reach decisions as a result of a group process. The role of the lecturer in this process is in my opinion therefor not so much to teach the best solution, but to show the variety of possibilities and to talk about their consequences. In my introductory lession I try to discuss two particular problems in detail because they seem to be crucial for the use of computers in historical research. First, the definition of an input format. As the input format decides what information of the original source will be included and what will be excluded from the entire process of electronic data processing, it is in my view of enormous importance to have an idea of the problems and benefits of free or fixed field input, of entering data in original or precoded form, and so on. Second, the transformation of the raw data file to an edited and finally to an analytical file. Rational ways to find and correct errors; creating thesaurii; the knowledge of various coding systems and of general coding conventions — all these topics are obviously of large influence on the quality of the final analysis as on the quantity of time consumed.

For both these items it seems to me of importance to get a broader view of the abilities of locally available software products such as text processors, editors and statistical packages. As this seems to me impossible without at least a little practice with such products, about a third of the course consists of practical exercises in the use of computers. As a first step students do this by entering the data, as a second step by actually writing and running little programs.[4]

Of course this is a huge program for an introductory course. Looking at the results it becomes quite clear that such a course is not able to create any routine in computing historical sources. But — as I hope — it can at least create a consciousness of the main problems in data processing and give the participants the small amount of practice which might enable them to start their own individual learning processes of trial and error outside blind alleys.

Notes

1. Gerhard Botz, 'Quantifizierende Geschichte als Gegenstand (inter-) universitärer Weiterbildung', *Bericht über den 16. österr. Historikertag in Krems/Donau 1984*, Vienna, 1985, pp. 667–75.

2. Gerhard Botz, '"Quantkurs" am Scheideweg', *Historical Social Research/Historische Sozialforschung*, 29, 1984, pp. 86–94.

3. Josef Ehmer, 'The Vienna Data Base on European Family History', in R. F. Allen, *Databases in the humanities and social sciences*, Osprey, 1985, pp. 113–16.

4. Josef Ehmer, 'Erfahrungen mit EDV-gestützten Projekten als Grundlage für die Konzeption einer Lehrveranstaltung "Einführung in die EDV für Historiker"', *Bericht über den 16. österr. Historikertag in Krems/Donau 1984*, Vienna, 1985, pp. 676–83.

Teaching First Century History by Microcomputer

The aim of the demonstration was to show that question and answer methods of teaching and multiple choice methods are more flexible than many people believe. In the former case it is possible to scan the answers and to report to the student how much of a one or two word answer matches the expected answer. Comment on the correct answer is easily included as is general comment in anticipation of the usual crop of erroneous replies. In the case of multiple choice question and answer sessions it is possible to provide comment on each of the answers whether they are deemed correct or not by the author. The possibilities are wide, and quite long comment can be offered. Sample sets of questions covered a number of topics including some on the social history of Judaea in the early Roman imperial period.

The demonstration used a programme developed for several subject areas in Edinburgh. The machine used at the conference was a Sirius, though the programme has been further adapted for a Vax in St Andrews and for an Apricot micro. The earliest version was used for teaching Biochemistry in Edinburgh, then for teaching Latin, then for Greek and First Century History. The original author was Dr A. P. Ryle, the programme was much adapted by Professor H. Hine, and was further modified to take Greek by the present contributor with the help of Professor Hine. The programme is written in ucsd-p pascal and the micro version runs on the p-system on Sirius or Apricot micros. The interaction of the programme with a Greek font is at present only possible on those two micros. Further details of the programme are available from the contributor.

Cursus

Cursus is a small data-base program which at present exists in 'prototype' form. The Latin word 'cursus' means race, 'race for office', or career. *Cursus* contains 150 careers of Roman administrators and army officers of the first two centuries A.D. Each entry includes name, origin (social and geographic), period and office held, and the data can therefore be interrogated from several different angles.

A knowledge of military and administrative institutions, and the part different social groups (e.g. senators, *equites*) played in the functioning of the empire, is naturally essential to any proper understanding of the Roman world. *Cursus*' contribution is to enable students to examine the primary evidence for themselves, and from it to build up a picture of the Roman imperial system. A session with this program should significantly enhance a student's understanding of the functioning of the Roman empire, whether from the viewpoint of a comparative newcomer to the subject, or that of someone wanting a more detailed insight into a specific aspect (e.g. how much military experience did the average Roman general have?).

The program is easy to use. It also has a swift response time, making it convenient for teaching situations. It has been written on the B.B.C. 'B' microcomputer, and some size has therefore had to be sacrificed to speed. The data-base is large enough to achieve its purpose as a teaching aid, however, and although it is intended to make it available on IBM, it will remain substantially unchanged. Little would be gained by increasing the amount of data unless a research tool were envisaged, and this would require a program on a much larger scale.

Quantitative Methods

54 *Peter Wardley*

Teaching Computing to Historians at Durham

Introduction

The main concern of this chapter is teaching computing to historians on mainframe computers. In particular, it relates my experience of teaching historians at Durham University, though this conforms with my experiences at other universities. Although the ideas expressed here are unoriginal, they may assist those considering the design of a computing course for historians. It is also hoped this discussion of practical issues might aid those who are tempted to introduce a computing course for historians but have no experience in this field.

There are at least five essential items which should be considered when the development of a computing course is being contemplated:

1. Access to the computer. This should include an assessment of the availability and location of computing facilities used for teaching purposes and of those used by students during times of their choice.

2. Nature of the service provided by the computer system. What features are expected to be used by students and are there restrictions on the use of either hardware or software?

3. Quality of output. This should include an assessment of the products which students will be able to produce by their labours.

4. Applicability of packages. This should include an assessment of the demands students are likely to make in the course of their historical studies and the suitability of available software.

5. Backup services. What additional support can the students expect

from the local Computer Centre ?

Each of these points should be considered when a computing course is being designed or re-assessed. This report, though strictly confined by space limitations, attempts to address these aspects.

The penultimate section describes some of the difficulties which occurred during my demonstration at the inaugural Association of History and Computing Conference. In addition to being a record of one session, as seen through the eyes of the presenter, it graphically illustrates some of the potential pitfalls which face demonstrators using alien equipment at a remote site. As a result the author would offer the strongest recommendation that those intending to give such demonstrations arrange for the completion of a practise session before setting out from their host site.

Finally a conclusion highlights three practical aspects of teaching computing; these points are straightforward and relevant whenever the teaching of computing is considered.

Computing with the mainframe at Durham University

The universities of Durham and Newcastle, along with Newcastle Polytechnic, participate in the Northumbrian Universities Multiple Access Computer organization (NUMAC). This system uses the Michigan Terminal System (MTS) and the campus network is known as NUNET; a variety of services can be accessed from NUNET. The local mainframe service at Durham University is known as DUR.MTS and is provided by and from the Computer Centre. The attitude of the Computer Centre management is liberal; all legitimate uses of the computer are encouraged. In addition, the output produced on the Durham mainframe is of the highest quality; in particular a laser printer offers the opportunity to produce 'print-ready' copy. Students, as well as staff, can generate output which looks very 'professional'.

Background to the Course

Towards the end of the second year of a three year stint at Durham University I suggested to members of the Economic History Department that I was prepared to offer a course on computing and statistical methods during the academic year 1985/6. My colleagues responded to this proposal with some enthusiasm and decided that such a course would be useful. It was agreed that an optional course should be provided for second year undergraduates which offered them an opportunity to use the University mainframe computer. Most students who took economic history at Durham were expected to complete a dissertation at the end of the summer vacation before the third year. It was hoped a computing course might be attractive to second year undergraduates because it would provide them with a set of skills which would be useful when they undertook this task. Original plans to offer a certificate at the end of the year were not pursued so the course started as an unexamined option offered to second year students. In the meantime the Economic History Department merged with the History Department and it was agreed that the course could be offered to second year students in the new Department of Modern History.

The stated objectives of the course were to increase the student's general awareness of the potentialities and pitfalls which face historians when computers and quantitative methods are used. The initial level of competence which was assumed was nil.

The general aims were to: instil a basic technical competence; increase confidence in the application of basic quantitative methods and computing; facilitate informed critical assessment of the historical literature which makes explicit use of these methods; and provide skills which students could use in their graduate careers as well as in an academic context. The specific aims were to promote: intelligent collection of historical data; informed analysis and considered presentation of information; and competent use of computer packages for statistical analysis, text processing, graphics and cartography.

The group who attended the course comprised four distinct, though compatible, types of participants. Firstly, there was the target group of second year undergraduates who made up the bulk of the group. Secondly, there was a pair of third year students, both female, who had become inquisitive about the methods employed in Quantitative Economic History during their second year and had expressed an interest in a computing course. Thirdly, a history undergraduate from a German university undertaking one year's study at Durham University persuaded me by his enthusiasm and persistence that he would benefit from the course. Fourthly, two colleagues, lecturers in the History Department, requested admission to the class on the grounds that they were absolute beginners who wished to take advantage of an opportunity which would not be repeated.

Given the heterogeneous nature of the group it would be useful to assess the success of the course before any further details are provided. Sixteen second year undergraduates started the course. All of them managed to master the basics but a realistic assessment of their performance would suggest that about half the group reached levels of competence which allowed them to use the computer constructively in their historical studies. One point expressed by these students was disappointment that they would not be examined and, therefore, would not be able to gain a certificate at the end of the course. Individually, and collectively, the second year students held strongly the view that proof of their exposure to computers and competence in computing would be very advantageous in their search for employment. The lack of a direct 'pay-off' in the form of a qualification diminished the incentive for some of these students.

Generally, the two third-year students acquired computing skills more quickly than did the second year students. One of the third-year students gained entry to a postgraduate course partly because she was able to convince her interviewers that she had some experience of computing and was enthusiastic about that experience.

Thirdly, I benefited from my admission of the German student. As things turned out he elected to take an economic history course and I taught the tutorial group of which he was a member. I received his first essay at the end of his first month in Durham. The essay had been typed to a file on the mainframe, formatted with the text processing package, and produced on the laser printer. I was very impressed that someone could produce his first essay at a new university in a foreign language on a computer system with such limited experience; particularly as he had no computing background and no experience of writing English for academic purposes at any level. My only consolation, being a guilty monoglot, was that his written English, while good, was not perfect and I could claim to have contributed to his skills ! During the year this student used the computer to compile and analyse a data set for the occupational structure of Durham constructed from the ninteenth century censuses which he intended to use in his undergraduate dissertation.

Finally, the most dedicated participants were my two colleagues from the History Department. If I can make the point without offending them, they proved easily that age and experience in the more traditional activities undertaken by historians was no barrier to the acquisition of new skills. Computing will now play a part in the teaching of at least one special study provided to third year students in the History Department at Durham University and future postgraduate students in British political history will be encouraged to acquire computing skills as a high priority.

The course taught the students how to edit and manipulate files. Once these basic skills had been acquired the students were introduced to packages which would facilitate the analysis and presentation of information. The packages used on the course included two graphics packages (EASYPLOT and GIMMS), a text processing package (TEXTURE), and an econometrics package (TSP) which has the advantage of very flexible data manipulation facilities which are easy to use. Although each student had different interests, for example some were more interested in graphics than others, most acquired sufficient technical skill to complete the tasks they required.

Course Details

The first priority was to provide basic skills which would allow students to edit and manage their files. Each student was provided with a summary guide to MTS which explained signing on, signing off, file space security, file management, line editing, screen editing, and job submission (Inclusion of the handout is precluded here by lack of space but requests for copies will receive a sympathetic response from the author). An on-line copy of the guide was available to students in the History group file library. As with other files in the group library, this could be copied, or 'imported', into the student's file space; once acquired, information could be added or subtracted as the student developed a customized information file to meet her personal requirements.

Teaching sessions were informal and varied in nature. Each session began with a review of previous work; it is important to maintain continuity when teaching skills which have to be acquired sequentially. Techniques were demonstrated using two large television monitors which revealed to the group what the teacher was doing and how results were obtained. After the formal demonstration students returned to their individual terminal to try out the new techniques.

Examples of the new techniques, in the form of files which had been prepared before the session, were available for the students to 'import' from the History group library. Students were also encouraged to select information that arose in their historical studies which could be adapted as examples; ideally these would be deployed in their course work.

An Illustration of Practical Examples

Two of the examples used in the course are presented here. These illustrate the simple structure of the files required to produce graphs; they also demonstrate the development of standard files to produce 'customised' graphs. Once a student has grasped basic principles, she can produce graphs which demonstrate relevant historical points by adaptation of an example file.

The first example produces a line graph using an 'in-house' (DUR.MTS specific) package called EASYPLOT. Needless to say, its name has been doubted by first-time users; nevertheless it is a useful package which can be used by unambitious graph designers who are prepared to build up patiently the features of their product. Example I is an input file which produces a simple line graph; the instructions which comprise the file can be explained by reference to line numbers which serve only as labels.

Our subject is a graph of the population, in thousands, of the major urban centres in County Durham since 1801. The instructions start with line 10, which specifies the output device on which the graph will be produced, and terminate with line 30. The number of variables to be plotted is stipulated at line 20. A graph would be drawn by a file which contained just these three lines and the associated data but additional commands allow refinement and improvement of the graph.

A grid is drawn across the graph unless the default is suppressed: this is done by line 110. Line 120 provides the title heading for the graph. Lines 130 to 133 provide the labels for the Y axis; in this case names of the urban centres the population for which are listed after line 30 (i.e. the population of Sunderland in 1981 was 196,200).

The relative dimensions of the graph can be changed by specifying the lengths of the axis; line 140 sets the y axis length. Line 141 generates a y axis which has a minimum value of zero, a maximum value of 250 thousand, and has a vertical scale marked in units of 50 thousands. The PLOT commands at lines 160 and 161 specify solid (LWSY) or dashed (DAWS) lines between data points and the symbols for each urban centre are selected from a range of options by lines 170 and 171. Finally, the size of characters (LETSIZ) for the labels and the size of the symbols (SYMSIZ) are specified in line 180. With the addition of the extra commands a much more effective graph is produced.

Example II illustrates the construction of pie graphs using a general purpose cartographic package called GIMMS; line graphs, bar charts, diagrams, and maps can also be produced with GIMMS which is a very flexible plotting system. The development of a program is illustrated here by two pie charts which illustrate some of the features available with GIMMS;

Example 1   *Durham Easyplot Program: Population Size in Thousands*

```
    10    &OPTS DEV='TEK'.

    20    NY=4.

   110    GRID='NO'.

   120    HEAD='URBAN CENTRES IN COUNTY DURHAM'.

   130    YLAB(1,1)='DURHAM'.
   131    YLAB(1,2)='GATESHEAD'.
   132    YLAB(1,3)='SOUTH SHIELDS'.
   133    YLAB(1,4)='SUNDERLAND'.

   140    YLEN=8.
   141    YMIN=0.0, YMAX=250, NYDIV=5.

   150    XMIN=1801.0, XMAX=1981.0, NXDIV=9.

   160    PLOT(1)='LWSY', PLOT(2)='DAWS'.
   161    PLOT(3)='LWSY', PLOT(4)='DAWS'.

   170    NSYMB(1)=11, NSYMB(2)=2.
   171    NSYMB(3)=1, NSYMB(4)=6.

   180    LETSIZ=0.25, SYMSIZ=0.1.

    30    &END
```

```
           1801     7.5       8.6      11.0      25.0
           1811     8.0       8.8      15.2      25.8
           1821     9.8      11.8      16.5      31.9
           1831     9.3      15.2      18.8      40.7
           1841     9.6      20.1      23.1      52.8
           1851    13.2      25.6      29.0      67.4
           1861    14.1      33.5      35.2      85.8
           1871    14.8      48.6      45.2     104.5
           1881    14.9      65.8      56.9     124.7
           1891    15.3      85.7      78.4     142.1
           1901    16.2     109.9     100.9     146.1
           1911    17.6     116.9     108.6     151.2
           1921    17.3     125.1     118.6     182.2
           1931    18.1     122.4     113.5     185.9
           1951    19.3     115.1     106.6     206.8
           1961    20.5     103.3     110.0     218.6
           1971    24.7      94.5     100.5     216.9
           1981    26.4      81.4      87.2     196.2
```

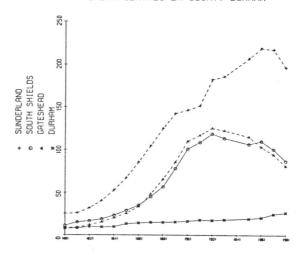

URBAN CENTRES IN COUNTY DURHAM

once more the line numbers are for reference purposes only. GIMMS job are controlled by command statements which start (lines 10, 20 and 21), end (lines 30 and 31), and control the system.

The basic illustrative example (lines 110–180) shows the percentage of the votes cast for the various parties at the 1983 election; the relative proportions are specified at line 140. The intensity of shading to be employed for each segment is stated at line 150. A 20 by 20 unit frame is specified at line 110 for reference purposes; each of the labels added to graph are located by a pair of x and y co-ordinates within this space. The relative size of the text for each label is specified by the height (HT) variable. As two portions of the graph are shaded the labels indicating the percentage within those segments are 'shielded' by lines 120 and 121 before the graph is drawn; this prevents over-shading.

The second pie chart was adapted from the first. It depicts the relative

Example 2   *An Illustration of GIMMS Commands*

```
10    *SYSPARM INTERACT

20    *PLOTPARM PLOTTER

21    *GRAPHICS

110   *NEWPAGE 20,20 FRAME

120      *TEXT SHIELD X=12 Y=11.5 HT=0.4 '28.3%'
121      *TEXT SHIELD X=7  Y=10   HT=0.4 '43.5%'

130   *PIE RADIUS=5

140   DATA=28.3,26.0,43.5,2.2

150   SHADING=2,0,4,11

160      *TEXT X=11 Y=7  HT=0.4 '26.0%'
161      *TEXT X=14 Y=14 HT=0.6 'LABOUR'
162      *TEXT X=14 Y=5  HT=0.6 'ALLIANCE'
163      *TEXT X=1  Y=4.5 HT=0.6 'CONSERVATIVE'
164      *TEXT X=8  Y=15.5 HT=0.6 'OTHER'

170      *TEXT HT=0.8 X=1 Y=1 '% VOTES - 1983 ELECTION'

180      *TEXT Y=17 X=1 HT=1.2  'E.G.- PIE GRAPH'

199      *SHIELD=OFF

210   *NEWPAGE 20,20 FRAME

220      *TEXT SHIELD X=12 Y=10 HT=0.4 '47.2%'
221      *TEXT SHIELD X=6  Y=10 HT=0.4 '25.9%'

230   *PIE RADIUS=5

240      DATA=47.2, 17.3, 25.9, 9.6

250      SHADING=2,0,4,11

260      *TEXT X=16 Y=10 FONT=33 SHADE HT=0.6 'LABOUR'
261      *TEXT X=3  Y=5  FONT=17 HT=0.6 'RESIDUAL'
262      *TEXT X=3  Y=4  FONT=17 HT=0.6 'PRODUCTIVITY'
263      *TEXT X=6  Y=6  HT=0.4 '17.9%'
264      *TEXT X=1  Y=13 FONT=32 HT=0.6 'CAPITAL'
265      *TEXT X=1  Y=13.5 HT=0.6 'LAND'
266      *TEXT X=6  Y=13.5 HT=0.4 '9.6%'

270      *TEXT FONT=62 X=1 Y=2 HT=0.6 'DAVIS ET AL. TABLE 2.12'
271      *TEXT FONT=52 SHADE X=1 Y=1 HT=0.6 'AMERICAN ECONOMIC GROWTH'
280      *TEXT FONT=62 SHADE X=1 Y=18.75 HT=1.0 'U.S.A. - SOURCES OF'
281      *TEXT FONT=62 SHADE X=1 Y=17.25 HT=1.0 ' GROWTH, 1840-1900'

30    *END
31    *STOP
```

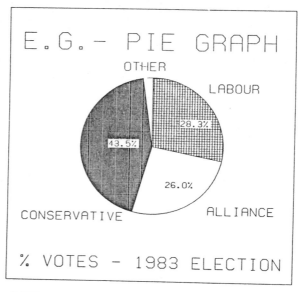

sources of growth for the economy of the United States between 1840 and 1900. As the program is written both graphs would produced by running the file. Note, however, that it would be easy to edit a file which contained lines 110 to 180 to produce a file which specified lines 210 to 280; inspection will reveal concordance between the two sets of instructions.

Construction of the second pie chart commences at line 210 but it should be noticed that the previously specified shielding is 'turned' off by line 199. Once the position of the segments has been established the text can be located within the new page by the co-ordinates. Apart from demonstrating the ease with which pie charts can be adapted from the original example, the second example also demonstrates the range of 'fonts' or alphabets which are available with GIMMS.

The course employed similar examples to demonstrate the statistical and text processing packages but, obviously, the graphics packages are the most striking illustrations. The common theme is a simple file, provided as an example, which can be altered and adapted in an experimental way by the student until, after sequential development, the final specification is achieved.

Presentation at Westfield College

When the History Department at Durham University received the notice announcing the 'History and Computing' conference the immediate response of my colleagues was to suggest that I should offer a summary of my experiences of teaching computing. My proposal to discuss the course and demonstrate teaching methods in a practical session was accepted by the organisers of the conference. This involved the use of the JANET (Joint Academic NETwork) link which would allow the use of computing facilities at Durham while working from terminals at Westfield College. My intention was to explain the 'spirit' of the course and to replicate the use of exercises employed as teaching aids during the year. This might be accomplished if the anticipated audience could be persuaded to participate in a practical session which took them through some of the activities which had been undertaken by students taking the course. In short, I was looking for guinea pigs who could illustrate the ease with which jobs could be undertaken with the minimum information about the computer system they were using. This, I hoped, would demonstrate how students taking the course had been taught.

There were, however, three problems which immediately confronted me. Firstly, only one link was available to Durham. Although there were five terminals in the demonstration area, four of them were 'enslaved'; the slave terminals could only be used as monitors which would display the work done on the one active terminal. This precluded the envisaged practical session. Secondly, it would be agreed by all concerned that the quality of output achieved with the graphics terminal which had been specially provided for the demonstration was poor. The clarity fell far below the standards I had become accustomed to and had hoped to reproduce in the session. The poor quality of the graphical display greatly hindered the demonstration and dampened my enthusiasm. Thirdly, the screen editor was inoperative over JANET. As a new set of screen editing commands had been implemented at Durham on the grounds that they were compatible with the universal standard adopted for use over JANET, I had assumed the screen edit facility was available over JANET. I was wrong. Or rather my attempt anticipated the implementation of this facility which is available now.

Under these circumstances much of the intended demonstration had to be abandoned. I was restricted to a description of the course, an illustration of the graphics packages discussed above, which entailed use of the line editing facilities, and an impromptu demonstration of the MINITAB package which is available at Newcastle (NCL.MTS).

Although the positive response of my audience restored my flagging confidence, and diminished my disappointment in the face of adversity, things had not gone as intended. I was not convinced, at the end of the session, that I had done justice to the course nor had I conveyed the full merits of teaching computing to history students. In particular, I am sure that some of those present who expressed doubts about the abilities of history students to acquire skills sufficiently quickly or overcome fears of computers might have been more reassured if they had been able to try out some of the exercises used in the course. On the latter point, it is my experience that lecturers have a fear of computers which greatly exceeds that experienced by students.

The moral to be drawn from this story is that if you plan to give a demonstration at a remote site using alien equipment you should insist on a dummy run before you leave your host site.

Conclusions

In general the course achieved its objectives, though it could have been improved. Some of the students did not make the most of the facilities available to them; how much this was due to my failure to explain the full potential of the system remains unknown. If it is all too easy to underestimate the time required to learn a new set of skills (or complete a task using a computer); it is even easier to forgot how long it took to master the skill you are attempting to propagate.

At the end of the course a questionnaire was sent out to the participants in an attempt to gauge the consumer's view; this was returned by three quarters of the students. The replies were enthusiastic and, by offering constructive criticism, positive; obviously the students had enjoyed the course. The most frequent comment was an expression of regret that they had not been examined on the skills they had acquired. In particular, the students thought the course had been useful and appreciated the efforts which had been made on their behalf. Oddly, among the students who did not respond were some of the most extensive users of the computer both during and after the course. Overall I would assess the course a success, though it should be noted that the participants who benefited most were *not* the original target group.

One attractive aspect of the course was the collective identity that the group developed; this generated mutual support within the class and discovery of aspects of the system by the students which were not included in the course. One aspect of a good mainframe system is the constant discovery of new facilities and novel short cuts which allow the more efficient completion of tasks. Although the two lecturers who attended the group did not teach any member of the group, I suspect their presence fostered a realization on the part of the students that computers had a positive role to play in the study of history. Certainly the examples provided by my colleagues, both of whom are political historians, illustrated the breadth of potential use. From a personal point of view the course was very rewarding to teach and generated a great deal of job satisfaction; though it should be noted this was not gained without effort. The 'Computing for Historians' course required a lot of preparation and was very time consuming. All the general facets of teaching computing mentioned above would also be supported by my previous experience. In general, three points should be emphasised:

1. Learning by doing.
2. Need to know.
3. Reinforcement of skills by practical application.

First, it is important to recognise that the skills acquired by students are learnt by hard work and the accumulation of experience at a terminal is essential; 'learning by doing' is the only way to acquire these skills and time must be spent if this experience is to be gained. This requires intelligent application and a realisation on the part of the student that the repetition of basic tasks is an unavoidable aspect of this process; these are frequently caused by mistakes which could be made by any user, but are particularly likely to afflict a novice in the early stages of learning a new craft. There is a salutary lesson here for all teachers. The instructor is quickly reminded that students acquire skills at very different rates; something which is more obvious in this setting than in teaching 'history' *per se*. While it is very useful to be reminded of this there is, fortunately, a corollary that the rate at which skills are learnt is not a particularly good guide to the sum total of skills which any individual can acquire and develop.

Secondly, it can be argued that students should be presented with information when they require it. At the beginning of the course they should be provided with sufficient information to start using a system. Consolidation of basic skills is essential even if this means there is a short delay before they can produce material which is immediately relevant to their academic work. A carefully designed course will minimise the delay before the student can produce historical material with the assistance of the computer and ensure rapid progress by providing sequential steps which increase the student's confidence.

Thirdly, computing offers students a new set of skills and access to a computer allows them to use additional techniques. These skills should be provided to enhance the history produced by the student. History students engage in historical studies in their degree courses; the computer offers the student an extra 'toolbox' which should enable them to produce a better quality product. For these skills to be employed to the best effect reinforcement is necessary in the form of opportunities to deploy them for historical purposes. If this is to occur lecturers must emphasise the use of appropriate techniques of presentation and analysis, as well as actively encouraging students to obtain the most from the facilities which are available to them. In itself, there is nothing novel in this prescription; throughout the ages historians have expressed the desirability of this ideal. Access to a computer merely adds to the techniques which can be employed and makes available additional resources. For the historian, *per se*, computing skills are a means to an end, not an end in themselves.

Finally, it should be stressed that computers are extremely useful tools which are designed to assist in the collection, presentation, and analysis of data. The historian should be grateful that these characteristics are just those required by those engaged in the production of history at any level.

55   *David Taylor*

Prime Numbers: the Teaching of Statistical and Computational Methods

The research-oriented papers delivered at this conference demonstrate clearly the immense benefits that computers can bring to the historian. However, at present, there are very few courses specifically designed for history students which will enable these new and desirable skills to be acquired. In this paper I wish to look at some of the practical difficulties that have been encountered in using computers to introduce graduates to the use of statistical methods as part of the M.A. in Local History offered at Teeside Polytechnic.[1]

The structure and content of the course (and, indeed, the whole teaching method) was determined by two basic beliefs. First, the course had to be clearly relevant to the needs of the students and not appear to be alien and imposed from without. To achieve this a style of joint- teaching, involving expertise from other disciplines, was developed but with a strong emphasis on historical content.[2] Second, the course had to overcome the understandable, if at times misplaced, fears of both numbers and computers. Hands-on experience in a controlled progression provided the key. As the result of experience since 1979, when the course first ran, statistical methods and computer usages are introduced in parallel. This means that essential 'keyboard' skills are introduced at a time when the mathematics is basic while more complex statistical techniques are developed when students have some familiarity with the computer. At all times the watchwords remain — relevance and reassurance!

The course itself breaks into two uneven parts.[3] In the first block students are shown (a) how to login to PRIME and how to call up MINITAB (and MINITAB worksheets previously prepared by the staff) and (b) how to carry out basic operations with various tabulation techniques (histograms, scatterplots etc.) and elementary descriptive statistics (means, standard deviations etc.). Students are provided with work sheets, including worked examples and problems all using historical data, as well as booklets detailing the underlying statistical principles involved. The first block finishes with a consideration of sampling and its attendant problems.

The remainder of the course is given over to a number of specific case studies. The approach is deliberately and necessarily selective. The intention is to demonstrate the potential of computational and quantitative methods for the historian rather than provide a whistle-stop tour of the statistical landscape. The case studies — three are used normally — vary from year to year but all have certain common features. First, the starting point is always a specific historical problem and usually related directly to work done elsewhere on the M.A.. At this stage the emphasis is very much on the complexities of the historical question and the problems that arise from imperfect data. In this way the artificiality that surrounds much teaching of statistics is avoided. More importantly it confirms the need for the historian to be in control, specifying the problem and evaluating evidence, from the outset. Second, having set up the problems, each case study involves a careful consideration of the principles that underlie the particular statistical technique(s) that will be used. Although computational and statistical techniques are presented as means to an end, it has always been the intention to make our students critical consumers and users which necessitates an awareness of how the statistician works and the expectations she/he has of the data. Only after this stage are students introduced to the relevant MINITAB feature and calculations completed. Finally, each case study ends with an evaluation and interpretation of the results. Once again the emphasis is on the crucial role of the historian, relating the statistical findings to the substantive historical problem.

To give a specific example: one case study is devoted to the question of nineteenth-century voting behaviour. Starting with a review of the work carried out by people such as Nossiter and Fraser, the whole question of socio-economic determinants of voting behaviour is examined. Students, many of whom will have taken a course on local politics in the second half of the nineteenth century, are asked to consider the practical difficulties involved in putting values on the relationships claimed to exist by various writers. Hand-in-hand with this goes a consideration of the evidence available to the historian. This involves, unsurprisingly, an evaluation of poll-books, directories, census-enumerators' books and the local press as sources.

Once again there is a direct link with another element in the degree — this time a course on nineteenth-century sources. Particular attention is paid to the problems associated with (a) determining socio-economic status and (b) ascertaining religious affiliation. Having clarified the issues involved, assessed the evidence and decided that it is worthwhile to proceed, the next stage is to look at the various measures of association from χ^2 through Spearman's *Rho*, the Pearson product- moment correlation to multiple regression analysis. While students are shown the way in which to calculate these measures of association, the prime concern is less with 'number-crunching' but more with the underlying principles and the data requirements involved. Necessarily, this is the most theoretical phase and the one most removed from historical detail. Nonetheless, it is firm view of both staff involved in the teaching of this course that it is an essential phase if students are to become critical users rather than unthinking button pushers! Button pushing (or more accurately key pressing), however, comes into its own as students are shown how to calculate χ^2 etc. using MINITAB on pre-entered data sets. As indicated above, the final stage is to analyse the print-outs in statistical and, more importantly, historical terms.[4]

Although the course has changed quite considerably over the years, a number of general observations can be made on its strengths and weaknesses. From the outset the course was seen to be ambitious and it is probably true to say that there has never been quite enough time to achieve all that was hoped. Equally, it has not proved possible to remove all fears and scepticism, though this has varied from intake to intake and from individual to individual. Overall, however, the evidence of written work produced by our students suggests that they have developed an awareness of what can and cannot be achieved. But as well as being critical consumers, others (albeit a minority) have demonstrated in their dissertations that they are critical and capable users of computational and quantitative methods.

Looking more specifically at the use of the computer, one arrives at a similar conclusion of qualified success though, as ever, the rider 'could do better' has to be added. There can be little doubt of several considerable advantages that accrue from the use of the computer. First, large volumes of data can be handled. The importance of this lies in the ability to approximate more closely the real world and reduce the artificiality that bedevils much teaching of elementary statistics. A second clear benefit is the ease of access to powerful statistical techniques afforded by such packages as MINITAB. Moreover, large and complex calculations can be carried out with both speed and accuracy. The reduction in drudgery as well as the lessening of error are very real gains in themselves but, perhaps more important, is the consequent gain in time which allows for more experimentation with data which can only enhance the quality of the statistical analysis and for more detailed evaluation and interpretation of results which can only enhance the quality of the historical analysis. Finally, accessibility and familiarity go a long way in reducing the mystery surrounding both computers and statistical methods and thereby diminishing fears and uncertainties among students who, for the most part, have a limited background in mathematics and little faith in their own abilities to handle numerical data. These advantages have been noted before in other spheres of study but this makes them none the less valuable. However, there is a danger of overlooking some of the practical problems that are encountered on such courses. While many of these problems are mundane in nature, there are a number of more substantial worries to note.

The first point to make is the time-consuming nature of this type of course. Preparation times have proved to be longer than anticipated while the decision to joint-teach the course further added to total staff input. More importantly the time required by students to master new techniques can easily be underestimated. 'Simple keyboard skills' are only simple when they have been mastered and many frustrating and dispiriting moments can be spent at a terminal, especially in the early days. Given the different nature of the learning process for most history students it is essential to provide time for practice. More could be made of worked and part-worked examples, though this will add to the staff load, in the short-run at least. Certainly, time for practice can help to offset the uneven rates of learning that are inevitably encountered and which can present real problems in an intensive course in which students are seen on only one evening a week.

There are, however, other problems that arise once these initial difficulties have been overcome and which, paradoxically, stem from enthusiasm and commitment. Despite repeated exhortations to the contrary, there is a tendency on the art of some students to see the computer as a panacea. This manifests itself most obviously in the tendency to use any data that happens to be to hand and to produce every conceivable table and statistic irrespective of its value to the substantive issue under consideration. It cannot be stated too firmly or too often that the computer (and its software) cannot make good deficiencies in the original data — the old warning, 'GIGO', garbage in/garbage out, still holds good — nor will quantitative methods provide answers. It is for the historian to evaluate evidence and to interpret results at all times.

There is a further dimension to this question of uncritical usage which deserves emphasis. As was noted above, powerful techniques are now available to anyone willing to master the basic keyboard skills required to use a package such as MINITAB. Familiarity reduces fear but, proverbially, it can also breed contempt and there is a very real danger that historians will pay insufficient attention to the data requirements of these statistical techniques. Do historians, for example, ensure that their two sets of data are normally distributed and have similar variances as well as having a linear relationship when calculating the Pearson product-moment correlation coefficient? Are they aware of the dangers involved in bending the rules? One suspects that the enthusiasm to apply new techniques to the flawed data from the past has lead to some dubious calculations being made. This is not to lend support to the Eltons of this world but rather to stress the need for a proper concern for the requirements of the new techniques that are being adopted.[5]

Having stressed the problems encountered in running this course, it is important to keep matters in proportion. The evidence of work produced by our students (and their comments) demonstrate that, on balance, the strengths have outweighed the weaknesses. As long as the historian remembers his/her responsibility to specify the problem, evaluate the evidence and techniques to be used and interpret the results then computational skills will be a major addition to the tools of the trade. However, in the final analysis, the computer is a fashionable and fast-working moron — the role of the user is of paramount importance. The computer greatly facilitates the use of statistics but, in itself, this will not turn the indifferent or careless practioner into a great historian; but the good historian can greatly enhance his/her skills and in so doing advance historical understanding through the thoughtful application of new technology along side more traditional skills.

Notes

1. Although the use of micros was considered it was decided to utilise the Polytechnic mainframe computer (PRIME). With regard to packages, SPSS was initially used but this was felt to be too complex and intimidating on an introductory course. Consequently, the more user-friendly MINITAB was adopted.

2. For an account of the teaching methods adopted on the course see D. Taylor and G. E. Skipworth, 'Utility through Collaboration: a problem-oriented approach', *Proceedings of the First International Conference on Teaching Statistics* ii, 1982, pp. 232–7.

3. The course is offered to part-time students, who attend for one three hour session per week, and lasts for twelve weeks. An individual back-up service is provided and further tuition provided as and when required by students during the preparation of their dissertations.

4. Other case studied have included the performance of the local iron and steel industry *c.*1870–1914, real wages and living standards in Edwardian Middlesbrough, the incidence of crime on Teesside between the wars. Work is in progress on aspects of early modern demographic change.

5. G. R. Elton, *The Practice of History* (1967), p. 34. See also J. P. Kenyon's warning not to yield to the temptation of 'whoring after the exotic delights of . . . computerisation', *Times Higher Education Supplement*, 18th May 1983. An alternative case is argued by R. Floud, 'Quantitative History and People's History', *History Workshop*, xvii, 1984, pp. 113–24. See also my brief contribution 'Percentage Play: or is there safety in numbers?', *Cleveland History Workshop*, i, 1986.

56   *R. B. Weir*

The Teaching of Computing and Quantitative Methods to Economic History Undergraduates

By comparison with the earlier papers in the conference which have described fascinating work at the frontier of research this paper is particularly modest. It describes an undergraduate course in computing and quantitative methods — Elementary Quantitative Methods — which is taken by second year students in economic and social history at the University of York. The course was introduced as a response to problems posed by the increasingly quantitative and theoretical nature of the literature in economic and social history, and the paper is offered in the belief that amongst the aims of this conference is a desire to make the methods and results of advanced historical scholarship accessible to undergraduates, the majority of whom are not going to become professional historians. The course is not presented as the ideal solution to this problem but rather as a possible solution which may be applicable elsewhere.

During the last two decades advanced historical study has undergone significant change. Key features of this have included the use of large data sets, the application of computers to extract information from such data sets, and the testing of hypotheses about behaviour in the past by a combination of theory and statistical methods. Of all the many branches of history represented at this meeting, economic and social history has probably been the most profoundly affected by this change. The conventional interpretation of many key topics has been radically altered by the techniques of 'the new economic history' and this has posed a severe problem for teachers. Initially, much of the innovatory work was confined to research seminars and postgraduate teaching but, as the results have filtered in increasing volume into the literature, it has become important for undergraduates to know about computing and statistical techniques so that they can assess for themselves the content of this advanced work. Just as a knowledge of German is essential for an advanced study of German history, so a knowledge of computing and statistical methods is vital for the study of economic and social history and must be taught to undergraduates so that they can undertake such study.

In British universities the response to the invasion of theory and quantification into economic and social history has been varied. The survey undertaken by Clive Lee for the Social Science Research Council in 1983 shows that some historians have chosen to ignore it, some to develop new courses and others have simply quoted the findings of the research to undergraduates without attempting to explain the methods.[1] This last response was not, and is not, adequate for two reasons. The first is that a common problem researched by two scholars can produce quite different results.[2] How are students to assess the validity of the results if they do not understand the method? The second is that the intellectually curious student is not going to be fobbed off by being told that the methods are too difficult: the good undergraduate wants to know, and deserves to know, how the results were achieved. And that raises the problem of skills.

For this advanced work to be accessible to undergraduates new skills have to be acquired particularly, though not exclusively, in numeracy and computing.[3] One problem at York (and probably common to most economic history departments in Britain) is that a relatively small percentage of the intake — 12% in 1984/5 and 18% in 1985/6 — has 'A' level Mathematics.[4] All are required to have an 'O' level pass (this requirement is often waived for mature students) but the time lag between 'O' levels and entry to university creates a considerable fear and apprehension about quantitative work at university level. Rusty mathematical skills, the fear that poor performance in quantitative work will have a detrimental effect on final degree results and the fact that some students are attracted to economic history because they believe it to be a literary, non-quantitative discipline can create a high threshold of resistance to quantitative work.[5]

At York the response to this situation was to introduce a compulsory quantitative methods and computing course to the second year of the economic and social history degree. Economic and social history is part of the Department of Economics and Related Studies and by their second year, students had already taken an introductory statistics course. The outline syllabus is shown in Table 1.

Table 1   *Part One Statistics Syllabus*

Autumn Term: Descriptive statistics and basic theory
—The role of statistical analysis in social and economic investigation. Different kinds of data and levels of measurement.
—Description and summarisation of a set of values of a single numerical variable; summary statistics and frequency distributions; index numbers and their application.
—Use of transformations to achieve symmetry
—Relationships between numerical variables. The descriptive use of regression analysis. The correlation coefficient.
—Simple time series analysis. Plotting, identifying and measuring trend, seasonal and other components.
—Introduction to the normal distribution. Introduction to the ideas of probability.

Spring Term: Statistical estimation and Hypothesis testing
—Probability and its interpretations. The relationship between population and random sample. Probability distribution of sample mean.
—Using sample information to estimate the characteristics of a population.
—Sample survey methods.
—Hypothesis testing. Introduction to statistical modelling.
—Contingency tables and the analysis of categorical data.
—Introduction to multiple regression analysis.

Summer Term: Case-studies
—Statistical analyses of the U.K economy
—Project

Teaching hours
  Autumn term: 9 lectures, 8 tutorials
  Spring term: 9 lectures, 9 tutorials
  Summer term: 3 lectures, 3 tutorials
  Total: lectures 21 hours, tutorials 20 hours = 41 hours

The second-year course for economic historians built on work covered in the first year so that revision would reinforce the statistical methods already encountered. In designing the syllabus emphasis was placed on the techniques most commonly used in the New Economic History, particularly regression (Table 2).

Table 2   *Syllabus of Elementary Quantitative Methods Course*
                          First Term

Topic	No. of lectures	No. of tutorials
Index numbers	2	1
Growth & fluctuations	1	1
Correlation	1	1
Regression	2	1
Hypothesis testing	3	1
Revision	-	1
Total teaching hours	9	6

Two principles were adopted: one was that all the statistical techniques should be taught using historical data, so that students would see the relevance of the particular statistical technique for economic history; the other was that tutorials would include statistical exercises and a detailed examination of a single journal article. Questions about the article, almost on a line-by-line basis, are distributed before the tutorial with the purpose of focusing students' attention on the statistical technique being used. This device has the virtue that it prevents students skipping over 'the difficult bits' of an article. Another — implicit — principle was that the course should be taught by economic historians and not by the statisticians in the belief that we should not expect students to do anything we are not prepared to do ourselves.

With a foundation in statistical technique the second term of the course introduces students to the computer as well as extending their reading in the literature of the New Economic History and preparing a group project (Table 3).

Table 3   *Syllabus of Elementary Quantitative Methods Course*

Second Term

Computing:
Session 1: using a terminal; problem solving games.
Session 2: description of the interactive programme, Statpack; running the programme; data input; file creation; use of the commands 'Desc', 'Basic', 'Hist', 'Bargr'.
Session 3: Statpack: coefficient of variation; correlation; regression; interpreting the regression output; assigning output to the line-printer.
Session 4: Statpack: Spearman rank correlation; multiple regression.
Session 5: Statpack: multiple regression. Use of the editor, SOS.
Session 6: Distribution of the Group Project.
Session 7: Tutorial
Session 8: Tutorial
Session 9: Report of results of Group Project

Teaching hours:
Computing: 5 sessions of 3 hours = 15
Tutorials: 2 sessions of 1 hour = 2
Project: 2 sessions of 2 hours = 4[a]
Total: = 21

a. This records staff time only. Students are recommended to allocate at least six hours to the project.

The ultimate objective of the second term is to equip students with the skills that will enable them to replicate some of the research work reported in the journals. The computing sessions use STATPACK an interactive programme available on the mainframe. The programme prompts the user and the user can ask for additional information by using the 'Help' command. The package contains a wide variety of statistical and graphic display commands, and is suitable for use by people with very little computing experience. Students are also taught to use a file editor, in this case SOS. As in the first term, historical data are employed, often in original documentary form. This reflects a belief that the historian's traditional skills of interpreting documents, marshalling, selecting and organising evidence should be linked to computing. By the end of this part of the course students are able to take data sets from journal articles and reproduce the findings.

The last four weeks of the course are devoted to a Group Project, introduced two years ago, in order to get teams of students into the habit of working together on a common problem. An important feature of the report that the groups prepare is that they are required to explain how they organised themselves as group. This year the topic chosen for the project was the Report of the Royal Commission on the Depression of Trade and Industry (1886). The Report lists some sixteen causes of the depression, for example, inflation of credit and foreign competition, and the project teams are asked to select one of these causes, formulate a hypothesis, collect the data and analyse and test the hypothesis using the computer.

An important feature of both terms is that the course does not form part of assessment for finals. Students are required to attend all classes and to complete the weekly exercises. Provided these requirements are met, students are entitled to a certificate stating that they have 'duly performed the work of the class'. This certificate has to be obtained before students can take their final examinations in the third year. By using this old device (borrowed from the Scottish universities) it is possible to reward genuine effort, even though the student may have considerable difficulty with quantitative techniques, and to lessen the resistance to quantitative work when it impinges on final degree classification.

What have been the results of the course? For the first three years after the course was introduced a questionnaire was circulated to assess students' response and to adjust the course content. These surveys showed

1) the integration of statistical methods and computing in the second term made statistics 'more palatable';
2) because the course was not assessed for finals some students felt that they should give it a low priority in allocating their time; on the other hand, the fact that it does not count towards finals assessment made most students feel more relaxed about tackling quantitative work and more willing to reveal their difficulties;
3) the course had helped students to overcome their fear of quantitative work and computing;
4) computing was regarded as a very welcome change from 'ploughing through books in the Library';
5) there is a demand for more time to be allocated to computing;
6) there is a problem for many beginners arising from the lack of basic keyboard or typing skills.

Other attitudes, revealed in less systematic discussions with participants, include strong support for working in groups — 'a welcome change from the usual individual approach to history'; the replacemement of a fear of numbers by a distrust of the reliability of numbers, and a more critical approach to some of the findings of the 'New Economic History'; an awareness of the relevance of numeracy and computing skills to future employment prospects.

These benefits are not, of course, costless. The Elementary Quantitative Methods course is expensive in terms of staff time, not least in the preparation, duplication and assessment of the many exercises required for the tutorials and computing classes. Nor can it be argued that this style of course is immediately adaptable to different institutional circumstances. The University of York is well served by an excellent Computing Service and time on the mainframe is centrally funded so the cost does not fall (directly) on the department's budget. Also, the fact that most economic history students have already completed a year's introductory statistics course is unlikely to be true of most history students in other universities. Finally, it cannot be claimed that the course has resolved the issue raised by Clive Lee in his 1983 survey:

. . .the secondary but vital question as to how far such courses, even if compulsory, are reinforced and even justified by the exposure of students to statistical and theoretical literature in other courses. . . [6]

Notes

1. C. H. Lee, *Social Science and History: an Investigation into the Application of Theory and Quantification in British Economic and Social History*, SSRC, 1983.
2. There is a view that the New Economic History has generated rather more controversy than definitive results.
3. A knowledge of economic or sociological theory would be an obvious addition to the list of skills.
4. These figures relate only to the economic history intake. The Department of Economics and Related Studies in which economic history is located also admits economics and statistics students where a far larger percentage have an 'A' level in Mathematics or Statistics.
5. For attitudes towards economic history at 'O' and 'A' level see R. G. Wilson and J. F. Hadwin, 'Economic and Social History at Advanced level', *Economic History Review* XXXVIII, 1985, pp. 548–68.
6. Lee, *op. cit.*, p. 28.

The views expressed are those of the author and not necessarily shared by his colleagues, Charles Feinstein, Mary Morgan and Peter Solar, who also teach the course.

Index of Software

This index lists the generic names of software, including programming languages, cited in the text.

SUPERFILE

The Multi-user database manager that lets the micro do mighty serious work

The hot phrase in software is 'multi-user database manager'. There are not many about; none with Superfile's unique combination of advanced features, user-friendliness, speed and the reliability that comes from a native UK product with 5 years of development behind it.

☐ Fast – find a Record in 20,000 in 2 secs ☐ Text Fields in Forms
☐ Free-form database – can be changed in use ☐ Easy to set up,
multi-screen, windowing forms generator ☐ Database manager
and forms generator callable from most languages
☐ Runs Multi-user under 3Com, Hi-Net, Novell, Torus,
MS-Net, MCCP/M, Xenix and others
☐ Full technical support, training, consultancy.

The total database system